HITLER'S GENERALS

Richard Brett-Smith was born in Oxford in 1923 and educated at Rugby and Christ Church, Oxford. He served in the Army from 1942 to 1947, retiring with the rank of Captain, 11th Hussars, having fought in Italy, France, Belgium, Holland, and Germany. After the war he served in Berlin and B.A.O.R.

After a year on the *Oxford Mail,* he went to the *Daily Telegraph* and for 14 years acted as foreign correspondent in Berlin, New York, Washington, and Central Africa. He travelled widely as that newspaper's first defence correspondent between 1959 and 1963. He also worked in industry and the Civil Service.

Even before the war, in his teens, Richard Brett-Smith visited Germany and made many friends there. Nine years later he was among the first British troops to enter Berlin, and his experiences there resulted in his first book, *Berlin '45.* He knew Germany and its people as friend, enemy, and student, and from this intimate knowledge wrote this fascinating account of the country's military leaders at the time of its greatest victories and most total defeat.

By the same author

Berlin '45
The Eleventh Hussars

BRETT-SMITH, Richard. Hitler's generals. Presidio Press, Box 3515, San Rafael, CA 94902, 1978 (c1976). 306p ill maps bibl index 77-085481. 12.95 ISBN 0-89141-004-9

CHOICE   OCT. '78

History, Geography & Travel

Europe

Brett-Smith discusses 82 generals in a monograph of less than 300 pages. Although the major figures are treated at some length, others are discussed in a page. A brief biographical sketch and summary of their combat or command record is often too brief, as is his discussion of the differences between the high command and the field officers. His evaluation of the best of these men is traditional in that he gives Manstein the highest praise with Rundstedt, Rommel, and Kesselring given secondary honors. He cites other authorities to support or oppose his views and he is not reticent in his criticism of various officers. The general brevity of the book, however, is its major weakness. This subject has been dealt with by many writers, but no one has undertaken to date such an ambitious task of biographical career analysis. For related works consult B. H. Liddell-Hart, *The German generals talk* (1948), Richard Suchenwirth, *Command and leadership in the German Air Force* (1960), and E. L. Hart, *Hitler's generals* (1944). Lower-division undergraduate and public library level.

HITLER'S GENERALS

Richard Brett-Smith

Presidio Press
SAN RAFAEL • CALIFORNIA

Published in 1977 by
PRESIDIO PRESS
1114 Irwin Street
San Rafael, California 94901

Copyright © 1976 Richard Brett-Smith

First published in Great Britain in 1976 by
Osprey Publishing Limited — ISBN 0-85045-073-X

ISBN 0-89141-044-9

Library of Congress Catalog Card Number 77-085481

Printed in the United States of America

Contents

Illustrations

Oak Leaves and Crimson Stripes

In Germany the Army has always been the senior Service, and has always enjoyed immense domestic prestige. Although it purported to keep itself removed from politics, in fact it commanded, and on occasion used, considerable political power. In the years of the Weimar Republic under the leadership of Colonel-General Hans von Seeckt, the Army became the most powerful political factor in the Reich, and through von Seeckt's skilful machinations Germany managed illegally to evade most of the arms clauses of the Treaty of Versailles. A famous field-marshal, Paul Hindenburg, was elected President in 1925 in his seventy-ninth year, and two lieutenant-generals, Wilhelm Gröner and Kurt von Schleicher, of whom the latter was an out-and-out politician, were successive Ministers of Defence. Von Schleicher destroyed the Brüning government, and briefly became Chancellor himself.

None of these things could have happened in England, where not since the days of Cromwell's major-generals have serving officers been allowed to engage in party politics. Under Gröner and von Schleicher in Germany, however, the Army only divulged to the Reichstag such information as it thought harmless. It had been limited by the Allies to 100,000 men, and any attempt by civilian politicians to go deeply into this question or that of munitions was met by a blank wall. 'As a result', to quote Wheeler-Bennett, 'Hitler, when he came to power, found a firm foundation of rearmament on which to rebuild the German military machine.' In this he was largely aided by the Army's chief representative, Colonel-General Werner von Blomberg, who was to become in 1936 the first field-marshal since Imperial days. Blomberg thought—and very many senior Army officers agreed with him—that the Army could use Hitler to improve its own situation. But in the result it was Hitler who used the Army. After the bloody murders of S.A. leaders and two of its own generals on 30 June 1934, the Army ought to have learned its lesson. But so relieved were the generals by the erasure of the threat to themselves, as they saw it, of Ernst Röhm and his bully-boy gangsters, that they played along with Hitler as before. In 1933 there was in German politics, and even to some extent in the Army, a frenetic atmosphere, that Hermann Rauschning called 'a fear, a neurasthenic fear, of "missing the bus", being left in the cold and out of everything'.

Hitler, on his side, needed the army to establish his power and make

1

Germany strong again, able to back her bids in the world's market-place by force if necessary. The Army provided one of the two classes—the other being organised labour—which had, in Rauschning's words, 'the most definite standards and criteria'. If Hitler was never entirely to conquer either class, both were vital to his plans.

There is no doubt that the majority of the men who figure in this book must have welcomed Hitler on his arrival in power because he stood for German rearmament and expansion of the Army. Some of the bitterest plotters against him, such as Major-General Henning von Tresckow and General of Artillery Eduard Wagner were, early on, much drawn to Hitler's cause. Rauschning is illuminating on the part the Army played in those early Hitler days:

'Later I frequently heard it said in service circles that they desired nothing better than to have Hitler thrust himself into the foreground as he did, and so take responsibility for all measures, virtually representing them as his own personal ideas and decisions.

'In the ranks of the higher officers there were other men, with a sense of responsibility, who felt it to be a genuine patriotic duty to recover for Germany what William II called her "place in the sun". Such men were far from any idea of preparing for another war, because they were only too well aware of the risks and sacrifices it involved, but it was inconceivable to them that Germany should permanently play subordinate part to nations like Poland and Czechoslovakia.'

But to Rauschning, as he writes in *Makers of Destruction*, the new chiefs of the Army, men like von Schleicher, seemed to lack something of the old school, to be too pragmatic in their approach, with no steady principle. This hand-to-mouth philosophy was to become prevalent as Hitler's reign went on. 'In the Reichswehr under the Republic and in the new army of the Third Reich, the chief virtue of the old Prussian army was lacking—the strong spirit of independence of the higher officers.'

It is worth pondering that remark when one thinks of the Faustian bargain that the generals drove with Hitler. Of course there were some, like von Reichenau and Keitel, who genuinely favoured Nazism. Most were willing to give it a try, and all were impressed by the fact that Hitler appeared to be on the side of the Army. Many honourable soldiers will appear in the following pages. But there were some, too many, who sold themselves to Hitler for promotion, higher pay, decorations, or glory, and some who denied their real views from fear for their own or their families' safety. It is instructive to compare with Rauschning what Ambassador Ulrich von Hassell wrote in his diary for 20 April 1943:

'The longer the war lasts the less I think of the generals. They have undoubted technical ability and physical courage, but little moral courage, absolutely no broad world vision, no spiritual independence or that strength of resistance which rests on a genuine cultural basis. For this reason Hitler was able to make them subservient and bind them hand and foot. The majority, moreover, are out to make careers in the lowest sense. Gifts and the field-marshal's baton are more important to them than the great historical issues and moral values at stake. All those on whom we set our hopes are failing, the more miserably so since they agree with all they have been told and permit themselves to indulge in the most anti-Nazi talk, but are unable to summon up enough courage to act.'

Some did act, however, even if belatedly and in a makeshift manner. Their courage led to a second and even more ghastly, because so vindictive, 'Night of the Long Knives'. If the tragedy of the German resistance was that its various groups lacked co-ordination, the tragedy of too many senior German generals was that they were prepared only to stand on one side and wait for someone else to act. In their hands the white, red and black of the German flag signified not so much glory as Tamburlaine's terms of surrender.

It should not be doubted that many of these expert professional military leaders—Colonel-General Franz Halder, Chief of Staff under Hitler for four years, for one—had to wrestle with their conscience because the oath of loyalty they had taken to Hitler weighed heavily upon them. But it occurred to many of the more intelligent and far-seeing that there might be a greater disloyalty to their country in continuing to serve an evil genius than in disobeying him. In the comparatively straightforward matter of military decisions, many were tempted to disobey—and some few did—direct orders from the Führer that made military nonsense or at least conflicted with what the commander on the spot thought to be in the best interests of his soldiers. Of the anti-Hitler generals who eventually acted (of whom more will be written later) most paid with their lives and all, with very few exceptions, were vilified in public at the time. Today, over thirty years later, it is more likely that their motives are understood by their fellow Germans, and in many cases their heroism has been recognized.

It is, however, presumptuous for anyone who did not live through the terrible years in Hitler's declining Germany to pass judgement idly on the vast majority of decent professional soldiers who kept clear of the plot, of which many indeed were ignorant in detail. It was a tricky matter to decide what constituted treason in wartime Germany; but it does say something for the non-participating generals who were approached in dozens of cases that never once did any of them make the slightest move to betray the trust imposed in them by their colleagues, and, more important, by outside civilian leaders. It does remain a pity that not more of them followed the advice that Diogenes Laertius attributes to Solon: 'Consider your honour as a gentleman of more weight than an oath.'

The oath here in question was that introduced to the Army on 2 August 1934 which to Lieutenant-General Ludwig Beck, who could foresee its consequences, was the blackest day of his life. Under the Weimar Republic the German soldier's oath had been sworn to the Constitution, not to the Head of State as in the days of the Kaisers. Major-General Walther von Reichenau, Head of the Armed Forces Office and at that time still an ardent Nazi, drafted the new oath, which was taken by officers and men alike. It read: 'I swear by God this holy oath, that I will render to Adolf Hitler, Leader of the German nation and people, Supreme Commander of the Armed Forces, unconditional obedience, and I am ready as a brave soldier to risk my life at any time for this oath.'

This was uncompromising. Yet some of Hitler's generals might have salved their consciences later on by remembering that Hitler also had taken an oath, before President Hindenburg and Vice-Chancellor von Papen, in the Garrison Church at Potsdam—an oath to respect the Constitution and guarantee the rights of man and political freedom in Germany.

With the emergence of a flourishing National Socialist state, and the growth of the S.S. and the Gestapo under Himmler, and of the Luftwaffe under Göring and Milch, the Army found that, though it continued to expand, its political power and its dominance in German domestic life did not keep pace. There was even to some extent a revival of the S.A. as a useful rallying-ground for veterans, and the Hitler Jugend and Bund Deutscher Mädel caught the imagination of the young, as I saw when I was fortunate enough to visit Nazi Germany in 1936, the year of the Olympic Games in Berlin. Even then uniforms abounded; and Hanover, where I stayed, was a particularly Nazi area. The S.A.'s brown shirts were much in evidence, the black shirts of the S.S. less so at that time.

The Army on the whole kept out of sight in its barracks, but the gaily coloured caps of the various student corps abounded in the streets, and all combined to give the unmistakable effect, even to a teenager, of a military State. And by then Germany was a military State: where in 1934 there had been only ten Army divisions on the official strength, by 1936 there were fifty, three of them the new Panzer divisions. The days of the 100,000-strong Army had long since gone. The infantry weapons and the training of the German Army were already better than those of their French and British counterparts, and the latter had as yet no fully organised armoured division.

The occupation of the Rhineland in 1936 and the seizure of Austria in 1938, followed by Munich, set the seal on Hitler's ascendancy over the generals. Very few dared question his judgement after these successes, though still the great majority were against a war with France or England. The German generals over-estimated the strength of the French Army

4

as much as did the British politicians. Poland was a different matter. Most senior generals felt no compunction about a war with Poland, and a few even looked upon it as a sacred duty.

In the old Imperial Prussian Army the influence of the Guards and Cavalry, as in Britain, had far exceeded their numerical strength. The Kaiser had reputedly spent all his military time with the Guards or the Navy. In Hitler's age the influence of the Guards and Cavalry lingered on in the persons of a few senior generals, such as von Hammerstein-Equord, von Bock, and von Kleist, but to no noticeable extent. On the other hand the Army, of the three Services, had always attracted by far the largest numbers of the aristocracy and landed gentry to its ranks. At the beginning of the last war something like a third of the officers of general rank had a 'von' before their name. At one time 60 per cent of the officers in the Reichswehr came from 'Ostelbien'– Pomerania, Silesia, East Prussia, and Mecklenburg, with their large estates. By 1945 the number of 'vons' among the serving generals represented a considerably lower percentage, though many, of course, had been killed in action, executed, or had died. In this context it is worth noting that in book after book by otherwise accurate authors some German generals have been labelled 'von' carelessly, as though the prefix went with the rank. Those who have been so misrepresented most commonly include Halder, Busch, Paulus, and Blumentritt. In this book I have tried to be completely accurate about names, and also about ranks. All too often a German general has been given a permanent rank, usually the last that he held, in serious attempts at history by some writers who appear not to bother about consistency of dating. I have tried everywhere to give the man the rank that he held at the time in question.

Promotion under Hitler was often rapid. For that reason it has been worthwhile to examine the careers of some of the younger generals. Equally there were infinitely more casualties under Hitler than in, say, the British Army of 1939–45. There were three main causes of a German general's loss of command or appointment. By far the commonest was the displeasure of Hitler, which almost invariably led to dismissal. Secondly there was death in action, capture, or incapacity from wounds. And thirdly, death from natural causes, suicide, execution, voluntary retirement and ill-health, the last two normally going together. Merely because one disagreed with Hitler or the O.K.W. did not entitle a general to resign, as Brauchitsch, Halder, and even Keitel found, as well as many others. If, on the other hand, Hitler once got his knife into a man, at best his career would be relegated to the sidelines, as in the case of Colonel-General Blaskowitz, or General of Infantry Gustav von Wietersheim, who finished up as a private in the Volkssturm.

The battle casualties of German generals were high, much higher than in the American or British Armies. In view of the nature of the fighting in Russia this is perhaps not surprising. Twenty-four generals were captured at Stalingrad alone, but many more died or were severely wounded in the fighting elsewhere. There were numbers of generals killed in Poland, France, the Western Desert, the Balkans, and Germany itself, many by aircraft action or in plane crashes but many on the battlefield itself. Others, such as Field-Marshal von Reichenau, Colonel-General Dollmann, and General of Panzer Troops Stumme had fatal heart attacks in the field. Others lost their health through battle fatigue or Hitler's nagging; and there was a surprisingly high rate of suicides, especially in Russia. Others still, some score of them, were executed after the July Plot.

The dismissal rate was far too heavy for the well-being of an Army, and was due almost entirely to Hitler. As a direct result of the Russian winter campaign of 1941−2 before Moscow, no less than thirty-five corps and divisional commanders were sent home in varying degrees of disgrace. By malevolently exercising his supreme authority Hitler in many cases deprived himself of the services of his ablest commanders. Colonel-General Erich Höpner, dismissed in disgrace, was a Panzer leader thought by many of his contemporaries to be the equal of Guderian. Lieutenant-General Hans Graf von Sponeck, commander of XLII Corps in the Kerch Peninsula in 1941, was quite wrongly court-martialled and reduced to the ranks for withdrawing a division in a hopeless position contrary to a Führer order. He was at first condemned to death but then given seven years' fortress detention. What in fact von Sponeck had done illustrates the dilemma of the German generals; he had reacted to a dangerous situation not by blindly following Hitler's *diktat* but by making a military decision in the light of his Prussian General Staff training.

Von Sponeck was one of the finest of the younger generals, a former officer in the Imperial Guards, who had won the Knight's Cross in Holland and shown outstanding gallantry during the crossing of the Dnieper. After 20 July 1944 he was shot without trial and for no good reason by Himmler's thugs.

In two cases when staff officers carrying important papers came down in a plane behind enemy lines a senior general was dismissed, and in one of them sentenced to fortress detention. They were General of Fliers Helmuth Felmy in 1940 in France, and General Stumme in Russia in 1942. In neither case could any reasonable person hold the general to blame. Felmy was subsequently given another appointment after a period of disgrace, and Stumme, due to the good offices of Göring and von Bock, soon got out of confinement and was posted to Africa. But instances such as these could be multiplied.

Such arbitrary and unjust procedures are bound to affect badly the morale of an officer corps and soldiers alike. This is not to say that none of Hitler's dismissals was justified, or those of commanding generals, for in every army there are incompetent generals, and it would have been surprising not to find some in an army as large as Germany's.

On the whole the standard of German leadership and generalship was high. The German generals tended to keep well up with their troops and to be seen more than their Allied counterparts. This was especially true of the Panzer leaders, almost by definition; of the Parachute generals; and of the generals of mountain troops.

One needs to remember that out of a nation of some 80 millions the German Army grew to a size much greater than the population warranted compared with those of France and Britain. All of Gort's or Montgomery's divisions in 1940 or 1944 would only have composed one sizeable German army in Russia, it may be healthy to recall. The ratio of fighting men to 'tail' was higher than among the Allies. Admittedly, from mid-1942 onwards, at least, many German formations were under strength and remained so, but for several years Hitler could rely upon a huge number of well-trained and well-equipped divisions. The pre-war Wehrkreis system of a score or so regional military districts ensured that there was a steady flow of manpower and replacements, and there was a special Replacement Army under Colonel-General Fromm to supply reserves.

From the winter of 1941 these reserves began to be lacking because of the casualty toll in Russia. Anyone who visited German churches immediately after the war will remember the wreaths and memorial tablets so very often in memory of a soldier, 'Im Russland gefallen', compared with the not inconsiderable numbers of those who had been killed in Africa, France, or elsewhere. In Britain we still may not fully have grasped the enormous scale of the fighting in Russia compared with that of other campaigns—which is why much of this book deals with the fighting in the Soviet Union.

In the course of research over the years I have made notes in greater and lesser detail of the careers of some 800 generals, more when including admirals and Luftwaffe commanders. Not a large number emerge, in my opinion, as being in the very front rank of commanders, although I would place Field-Marshals von Manstein and Kesselring, and possibly Model, in it. But a great many German generals seem to have been in the forefront of the second class, or good enough to be called first class without being among the greatest captains. In other words the standard was very high, and it is worth remembering that these men controlled and ran most of western Europe for years in many countries over thousands of square miles. Where a German general walked lay a path of fear, obedience and healthy respect. When one considers how comparatively few troops the Germans had with which to control Europe it is an astonishing feat. To have conquered it in the first place was another. These men, as those who have fought against them know, were thorough-going professionals. Even in defeat their discipline was mainly steadfast, and if given any respite they were superb improvisers.

Good generals are not uncommon, nor are good staff officers. The combination of both is much rarer. In England one thinks of Field-Marshal Sir Alan Brooke, though his field command was fairly brief; of General Sir Richard McCreery, who had been Chief of Staff to Alexander and then commanded 8th Army in Italy; and of Lieutenant-General Sir John Harding, who commanded a division and a Corps with distinction in Africa and went on to be a very successful Chief of Staff to Field-Marshal Alexander. But not of many more, perhaps because the opportunity did not often arise. The Germans can point to more who combined that flair for staff work with real operational brilliance which has stood the test of time. Manstein is the prime example; but Model started the war as Chief of Staff to Busch at 16th Army, and there are General Erich Marcks, Colonel-General Hans von Salmuth, Generals Günther Blumentritt, Theodor Busse, Georg von Sodenstern, Otto Wöhler, and Lieutenant-General Fritz Bayerlein. Marcks and Bayerlein were distinguished divisional and corps commanders, and all the others successfully commanded Armies after holding extremely important posts as Chiefs of Staff. One can think of others, and whatever view one holds of Guderian's having accepted the post of penultimate Chief of Staff of the Army from Hitler, it is a fact that Guderian wore with pride the double crimson stripes on his breeches of the General Staff and that he, predominantly an attacking Panzer commander, was certainly up to the job.

The old General Staff excelled in training thoroughly competent officers, and the excellent equipment and availability of ample training grounds for manoeuvres ensured that commanders had good peacetime practice in moving large formations in realistic exercises. Major-General Sir Francis de Guingand has recorded how impressed he was, during a visit to Germany in 1937, by the relationship he found between officers and men and by the Infantry School at Döberitz. The German Army before the war, at any rate since Hitler's advent, had not suffered from the penny-pinching that afflicted the British. German tank men had in some cases trained in Russia, and between 1936 and 1939 the Luftwaffe had been able to try out its strength in Spain, where such senior Army officers as Colonel Ritter von Thoma had also gained valuable experience.

Hitler conducted a love-hate relationship with the Army. He had served bravely in the Great War, winning the Iron Cross both first and second class, and there is no evidence that he was one of those soldiers who took violently against officers as a class. 'All of us worshipped Lieutenant-Colonel Engelhardt', Hitler wrote in a letter of 5 February 1915, of his commanding officer, whose life he may have saved and who had recommended him for the Iron Cross. In later days he was to find a sinecure for his former company commander.

But Hitler's experience in the trenches was bound to disillusion him with the old Imperial generals, and his own interest in developments in military equipment, including naval and air equipment, coupled with his photographic memory for the details of armaments such as gun calibres, rate of fire, weight, and range, led him unerringly to believe that he could certainly do as well if not better than his own generals in the field. This was a fatal error. Hitler had little education or knowledge of foreign countries, and no General Staff training. He could easily move about arrows representing formations on a map—and often did so to the consternation of his commanders—but he lacked any real tactical sense and the peasant in him would very seldom permit ground to be forfeited even temporarily, unless the crisis was so overwhelming that there was no other way out. He also tended to panic in adversity, as in the case of the invasion of Norway, which at one stage he wanted to call off. Technically Hitler could talk on equal terms with the generals on the surface, but he failed disastrously to get new jet fighters into production early enough, to concentrate sufficiently on a new U-Boat production programme, to build four-engine bombers, and to speed up the V-weapons rocket programme. It is too facile to lay all the blame on Hitler's shoulders, as some German generals (Halder, for one, in *Hitler als Feldherr*) did after the war. But in spite of his many successes—and for a time his strategy worked brilliantly—he made too many mistakes and interfered far too much with the conduct of operations on the ground not to bear the brunt of the responsibility for Germany's failure. Hitler made three cardinal mistakes. The first was to start the war before the Navy had enough submarines. Grand-Admiral Erich Raeder had been told to be ready for war by 1944, and by that time his U-Boat force would have been truly formidable. As it was, he started the war with less than forty-five sea-going submarines, and production never gained the proper ascendancy over losses.

What might have happened if Hitler had not advanced his timetable, presumably in fear of Soviet attack, is a chilling thought, when one considers how nearly the British lost the Battle of the Atlantic.

Hitler's second grave mistake was to invade Russia and commit himself to a war on two fronts, something which he had always previously rejected. His third was to assume personal military direction of the war and never to leave alone his senior commanders, but constantly to interfere in their conduct of operations, even down to battalion level at times. Since Hitler sat most of the time in East Prussia or Vinnitsa, he was not in a position to judge events on the ground in Russia. Having entrusted the conduct of the Russian campaign to O.K.H., leaving O.K.W. responsible for all other theatres, he should have left them to it. This, of course, was the one thing that Hitler could not bear to do—not to interfere. A fourth grave mistake, the imbalance and decline of the Luftwaffe, may rather be laid at Göring's door than attributed to Hitler; but that too had fatal results.

Hitler was fond of saying: 'I have a reactionary Army, a Christian Navy, and a National Socialist Air Force.' The first two epithets sometimes varied to become 'monarchist' and 'imperial'. The Army, despite an influx of younger, ardent Nazis as the war went on, was basically conservative in its leadership. The Navy, which Raeder controlled absolutely from 1928 to 1943, was, like various other navies, mostly a law to itself in its actual administration and the promotion of its leaders, but here again Hitler interfered with disastrous results. He did not understand naval warfare, and was indeed rather frightened of the sea (he paid few visits to warships at sea and there are few photographs recording such). He demanded much of his capital ships, but was reluctant to risk them; and when Raeder was forced into retirement they ceased to influence the war. Hitler ignored many of Raeder's sound strategic ideas, most damagingly the capture of Malta, which Field-Marshal Kesselring also saw as a prerequisite to controlling the Mediterranean and winning the war in Africa. He failed to force Göring, as he should have done, into giving proper air backing to the Navy, or to resolve the constant bickering that went on between him and Raeder. Nevertheless, the German admirals enjoyed on the whole an autonomy denied to their Army counterparts, and the Navy was considerably more National Socialist in outlook than the Army, perhaps because it had less aristocratic leaders.

The Luftwaffe was entirely a National Socialist creation, and though most of its senior officers had served in the old Army its loyalty to Hitler was never in doubt. Hardly a Luftwaffe officer figures among the conspirators of 20 July 1944. A Nazi air force was to some extent an insurance for Hitler, especially since the Luftwaffe controlled both the parachute and the anti-aircraft arms, which was not the case in Britain. Göring could therefore muster a strong force of fighting-men in ground divisions, but their use was to cause continual headaches to the Army generals who controlled them in fighting operations, since their administration, equipment, and discipline came under the Luftwaffe. Although the parachute arm won striking successes in Holland, Belgium, and Crete, Hitler was so disturbed by the casualties in the Crete campaign that he failed thereafter to use it in its proper role to any large extent—as for example, against Malta.

There remains the S.S., of ill repute. This book is concerned only with the Waffen S.S., again led in the main by former Army officers. The Allgemeine S.S., the S.D., and the Gestapo contained so-called generals within their ranks, but they were mostly jumped-up bureaucrats and street-corner politicians, bully-boy thugs, promoted policemen, adventurers, and fanatics. Many of them should have been in gaol or asylums, and few were worthy to wear military uniform. The Waffen

S.S., despite its excesses against civilians, and sometimes soldiers, in Poland, Russia, the Balkans, Italy and France, was a military organization. Again it was a sore trial to the Army in that its discipline, organization, equipment, and administration were jealously supervised by Himmler and his minions, although in fighting S.S. divisions and corps took orders from the Army. The Waffen S.S. tended to receive the latest and best equipment and the cream of reinforcements; but from 1942 or so onwards its volunteer character was disappearing, and by the end of the war S.S. divisions were much less noticeably distinct from their Army counterparts than earlier on. In Poland, France, and during the first part of the Russian campaign, there were several examples of S.S. formations faring badly or putting up poor performances, but in general the reputation for ruthlessness, courage, and fanaticism that the S.S. soldier earned was a deserved one, as those who fought against him will remember. In one case in Normandy the S.S., whether drunk or drugged, attacked British troops with swords.

Apart from the egregious Himmler, who indulged his fantasies of military glory between January and March 1945, but put up so pitiful a show that he had to be replaced, no S.S. leader ever commanded an Army Group. But there were able generals amongst them, notably Colonel-Generals Paul Hausser, Joseph 'Sepp' Dietrich, and Felix Steiner.

From 1933 the Army thought to tame Hitler, but he proved an intractable tiger. 'It was natural', Rauschning thought, 'that a nobility of blood, a nobility with a past record of service to the State, with its sense of tradition and blue blood and high caste and honour and special obligations, should feel some kinship with the Nazi doctrine of the inequality of human races, of political leadership, and of the rule of a special *elite.*' But by 1945 the honour of the German Army stood rooted in dishonour, and it had fatally compromised itself by long witnessing and sometimes partaking in excesses which no general should be asked to condone. Many atrocities in Russia and elsewhere were committed not by the Waffen S.S. alone but by ordinary Wehrmacht soldiers.

What sort of men were the generals? They varied enormously, as in any other nation. The popular image of the ramrod-stiff, ruthless, humourless Prussian did exist, but not in large numbers. Of all the leading generals, Field-Marshal Fedor von Bock seems to come closest to this picture. The qualities which most of these men shared were high professional skill and staff experience, physical toughness, smartness, resilience, opportunism, and ruthlessness. Field-Marshal Montgomery did not idly hang portraits of Rommel, Rundstedt, Model, and Kesselring on his caravan walls. He studied them, and in many of the photographs in this book, even in the posed ones, may be seen the toughness and ruthlessness of the German generals. In some the underlying flaw of character may be caught, and it is not hard to guess the S.S. commanders.

To all but military historians many of the names in subsequent pages will be unknown. The German generals best known to the British public are probably Rommel, Guderian, von Rundstedt, and perhaps Kesselring, in that order. These were household names in Germany, but there were many more, and the relentless propaganda machine of Dr Göbbels often went to work to puff up the favourite of the time, whether von Bock, von Reichenau, von Kluge, von Manstein, Student, or 'the lion of the North', Colonel-General Eduard Dietl, victor of the Norwegian campaign. In the Luftwaffe Colonel-General Ernst Udet had been well known as a stunt flier and war hero long before the second World War; and Wolfram, Freiherr von Richthofen, bearer of a famous name, won fame as a Luftwaffe field-marshal.

The Kaiser had created only five field-marshals, Ludendorff not being among their number. Von Blomberg became Hitler's first field-marshal and Minister of Defence, but after him only Göring was awarded the rank, for political reasons in 1938, before the war. As Reichsmarschall, a title created on 19 July 1940, Göring then outranked all others and became the senior serving general. Before his retirement in 1938 von Rundstedt had been the senior Army officer, succeeded by von Bock when Hitler put on the shelf so many senior generals in February 1938. Nearly all returned for the war.

Hitler was lavish with his promotions, which he saw as one means to bind the senior generals to him. By the end of the war he had created no less than twenty-three field-marshals, twelve of them on 19 July 1940; and some forty Army officers and ten Luftwaffe ones were advanced to the rank of Colonel-General (which does not exist in the British Army). A colonel-general commanded at least an Army, and often an Army Group; the equivalent rank in the Waffen S.S. was Oberstgrüppenführer. It has become customary to equate a colonel-general with a full or 'four-star' general in the British and American Armies, and in one sense this is correct. But if the pattern is followed a German major-general is the equivalent of a British brigadier or American brigadier-general, a German lieutenant-general merely of a major-general. Various books have followed this system of equivalent ranks, but however logical it may seem in theory it does not correspond with the facts. Thus before the war, out of some fifty German divisional commanders, thirty were lieutenant-generals and twenty-one major-generals. This pattern continued throughout the war. The normal command in the German Army of a major-general, if he was not on the staff or special duties, was a division, not a brigade. A lieutenant-general sometimes commanded a division, sometimes a corps, according to his seniority. A full general normally commanded an Army, very occasionally an enlarged corps, quite often a corps group. There were indeed various occasions on which German divisions, albeit sometimes under-strength ones, were commanded by a full colonel. This would occasion no surprise. The lower ranks among German officers often had more responsibility and authority than their British counterparts, especially on the Staff; thus a colonel would be the normal rank of a Corps Chief of Staff or often even of an Army one, and of the Chief of Operations, whereas in the British and American Armies such posts in an Army would probably be held by a brigadier. In Gort's B.E.F., the Chief of Staff was a lieutenant-general. The Chief of Staff of a German Army might be a colonel or a major-general, the Chief of Staff of an Army Group usually a major-general, occasionally a lieutenant-general. But these officers had considerably more authority and prestige than most of their rank. It was also not infrequent for the Chief of Staff to take over active command when his superior was away or out of action, whereas in the British Army this would be unlikely, the senior corps or divisional commander being brought in. On a junior level it was not uncommon later on in the war for a captain to command a battalion.

I suppose that it was the secret dream of every British troop leader of armoured cars or tanks to overrun a German headquarters and capture a general. In Normandy, and later, some of us had several near misses; I remember with regret one small château which a few hours before had housed Oberstgrüppenführer Hausser. The 3rd Royal Tank Regiment of 29th Brigade in 11th Armoured Division, which captured Amiens on 29 August 1944, actually pulled it off and took prisoner General of Panzer Troops Heinz Eberbach, then commanding the remains of 5th Panzer Army. It was a fitting and much appreciated reward.

With two other subalterns at the end of the war I had to be content with accepting the surrender of a senior major-general and his staff, with the best part of a division in full fighting trim, at Brunsbüttel, where the Kiel Canal meets the Elbe. We were rather dishevelled in battle-dress. The general and his staff, on the other hand, might have been on parade in Unter den Linden—their shining black boots, red-striped breeches, and heavily medalled tunics of grey-green were immaculate. I shall never forget the stiff, stern, unsmiling faces that showed hardly any emotion, and the few, brusque, harsh-sounding orders that the general rapped out after we had told him where his troops had to go. The same sort of scene during those days was being repeated in many areas of Germany. The Nazi régime was at an end. With it had died the hopes and the ambitions of a ruling class, and something more—the fear, domination, and even terror that the German Army in the West had for so long inspired. It was indeed the end of an era.

Since then I have met several German generals of both Army and Luftwaffe, and admirals who fought in the last war; and today, of course, the Bundeswehr is a trusted and needed ally in N.A.T.O. Some of the younger generals of the war have made notable contributions

13

to their country's defence—like Generals von Manteuffel, Heusinger, de Maiziere, Châles de Beaulieu, Pemsel, and Trettner; and from the Luftwaffe Galland and the former Colonel, now General, Johannes Steinhoff. When first I saw General Heusinger—who had been Chief of the Operations Branch of the O.K.H. from 1940 to 1945; who had supervised the planning of the proposed invasion of England; and who had stood near Hitler's side when the bomb went off in July 1944, and been himself a casualty—in the new uniform of the Bundeswehr, easily identifiable yet so reminiscent of the old German uniform, I confess that my heart missed a beat. This was in Washington; later at Fontainebleu I was to be given a most rewarding interview by General Dr Hans Speidel, once Rommel's Chief of Staff in Normandy, in his capacity as C-in-C of N.A.T.O.'s Ground Forces. I trust that he did not catch me staring at his Iron Cross and Knight's Cross when I entered his office. My mind went back to those happy, peacetime days in Hanover in 1936, and I wondered ruefully how many of my German friends of those days now lay buried for ever on some Russian steppe, in the sands of Africa, or in graves in Italy, France, and Germany itself.

Fritz Thyssen, the armaments millionaire, once voiced the thoughts of many Germans when he wrote: 'Up to the eleventh hour I thought it would be possible to avoid war. I consoled myself by imagining that the responsible generals would succeed in restraining Hitler.' But by then it was too late. The generals had long since lost any political power, as von Hassell saw, though there were 'excellent people' among the Army leaders. He instanced von Rundstedt, Blaskowitz, von Bock, von Leeb, von Witzleben, and List—but they were too far away from the centre of things to wield any power outside their local commands. Hitler, the corporal of the Great War, had become the military as well as the political overlord by the summer of 1934 and the fateful oath of allegiance.

It took nearly six years to defeat the Germans, and to beat them, moreover, in their own fields. Without the high abilities of many of these men it would have taken less time. Yet they were early discredited by their own leader, and in the end most were soldiering on, if they had not been dismissed, automatically and from an obstinate sense of duty. They had lost everything but their professional pride. Let a German general himself have the last word. General of Panzer Troops Leo Frëiherr Geyr von Schweppenburg, who knows the English well, summed up: 'One thing is certain: during the last 200 years of Prussian-German military history, no body of generals was ever so thoroughly divided, watered down, disunited and internally disintegrated, as it was in the Third Reich.'

The Old Guard

In September 1939, at the outbreak of World War II the man who was to become better known to the world than any other German general except Rommel was already in retirement and approaching his sixty-fifth year. This was Colonel-General Karl Rudolf Gerd von Rundstedt, an infantryman, who came from an old Prussian family from Mecklenburg, though he himself was born at Aschersleben, near Halle. Von Rundstedt's father was a Junker and a major-general, his mother of bourgeois stock.

At 17 Rundstedt had joined Infantry Regiment No. 83 as an ensign at Kassel, and in 1893 became a lieutenant in Infantry Regiment No. 171 (the 2nd Upper Alsatian Infantry Regiment). In 1907 he joined the General Staff, and it was as a staff officer that he made his reputation in the Great War on both Western and Eastern fronts, especially as Chief of Staff to XV Army Corps; his outlook was enlarged by a spell of duty under the Turkish General Staff.

Rundstedt, coming from a typically conservative, monarchist Prussian family with roots in the 'Altmark' of Brandenburg, and married to another aristocrat (his wife was a von Götz), was dedicated to his country and to the Army, and placed service and obedience to duty above politics. He was a sound disciple of Colonel-General von Seeckt, who had so masterfully led the rearmament of the German Army in the days of the Weimar Republic. To him indeed Seeckt's sanctimoniously cynical ruling that the German soldier should have no part in politics was sacrosanct, even as he believed Seeckt's words: 'The Army should become a state within the State, but it should be merged in the State through service; in fact it should itself become the purest image of the State.'

To such a man as Rundstedt the Nazi leaders and their doctrines could only seem vulgar and antipathetic, and those who promised to break down all barriers of class distinction no better than upstarts. Yet, like so many of the senior generals anxious to restore German military might and circumvent the *diktat* of Versailles, it suited Rundstedt to play along with Hitler's policy of rearmament. He could have shed no tears at the demise in 1934 of Röhm and his fellow Brownshirts, after which the S.A. ceased to be a practical rival to the Reichswehr. As Liddell Hart has written of von Rundstedt: 'He despised politics, but they kept on intruding into his seclusion.'

For three years after the Great War, between 1920 and 1923, Rundstedt as a lieutenant-colonel on the Staff investigated the reasons for Germany's collapse in 1918, and found that the economic power of Britain had been the chief cause of Germany's military downfall. As a colonel in the mid-twenties Rundstedt showed ruthlessness in suppressing left-wing and communist groups in Thuringia in central Germany. When he became Chief of Staff of the 2nd Army District (Wehrkreis) with headquarters in Stettin he encouraged the nationalism which he found in Pomerania, perhaps the leading militaristic province of Prussia, though he himself was a nationalist loyal only to the Army.

What Rundstedt thought of the murder by the Nazis in 1934 of Lieutenant-General von Schleicher, the former Chancellor of brief duration, is not recorded, but it must surely have sounded off warning bells in his mind. The two men had been close friends, and just as Schleicher was behind Rundstedt's first appointment to divisional command, that of the 2nd Cavalry Division at Breslau in 1928, so Rundstedt was something of a force, in his non-political way, behind Schleicher's bid for the Chancellorship. In 1932 Rundstedt, now a lieutenant-general, 'arrived' as a force in the new Germany Army with his appointment to be Commander of Army District III, soon followed by his promotion to General of Infantry and Chief of the important First Army Group, based in Berlin. It fell to him in this capacity to remove, under Chancellor von Papen, the Social Democrat Ministers of Prussia when they refused to give up office.

For the next six years Rundstedt dedicated himself, with all those characteristics of thoroughness, forcefulness, precision and prestige that were later to lead him to high victories, to the re-organisation and modern rearmament of the German infantry. He achieved a triumph, for while it is often remembered how superior were German tanks to most of their British and French opponents in 1940 and later, it is usually overlooked that in weaponry, training, initiative and equipment also the German infantryman of 1939, 1940, and 1941 started off at an advantage over his counterpart in the Polish, French, British or Soviet Army. Rundstedt worked successfully to dispel the 'neurosis against the machine-gun hail' which remained after 1918. To dislodge the remnants of this paralysis he favoured the large-scale introduction of lorried infantry, greater fire-power, emphasis on individual training and development as well as upon the traditional Prussian discipline of line infantry regiments, and more motorization. Although the German Army in Hitler's War was to win its greatest fame for armoured Blitzkrieg-type victories, it is interesting to recall that, even as late as 1944 and 1945, a heavy proportion of its supplies and equipment were still reliant upon horse-drawn transport, as those who have had to fire or lay down artillery barrages against them will remember vividly with regret.

Rundstedt, unlike some of his contemporaries (Beck, and some who later made their own names in handling tanks, such as von Kleist) was never sceptical of armour, but believed strongly that it should work closely with infantry and that armour should not be expanded at the expense of the ground troops. But his holding back of armour near Dunkirk in 1940 was to cost Germany dear, and it may be thought that as a traditional infantryman he was slow to appreciate the new and decisive threat that daringly controlled panzer thrusts could pose in the hands of tank experts like Guderian, Hoth, Höpner and Kirchner.

In March 1938 von Rundstedt was promoted colonel-general, and became second only to his Commander-in-Chief, von Brauchitsch (whose promotion to that post and rank dated from a month earlier), as the senior serving soldier in the German Army. But with the dismissals of von Blomberg and von Fritsch after the Nazi-induced scandals concerning them that same year, his own position with the Nazis became eroded. This was partly because he honourably backed Fritsch and protested to Hitler about Fritsch's treatment, and partly because he subscribed to the memorandum forecasting general war that General Beck had put up to von Brauchitsch, Fritsch's successor, and Hitler in May 1938. In November 1938, with more than a dozen senior Army generals (nearly all of whom were to be re-employed at high level when war broke out), Rundstedt resigned, with the sop of appointment as Honorary Colonel of the 18th Infantry Regiment, which he had once commanded.

His retirement, the first of four, was to be short-lived. On 1 June 1939 Rundstedt was recalled to duty, and when Germany invaded Poland in August he led well over half a million men in Army Group A to some of the outstanding and decisive successes of that short campaign. It may be wondered why he chose to return; but while opposed to the idea of war with Britain, Rundstedt—like many of the senior generals, including von Bock, von Leeb, Blaskowitz, and von Kluge—believed, as even von Fritsch had believed, in the nullification of Poland and the destruction of the Polish Corridor through East Prussia. To them a Polish campaign was little short of a sacred cause, and in following closely the plans and timetable once laid down by von Fritsch, von Rundstedt was doing nothing against his conscience. His campaign with Army Group South, launched from Silesia and Czechoslovakia, was studded with victories from Cracow to Lemberg, from Kutnov to Warsaw, and has been described by the analyst writing under the name 'W.E. Hart' as 'an almost flawless operation'. The opposition in Poland was hopelessly outclassed in air power, tanks, artillery and equipment so, although the fierce resistance of the Poles took its toll, the outcome was inevitable. Rundstedt controlled Colonel-General List's 14th Army, General Blaskowitz's 8th Army, and General von Reichenau's 10th Panzer Army. Two of the finest staff officers in the German Army were at Rundstedt's elbow—his Chief of Staff, Lieutenant-General von Manstein, and his Chief of Operations, Colonel Blumentritt. At the campaign's close Rundstedt found distasteful the triumphal entry and Caesarean antics of Hitler and coterie at Warsaw, which he bitingly described as 'Affentheater' ('Monkey theatre'). Blaskowitz, shortly to tangle with Dr Frank and the S.S. during the German occupation, was similarly astringent.

Rundstedt's next campaign, that against France, was to be his greatest. Yet up until late February 1940 his was intended to be a supporting drive, with the main thrust being made by Colonel-General von Bock's Army Group B, with over 40 divisions, including nine panzer and four motorized ones, through Belgium and possibly part of Holland. However, in his Directive No. 8 for the conduct of the war, issued from Berlin on 20 November 1939, Hitler stressed: 'All precautions will be taken to enable the main weight of attack to be switched from Army Group B to Army Group A should the disposition of enemy forces at any time suggest that Army Group A could achieve greater success.'

In the event, when the blitzkrieg finally was launched on 10 May 1940, the parts played by Bock and Rundstedt had been reversed. It was the latter's Army Group A, enlarged to forty-four divisions, including seven panzer and three motorized (from its original twenty-seven, with only one panzer division reluctantly granted by Hitler) that became the main spearhead. Bock in the north had to be content with twenty-eight divisions, including three panzer and one motorized, while Colonel-General von Leeb's Army Group C in the south, which was to contain if not breach the Maginot Line, mustered only seventeen infantry divisions.

The man behind the change of plan was von Rundstedt's Chief of Staff, von Manstein, who thought that an attack through the Low Countries would be too obvious, would set the Germans mainly against the British Army rather than the French, and would run into country not ideal for tanks in the polders and canal-studded low pastures, easily floodable at some points, of Belgium and Holland. Manstein therefore advocated an attack through Sedan and the Ardennes, at first sight unpromising tank country, but terrain he believed, after consultation with the armoured expert General Guderian, could be covered. Once navigated, it would lead into the far more promising rolling farmlands of northern France.

Manstein's plan did not at first find favour with either Colonel-General von Brauchitsch, his Commander-in-Chief, or with General Halder, the Army's Chief of Staff, who did not like Manstein. Nor, at first, did it find much favour with Hitler, though he was attracted enough by the possibilities of a Sedan thrust to add a panzer corps (Guderian's) to Rundstedt's command.

The Manstein plan clearly found no favour at all with the vain von Bock, who saw his star part in danger of being snatched away from him. Rundstedt and Manstein continued to press their views, with various modifications, both to Brauchitsch and Halder; and Rundstedt took at least one opportunity to press his claims for a stronger southern wing with Hitler himself, but nothing decisive emerged. Instead, mainly because of continuing bad weather throughout the winter months, one projected offensive after another had to be postponed.

In February 1940, perhaps as a result of his opponent's intrigues, Manstein was removed from his post at Rundstedt's side, and 'promoted' to command XXXVIII Corps in the 2nd Army of General Baron von Weichs, which had in the initial assault been given only a follow-up part. He was replaced as Chief of Staff, Army Group A, by Lieutenant-General von Sodenstern, a protégé of Halder, whom, not unjustly, Guderian thought efficient but 'more prosaic' than Manstein.

If the anti-Manstein faction of O.K.H. hoped to sidetrack his plan thus, the attempt failed for, ironically enough, when Manstein was a guest at a dinner given by Hitler for new commanders he took the chance to expound his ideas for an Ardennes breakthrough in detail. Hitler became enthusiastic, and the upshot was that the unlucky Bock lost most of his armour, and two armies, von Weichs's 2nd and von Kluge's 4th, to von Rundstedt. Brauchitsch gave the latter even more strength than Manstein had contemplated, so that the main *Schwerpunckt* was now to come in the south centre; while Bock's objective, still important enough, was to cut off the Allied strength in the north, which included the British Expeditionary Force.

Major L.F. Ellis, the official War Office historian, is inclined in his *The War in France and Flanders 1939–1940* (p. 341) to give the main credit for the shape of the final German plan to von Rundstedt, with some part to Manstein and some to Hitler, but not much to the O.K.H. General Staff, which drew up the final operational orders. Most German generals, however, have awarded von Manstein the lion's share of the credit, which he certainly deserved. It is arguable that without the intelligent backing of Germany's most prestigious general, von Rundstedt, he might never have succeeded, but the plan was his own creation. According to General Blumentritt after the war, as quoted by Liddell Hart, 'The opposition was finally overcome and the plan changed owing to definite news, emanating from Brussels, of the Allied plans'.

The high respect which men such as Rundstedt and Leeb had held for the French High Command, and General Gamelin in particular, proved to be ill-founded. Rundstedt had feared a French counter-attack from the Verdun area against his left flank while he was pushing his divisions through the Ardennes, but it never materialized. The execution of the plan could hardly have gone better, and the Germans made progress far beyond their hopes.

Even so, Hitler, to whom the scale of success beyond his dreams brought a rash of nerves, worried continually about the left flank of the advance that was cutting the Allied forces in two and pinning the bulk of the B.E.F. and of the French 1st Army back against the Channel. The first jolt caused to the advancing Germans was near Arras when two British tank regiments, both of the Royal Tank Regiment, counter-attacked supported by infantry from 50th Northumbrian Division, and with the help of a small French force on 21 May. This attack, small in scope and with limited objectives, had a much greater deterrent effect upon the Germans than its brave but restricted force warranted—the best of the 74 tanks available were slow-moving Matildas. The attack, led by Major-General Giffard Martel, fell mainly upon Major-General Erwin Rommel's 7th Panzer Division. Rommel and his superiors greatly over-estimated the British strength and thought that elements of several armoured divisions were involved. Rundstedt told Liddell Hart after the war, as recorded in *The Other Side of the Hill*: 'A critical moment in the drive came just as my forces had reached the Channel. It was caused by a British counter-stroke southward from Arras towards Cambrai, on 21 May. For a short time it was feared that our armoured divisions would be cut off before the infantry divisions could come up to support them. None of the French counter-attacks carried any serious threat as this one did.'

Thus Colonel-General von Kluge, commanding 4th Army, delayed further westward advance from Arras until the situation had been cleared up. General von Kleist, commanding the Panzer Group, slowed down, from excessive caution, the drive made by Guderian's XIX Corps, which had reached Abbeville and the Channel on 22 May, towards Dunkirk, Calais and Boulogne. Indeed at this time the leading panzers were nearer to Dunkirk than were the British fighting troops.

Rundstedt himself could not have been unaffected by the Arras counter-attack. He was in control of four armies and two large Panzer Groups strung out over hundreds of miles. His armour in particular was scattered; some of his armoured divisions had suffered about 50 per cent casualties and breakdowns, others up to 30 per cent. Some of his infantry divisions were already heavily engaged, others were lagging behind the armour, and there was always the danger, if not the likelihood, of another and bigger counter-attack—indeed Rundstedt still expected one from Gamelin, and perhaps from the British on the Canal Line. The next moves in France, moreover, had to be contemplated, for there still remained Paris and much of the hinterland to conquer.

It was thus that on the evening of 23 May Rundstedt decided to close up his armour on the Canal Line front before continuing the attack. Evidently the worst was over, and when von Bock's Army Group B, still some forty miles away, drove back the Allies' left wing they would be hopelessly caught between the two German Army Groups. Or so it seemed. Rundstedt therefore consulted von Kluge, whose 4th Army controlled both von Kleist's and General Hoth's Panzer Groups, who said that 'the troops would be glad if they could close up tomorrow'. 4th Army War Diary recorded that it would 'in the main, halt tomorrow in accordance with Colonel-General von Rundstedt's order'. Brauchitsch seems to have seen the situation more correctly than anyone, for he now ordered, as Commander-in-Chief, that early on 24 May Kluge's 4th Army should transfer to Bock's control, with the latter co-ordinating all the final encircling movements. Halder recorded his disapproval of this measure.

Rundstedt had doubtless intended his 'halt and close up' order only to be temporary, but when Hitler visited him on 24 May the Führer at once endorsed it without consulting von Brauchitsch, and countermanded the latter's sensible order about 4th Army. On 25 May O.K.H. early authorized the armour to cross the Canal Line, but Rundstedt ignored this order, and when Brauchitsch proposed a new armoured attack Hitler opposed it but left the decision to Rundstedt, who also opposed it, since he seemed more concerned with resting and refitting his tanks and their crews.

Thus nothing happened on 25 and 26 May, and it was Rundstedt, not Hitler, who was responsible, though Hitler endorsed Rundstedt's views. It was Hitler, however, not Rundstedt, who ordered a resumption of the attack on 27 May, by which time invaluable breathing-space had been afforded the Allies and Dunkirk been made possible.

Since the war the German generals have closed ranks to put all the blame on Hitler. Rundstedt feared an Allied counter-attack, and Hitler was mistakenly swayed by his own fears (encouraged by the personal reminiscences of General Keitel) that his tanks would get bogged down in the marshy Flanders terrain. By 26 May Rundstedt was satisfied that there was no danger of a strong counter-attack, and was discussing the resumption of his advance with Kluge. He was therefore at one with Hitler's decision to renew the attack, but—significantly—nowhere in the German War Diaries is there any suggestion that he was at odds with Hitler's extension of his own original halt order.

After the war, however, Rundstedt claimed differently. He told Liddell Hart that on 23 May, when Boulogne and Calais were already cut off and Lieutenant-General Reinhardt's tanks reached the Aire-St Omer Canal, less than twenty miles from Dunkirk, that: 'At that moment a sudden telephone call came from Colonel von Greiffenberg (Chief of O.K.H. Operations Section, and later Chief of Staff to both Bock and List, and a General) saying that Kleist's forces were to halt on the line of the canal. It was the Führer's direct order—and contrary to General Halder's view. I questioned it in a message of protest, but received a curt telegram in reply, saying: "The armoured divisions are to remain at medium artillery range from Dunkirk (a distance of eight or nine miles). Permission is only granted for reconnaissance and protective movements."' Kleist, who was Reinhardt's superior, found no sense in this order and ignored it, until firmly told to withdraw his tanks behind the canal, where they stayed for three days. Later, when he mentioned to Hitler the great opportunity that had been missed of reaching Dunkirk before the British got away, Hitler replied: 'That may be so. But I did not want to send the tanks into the Flanders marshes and the British won't come back in this war.' Hitler was confident then that Britain would agree to peace, an aim to which Rundstedt thoroughly subscribed.

Milton Shulman, in his excellent *Defeat in the West* (pp. 42–43) has recorded an even more forcible blaming of Hitler by von Rundstedt in October 1945. 'To me Dunkirk was one of the great turning-points of the war,' the Field-Marshal told Shulman. 'If I had had my way, the English would not have got off so lightly at Dunkirk. But my hands were tied by direct orders from Hitler himself. While the English were clambering into the ships off the beaches, I was kept uselessly outside the port unable to move. I recommended to the Supreme Command that my five panzer divisions be immediately sent into the town and thereby completely destroy the retreating English. But I received definite orders from the Führer that under no circumstances was I to attack, and I was expressly forbidden to send any of my troops closer than ten kilometres from Dunkirk. The only weapons I was permitted to use against the English were my medium guns. At this distance I sat outside the town, watching the English escape, while my tanks and infantry were prohibited from moving.

'This incredible blunder was due to Hitler's personal idea of generalship. The Führer daily received statements of tank losses incurred during the campaign, and by simple process of arithmetic he deduced that there was not sufficient armour available at this time to attack the English. He did not realize that many of the tanks reported out of action one day would, with a little extra effort on the part of the repair squads, be able to fight in a very short time. The second reason for Hitler's decision was the fact that on the map available to him at Berlin the ground surrounding the port appeared to be flooded and unsuitable for tank warfare. With a shortage of armour and the difficult country, Hitler decided that the cost of an attack would be too high, when the French armies to the south had not yet been destroyed. He therefore ordered my forces be reserved so that they could be strong enough to take part in the southern drive against the French, designed to capture Paris and destroy all French resistance.'

Thus Rundstedt, unfairly, laid all the blame on Hitler. It may well be—as Sodenstern, naturally loyal to his chief, put it—that the original halt order was only intended to bring the motor to a halt, idling or ticking over, not to *stop* it, but for the results and the unnecessary prolongation Rundstedt must bear a large share of the blame.

In the second stage of the Battle of France, Army Group A had to pierce the Weygand lines on the Aisne and the Marne. Only on the Aisne was French resistance really tough, and once that was broken the rest of the campaign, which was to end in the enslavement of France for four years, was comparatively easy. Rundstedt summed it up laconically in talking to Liddell Hart:

'There was tough going for a few days but the issue was hardly in doubt. The offensive was opened by Bock's Army Group B, on the right wing. I waited until his attack had made headway, across the Somme, before joining in the offensive. My armies met with strong resistance in crossing the Aisne, but after that it was easy. The vital thrust was that made over the Plateau de Langres towards Besançon and the Swiss frontier, behind the back of the French right wing in the Maginot Line.'

It was Hitler's belief that, after the fall of France, Britain would have to make peace and would be prepared to do so, on 'honourable' terms which he was, at that time, prepared to grant her. His intention was to gain a free hand on the Eastern Front, and even, perhaps, come to some sort of agreement over spheres of interest with Britain, if not quite making her an ally against Russia. Hitler was puzzled by the continuing British refusal to talk peace terms, and, as one result, his timetable for a proposed 'Sea-Lion', an invasion of Britain across the Channel, was inevitably delayed; and had an invasion actually occurred, it would have missed the best weather for a seaborne crossing. In fact, detailed preparations and full-scale planning did not properly start until after the French capitulation (Paris fell on 14 June, the Armistice was signed on 22 June), although Grand-Admiral Raeder had told Hitler of contingency studies for an invasion of England as early as 21 May. Hitler had not reacted with enthusiasm to the idea, nor did he, apparently, when Raeder reverted to it on 20 June. But on 2 July he had changed his mind and decided that an invasion was possible given air superiority and 'certain other necessary conditions'; and on 16 July Hitler's Directive No. 16 was issued, which began, with evident caution: 'Since England, in spite of her hopeless military situation, shows no signs of being ready to come to an understanding, I have decided to prepare a landing operation against England, and, if necessary, carry it out.' Note the reservation. It is also noteworthy that on 15 June O.K.H. had been ordered to reduce the Army's strength to 120 divisions, i.e. by about a fifth, to return men to industry and the land, just as had been done to a lesser extent after the conquest of Poland.

The size of the landing force was not specified in Hitler's directive, though O.K.W. had been thinking at first in terms of between twenty-five and forty divisions, possibly using some airborne forces. The landing zone was to extend from near Ramsgate to west of the Isle of Wight. In the event, before the whole thing was allowed to fizzle out, the number of assault divisions was reduced to thirteen, presumably because of lack of sea transport; but, as Peter Fleming has pointed out, it makes no sense to believe that forty or even twenty-five divisions are needed to conquer an island in mid-August and only thirteen a month later!

In Berlin on 19 July, in a colourful scene in the Reichstag, Hitler had made his peace offer to Britain, and had then created at a blow a dozen Field-Marshals. Nine were from the Army, including von Rundstedt; and three from the Air Force, with Göring given the special promotion, unique, to Reichsmarschall, thus out-ranking all the rest. Of the senior members of the 'Old Guard' besides Rundstedt, Colonel-Generals von Brauchitsch, von Bock, and Ritter von Leeb were awarded their batons, as were Generals of Infantry List and von Witzleben. Slightly younger were two more new Field-Marshals—von Reichenau, once an enthusiastic Nazi, and von Kluge, still a tepid one, both Generals of Artillery in their mid-fifties. The most undeserved promotion was that of the arrant Nazi and Hitler lackey, Colonel-General Keitel, head of the O.K.W. and general factotum and military dogsbody to Hitler. The three Luftwaffe Field-Marshals were Generals der Flieger Milch, Kesselring, and Sperrle, the former the real architect of the German Air Force and the latter two Luftflotten commanders in France and previously in Poland. Had there been any justice, General of Infantry Blaskowitz, who had been an Army Group commander before the war, would have been in the list, but he had made himself unpopular with Hitler by his criticisms of the behaviour of the S.S. and Party function-aries in Occupied Poland. So too would have the Army Chief of Staff, General Halder, but he had had his brushes with Hitler, to whom he was prepared at times to speak brusquely.

It was now to fall to von Rundstedt to command the assault Armies in the invasion of England. These were to be Reichenau's 6th Army, and the 9th and 16th Armies of Colonel-Generals Strauss and Busch respectively, all in Army Group A. As the summer lengthened, however, and more and more difficulties were raised by the Navy, and modifi-cations to the plan multiplied (Reichenau's 6th Army being converted to a follow-up role, for example), it looked clear to the always sceptical Rundstedt that the invasion was not going to come off. He had always doubted its practicality since he had had a private talk with Hitler on 19 July, as a result of which he tended less and less to take the prospect seriously, dismissing it as 'nothing more than a political bluff'. So he left much of its planning to Busch at 16th Army, who actually signed the only 'Invasion Order', and even the conscientious von Soden-stern was allowed to be frequently absent from his headquarters.

As the weeks passed without invasion coming visibly nearer, Rundstedt was heard to refer to 'Sea-Lion rubbish', and when von Brauchitsch and Halder arrived at his H.Q. on 10 September on a tour of inspection of invasion preparations they found the prospective Julius Caesar away on leave. To Liddell Hart after the war Rundstedt explained: 'The invasion was to be made in August if possible, and September at the latest. The military reasons for its cancellation were various. The German Navy would have had to control the North Sea as well as the Channel, and was not strong enough to do so. The German Air Force was not sufficient to protect the sea crossing on its own. While the leading part of the forces might have landed, there was the danger that they might be cut off from supplies and reinforcements.'

To Shulman he spoke even more strongly: 'The proposed invasion of England was nonsense, because adequate ships were not available. They were chiefly barges which had to be brought from Germany and the Netherlands. Then they had to be reconstructed so that tanks and other equipment could be driven out of the bows. Then the troops had to learn how to embark and disembark. We looked upon the whole thing as a sort of game, because it was obvious that no invasion was possible when our Navy was not in a position to cover a crossing of the Channel or carry reinforcements. Nor was the German Air Force capable of taking on these functions if the navy failed. . . .

'I was always very sceptical about the whole affair. I must admit that serious preparations were made, but we only had very few paratroops at the time—one airborne division.

'I have a feeling that the Führer never really wanted to invade England. He never had sufficient courage. He used to say, "On land I am a hero, but on water I am a coward". Hitler definitely hoped that the English would make peace overtures to him.'

For nearly a year from 25 October 1940, therefore, Rundstedt, as the ranking general in France, was Commander-in-Chief West. His next assignment was to take him back to the east, where he had served in the Great War, and it was one that he did not favour—invasion of Russia. Nor did von Brauchitsch and Halder. They did not believe in a two-front war in Europe, and while England was at present dormant from the Army point of view, though certainly not in the Battle of Britain and on the high seas, if there were to be an extension of the war the Mediterranean area seemed to them, as to Raeder, to offer the best chances of success. But at the end of July Hitler, whose real ambitions and intentions had always leaned towards the east, was determined to crush Russia in a short war that would begin in the spring, probably May, of 1941. To this end plans for a Russian invasion were ordered to be made in detail, enlarging contingency O.K.H. studies already in existence. The senior planner was the able Major-General Erich Marcks, who submitted the first comprehensive plan to Halder on 5 August which envisaged the use of 147 German divisions, including twenty-four panzer and twelve motorized ones.

A further study was made for Jodl by Lieutenant-Colonel Bernhard von Lossberg (later a Major-General) and completed by 15 September. This bore the proviso, which must have been much in the minds of many General Staff officers and commanders: 'Finally it remains to be examined whether and to what extent a campaign against Russia really must be prepared during the coming autumn and winter even if England is not yet defeated. It is important that Russia must not be made aware of the threatening danger before the conquest of England, and thus provoked into counter-measures (Rumania, stopping of economic deliveries)'.

From this it is clear that the General Staff had by no means abandoned the idea of Sea-Lion. But Hitler had, and in his mind the earlier defeat of Britain was not now a prerequisite for his attack on Russia, mainly because he felt that Russia was ever growing stronger and was exploiting its position through his own conquests. Whether the final decision was made, as seems probable, by Hitler by the end of July, 1940, or in September, or in November, those who, like Rundstedt, saw no point in attacking Russia were finally overruled.

It has often been said that the Germans underestimated Soviet strength. In one sense they did, by making insufficient allowances for the vastness of the country and the resilience of its people. But the senior generals had paid attention for some years to the able reports of the German Military Attaché in Moscow, Major-General Ernst Köstring. He was against a war with Russia; it was Hitler who ignored his warnings. As to questions of logistics, supply, communications, and even maps, it is now evident that the German Army was not adequately equipped in these respects for such a war, and that these branches of the Army (not through their own fault), had not kept pace with the modernizations of the armoured, infantry, and artillery forces.

As recently as 26th July General of Signals Erich Fellgiebel had made the damaging admission that signals networks for Sea-Lion and for Russia could not be readied simultaneously.

Worst of all, Hitler thought that the campaign could be won speedily by autumn 1941, with the result that proper preparations for the winter, let alone a long campaign of several years, were not undertaken. The most obvious example of this was the scandalous lack of winter clothing for the German troops in 1941–2, many of whom died from exposure or frostbite as a result.

Ironically enough, Lieutenant-General Friedrich Paulus, who succeeded Lieutenant-General Heinrich von Stülpnagel in the summer of 1940 as Deputy Chief of the General Staff (Oberquartermeister I), was given the task early in September of revising Marcks's plan. He reduced the number of divisions allotted by Marcks to the Army reserve, while lumping the main forces into three separate Army Groups which had as their targets Leningrad, Smolensk and Moscow, and Kiev and Kharkov. The central Army Group was to be the strongest, and a 'decisive' advance on Moscow was anticipated in the sixth or seventh week of the invasion. Hitler, however, refused to make Moscow the chief target, and stipulated that it was to be attacked only after the destruction of enemy forces in the Baltic states and the capture of Leningrad and Kronstadt.

'We have only to kick in the door and the whole rotten structure will come crashing down!' Hitler had told Jodl. The German generals, warned not to interfere in politics of which they were ignorant, had been told that the Russian people would rise against Stalin and that there would be a political upheaval when the Red Army was defeated. This was one serious miscalculation. Another, as we have seen, was the inability of the logistical support to cope with the huge advances made, and the lack of good roads (often not at all like those shown on the map), and suitable railways. A third was the stretching, after initial successes, of the Luftwaffe. Even more serious were the under-estimation of the Russian will to resist, and the quality and numbers of new Soviet tanks coming into production.

It may be that—had the O.K.H. been permitted to function freely with a supreme commander (either Rundstedt, Leeb, or Bock) of its own choosing, in whom it had confidence—these serious difficulties might have been overcome. But after France, Hitler's prestige was enormous, and by promotion, honours and, in some cases, gifts of money or estates he was able to convert the waverers among the generals to his side. Halder, as Chief of Staff, produced no personal iron-cast plan for 'Barbarossa', and was already on poor terms with Hitler, while the part played by the Commander-in-Chief .of the Army, von Brauchitsch, was now, all too often, reduced to that of Hitler's executive or even whipping-boy. So the O.K.H., in nominal charge of the Russian campaign, could never evade Hitler's authority for long; while Keitel and Jodl, the senior figures of O.K.W., possessed Hitler's ear and, at least in the former's case, all too often sychophantically supported his arbitrary conduct of the war.

The Italian invasion of Greece and then the German invasion of Yugoslavia set back the date of the attack by at least four, probably five, and possibly six weeks with disastrous results for a campaign intended to be completed by winter. As a result of the Balkans inter-vention von Rundstedt's Army Group South, for example, was initially deprived of about one-third of its tank strength; and when the tanks were returned, many of them needed overhauling. The German attack on Crete in late April delayed the return to Poland of the 8th Air Corps; and more important, because of the heavy German casualties in aircraft and parachutists at Crete, Hitler refused to sanction any of the envisaged large-scale airborne operations which might have been of great importance at stages in the Russian campaign. And in 1941, to cap it all, the Russian winter came early.

Rundstedt's task in the invasion of Russia was the hardest. His Army Group South, consisting of three German Armies—the 6th (Reichenau) the 11th (Colonel-General Ritter von Schobert) and the 17th (General Heinrich von Stülpnagel); Colonel-General von Kleist's Panzer Group I; and the Rumanians (and from mid-July the Hungarians), the whole supported by General der Flieger Alexander Löhr's 4th Air Fleet, was operating between the Pripet Marshes and the Carpathians. They had crossed the Soviet frontier from South Poland and Galicia on 22 June 1941, to find the Russians unprepared, despite the urgent British warnings delivered to Stalin personally by Sir Stafford Cripps well in advance of the invasion, but ignored by that dictator. It was Rundstedt's task to destroy the Russian forces in Galicia and the western Ukraine, secure the crossing of the Dnieper, and capture Kiev, with his twenty-five infantry, five panzer, four motorized, and four mountain divisions.

Rundstedt had left France in April 1941 to ready his Army Group for the assault, and he felt strongly that it should begin no later than May. The Balkans affray was to him 'a very costly delay'. When he did attack the Bug and San rivers (in Soviet-occupied Poland) on 22 June, Rundstedt was to find the Russian opposition better organized and stronger than he had been led to expect. After ten days' hard fighting Kleist's armour had penetrated only sixty miles into Russian-held territory.

The Russians managed to evade a planned German encirclement north of the Dniester and withdrew in good order to the strongly fortified Stalin Line which, in the part below the Pripet Marshes which separated Rundstedt's and Bock's Army Groups, protected Vinnitsa, Zhitomir, and Kiev. But Kleist, greatly inferior in tank strength though not in expertise, managed to break through the Stalin Line on 7 July in the Zvyagel area, and Major-General Ludwig Crüwell, later of Africa Korps fame, captured Berdichev with his 11th Panzer Division. Two days later the 16th Panzer Division under Major-General Hans-Valentin Hube broke through again at Lyuban, helped by continual bombing and Stuka sorties by the 4th Air Fleet.

On 16 July Kleist's tanks reached Belya Tserkov, an important centre south of Kiev. But further north Rundstedt's troops were hardly making spectacular progress, and when August came had still to get beyond Zhitomir, over eighty miles west of Kiev and the Dnieper river. Rundstedt decided, therefore, to strike south-east and, after Kleist had taken Novo Arkhangelsk on 1 August, trapped parts of three Soviet Armies between Kleist's Panzers at Uman, south-west of Kiev, and infantry divisions from his 11th and 17th Armies. It was not a complete victory, although 103,000 prisoners were taken, but it opened the way east towards Krivoy Rog and its iron ore, the Black Sea ports of Odessa and Nikolayev, and above all to the lower Dnieper. Moreover there was now a chance of a great encirclement battle round Kiev, and Hitler therefore decided to divert Colonel-General Heinz Guderian's 2nd Panzer Group from von Bock's control to join with Rundstedt in that area.

By the end of August Rundstedt's troops were keeping the Russians busy on the lower Dnieper. They had captured Dniepropetrovsk and were laying siege to Odessa. On 10 September Kleist's XLVIII Panzer Korps, under Lieutenant-General Werner Kempf who had commanded 6th Panzer Division successfully in France, reached the western banks of the Dnieper near Kremenchug, and next day a small bridgehead was established. In the north, after a terrible battle on the Desna river, Guderian's XXIV Panzer Corps, under General Baron Geyr von Schweppenburg, sent Lieutenant-General Walter Model's 3rd Panzer Division between two Soviet Armies. Exploiting the gap he had torn, Model pushed on, and though there was still a distance of thirty miles between Guderian's and Kleist's Groups, the two managed to link up, and had by the evening of 14 September virtually cut off the Russians at Romny, east of Kiev. By 19 September Kiev had fallen to the XXIX Corps of Reichenau's Sixth Army, and Marshal Budenny's Armies had been smashed.

It was a staggering defeat for Stalin, who had contributed to it in the Hitler style by forbidding Budenny to retreat while retreat was possible. But the main credit must go to Guderian, Rundstedt, and Kleist. Hitler was ecstatic, calling it 'the greatest battle in the history of the world', and O.K.H. put Russian losses at 665,000 prisoners, 3,718 guns, and 884 A.F.V.s. General Kempf's XLVIII Panzer Corps alone took over 100,000 prisoners.

The main result of Kiev was Hitler's decision to attack Moscow on 2 October. But time was already running out. In the south the elimination of several Russian armies now allowed Rundstedt to occupy the Ukraine, push into the Crimea, and reach the Donets Basin. In these operations Army Group South destroyed or captured 753 Russian tanks, 2,800 guns, and took another 400,000 prisoners.

Rundstedt was not in agreement with Hitler, and nor was Brauchitsch. 'We ought to have stopped on the Dnieper after taking Kiev,' the Field-Marshal told Liddell Hart, and he argued the case strongly. But Hitler was flushed with success, and Field-Marshal von Bock, whose forces were to take Moscow, was naturally eager for his own lion's share. Bock and many other generals, including Guderian, had wanted to concentrate the attack on Moscow rather than Kiev, but Hitler had overruled them in his passion for the Crimea.

Colonel-General von Schobert's 11th Army, which, starting the invasion from Rumania, had played no part in the Kiev battle, was now ordered 'to capture the Crimean peninsula with some of its forces, and with the bulk of its forces will drive towards Rostov along the northern edge of the Sea of Azov'. This order coincided with a change of command, for on 12 September Eugen Ritter von Schobert, a Bavarian aristocrat who was strongly pro-Hitler, became the first Army commander to become a casualty, though by no means the last. His Fieseler Storch spotter-plane, attempting a forced landing, came down in the middle of a Russian minefield and was blown to pieces.

Before forming the 11th Army in October 1940, von Schobert had led the VII Corps as a General of Infantry in the Polish and French campaigns, having commanded it from Munich since 1938. This Corps had been earmarked as one of the assault formations for England, and had even adopted a new march written for the purpose called 'England zerkrache!'—loosely translatable as 'England, burst!'

Schobert's successor was General von Manstein, who had been commanding LVI Panzer Corps in the north with conspicuous success.

Hitler was aware that control of the Crimea meant control of the Black Sea. It also introduced political leverage over Persia and, in particular, Turkey. The dream of a link with the Mediterranean and African forces did not seem too fanciful. Seizure of the Crimea and Rostov would provide a springboard for Rundstedt in his attack on the Donets Basin industrial area.

It soon became clear that too much was being asked of 11th Army, although their scope was limited to the Crimea while the capture of Rostov was allocated to Kleist's 1st Panzer Group, now promoted to 1st Panzer Army. By 28 October all units had reached the Mius river, and von Stülpnagel's 17th Army had reached the Donets. On 24 October, von Reichenau's 6th Army further north had captured the industrially important city of Kharkov. Then everything was halted by mud. It was not until 17 November that General of Cavalry Eberhard von Mackensen's III Panzer Corps started its attack against Rostov, 'the gateway to the Caucasus' and a vital communications centre and staging post for British supplies arriving in Russia from the Persian Gulf. Three days later Mackensen could report the capture of Rostov, a feat which must have inspired in Hitler's mind visions of gushing Soviet oil. But the Russians were not going to let things go, and exploited the gap between Kleist and Stülpnagel to counter-attack. Mackensen was forced to divert some of his armour to deal with this threat, whereupon the main Russian counter-attack fell on his weakened Corps on 25 November 1941. His front was seventy miles long and could not be held with the forces available. Rundstedt therefore rang up Halder at Hitler's headquarters and asked permission to abandon Rostov. To Hitler, of course, this was out of the question, and Rundstedt was ordered to hold where he was. His own account of the matter to Wilmot follows:

'After accomplishing my first objective, which was the encirclement and destruction of the enemy forces west of the Dnieper, I was given my second objective. It was to advance eastwards and take Maikop and Stalingrad. We laughed aloud when we received these orders, for winter had already come and we were almost 700 kilometres away from these cities. Hitler thought that with the frost making the roads hard we could advance towards Stalingrad very quickly. At the same time I was told to advance towards Maikop because oil was urgently needed and I was also expected to clean up the Crimea in order to deprive the Russians of their airfields in this area. With my forces split in these three drives, we nevertheless managed to get a tank force as far east as Rostov. This meant that I had a terribly long left flank with nothing to protect it. The Russians attacked at Rostov from the north and south about the end of November, and realizing that I couldn't hold the city I ordered it to be evacuated. I had previously asked for permission to withdraw this extended armoured spearhead to the Mius river, about 100 kilometres west of Rostov. I was told that I could do this and we began to withdraw very slowly, fighting all the way. Suddenly an order came to me from the Führer: "Remain where you are, and retreat no further," it said. I immediately wired back, "It is madness to attempt to hold. In the first place the troops cannot do it and in the second place if they do not retreat they will be destroyed. I repeat that this order be rescinded or that you find someone else." That same night the Führer's reply arrived: "I am acceding to your request," it read; "please give up your command." I then went home.'

This was on 1 December 1941, shortly before Rundstedt's sixty-sixth birthday. Perhaps he was not sorry to leave, for the toll of the campaign had affected his heart. When he left Army Group South headquarters every single officer turned out to say goodbye to him. He was succeeded in command by Field-Marshal von Reichenau, from 6th Army, who instantly stopped the retreat. Twenty-four hours later, however, he too had to ask Hitler's permission to shorten the line, in other words withdraw to the Mius, exactly as Rundstedt had desired.

Hitler had now seen for himself something of the situation, having flown to the Army Group a day or two earlier, where he had been given an unequivocal briefing on the dangers of the situation by von Sodenstern and had made fulsome enquiries about Rundstedt's health. So he sanctioned the abandonment of Rostov, and Reichenau's withdrawal. This may have been the German Army's first major setback of the war, but as Rundstedt pointed out later: 'Significantly, the Mius river line was the only sector of the front that was not shaken during the winter of 1941–2.'

Rundstedt had always doubted Russia's aggressive intentions against Germany, and had found no evidence of them when he crossed the frontier. He thought the deep drive of his own Army Group a misconceived strategic move. The main effort, he thought, should first have been directed at Leningrad, not at Moscow, to link up with the Finnish Army, followed by an all-out drive on Moscow from the north in company with the advance from the west of the most powerful Army Group, von Bock's Centre one.

Brauchitsch had been in accord with Rundstedt's request to withdraw to the Mius. He also agreed that it would be wise to conduct a wholesale withdrawal in the face of the oncoming winter, thus enabling the Armies to be re-equipped and refreshed before launching new offensives in 1942. Rundstedt and von Leeb actually favoured going back as far as Poland. Hitler ruled that there should be no withdrawals. Whether this decision is remarkable as displaying 'iron nerve' or 'the peasant in him that refuses to give up an inch of ground' is arguable. Many commentators and generals, including German ones, have found that Hitler was exactly right to stand where he did and thereby saved the situation. It is my belief that the exact opposite is true, and that future disasters would have been avoided if the Germans had withdrawn considerably, shortened their line, and prepared properly thought-out new attacks, principally on Moscow, in 1942 rather than continuing their 1941 attacks for so long. The lack of winter clothing alone is an outstanding argument for withdrawal in 1941. The argument that any withdrawal might have turned into a panic retreat is not defensible with troops as hardy, experienced, and well-disciplined as the Germans then in Russia. Rundstedt summed up: 'It was Hitler's decision for rigid resistance that caused the danger·in the first place. It would not have arisen if he had permitted a timely withdrawal.'

The war in the east, however, was no longer directly to concern Rundstedt. In March 1942 he celebrated his fiftieth year in the Army by being recalled to duty as acting Commander-in-Chief West and C-in-C Army Group D. These appointments were confirmed on 1 May, and from then until the Allied invasion in June 1944 von Rundstedt could take things comparatively easily in the comfort of his villa at St-Germain-en-Laye near Paris. This suited him well enough at his age, for he was something of a Francophile through his mother's Huguenot blood, and friendly disposed towards Marshal Pétain. He spoke French very well.

His actual powers, however, were strictly limited. General Baron von Neubrunn, who was German military representative at Vichy between 1940 and 1944, a decent old soldier, is quoted to the point by Richard Griffiths in his biography of Marshal Pétain (pp. 323–4): 'Unfortunately Rundstedt held himself apart from any exertion of political influence. Through this the administrative task of the military commander, General Heinrich von Stülpnagel, was likewise made more difficult. I have heard many a complaint from this passionate opponent of Hitler's policies, about the passive behaviour of the Commander-in-Chief. The executive power in France was moving over more and more to the Embassy, the S.S., the Gestapo, and the Party organisation.'

Rundstedt, of course, was supremely the non-political general. This explains why one can never envisage him as a collaborator with the anti-Nazis of the Resistance, sympathetic though he may have been to their aims. His age, too, should be remembered. He thought himself, rightly, too old to dabble in underground plots or assassination attempts, though, as the first high commander to be dismissed by Hitler, he felt no love for his Führer, whom he preferred still to think of as an ex-corporal rather than a present Commander-in-Chief. Thus when approached, as he frequently was, by one or other Resistance plotter or anti-Nazi general like Heinrich von Stülpnagel, Rundstedt would be sardonic but distant. As Schlabrendorff recalled: 'Our talk revealed that he was quite ready to use strong words against the Nazis, but that he was equally determined to take no action against them.' So when Alexander Freiherr von Neubronn thought of the attempts to get Laval dismissed he said: 'When I told him [Pétain] that the General [von Rundstedt] too hard to go through the Embassy, the Marshal resigned himself with a bitter smile. He must have seen that his plan to set Laval aside was not to be achieved with the collaboration of German military circles. It was shaming for me to have so openly to admit the powerlessness of the highest military authority in France.'

Later, Rundstedt used to joke that he could not change the guard in front of his house without permission from Berchtesgaden. His attitude towards the anti-Hitler conspiracy has been well put by one of the former Chiefs of Staff to both von Stülpnagel and Rommel, General Dr Hans Speidel:

'Rundstedt was an eminent strategist, a master of the rules of war, but in the last few years he had lost with advancing age the creative impulse and the clear sense of responsibility towards the nation. Symptoms of this lapse were sarcastic comments or indifference. Of course he despised Hitler and referred to him in all private conversations, as Hindenberg did, with the nickname of "the Bohemian corporal". But he seemed to think that the height of wisdom was to make studied representations and write grave situation reports. He left action to others. When Rommel sought to move him to send joint demands to Hitler, Rundstedt exclaimed: "You are young. The People know and love you. You do it!"

This reveals a flaw in character. As early as February 1940 Hasso von Etzdorf of the Foreign Office, whose job was liaison with the General Staff, had told Ambassador Ulrich von Hassell that he thought Rundstedt 'soft in the head'.

As Commander-in-Chief West in 1944 von Rundstedt had only about sixty divisions, many of them of second-rate quality, to defend a coastline from the Italian frontier in the south to the fatherland in the north. This was obviously an absurdly low strength. The much-vaunted Atlantic

Wall, moreover, was little more than a grand illusion, though Rommel since his appointment to Army Group B in late 1943 energetically did much to strengthen coastal defences, especially in the Pas de Calais and north-western France. It was clear to Rundstedt, however, that there was not much hope of preventing an Allied landing in strength from gaining a firm foothold in France. He saw the best chance of defeating it, or at least of holding it back, by concentrating his armoured strength some way behind the invasion beaches and launching a powerful counter-attack at a time and place of his own choosing.

In this theory he was supported by the field commander of the bulk of the German armour in France, General of Panzer Troops Baron Geyr von Schweppenburg, a former military attaché in London, who had commanded an armoured Corps with distinction in Russia, and was now G.O.C. Panzer Troops West. The theory was perfectly justifiable, but neither Rundstedt nor Geyr fully anticipated the enormous effects of total Allied air superiority over the beach-head and in the hinterland, so that it became virtually impossible to move up a division, especially a panzer division, in daylight without suffering crippling casualties from bombing and rocket attacks. Rommel, who confessed to having had to be 'very rough' with von Geyr to get his own way, apparently did see the danger. At any rate he was firmly convinced that the Allies must be beaten back right on the beaches and that his armour must be kept as far forward as possible to achieve this result. It is now evident that Rommel was right, and Rundstedt and von Geyr wrong.

In the event, however, neither side in the controversy was fully to get its way. Rommel was allowed to place his armour close to the coast, but that only involved three panzer divisions, with whose dispositions Rundstedt did not attempt to interfere. The remaining dozen in all France came under von Geyr, who was responsible operationally to Rundstedt, and were kept, with the exception of Panzer Lehr, the most formidable of the lot, well back, ready for a concentrated armoured counter-stroke when the occasion came. But even here there was a grave snag. In fact neither Rundstedt nor von Geyr had freedom to move any of these divisions without express permission from Hitler back in Berlin, a ludicrous situation. The one thing which the Allies who fought in Normandy constantly expected and were relieved never to have to withstand in the early days was a concerted, concentrated all-out counter-attack on our weak spots with masses of Panthers, Tigers, and Mark IVs supported by Panzer Grenadiers. For this they could thank first our overwhelming air superiority, and secondly, Hitler. As things turned out, although the British tied down as many as nine panzer divisions on the Normandy front, the counter-attacks came in small bursts rather than in one big push, and were thus easier, although not easy, to deal with.

Rundstedt admitted to having been wrong about the site of the invasion, which he thought would come at first between Le Havre and Calais, especially between the Somme and Calais. Only Hitler had thought consistently that Normandy was the likeliest locale, though he shied away from that choice shortly before it came true. Rommel was right in thinking Normandy, but as a last-minute convert to that school. The general opinion was that any landing in Normandy would have a limited objective—Cherbourg.

Even before 6 June 1944, Rundstedt, because of his troops' weakness, had favoured a drastic regrouping in France. 'Before the Allied invasion,' he told Liddell Hart, 'I had wanted to evacuate the whole of southern France up to the Loire, and bring back the forces there to form a strong mass of manoeuvre with which I could strike back at the Allies. This would have provided ten or twelve infantry divisions and three or four armoured divisions to fight a mobile battle. But Hitler would not listen to such an idea—though it was the only way in which I could hope to form a proper reserve. All the newspaper talk about "Rundstedt's Central Army" was sheer nonsense—that army did not exist. Worse still, I was not even allowed a free hand with the handful of armoured divisions that were available in France. I could not move one of them without Hitler's permission.'

When, some ten days after the Normandy landings, the Allied strength ashore had reached nearly half a million men, and several armoured divisions, Rundstedt tried to revive this plan, and advocated that all German divisions in southern France and along the Atlantic coast be pulled back and sent north of the Loire. He told Shulman later: 'With these divisions I planned to hold a position along the Loire and Orne rivers, relieve the panzer divisions, and with them push forward with a counter-offensive. Such a policy, of course, meant the abandonment of all of France south of the Loire, and this decision was considered politically impossible at Berlin. With insufficient infantry at my disposal I was unable to remove the armoured formations facing the Allied bridgehead.'

On 1 July II Panzer Corps, using elements of four divisions, tried in bad weather for not the first time to break through the British front at Caen. The British held the attack, even without being able to call on air support.

That night when Rundstedt reported failure over the telephone to Keitel in Berlin, the chief of the O.K.W. moaned: 'What shall we do? What shall we do?'

'Make peace, you fools,' replied Rundstedt. 'What else can you do?'

This not tactful remark may well have been the immediate cause of Rundstedt's removal from command the next day. Again he went into retirement, to be succeeded by the egregious von Kluge from the Russian front. Baron von Geyr, who had been wounded when his

Panzer Group West forward headquarters near Caen had been pin-pointed and bombed with heavy casualties to his staff, followed Rundstedt into retirement on 5 July.

But for being wounded in another air action, near Ste Foy de Mont-gommery, ironically enough, Rommel would almost certainly have joined the pair. In their short partnership Rundstedt and Rommel had learned to work harmoniously together, though they were utterly different in character. Von Rundstedt did not interfere in Rommel's tactical disposi-tions, though he tended to regard him as only really capable of small operations and not fully qualified for high command. This may well have been inherent career or Prussian snobbishness on Rundstedt's part. On his side Rommel always faithfully obeyed a Rundstedt order. Neither was to blame for the defeat in Normandy, which it is highly doubtful if any general, however gifted, could have prevented at length, after the Allied build-up and in view of Allied air and naval superiority. It should not be forgotten that the guns of the Fleet wrought great execution on the defenders and their gun positions. And on their morale.

Little over two months later, on 4 September 1944, von Rundstedt was recalled to the top job, in succession to von Kluge and Model. Neither of these men had been able to stem the Allies, who had now reached Holland, the German frontier, the Vosges, and the Swiss frontier. Since neither at Soissons nor at Margival had Rundstedt and Rommel been able to convince Hitler that the German armies must be withdrawn across the Seine, the killing cauldron of Falaise had taken place and the Germans had been driven into helter-skelter retreat. The calm, authoritative hand of Rundstedt was called for, and in one of his more impressive achievements the ageing general imposed rapid reorganisation upon his soldiers and re-established a more or less stable continuous front.

The last great offensive mounted by the German Army, which became known as the Battle of the Ardennes, was conceived by Hitler and controlled by him, though it was popularly supposed at the time to be the work of von Rundstedt. This was not the case, for the Field-Marshal was only nominally in command of it, and the actual operational conduct of the battle was in the hands of Field-Marshal Model and of S.S. Colonel-General Sepp Dietrich, commanding Sixth Panzer Army, and General of Panzer Troops Hasso von Manteuffel, commanding 5th Panzer Army. For once the Luftwaffe scraped together enough aircraft to make some contribution when weather permitted, but after losing 270 planes in the massive sweeps against Allied targets on 1 January 1945, it made no effectual contribution. The actual Ardennes attack started in misty weather on 16 December 1944, achieved initial success, but had shot its bolt by early January 1945. By the end of that month all the ground lost originally by the Americans had been recaptured, and though casualties were heavy on both sides the

Germans came off worst and they could not afford the toll.

Antwerp and Brussels were the main objectives of Hitler. Both Rundstedt and Model thought these over-optimistic, but pressed for more limited and realistic objectives in vain. They were backed up by Manteuffel. In Rundstedt's words (to Liddell Hart): 'When I received this plan early in November I was staggered. Hitler had not troubled to consult me about its possibilities. It was obvious to me that the available forces were far too small for such an extremely ambitious plan. Model took the same view of this as I did. In fact, no soldier believed that the aim of reaching Antwerp was really practicable. But I knew by now it was useless to protest to Hitler about the *possibility* of anything. After consultation with Model and Manteuffel I felt that the only hope was to wean Hitler from this fantastic aim by putting forward an alternative proposal that might appeal to him, and would be more practicable. This was for a limited offensive with the aim of pinching off the Allies' salient around Aachen.'

Rundstedt found it a continuing source of annoyance after the war that his name was always linked with the Ardennes offensive, the more so because he had protested so vigorously against it. But his suggestion of the Aachen salient was turned down by Hitler, as were all his other modifications. He summarized to Shulman: 'It was only up to me to obey. It was a nonsensical operation, and the most stupid part of it was the setting of Antwerp as the target. If we reached the Meuse we should have got down on our knees and thanked God—let alone try to reach Antwerp.'

Surprisingly enough, perhaps, the most vociferous protest came from Hitler's old friend and strong-arm merchant, Sepp Dietrich, who by now was more than disillusioned with his Führer's conduct of the war. He told Shulman sarcastically: "All I had to do was to cross a river, capture Brussels, and then go on and take the port of Antwerp. And all this in December, January and February, the worst three months of the year; through the Ardennes where snow was waist deep and there wasn't room to deploy four tanks abreast, let alone six armoured divisions; when it didn't get light until eight in the morning and was dark again at four in the afternoon and my tanks can't fire at night; with divisions that had just been reformed and were composed chiefly of raw untrained recruits; and at Christmas time.' Dietrich took his protests to Jodl, but they achieved nothing.

As early as 24 December, when the Germans had failed to capture the vital communications centre of Bastogne, Rundstedt urged that the offensive be called off; but Hitler would have none of this. And so it went on, with immense and irreparable losses to Germany, not least in morale. In physical terms nearly 600 tanks, tracked guns and assault guns were lost, and over 1,600 aircraft. Rundstedt summed up to Shulman about this costly and wasteful battle:

'It must be remembered that the Ardennes offensive was planned in all its details, including formations involved, objectives and so on, by the Führer and his staff. All counter-proposals were rejected. Under such circumstances, there could be little faith in its success. Even during the attack the Supreme Command conducted the operations by means of liaison officers and direct wireless orders to the armies involved. I received few reports from 'Sepp' Dietrich of the Sixth S.S. Panzer Army, and what I did receive was generally a pack of lies. If the S.S. had any problems they reported them directly to the Führer, who would then make them known to Model. The execution of the operation was also made much more difficult by the strict order from above that every place, including sectors that had been cut off, was to be held. And even towards the end, when Fifth Panzer Army was being attacked by superior enemy forces from both the north and south, any and every proposal made by me for a timely withdrawal to a defence line was flatly turned down.'

Rundstedt, therefore, can bear no blame for the Ardennes failure. 'As far as I was concerned, the war was ended in September,' was, in any case, his view.

It is ironic that Rundstedt was first dismissed when his reputation was at its height; and as a commander he was, in the eyes of most of his colleagues, unrivalled in the German Army. He was out of a job when Hitler went through the motions of congratulating him in March 1942 on celebrating his half-century in that Army. It is significant, in examining Rundstedt's record as a commander, that Hitler felt it necessary to recall him twice. This shows the influence and authority which he wielded in the Army. It cannot be claimed that Rundstedt rose to the very first rank of military commanders, nor that he was in any way intellectual or a particularly original general. He was intelligent, excellently trained, experienced, calm, unhurried, with that rare gift for improvisation denied to so many generals. An orthodox commander, perhaps, but one well able to exploit his opportunities in an offensive, and, judging by his Chiefs of Staff and Army commanders, a good picker of men. Perhaps his success may best be explained by the fact that he had *character*, and this won him the respect and indeed the fondness of his subordinates, though he never played to the gallery or tried to win favourites. It was typical of Rundstedt that he was, though invariably turned out impeccably, one of the only two or three German generals who usually wore not the gold Oak Leaves of a general on his collar but the simple badges of a colonel of a regiment.

If Rundstedt does not rank among the highest, he must rank high. His conduct of his campaigns in Poland and in France in 1939 and 1940 ensures that. His comparatively brief spell in Russia produced one great success, if it failed in over-ambitious objectives for which he himself was not responsible. It is hard to see that Rundstedt did anything very wrong in Russia, but from that period on he was fatally hamstrung by Hitler's personal handling of the war. Rundstedt's successes in the Ukraine and in the south of Russia were certainly greater than those of Leeb in the north. And over the reason, or at least the overt reason, for his dismissal, the withdrawal to the Mius, he was proved right. It is my view that he was also right about a general withdrawal in that first winter in Russia.

Of Rundstedt's conduct of the defence of Normandy in 1944 one can justly say that again he was hopelessly hampered by not having a free hand. He was not successful, but it is doubtful if anyone else in his place would have done much better. His restoration of the situation in forming an orderly line in September was a real achievement, for there had been a danger of collapse. His part in the Ardennes offensive was nominal, as we have seen, and although he directed Germany's last offensive of the war, the small one in Alsace in January 1945, this was fairly easily contained by the Americans and French. By the time that Rundstedt was finally replaced on 10 March 1945 by Field-Marshal Kesselring and went into retirement, there was nothing that he or anyone else could have done to stem the final victorious advance of the Allies.

Of his mistakes, two stand out. He was badly wrong—not to halt and tidy up the German armour in France in May 1940—but to prolong that delay, and thus he missed a great chance before Dunkirk. Equally, he was wrong in his disposition of the German armour before the invasion of June 1944, and in his overall command arrangements it would have been wiser to listen more to the vigorous Rommel. Even so, with the very telling air superiority of the Allies in Normandy it is doubtful whether he could ever successfully have beaten back the invaders.

Sir Basil Liddell Hart, who had great experience of generals, thought more and more highly of Rundstedt the longer he talked to him; and Liddell Hart was not easily duped. His subordinates on the whole revered and liked him, and preferred, for example, to serve under him than von Bock, a difficult man. His political outlook has been called ruthless and narrow, but it stemmed from his fierce sense of duty and his patriotism. His loyalty, even under great provocation, to Hitler remained untarnished even if in private he condemned the whole Nazi gang. Whether he should have thrown in his lot with the conspiring generals is hard to say, but his typical Prussian character, and devotion to duty as he saw it, makes it plain why he did not. Few seem to have thought the worse of him for standing aside. He was something of a disciplinarian, who could treat his own soldiers severely. He was strongly against looting and thieving in Poland and Russia.

He could be severe, too, with people in the occupied countries. For example, at Ascq in France in 1944, seventy-seven men ranging in age from 15 to 74 were shot, having been chosen indiscriminately from the population, after a railway line was destroyed by the Resistance. Rundstedt then declared: 'The population of Ascq bears the responsibility for the consequences of its treacherous conduct, which I can only severely condemn.'

In 1948 Rundstedt was notified, with Field-Marshals von Brauchitsch and von Manstein, and Colonel-General Strauss, that he would be tried by the British military authorities in Germany for war crimes. He was then nearly 73. The justification for such a trial presumably rested upon incidents such as that at Ascq, and on a statement attributed to Rundstedt by *Picture Post* of 24 April 1948. 'We Germans must number twice the population of our neighbours. Therefore we shall be compelled to destroy one-third of the population of all adjacent territories. We can best achieve this through systematic malnutrition—in the end far superior to machine-guns. . .starvation works more effectively, especially among the young.'

This so-called statement rings altogether false, and in harking back to the 1948 notice of incitement one may comment that if asked to select four representatives of much that was best in the old German Army one could hardly do better than choose Rundstedt, Brauchitsch, Manstein and Strauss. *The Times* thought that these generals had been held far too long in captivity without trial, and that the handling of the Field-Marshals' cases could be 'legitimately censured'. In the event Rundstedt never did come to trial as a war criminal, because of illness, and the case against him was dropped in 1949.

He died in 1953. Lean, spare, erect, with a formidable dignity but a pleasing if rather sarcastic sense of humour, Rundstedt still stands out as one of the ablest soldiers in the German Army this century. It is pleasant to know that he was an excellent mimic who could speak in practically every known German accent. If his military powers declined during the war, their falling-off was not noticeable. It was indeed true to say of him, as did W.E. Hart, that he was 'accomplished in theory and proved in action', and the gloss on that verdict may be found in the biography written by one of his Chiefs of Staff, General Günther Blumentritt, himself a gifted soldier. Hart thought that 'the thin, intellectual features might be those of the priest if the outward alertness of the soldier were absent', and the nickname by which von Rundstedt became known in Germany was not inapt 'the high priest of strategy'.

General Baron Geyr von Schweppenburg described Rundstedt as 'incredibly idle. . . clever but horse-minded', the latter presumably in the sense of being out of date. It is true that Rundstedt did not belong to the thrusting school of the new, young, forceful panzer generals such as Rommel, Model, von Schwerin, and Balck. But, before cynicism set in and, with old age, combined to advocate the path of least resistence, the abilities, character and sagacity of Field-Marshal Gerd von Rundstedt had placed him firmly among the outstandingly expert though not among the greatest of German military commanders.

Germany's last professional Commander-in-Chief of the Army, Walther von Brauchitsch, was an artilleryman who had served throughout the Great War on the General Staff. When the Nazis achieved the discrediting and downfall of his predecessor, Colonel-General von Fritsch, it had been Hitler's wish and intention to get von Reichenau promoted in his place. But this the Army, led by von Rundstedt, would not accept, so the post went to von Brauchitsch who was acceptable to all and popular throughout the Army. He was several years junior in age and seniority of rank to von Rundstedt, but was promoted Colonel-General on the day of his appointment, 4 February 1938, and became Field-Marshal in the mass promotion Hitler ordained after the victory over France in July 1940.

Brauchitsch has been hardly, even severely, dealt with by many historians, particularly by Sir John Wheeler-Bennett ('a man of little moral courage and no strength of character'), Barry A. Leach, Walter Görlitz, and Colonel Albert Seaton, and his case has not been helped by the disloyalty to his Chief which Halder sometimes showed even during the war. It is time that at least a part of his reputation be re-established.

Brauchitsch was born in Berlin in 1881. In 1900 he became a subaltern in the 3rd Foot Guards, a famous regiment which nurtured one of his predecessors as Commander-in-Chief, Colonel-General Freiherr Kurt von Hammerstein-Equord, and Field-Marshal von Manstein. But the next year Brauchitsch, despite promptings to the contrary from his friend in the cavalry, von Kleist, transferred to the 3rd Guards Field Artillery Regiment. A major at the end of the Great War, he served as a staff officer in the Truppenamt from late 1922, and in 1925 commanded an artillery battalion. By 1928 he was a colonel, followed by further spells of duty in the Truppenamt in 1930 as Director of Army Training, a departmental head, and in 1932 as Inspector of Artillery. He became a Major-General in 1930; a Lieutenant-General in 1933, when commander of Wehrkreis I and the 1st Division at Königsberg; commander of I Army Corps at Königsberg from June 1935; a full General of Artillery in 1936, and commander of Gruppenkommando 4 in 1937.

An innovator in artillery methods and a thoroughly good gunner, Brauchitsch was not fenced in by traditional military beliefs and was, in fact, largely responsible for developing the formidable 88 mm. gun for dual-purpose work, that is as both an anti-tank and an anti-aircraft gun. The dual-purpose 88 mm. became the finest artillery piece of the war. As a former grammar-school boy he was not subservient to the tenets of the Junker class. When he was commanding in East Prussia Brauchitsch clashed with Gauleiter Erich Koch, an equivocal character, and with the S.S., elements of whom he ejected from Army manoeuvres. His appointment as C-in-C Army came as a great surprise, partly because he was by no means considered to be a Nazi sympathizer. Powerful though such an appointment might be, much of its strength was vitiated because Hitler chose the time of the demise of von Blomberg and von Fritsch to establish the Oberkommando der Wehrmacht, or O.K.W., under General Keitel, who had previously been head of the lesser Wehrmachtsamt and, in Blomberg's words, 'the man who runs my office'. Thus the new C-in-C Army became less of a power than he had been previously. His position with the Nazis was also weakened because in 1938 he divorced his first wife, and married a woman who was notoriously pro-Nazi. It was suggested at the time that possibly Hitler and certainly Göring had smoothed the way for this second marriage to take place, as conservative Army circles did not relish divorces in those days, and Brauchitsch was the son of a Prussian General of Cavalry.

Brauchitsch has been criticized for accepting his appointment before Fritsch's case was dealt with, for tamely accepting Hitler's new unification of command in the O.K.W., and for agreeing to some vital changes of personnel in the High Command. Jodl thought he would have accomplished most of the latter in his own interests anyway, but it remains true that more or less contemporaneously with Brauchitsch's promotion sixteen high-ranking generals lost their commands (though nearly all were to regain them within a year or so) and many others were transferred. In the view of Wheeler-Bennett, Brauchitsch was an appeaser who had sold the pass before he started his top job. Others may feel that he had a sincere desire to protect the Army from undue Nazi influence. He told Hitler in 1938 that the interference of civilians in military affairs invariably led to disastrous results, a warning which seems to have passed the Führer by; and he kept on von Fritsch's staff and remained on good terms with his predecessor. He did not think much of Keitel, and he was bold enough to threaten to challenge Dr Göbbels to a duel for spreading unpleasant rumours about his divorce.

Like others who had thought that they might tame the tiger, von Brauchitsch was to find Hitler an impossible customer to deal with. The tragedy is that Brauchitsch progressively weakened and eventually lost control of his own organization, to become merely a figurehead. The reasons for this were a certain weakness of character, the unstoppable success and undeniable orders of an emphatic Hitler, a misguided sense of loyalty, and the very considerable influence upon him of his '200 per cent' Nazi wife. It was thus that he became, in von Manstein's words, 'demoted from the status of military adviser to the Head of

State to that of a subordinate commander pledged to unquestioning obedience'.

In various ways Brauchitsch had a wider outlook than many of his colleagues. He was a well-educated man, spoke several foreign languages, and himself listed economic and political questions of the day as his outside interests. Like Raeder in the Navy, he tried to maintain the old religious traditions in the Army. He had very good manners, to those outside the Army as well as to his colleagues, and showed warmth and understanding towards his subordinates. As a result people liked to serve under him. He was particularly solicitous of the welfare of the troops, and paid attention to their housing and food. Militarily he had shown himself keen on new ideas in the 'twenties by organizing manoeuvres to test the co-operation of aircraft with motorized troops. Unfortunately, although not a Nazi in the sense that his more galvanic superior, von Blomberg, had been, he was when he came to his high post a warm personal admirer of Hitler.

Thus, in an order about the training of officers issued on 18 December 1938, he said: 'Adolf Hitler, our leader of genius, who has recast the great lesson of the front-line soldier in the form of the National Socialist philosophy, has built and secured for us the new Great-German Reich. Only he who can comprehend the yesterday, today and tomorrow in their full difficulty and immensity can appreciate the historic nature of the deeds of this man. The revolution has been stupendous in all fields. A new German being has grown up in the Third Reich, filled with ideas different from those of the generation which went before us. . . . Our loyalty to the man who has created all this, who by his faith and will has worked this miracle, is unshakeable, our confidence in him is firm. . . . The Armed Forces and National-Socialism are of the same spiritual stem. They will accomplish much for the nation in the future, if they follow the example and teaching of the Führer, who combines in his person the true soldier and National-Socialist.'

This was not at all the stuff to appeal to Colonel-General Ludwig Beck, Brauchitsch's first Chief of Staff, who, though he had resigned by the time of that order, had had to listen to much similar tub-thumping before. Beck was utterly against a war with the West, as indeed was Brauchitsch, but whereas Beck put his arguments in the most forceful way Brauchitsch managed only to convey weak protests to Hitler, though he himself had told a conference of senior generals that war would mean the end of German culture. Relations between the two men progressively worsened, and Beck finally did for himself in Hitler's eyes by a memorandum of 3 June 1938, in which he asserted that a war with Czechoslovakia would involve all Europe in a war, which Germany would lose. After several offers of resignation Beck finally went that August, to be succeeded by the Bavarian General Halder.

In Hammerstein's view Brauchitsch had no political sense, and, owing to the deliberate reorganization by Hitler of the High Command, no power. The opinion of this most anti-Nazi and intelligent of German generals, interestingly one who achieved the reputation of being 'red', is recorded by Ambassador Ulrich von Hassell as early as December 1938, and should be respected.

It is evident that Brauchitsch, in many ways a reformer, had the opportunity to put the German Army on a new track, but followed the wrong one. Had he made common cause with Beck and decent and respected pillars of the old school such as Rundstedt, Witzleben, Leeb, and Blaskowitz, and had he tried to win over Göring, with whom he was on good terms, and some of the ex-Army officers in the Luftwaffe such as Kesselring and Sperrle, and Raeder, who as a traditionalist presented no great problems, it is just possible that a last chance to head off Hitler from his path to destruction might have been created. Whether Brauchitsch thought, like some Army generals before him, that Hitler could be used, and did not see the dangers in this false belief until too late; or whether he genuinely believed that the Army and Nazism must walk hand in hand, is not certain. At all events, either from weakness when confronted with the extraordinary forcefulness of Hitler, or from compliance, he proved lamentably unable to stand up to Hitler, and not the man to lead an Army revolt against him. Not that the idea did not occur to him, for though Beck had learned to put no faith in him and the conspirators did not include him in their plans, Brauchitsch was well aware that there was a conspiracy. Beck had tried to get him to act, and had sought at least a free hand to act himself before it was too late and the West flared into war, but Brauchitsch had never consented. Political events had conspired, it seemed, to give Hitler one triumph after another, in the Rhineland, Austria, and Czechoslovakia. Brauchitsch, meanwhile, consoled himself with the trappings of office and a genuine but naive hope that all would turn out for the best.

It is significant of the weakness of his position that when the German-Soviet Pact was signed in late August 1939, Brauchitsch was not consulted, nor had he been given any hand in drawing up the 'Pact of Steel' signed between Italy and Germany on 22 May 1939, though the latter was a military alliance containing military clauses, and there were pronounced military undertones in the former.

Brauchitsch was not against the invasion of Poland, but only because he believed Hitler's assurance that it would not lead to general war. He was in charge of the planning of the campaign, but in fact this closely followed plans that had been laid down by von Fritsch. Brauchitsch was more worried about Russian intervention than anything else, for he had consistently urged Hitler to come to an accommodation with the Russians. He was well-informed about the strength of the Red Army.

Hitler did not interfere with the conduct of the Polish campaign, but he very much resented it when Brauchitsch reported that many German infantry units had not shown the same dash and discipline as had been noteworthy in the Great War. Brauchitsch was against the Norwegian venture, because he did not believe that the Royal Navy would allow a German force to reach Norway; as things turned out the major planning was done by Raeder and his staff, and Brauchitsch was proved wrong. He was also against the invasion of France, for having been at Verdun and other Great War battles he tended, like most Germans of his age and experience, to over-estimate the qualities of the French Army and of Gamelin's leadership. He was also afraid that the full weight of the British Empire would be brought into the war and would not prove easy to deal with. He and Halder became responsible, however, for the detailed planning of the invasion of France, and he resisted the changes proposed by Rundstedt and Manstein which took away the main effort from the German right flank and put it towards the left. When, however, he was overruled he went even further than Rundstedt and Manstein so that the former ended up with more divisions and much greater armoured strength than had originally been proposed.

In the famous 'halt' dispute before Dunkirk Brauchitsch emerges well. On 24 May 1940 he ordered that encircling attacks should proceed, and, more important, that the whole 4th Army, which controlled all the panzer divisions and was attacking the B.E.F. and the 1st French Army from the south and west, should be removed from von Rundstedt's Army Group A and given to von Bock's Army Group B which was attacking the Allies, including the Belgians, from the east. This would place Bock in command of the final encirclement drive, and had the advantages of nominating one ground commander to finish off the Allies in the north, and of using troops who were fresher than those of von Rundstedt.

Halder did not agree with Brauchitsch and, as was his right as Chief of Staff, expressed his disagreement by annotating the order to the effect that it went out without his signature 'to signify disapproval of the order and its timing'.

Hitler, however, heard Rundstedt's explanation of the 'halt and close up' order when he visited him on 24 May, and without bothering to consult Brauchitsch countermanded his order and endorsed that of Rundstedt. This was both high-handed and discourteous; worse, it was a grave tactical error. Not unnaturally the atmosphere at Hitler's headquarters was very unpleasant when next Brauchitsch saw the Führer. It is also regrettable that the personal war diary (not the official one) of Halder, kept throughout the French campaign, sometimes contains unpleasant references to Brauchitsch, to whom he owed absolute loyalty.

Brauchitsch had had many arguments after Poland with Hitler, Keitel and Jodl, some of which had been bitter; he had actually offered to resign when Hitler called for a Saarbrücken offensive, and according to Allen Welsh Dulles 'told the conspirators, with whom he was still in touch, that he did not know whether he would arrest Hitler or Hitler would arrest him'. But he had given no encouragement to Beck when the latter tried to get him to act before the real war in the west began.

About 'Sea-Lion' Brauchitsch had mixed feelings, but he did believe that, given the right circumstances—which included a triumphant Luftwaffe, good weather, and proper naval preparations—it might well be feasible. He was certainly more optimistic than Rundstedt, and he might have shared the feeling in some Army quarters that the Navy were dragging rather cold feet about the prospect of invading England. Raeder wrote on 22 June 1940, the day the French armistice was signed: 'I told the C-in-C [Brauchitsch] that the operation would involve very great dangers indeed.'

Looking forward to the German occupation of Britain, Brauchitsch produced a series of instructions, some in considerable detail, called 'Orders Concerning the Organization and Function of Military Government in England'. They included matters of law, order, requisition, deportation, work, etc., of which the keynote, in Peter Fleming's words, is 'a drab, impersonal ferocity'. On 9 September 1940 Brauchitsch signed a directive which provided that 'the able-bodied male population between the ages of 17 and 45 will, unless the local situation calls for an exceptional ruling, be interned and dispatched to the Continent'. In other words, the bulk of the adult male English population were to become slave labour for the Nazis, and would probably never see their homes again. It shows how far Brauchitsch had progressed along the slippery path of Nazism that he allowed himself to sign an order like this.

Brauchitsch had instructed Halder to examine the possibility of a war with Russia as early as 2 July 1940, though it was not until 31 July at the Obersalzberg that Hitler told Brauchitsch and Halder of his intention to attack the Soviet Union 'the sooner the better, and preferably this year. With Russia defeated, Britain's last hope will be gone'.

To start with, owing to surprise, good weather, and the aggressive dash of individual German generals and their troops, things went remarkably well. But at the end of July 1941 a serious difference of opinion arose between the Commander-in-Chief and Hitler, a dispute which was to become even more acrimonious in August. It involved Moscow. Brauchitsch was, after the capture of Smolensk, in favour of an all-out effort to take Moscow and thus finish off Stalin and the war, for he thought that if the capital went the country would collapse. His opinion was shared by Halder, Guderian, Bock, Hoth, and all the other leading commanders on the Eastern front. And as O.K.H.

was charged with the conduct of the Russian war, it should have prevailed.

But Hitler disagreed. In his Directive No. 34 of 30th July 1941 he ordered Army Group Centre, which faced Moscow, to go over to the defensive. The main targets were given as, in the north, the encirclement of Leningrad and juncture with the Finnish Army; and, in the south-east, the destruction of strong enemy forces west of the Dnieper and the establishment of bridgeheads across that river. Hitler had always held that Leningrad should be captured before Moscow, and refused to consider a strike against the capital first. On 18 August Brauchitsch submitted his views on the conduct of future operations, but three days later Hitler replied tersely that they were not in accordance with his instructions.

'The most important aim to be achieved before the onset of winter is not to capture Moscow, but to seize the Crimea and the industrial and coal region on the Donets, and to cut off the Russian oil supply from the Caucasus area. In the north, the aim is to cut off Leningrad and to join with the Finns.'

Finally, on 23 August, Colonel-General Guderian, representing the views of Field-Marshal von Bock and Colonel-General Halder, flew to Rastenburg in East Prussia to put to Hitler the case for taking Moscow. Although forbidden by von Brauchitsch to broach the subject of Moscow himself, Guderian, when asked by Hitler if he thought his Panzer Group still capable of a major effort, found it easy to get on to the vital subject. Hitler heard him out in silence, then rejected the Moscow idea.

Brauchitsch was not present to protest, but it would have made no difference, for Hitler had ceased to consult him seriously. From the beginning of the Russian campaign he had opposed and then ignored the views of his General Staff, in particular their insistence that the best way to finish the war quickly was an all-out drive on Moscow to bring down the Soviet government. On 21 August Hitler had accused Brauchitsch of not conducting the offensive as he wished it, a fairly idle complaint since he was standing for no opposition to his own views.

In Directive No. 35, of 6 September 1941, the main objective was 'a decisive operation against the Timoshenko Army Group which is attacking on the Central Front'. On von Bock's front the attack against Timoshenko would take place at the end of September to destroy the Russian forces east of Smolensk and in the Vyazma area. Only when these had been defeated would his Army Group Centre be directed against Moscow 'with its right flank on the Oka and its left on the Upper Volga'. Von Bock's strength was raised to some seventy divisions by additions from Army Groups North and South, and the air forces covering him were also strengthened. Fourteen of his divisions were

Panzer ones, and eight Panzer Grenadier ones.

But Hitler had, by ignoring the advice of Brauchitsch and the experts, left it too late. In west and central Russia summer ends by early September at the latest, the autumn is short, and the weather breaks up—and so do the roads—in October, with heavy rains, hard frosts, thaws, and mud. By mid-November Hitler's Moscow offensive had ground to a halt, held up more by bad weather than by Russian resistance. At a conference at Orsha on 13 November the representatives of von Leeb and Rundstedt advocated going over to the defensive in the sectors of Army Groups North and South; Leeb, indeed, had already done so. Von Bock was in favour of resuming the Moscow offensive at once, and since Brauchitsch, Halder and Guderian had long striven without result for the Moscow objective, they too wanted to press on now that it at last was a reality. Even Brauchitsch's bad heart attack on 10 November did not change his views.

It was decided at Orsha that the attack on Moscow would be resumed on 19 November. It was, and in the face of fierce Russian resistance and further bad weather 'Operation Typhoon', as it was now called, made progress but at very heavy cost in casualties. Some advanced units and reconnaissance troops managed to reach the farthest of Moscow's outlying suburbs, but could get no farther. Exhausted, lacking winter clothing, and short of supplies, the troops of Guderian's Panzer Army could get no farther than a general line twenty miles from the capital, and there were no reinforcements now to make the breakthrough. On 5/6 December Guderian recalled his advance units and went over to the defensive. The attack on Moscow had failed. Two days later even Hitler realized this, though he put it down to 'the surprisingly early winter and the consequent difficulties in bringing up supplies'.

Heads now began to fall. Rundstedt had already gone; Brauchitsch was to be next, at an acrimonious meeting on 19 December 1941.

The dismissal of Brauchitsch was a watershed. Never again now was there to be a Professional head of the German Army during Hitler's war. Instead, contemptuous of the General Staff and convinced of his own military far-sightedness, Hitler himself assumed the chief command. He became Commander-in-Chief, in title as well as in effect, thus brooking even less interference or guidance than before. In fact the position of Brauchitsch had long been eroded, and since the summer of 1941, with the O.K.W. ventures in Yugoslavia and Greece, over which he was not consulted, and then Africa, Russia had been the only proving ground where the Army could have recovered its old authority. But even here, though it was officially an O.K.H. theatre of war, Hitler had constantly interfered, so that Brauchitsch was never able to fulfil his function as Commander-in-Chief, certainly not to the extent that he had in Poland and France.

It is facile to criticize him for weakness in not standing up to Hitler.

This was more difficult than it sounds, not only because the danger of dismissal, disgrace, and even prison always loomed in the background, but because it was simply not possible to argue with Hitler. On various occasions Brauchitsch had been prepared to resign, or offered his resignation, but either Halder persuaded him that they could best serve their colleagues—and their country—by remaining where they were, or Hitler contemptuously rejected it. His constant bullying and rudeness would have worn down most men—they were infinitely worse than anything Field-Marshal Sir Alan Brooke ever had to endure from Winston Churchill in his worst moments. Moreover, Brauchitsch genuinely suffered from a bad heart. It could not have been improved by the knowledge that in the east by December 1941, Germany had suffered three million casualties in soldiers dead, wounded, ill, or frostbitten. These figures were not disclosed to the public, but they weighed heavily on Brauchitsch, who was a decent man. A final cause of his dismissal was his belief that the German Army should conduct a large scale withdrawal to a safe winter line in 1941–2, west of Smolensk, to the Baltic states in the north, and to the west Ukraine in the south. Here he was only in agreement with his Army Group commanders. But, as always, Hitler would not concede ground.

For the remainder of the war von Brauchitsch was to be in sad retirement, though he was not forgotten, least of all by Hitler, who even on 15 March 1942 was referring to him as 'a nincompoop and a coward'. Assuredly Brauchitsch was neither. Göbbels, taking a leaf from his master's book, wrote in his diary on 20 March 1942 of the grievous German losses in the Russian winter of 1941–2:

'Brauchitsch bears a great deal of responsibility for this. The Führer spoke of him only in terms of contempt. A vain, cowardly wretch who could not even appraise the situation, much less master it.

'By his constant interference and consistent disobedience he completely spoiled the entire plan for the eastern campaign as it was designed with crystal clarity by the Führer. The Führer had a plan that was bound to lead to victory. Had Brauchitsch done what was asked of him and what he really should have done, our position in the east today would be entirely different.

'The Führer had no intention whatever of going to Moscow. He wanted to cut off the Caucasus and thereby strike the Soviet system at its most vulnerable point. But Brauchitsch and his general staff knew better. Brauchitsch always urged going to Moscow. He wanted prestige successes instead of factual successes. The Führer described him as a coward and a nincompoop. He also had tried to weaken the plan of campaign in the west. But the Führer was able to intervene in time. . . .'

After the war von Brauchitsch gave evidence at Nuremberg, and was himself listed as a war criminal. In the sense that every general staff has to prepare contingency plans for attacking other countries, it is hard to see how he could have been convicted, for he had steadfastly done his best to maintain the old traditions of the German Army, and to prevent excesses by the S.S., of whom he disapproved. But he never came to trial, as he died in 1948. Brauchitsch never joined or countenanced the anti-Nazi generals or their conspiracy, of which he was well aware. Equally, he never betrayed them although he once threatened to have General Georg Thomas, the Chief of War Economy and Armament, arrested if he did not cease his persistent intrigues against Hitler. Later, however, shortly before his dismissal, in November 1941 he seems to have relented, for Hassell records on 1 November 1941:

'Falkenhausen and General Thomas have visited Brauchitsch and report that he comprehends what beastliness is rampant. He is also gradually awakening to the fact that a share of the responsibility is his. If Hitler should be eliminated, he has decided to take action. This at least indicates some progress.' According to Hassell, Brauchitsch intervened to save von Falkenhausen from being dismissed from his post as C-in-C of occupied Belgium and north-western France, and Falkenhausen was one of the most consistent anti-Hitler plotters.

Brauchitsch was Commander-in-Chief for nearly four years. He is the classic example of the man who thought that, by going along with Hitler, he could save the Army and Germany. The result was failure and bitterness, and when he went the position of the Army became weaker than ever before. Now there was no one to intervene between Hitler and disaster, for Halder's days were numbered and he himself already a broken reed.

Brauchitsch cannot be rated in the high ranks as a *Hofgeneral*. This small, wiry, upright man, whose speech and actions were rapid and brisk, came to his high rank with the full support of the Army; when he left it, he had lost the goodwill of some and the respect of others, but he still maintained the confidence of a large body of his colleagues. Because he did not exercise strict personal control over the campaigns in which he was engaged, his abilities as a general are hard to assess. It must be granted, however, that as Commander-in-Chief of the mightiest Army that Europe had ever seen, the huge successes it achieved from 1939 to 1941 reflect no little credit on his own pre-war preparations as a professional soldier.

His tactical decisions, had they been freely carried out, seem to have been the right ones, notably his wish to push on in France in 1940, his desire to concentrate on the capture of Moscow in the summer of 1941, and his wish to withdraw to a safe winter line in 1941–2.

Had he been an outstanding personality, he might just have been able to stand out against Hitler. But whilst having the intelligence, he lacked the character. Hermann Rauschning gives a somewhat different judgement: 'I make no secret of the fact that I esteemed and sympathized with this man ... but his features did not bear the stamp of any extraordinary ability.'

Brauchitsch himself, paraphrasing words of von Fritsch, has summed up most vividly his quandary. 'Hitler was the fate of Germany, and this fate could not be stayed.'

In evidence before the Nuremberg Tribunal, Field-Marshal von Manstein stated that out of seventeen Field-Marshals in the Army, only one (presumably Keitel) managed to get through the war and keep his position as Field-Marshal, and that of thirty-six Colonel-Generals 'only three survived the war in their positions'. Although Manstein's figures may have been slightly out, his thesis was absolutely correct.

It did not do to cross Hitler, and perhaps if such an offence were to be committed, it was best to get it over early in the war. This must account for the case of Colonel-General Johannes Blaskowitz, who fell from favour with Hitler after the successful invasion of Poland, but nevertheless ended the war as an Army Group commander. As Blaskowitz, generally agreed to have been very much of the old school, was not one deliberately to toady, his professional ability must account for his restoration, though he sat out most of the war without active command. General Blumentritt described him as 'a fine soldier' and 'an able leader, admired by everyone, whose removal Rundstedt particularly regretted' (in 1944) but recorded that Hitler did not much like him.

Blaskowitz, an infantryman, was one of the most senior German generals. Born in 1878, by 1935 he was a Lieutenant-General commanding II Army Corps at Stettin, where he remained for three years. He was promoted General of Infantry in 1939, having survived the Army purge by Hitler in 1938, and given command of *Heeresgruppe* III at Dresden. Looking upon war against Poland as 'a sacred duty', Blaskowitz had no qualms about Hitler's invasion, in which he commanded the 8th Army under Rundstedt's Army Group South. Blaskowitz encircled the Poles at Posen and took part in the drive against Warsaw, and his handling of 8th Army was excellent, although he incurred Hitler's displeasure by having to withdraw once. On 27 September 1939 he received Polish envoys at his headquarters, where the surrender was signed next day. He was rewarded after the fall of Poland by being made C-in-C of the Army of Occupation.

But it was soon made clear to Blaskowitz that his duties were purely military, and the control of the country was put more and more into the hands of Gauleiter Koch, Governor-General Hans Frank, Alfred Rosenberg, and the Gestapo, S.D., and S.S., with resultant excesses and tyranny. To his credit, Blaskowitz was so appalled by these excesses and by the conduct of the S.S. that he sent a memorandum about them to Brauchitsch and Jodl, of which Hitler undoubtedly got to hear. The protests cut little ice, and Blaskowitz later gave up his job. According to Hassell he wanted to prosecute Sepp Dietrich. The most that came of Blaskowitz's protests was that Himmler admitted to Brauchitsch that some mistakes had been made by the S.S. in carrying out the 'ethnic policy' in Poland, and promised him a minimum of bloodshed in the future, a promise which, of course, was not kept. Himmler also stressed that he wanted good relations with the Army and had no desire to establish 'an army alongside the Army'—another untruth. In fact Brauchitsch maintained military control of the use of S.S. formations in Russia after the French campaign, in which, comparatively raw and untrained S.S. units had not always shone.

For the next four years Blaskowitz played no important part in military events (he held no fighting command in France or Russia) though by October 1943 he was commanding an Army Corps in the occupation of France. In the grand promotions of July 1940 he was not made a Field-Marshal, though senior to some who were.

When some of the less enthusiastic Nazis were considering how to end the war in 1943, von Papen put forward Blaskowitz's name as one likely to consider armistice proposals.

By 1944 Colonel-General Blaskowitz did have a really important command again, in France under von Rundstedt. This was Army Group G, responsible for all territory from the Loire to the Mediterranean and the Atlantic, consisting of 1st Army (General Kurt von der Chevallerie) with headquarters at Bordeaux, and 19th Army (General Georg von Sodenstern) with headquarters at Avignon. The Army Group, however, contained many second-line formations and only three armoured divisions, and when the invasion of southern France came in 1944 was heavily hampered by Maquis activities. And when Army Group B in northern France was shattered after the Normandy landings, Army Group G was in a hopeless position and had to head rapidly for the east to avoid complete encirclement. Not all of it got away. In September 1944, Blaskowitz was replaced by Colonel-General Balck, but later he was restored to command.

Later on in the retreat, Blaskowitz became responsible for the defence of the Saar and the Vosges Mountains front, but in late January 1945 he was put in charge of Army Group H in the northern part of the front, succeeding Colonel-General Student. Finally, when O.B. North-west was formed in April 1945 from Army Group H headquarters, under Field-Marshal Busch, Blaskowitz became responsible for all German troops remaining in Holland (25th Army). None of these were enviable commands, but the bitter resistance offered by the Germans, particularly by 1st Parachute Army which came under Blaskowitz's command for a time, even after all hope of final success had vanished, testifies to the strong grip and discipline which Blaskowitz kept. Indeed his order of 5 March 1945, testifies to the desperate situation:

'As from midday 10 March, all soldiers in all branches of the Wehrmacht who may be encountered away from their units on roads or in villages, in supply columns or among groups of civilian refugees, or in dressing-stations when not wounded, and who announce that they are stragglers looking for their units, will be summarily tried and shot. . . .'

At least he had the decency to give a few days' warning. It fell to Blaskowitz and the Reich Commissioner Seyss-Inquhart, who had known each other in Poland, to surrender north Holland, after the former had held the last German position on the Grebbe Line east of Utrecht. For some time they held out stubbornly against Eisenhower's emissaries, and Blaskowitz made difficulties about capitulating. But when Hitler's death was known there was nothing further that he could do.

To his contemporaries and to most historians Blaskowitz emerged as an able soldier and an upright man. He was never given the chance by Hitler to shine in high command. He is described by Curt Riess as a 'very good-looking man of noble family', though by 1945 Shulman found him rather battered 'with a flattened frog-like jaw, broad nostrils, and thinning hair', and described him sarcastically as 'a sterling product of the German General Staff'.

Blaskowitz was awaiting trial at Nuremberg as a minor war criminal when, thoroughly disillusioned like so many of the old guard, he committed suicide in February 1948. It is doubtful on what grounds he could properly have been convicted. There seems no basis to a story that he was murdered by ex-members of the S.S. working as 'trusties'.

Wilhelm, Ritter von Leeb, whose austere, intellectual features and long head with its high, domed forehead mark him as a thinker more readily than as a man of action, was considered to be the leading defensive strategist of the pre-war German Army. An artilleryman only one year junior to von Rundstedt, he had been born in 1876 and was thus 63 years old when war broke out. A sincere Catholic, he had been a supporter of von Fritsch although, rather curiously, he was also on good terms with his fellow gunner Keitel. As one of the old school, a monarchist and a Catholic, Leeb was neither a friend nor a follower of the Nazi Party, and indeed Hitler once referred to him as 'an incorrigible anti-Nazi'. He was one of those to lose his command in the purge of 1938, though he was restored the following year.

By 1932 Leeb was a Lieutenant-General commanding a division, and between 1934 and February 1938 he commanded Gruppen-kommando 2 as a full General of Artillery with headquarters at Kassel.

Although never a member of any of the conspiracies against Hitler, Leeb must have been one of the first important generals to have been put under surveillance by the Gestapo. He worked out his own ideas from the standpoint of an intellectual, and although ignorant of the plots of Beck and Halder in 1938 and 1939, came up independently with his own idea that, in 1939 when the invasion of France loomed, the three Army Group commanders, of whom he was one, should refuse to undertake the offensive, and tell Hitler so. He was dissuaded from this drastic course of action by the other two generals concerned, Rundstedt and Bock, who told him that such a step would amount to mutiny. Leeb may be seen from this episode to have been somewhat naive.

During the invasion of Poland Leeb, then a Colonel-General, was left in charge on the Western front, as the expert on defence, and must have been relieved that no Allied attack was made against his threadbare forces. He was not in favour of a policy of aggression in the west, and in October 1939 circulated a memorandum among his fellow generals prophesying that the whole world would turn against Germany if she, for the second time in twenty-five years, violated Belgian, and now also Dutch, neutrality. 'The entire nation is longing for peace', Leeb wrote. It was for this reason, and for his admirable personal character, that conspirators such as Hassell and General Thomas saw some hope in Leeb. In January 1940 Etzdorf, the Foreign Office liaison officer with the General Staff, thought Leeb the only one of the three Army Group commanders with whom something might be done. But Leeb was not forceful enough, and did not command sufficient backing in the Army, to be a successful catalyst; and by September 1941 Johannes Popitz, the Prussian Minister of Finance and a leading conspirator, told Hassell that he found Leeb 'almost fossilized'.

As C-in-C West in 1939, Leeb was naturally given an Army Group for the invasion of France, but Hitler saw to it that it was the least powerful one. For the first part of the *blitzkrieg* the 1st and 7th Armies of Leeb's Army Group C merely tied down the French forces opposite them in the south, and it was only after the encirclement of the British and French in the north that he penetrated the Maginot Line. Thereafter Leeb's seventeen divisions made good progress in the second part of the battle of France, but their achievements were overshadowed by the more spectacular Panzer breakthroughs in the north.

Leeb was promoted Field-Marshal on 19 July 1940, and on 25 October his Army Group headquarters was moved from France back to Dresden, in preparation for the coming invasion of Russia. In this campaign Leeb was given command of Army Group North, whose main objective was Leningrad, and which consisted of his friend Colonel-General von Küchler's 18th Army, Colonel-General Busch's 16th Army, and Colonel-General Höpner's 4th Panzer Group. Leeb was against the invasion of Russia, and protested about it to Brauchitsch, foreseeing for one thing the entry of America into the war against Germany. Nevertheless he took command of a formidable force of twenty-three infantry divisions, three panzer, three motorized, and three security divisions,

Although von Leeb's initial advance into the Baltic States from East Prussia was successful, and he crossed the Dvina River, he was unable to encircle the defending Soviet north-west front as it withdrew. Admittedly the Russians lost much *matériel*, but they husbanded their personnel. By the end of July, when Leeb's forces were getting close to Leningrad, opposition stiffened. The Finns in the north had retaken the ground they had lost in the Winter War of 1940, but did not press towards Leningrad or south of the Stir river. When Hitler changed his mind about Moscow in September, one result was to have a disastrous effect on Leeb's advance: he lost at the end of the month Höpner's 4th Panzer Group, a total of five panzer and two motorized divisions, to von Bock's Army Group Centre for 'Typhoon'; and also Richthofen's VIII Air Corps from Kesselring's 2nd Air Fleet, which returned to its parent formation in the centre.

Leeb's objections were overridden by Hitler with the assurance that Bock's successes would take the pressure off Army Group North and make its task easier. Rundstedt in the south also had to sacrifice nine divisions, two of which were panzer and two motorized, to Bock. This was at the very end of September and the beginning of October. By furious attacks Leeb's troops reached the shores of Lake Ladoga, but thereafter his offensive got bogged down, supply difficulties became acute as the Russian winter made itself felt, and the Finns showed no sign of crossing the Stir. By late November the Red Army was launching counter-attacks on Leeb, the strength of which surprised Halder, especially in artillery. Leeb was unhappy at the way in which the whole campaign was being directed, and on one occasion remarked sarcastically that Hitler seemed to be allying himself with Stalin.

On 6 December 1941 Leeb's Chief of Staff, Lieutenant-General K. Brennecke, reported to O.K.H. that Tikhvin was under threat of encirclement from the Russians, in such intense cold, sometimes as much as minus 35 degrees centigrade, that most of the German tanks could not fire their guns. In fact Army Group North had long since gone over to the defensive after the transfer of the bulk of its armour. For once Hitler gave permission for a withdrawal without making a fuss, though he stipulated that Tikhvin be kept within artillery range. It had become clear to O.K.H. that Leeb, like von Rundstedt, was over-extended and weaker than they had thought.

Why did Leningrad not fall, apart from the heroic resistance of the Russians? It should have been captured before Leeb lost his main armour. On 16th August Lieutenant-General Otto Sponheimer's 21st Infantry Division from East Prussia, part of I Corps in Busch's 16th Army, captured Novgorod which the Russians had made a 'last man, last round' citadel. Without stopping they had pushed on by the 20th to Chudovo and captured intact the railway bridges first over the Kerest river, then the more important one over the Volkhov which took the October Railway from Leningrad to Moscow.

It had been decided at O.K.H. that the main attack on Leningrad should be developed from the right flank, that is from the south-east. Meanwhile resistance at Luga, which lay astride the main road to Leningrad, was very fierce. Had Höpner been allowed to switch all his armour to the north-west, parallel to the Narva-Kingisepp railway, and attack Leningrad from the west, the chances are that he would have succeeded before Bock's autumn push on Moscow. This would have meant switching Manstein's LVI Panzer Corps from the Novgorod-Luga-Soltsy to join Reinhardt's XLI Panzer Corps between Luga and Kingisepp, on the lower Luga stretches. But when Höpner had established a springboard for the final seventy-mile advance to Leningrad east of Lake Peipus, the High Command held back his tanks for three fatal weeks. They wanted him to wait and join up with the bulk of 16th Army, coming up on the right, to envelop the Russians in retreat from the Baltic countries. Unfortunately this plan and the allocation of the weight of the attack on Leningrad from the south-east did not take into account the fact that on the right, where the ground was wooded and marshy, tanks could not operate nearly so freely as on the left, which was why Höpner had switched Reinhardt's Corps. All that Höpner needed for a successful attack were more infantry divisions to cover a long panzer thrust to Leningrad. At worst he could make do with Manstein's Panzer Corps. But Leeb was unable to persuade Rastenburg of the soundness of his theory, it being held that Reinhardt was not strong enough to attack Leningrad by himself. When reinforcements did arrive they were sent to the Lake Ilmen area on the right, not to the left.

Colonel-General Georg-Hans Reinhardt, as he became, later asked why Manstein's Corps was not switched to his wing. Leeb did try to have the decision to emphasize the right wing rescinded, but failed after weeks of argument during which the Russians were working night and day to strengthen their line. So a great opportunity was missed, the more so because Höpner and Reinhardt were two of the most experienced commanders of armour in the German Army, and von Manstein had already proved his worth in this role, though an infantry-man. On 30 July Reinhardt wrote in his diary: 'More delays. It's terrible. The chance that we opened up has been missed for good, and things are getting more difficult all the time.'

He admitted that it was necessary to improve the road system before the attack (how often were the Russians to be saved by their bad roads!) but this was a matter of days, not weeks: 'Time and again our Corps urged a speedy resumption of the attack', Reinhardt told Paul Carell, 'and asked that some units at least of Manstein's Corps should be switched over to us, especially as they were bogged down where they stood. But all was in vain.'

Eventually on 15 August, after a heated discussion between Höpner and Leeb, the latter agreed to give Reinhardt one of Manstein's motorized divisions. But this was hardly enough.

Between 15 and 23 August, Manstein's forces were heavily engaged in the south-east corner of Leeb's front, in the Lake Ilmen area and at Staraya Russa. Because of this crisis at Staraya Russa, Höpner had to hold his attack on Leningrad. Höpner had been advocating to Leeb since 15 August a switch of von Küchler's 18th Army from Estonia to the Luga front, so that Küchler could secure Höpner's northern flank.

Leeb, however, now gave Küchler two jobs: to destroy the Soviet 8th Army on the Baltic coast, then to capture the Russian fortifications along the southern coast of the Gulf of Finland. This double-headed order was a mistake, for it meant tying down forces on a secondary front when Höpner needed every division he could get for Leningrad. Now every day was important to the Russians digging defences, and it took eleven days for 18th Army to move from Narva to Opolye, only twenty-five miles in a direct line! Carell believes that Leeb was motivated by a wish to let Küchler, an old friend, share in the coming victory at Leningrad. But whereas Höpner and his 4th Panzer Group might well have taken the city in mid-August, when the morale of the population was very low in the face of German successes, it was a different matter by 8 September when the German attack finally began.

The Russian resistance was ferocious. The key to the capture of Leningrad was the fortress of Schlüsselburg, and this was taken by German infantry in a surprise attack, thus sealing off the city to the east. Despite severe Russian counter-attacks the Germans held on, and when the Duderhof Hills had been taken, and then Uritsk, it seemed that the end was near. But now came startling interference and a change of plan from Hitler. Reinhardt recalled to Carell: 'In the middle of the troops' justified victory celebrations, like a cold shower came the news from Panzer Group on 12 September that Leningrad was not to be taken, but merely sealed off. The offensive was to be continued only as far as the Pushkin-Peterhof road. The XLI Panzer Corps was to be detached during the next few days for employment elsewhere. We just could not understand it. At the last moment the troops, who had been giving of their best, were robbed of the crown of victory.'

On 17 September Höpner's Panzer Group was withdrawn from the Leningrad front, and so were all bomber formations. This at a time when one final push would have secured the city, invaluable as a port and supply base, as a factory area producing tanks, guns and ammunition, and as a point of juncture with the Finns. Its capture would have freed 18th Army for other operations; as it was, this army was contained round Leningrad until 1944.

One reason for Hitler's directive was the attitude of the Finns. Marshal Mannerheim did not wish to involve his troops in the capture of the city, or cross the old Russo-Finnish frontier in the Karelian Isthmus. But Hitler was to pay hard for his change of mind. Previously he had always insisted that Leningrad should be taken before the attack on Moscow. Now, despite the Kiev success in the south, he was to have neither Leningrad nor Moscow, and from the end of 1941 onwards the front between Leningrad and the Volkhov was to be a continuing threat and an expensive drain on the Germans. Indeed it may be said that never again did Army Group North gain any great success.

It is easy to see why and how von Leeb was so dissatisfied with the conduct of the Russian campaign. But a more forceful man would not have been put off or been so compliant as was Leeb. He does not emerge in any sense as a great commander. The fact was that the war in Russia was not for elderly gentlemen, it was for younger toughs like Model and Schörner. In their sixties men like Rundstedt, Bock and Leeb were too old and too set in their ways to stand up to Russian winters and hardships, and to an exasperating Commander-in-Chief playing the part of a sometimes hysterical back-seat driver.

It is also clear that Leeb's heart was not in the war. On 12 January a crisis arose when a large part of Busch's 16th Army looked like being cut off in the Demyansk pocket. Leeb therefore asked permission to withdraw II Corps, but Hitler refused. Leeb had the chance he had been looking for, and requested that he be relieved of his command. Hitler complied, and von Küchler succeeded to the command of Army Group North on 18 January.

In October 1948, when he was 72, Field-Marshal von Leeb was sentenced to three years' imprisonment as a minor war criminal. The court found that there was much to be said in mitigation for him. Today the verdict seems hard, and perhaps the best epitaph for this intelligent, conscientious Bavarian general remains, as the judges put it, 'He was not a friend or follower of the Nazi Party'.

Another Bavarian, Siegmund Wilhelm List, was among those generals (such as Rundstedt, Bock, Leeb, Blaskowitz, and Witzleben) who, in October 1939, von Hassell had characterized as 'excellent people'. But in his view they were, in their local commands, too far from the helm.

List had been Chief of the Army Training Office, and in the early days of 1933 inclined towards support of Hitler. In 1934 he was a Lieutenant-General commanding 4th Division at Dresden; and from 1935 to 1938 commanded IV Army Corps under von Bock from the same headquarters, being promoted General of Infantry in 1936.

Having escaped the generals' purge of 1938 the following year, he was promoted to Heeresgruppe 5 in Vienna, and in the war against

Poland he was the senior Army Commander, with the rank of Colonel-General (14th Army) under von Rundstedt's Army Group South. His troops linked up with those of Guderian from Bock's Army Group North at Wlodawa, south-east of Brest-Litovsk, in one of the great pincer movements of the Polish campaign on 17 September 1939.

A tall, rather bald, burly man, List was born at Oberkirch in 1880. During the Great War his service took him to eastern Europe where he made many friendships with Bulgarian and Turkish officers, and became something of an expert on the Balkans. This was to influence his career in the Second World War. In 1944 Curt Riess described him as 'a big, unpleasant-looking man with the aspect of a proletarian and an uncultured manner. A *petit bourgeois* who certainly did not belong. But he had been Colonel of Hitler's Regiment in World War I.' Paul Carell saw him rather differently as 'a man with an old Bavarian General Staff training and with distinguished service in the campaigns in Poland and France. . . . He was a clever, cool, and sound strategist—not an impulsive charger at closed doors, but a man who believed in sound planning and leadership and detested all military gambles.'

In the battle of France List again served under Rundstedt, commanding 12th Army. When Guderian, in a fury over the 'halt' order to the armour, offered his resignation to von Kleist, who accepted it, and then was about to fly to Rundstedt's headquarters to give his version of events, Rundstedt delegated to List the task of sorting things out. He could not have chosen better, for, after listening to the arguments, List gave an order to Guderian to which Hitler could hardly object but which, he knew, Guderian would interpret in his own way. This was: 'Reconnaissance in force to be carried out. Corps headquarters must in all circumstances remain where it is, so that it may be easily reached.'

List's 12th Army was mainly composed of infantry, but he increased his reputation for ability in the campaign by the speed with which he managed to move his troops. He was one of the glut of generals promoted Field-Marshal by Hitler on 19 July 1940. He had shown his personal fearlessness by being one of the first German commanders to force a gap in the Maginot line.

List's next assignment was to take him back to the Balkans. On 8 February 1941 he concluded a secret agreement with General Dascaloff, King Boris's War Minister, whereby Bulgaria would allow the passage of German troops on their way to Greece. King Boris believed in German victory, and the Bulgarians were avid for a slice of Greek territory to the south which would give them access to the Aegean. Late on 28 February German troops crossed the Danube from Rumania, and on 1 March Bulgaria, miscalculating again, joined the Tripartite Pact between Germany, Italy and Japan, already signed in Berlin on

27 September 1940. The Yugoslavs were not such easy meat as the Bulgarians but, bribed by the offer of Salonika, the Regent's Ministers signed the Pact in Vienna on 25 March 1941. Now, however, immediately they returned they were overthrown by a popular uprising in Belgrade which put young King Peter on the throne, and made clear German unpopularity with the Serbs. Hitler flew into a fury, and ordered Belgrade destroyed by waves of air raids. Shortly this was done.

The attacks on Yugoslavia and Greece on the ground began on 6 April, and von Weichs's 2nd Army, and List's 12th Army, which had mustered in the Graz area before moving to Bulgaria and Hungary, were the leading German formations. On 13 April Belgrade was entered by Weichs's troops and the Hungarians, and on the 17th the Yugoslav Army surrendered at Sarajevo. List's Army of fifteen divisions, four of them panzer, had entered Macedonia and divided their two opponents. The Greeks, who had made the Italians look absurd for six months, found the crack German troops a different proposition, and there were not enough British troops scraped up from Africa to influence the decision. Most decisive of all was the ruthless German use of dive-bombers against military and civilians alike, against which the Yugoslavs and Greeks had little or no defence. On 23 April the Greeks too were forced to submit, the British conducted a desperate evacuation of the remains of their four divisions, and on 27 April German tanks from List's Army rattled into Athens, and the swastika was hoisted atop the Acropolis.

Lieutenant-General Adolf Galland, the German fighter ace, in his book *The First and the Last*, has left an interesting account of this time when German air superiority was so formidable:

'The Reich had to intervene by force. Within a few days Weichs's army marched into Carinthia, Styria, and south Hungary; Kleist's armoured Corps occupied the Sofia sector; List's Army was standing in the mountain region on the borders of Bulgaria and Greece. On 6 April the campaign in the Balkans began. This was the last time that motorized German army units, perfectly co-ordinated with the air force, decisively defeated in the shortest possible time a courageous and well-mobilized adversary. The 8th Flying Corps under von Richthofen, a specialist in co-operation, proved itself once more. Strongly supported by Stukas, List broke through the well-designed and tenaciously held Metaxas Line. On April 9 he took Salonika. Weichs and Kleist advanced in a pincer movement from north and east toward the main concentration of the Yugoslav army. Nis fell on 9 April and Zagreb on the 11th. Belgrade fell on 13 April. With the unconditional surrender on the 17th this campaign came to an end. The Greek government together with the British troops which had been in Greece since March, escaped to Crete on 23 April. On 20 May the invasion of Crete from the air started. So far it was the greatest operation of its kind in

World War II. The conquest of Crete proved a brilliant success in spite of the heavy losses sustained by the Luftwaffe. On 2 June the last Englishman had been chased from the island.'

Hitler's Directive No. 31, issued from Führer Headquarters on 9 June 1941, 'As *Commander Armed Forces South-East*, with headquarters in Salonika, I appoint Field Marshal List.'

This was a big job for List, who held it until mid-October 1941, when he was succeeded by General of Pioneers Walther Kuntze, and later by Colonel-General Löhr of the Luftwaffe, who had been his air forces commander; later still by Field-Marshal von Weichs, and finally by Löhr again. List became the highest German commander in the Balkans, over all branches of the Wehrmacht, with full powers in all German-occupied areas, directly subordinate only to Hitler, though Keitel worked out some limitations of his powers vis-à-vis the Plenipotentiary of the Reich in Greece. List was responsible for the defence of German-occupied Serbia and Greece, including the Greek Islands, for the protection of Crete, and for liaison between the Italian and Bulgarian forces in the Balkans. He had the Admiral South-East and the Air Commander Balkans, who was also the Commanding General, Southern Greece (General of Fliers Helmuth Felmy) under him, and was the chief military administrator of a huge area. Crete was a new air base for the Luftwaffe designated by Hitler as 'a fortress' under command of a special Air Force Commander. Otherwise List was in charge of the Old Serbia area, where the Commanding General Serbia was General of Anti-Aircraft Artillery von Schröder (Luftwaffe), the Salonika area, and Lemnos, Mitylene, Chios, and Skyros (Commanding General Salonika-Aegean), and the Athens, Crete, Cythera, Anticythera, and Melos areas, under the Commanding General Southern Greece (Felmy).

In the summer of 1942 things were going well for the Germans both in Russia and Africa. Hitler grew over-confident and changed his plans. When in July or August he might well have taken Stalingrad had 4th Panzer Army been wholly committed and backed up by strong infantry forces, Hitler decided that he could capture that city without 4th Panzer Army and at the same time crush Timoshenko's armies on the lower Don, with Rostov as the centre of another battle of encirclement.

To this end Hitler split Army Group South into two parts, the newly-formed Army Group 'A', consisting of 11th and 17th Armies and 1st Panzer Army, and Army Group 'B', formed of 6th Army, the Hungarian 2nd Army, and 2nd Army. Later 4th Panzer Army was temporarily attached to Army Group 'A', which became known as 'the Caucasus front'. Field-Marshal List was given command of Army Group 'A', as Bock noted on 7 July 1942, adding, 'This means that the battle is being chopped in two.' Rostov was attacked by 17th Army and 1st Panzer Army, and fell after bitter fighting on 25 July; two days earlier Colonel-General Halder had tried hard to persuade Hitler not to split his forces in the south and wait until Stalingrad had been taken. Confident that the Russians were on the run, Hitler would have none of Halder's objections, and actually pulled five divisions of Manstein's 11th Army out of the Crimea, where they were ready for action in the Caucasus, to reinforce the Leningrad front, and sent back two crack S.S. Divisions, the Panzer Grenadier 'Leibstandarte' and the Motorized Infantry 'Grossdeutschland' to refit in France. Halder grimly noted in his diary: 'His persistent underestimation of the enemy's potential is gradually taking on grotesque forms and is beginning to be dangerous.'

Hitler's Directive No. 45, issued on 23 July 1942, began with a lie when it stated: 'Only weak enemy forces from the Timoshenko Army Group have succeeded in avoiding encirclement and reaching the further bank of the Don.' It then instructed Army Group 'A' to (1) encircle enemy forces which had escaped across the Don south and south-east of Rostov, and destroy them; (2) occupy the entire eastern coastline of the Black Sea, to force a passage of the Kuban, and to occupy the high ground around Maykop and Armavir; (3) capture the Groznyy area and thereafter occupy the Baku area by a thrust along the Caspian coast. Army Group 'B' meantime was to take Stalingrad.

A glance at the map will show the ambitiousness of these widely separate objectives, and it is no wonder that when List received them at Stalino on 25 July he shook his head. He and his Chief of Staff, Lieutenant-General von Greiffenberg, assumed that the Supreme Command must have some special information about the enemy's situation that they did not, and which made such plans feasible. List decided that the enlarged 17th Army, under General of Infantry Richard Ruoff, who had commanded V Corps under Kluge in France in 1940 and had been scheduled to play an important part in the second wave of the invasion of England, should advance almost directly south from Rostov towards Krasnodar, an important city in the Kuban not far from the Black Sea. Von Kleist's 1st Panzer Army, also under List's Army Group, should break out from bridgeheads on the Don and head for Armovir and Maykop, as the outer line of a pair of pincers designed to entrap the Russians south of Rostov. Obviously Kleist's forces would move faster than Ruoff's infantry, and their eastern or left flank was to be guarded by Colonel-General Hoth's 4th Panzer Army, itself directed on Voroshilovsk.

The Russians, however, had no intention of allowing more German encirclements, having learned the lessons of Smolensk and Kiev. Furthermore the Germans now encountered a new kind of terrain south of the Don, with mile after mile of steppe, many watering-points which determined the line of advance, and, far ahead, one of the greatest mountain ranges in the world, the Caucasus, running athwart their path from the Caspian to the Black Sea. They were on the edge of Asia.

When at the end of July and beginning of August the river Manych was crossed, and the experienced 3rd Panzer Division, commanded by the shrewd Major-General Breith, took Manych-Stroy itself, his troops from General of Panzer Troops Geyr von Schweppenburg's XL Panzer Corps, and those of General of Cavalry Eberhard von Mackensen's III Panzer Corps on their right, were now fighting in Asia.

Further north, however, things were not going so well. It soon became apparent even to Hitler that 6th Army, gravely short of supplies and faced by four Soviet armies, was not going to be strong enough to take Stalingrad on its own. On 31 July Hitler therefore pulled out 4th Panzer Army, less Geyr's Corps, and put it under Army Group 'B' to strike at the flank of the Russian front at Kalach, west of Stalingrad. But this force was not sufficient to allow Army Group 'B' to make sure of Stalingrad, while its removal naturally weakened List's hand in the Caucasus. The fact was that these two large-scale operations were far too separated, with resultant chaos in the supply situation. Now thousands of miles were involved, and those who recall the hundreds of miles daily churned up by lorries and 'water-bugs' in the African desert and from Normandy to the Rhine will appreciate the problems that beset the German staffs and commanders. In the south the Kalmyk steppe was itself a sort of desert.

Nevertheless, at first all went well for List. Mackensen's soldiers captured Salsk, just south of Manych-Stroy on 31 July, and on 9 August the 13th Panzer Division, under one of the more brilliant of the younger tank commanders, Major-General Traugott Herr, took the oil city of Maykop, though the storage tanks had been destroyed by the Russians, and much vital equipment removed. By 13th August the XLIX Mountain Corps under General of Mountain Troops R. Konrad, and V Corps under Lieutenant-General Wetzel, took Krasnodar and crossed the Kuban River. Further east Breith's 3rd Panzer Division captured Voroshilovsk in a surprise attack on 3 August, and to its west Lieutenant-General Rudolph Kirchner, a veteran of the French and Polish campaigns, pushed his LVII Panzer Corps south across the Kuban steppe, crossed the river, and established bridgeheads for Ruoff's Army following up.

In these operations the S.S. 'Viking' Division under S.S. General Felix Steiner, a former regular soldier who had transferred from the Army in 1933 when a major, was prominent. Two Panzer groups, under S.S. Lieutenant-General Herbert Gille and S.S. Major-General Fritz von Scholz, who later became responsible for Russian and Cossack volunteers in the German Army, crossed the Kuban River, the latter at Kropotkin. The 'Viking' Division was composed of German, Scandinavian and Baltic volunteers; it pushed on into the Maykop oilfields.

In merciless heat and sunshine—sometimes 55 degrees centigrade—the Germans drove south. They were gaining much ground, but they were not destroying the enemy formations, who found it easy to fight and run, or fade away before engaging battle. All the time the eastern flank grew longer, communications and supplies became more difficult. As a safeguard Lieutenant-General Ott's LII Corps was directed east towards the Caspian, and on 12 August took Elista, the biggest town on the Kalmyk steppe. To their west the Panzer crews were shortly to spot what at first they mistook for a white cloud; it was in fact the highest peaks of the Caucasus range, Mount Elbrus. By 10 August Geyr's XL Panzer Corps, now a part of 1st Panzer Army, had reached Pyatigorsk and Mineralnyye Vody, at the foot of the Caucasus, with only the Terek River in between. The same day V Corps from Württemberg reached the Krasnodar area further west behind them, having covered, as infantrymen, some 200 miles from Rostov to Krasnodar, capital of the Kuban Cossacks, in only sixteen days. When the town finally fell on 14 August the Muslim population flew crescent flags from their houses and welcomed the Württembergers as liberators!

List now directed Ruoff to the real strategic objectives of Army Group 'A'—the ports on the Black Sea of Novorossiysk, Tuapse, Sochi, Sukhumi, and Batum. Vitally important to the Germans as supply bases, their loss would cripple the Red Fleet, and prove in German hands a significant lever over Turkey. Novorossiysk duly fell to General Wetzel's infantrymen, and inland some extraordinary feats were accomplished by the Jägers and mountain troops, who showed in Russia as in Norway that they were some of the best troops the Germans had. The German and Austrian Armies had always had room for mountain experts, and trained them thoroughly. Many Germans and Austrians naturally learned to ski while still at school, and there was no lack of suitable country for them to operate in in Europe. Soldiers of the 1st and 4th Mountain Divisions planted a large swastika on Mount Elbrus, 18,480 feet high. Mountain Jägers fought engagements at heights of up to nearly 10,000 feet, and covered 120 miles on their way to Sukhumi. But when they emerged from the wooded slopes to within twelve miles of the Black Sea they lacked mules, ammunition, and air support. They could not reach their objective. It was the same at Tuapse, a vital objective; the troops of Major-General Rupp's 97th Jäger Division fought through to a distance of some thirty miles from the town, but they lacked the strength to take it. Well to the east von Kleist got three divisions, including the 23rd Panzer, across the Terek River at Mozdok, by 30 August, but he could make no further progress against fierce opposition.

The Terek was to mark the limit of List's Army Group 'A' advance. Tiflis was not after all to be captured, let alone Baku. List simply did not have enough strength to continue. Obsessed with the need to capture the oilfields, Hitler angrily blamed, as usual, his generals. On 7 September 1942 he despatched Colonel-General Alfred Jodl, Chief of Operations, O.K.W., to List's headquarters at Stalino to find out why the advance to Tuapse had got bogged down. When Jodl returned he supported the views of his fellow-Bavarian, List, who demanded a complete regrouping of the whole front on the grounds that his available forces were too weak. There was a terrible row, as a result of which Jodl, and with him Keitel, nearly lost their jobs. Hitler ordered the offensive in the Caucasus to be resumed, but it made heavy headway through the rest of September and October, and by mid-November bad weather had brought it to a complete halt—still with the Black Sea ports of Baku, Tiflis, and Batum untaken.

Field-Marshal List could not be saved, although he had scrupulously —and to his cost—observed all Hitler's directives. He went in disgrace on 10 September, to be followed later that month by the Army's Chief of Staff, Colonel-General Halder. For the time being Hitler took personal responsibility for the command of Army Group 'A'. Halder had supported List, despite Hitler's exceptionally vituperative attacks upon the Army Group commander, and the accusations of ignoring orders and not properly deploying his troops, which Halder knew to be groundless.

So went one of those able top commanders whom Hitler could not really afford to lose, sacrificed to petty spite and grandiose designs. In Africa, where he himself was in serious difficulties before El Alamein, Rommel heard the news, and wrote to his wife on 16 September 1942: 'I hear that Field-Marshal List is retiring. I thought particularly highly of him, as you know.' Rommel had, of course, witnessed List's performance in Poland and France.

Although an infantryman, List was good at handling his armoured commanders, and he made exceptionally good use of his mountain troops. He was essentially well-balanced, and not unfitted for tasks requiring diplomacy. List had little contact with anti-Hitler forces in or outside the Army, and after his dismissal faded into obscurity. It was rumoured but never proved that he had once turned down a gift of half a million marks from Hitler. Göbbels noted on 23 September 1943: 'Even of Wilhelm Walter List the Führer now has a more favourable opinion than several months ago. List, too, is ill; he was not equal to the wear and tear of a war lasting four years.' But Hitler did not re-employ List in high command.

In February 1948, List was given a life sentence by an American court at Nuremberg, chiefly for offences in Greece and the Balkans. He was, however, released and pardoned at Christmas 1952.

Of all Hitler's generals, none might more easily have been taken, in different circumstances, for an officer of the Brigade of Guards than Fedor von Bock. Tall, ramrod stiff, spare, and wiry, with a dignified, aristocratic air, von Bock was indeed a guardsman—a Prussian, whose father was a general, Bock was born in 1880 at Küstrin on the Oder, and in 1898 joined the 5th Regiment of Prussian Foot Guards. In 1910 he was posted to the General Staff and became a captain two years later.

Bock was always ambitious to get on in the Army, to which he had given his heart. As a boy at the cadet schools of Potsdam and Gross Lichterfelde he was unusually earnest and purposeful, just as later these qualities acquired for him the nickname 'The Holy Fire of Küstrin'. He became something of a zealot and a not always popular fire-eater. Not for him a perpetual Staff desk or a cushy command when the fighting came—Bock itched for glory. The handsome young Guards officer was to get it in the Great War. But he had to wait over two years; from 1914 to 1916 he served on the staff of Crown Prince Rupprecht of Bavaria's Army Group.

In the fighting on the Somme and at Cambrai he showed great gallantry, and in 1917 became commanding officer of a battalion of the 4th Prussian Foot Guards. His wartime career was crowned when he won Germany's highest award for gallantry, the Pour le Mérite—as, in a different theatre, did those more plebeian soldiers Rommel and Schörner. He also won the Order of Hohenzollern.

Bock thus came to high command in the Second World War with one great advantage over numerous other generals, most if not all of whose wartime service had been spent in not very dangerous Staff appointments. He had personal and successful experience of bitter infantry fighting and had successfully commanded a crack battalion in action. He had also picked up, through his fire-eating qualities, another nickname, this time one he was never to lose, *'Der Sterber'*, 'the fatalist', or 'the fanatical dier'.

After the Great War Bock was much concerned with recruiting a new army, and later with its illicit rearmament. From 1920 to 1923 he was Chief of Staff to the 3rd Military District in Berlin where, as one of von Seeckt's 'bright young men' he was ideally placed to get to know what was going on and to further his own career. He became a divisional Chief of Staff as a Lieutenant-Colonel, and in 1924 took command of the 2nd Battalion of Infantry Regiment No. 4 at Kolberg.

What exactly Bock's relations with the so-called 'Black Reichswehr' had been in the early 'twenties is hard to say exactly, but it is certain that he and some few senior officers in the Bendlerstrasse connived at the illicit rearmament of a large clandestine force operating within the Berlin-Brandenburg area, of which he was Chief of Staff. Whether he was connected with the goings-on of the revived Femegerichte ('Secret Courts' dating from medieval times) that sprang up and were responsible for some brutal murders of those suspected of betraying secret rearmament to the German or Allied authorities, is not known. The dealings of the 'Black Reichswehr' were, sensibly enough, not committed to paper. Bock's relations with them, particularly in his home town area of Küstrin, do not, on the face of it, appear to have reflected much credit on a regular officer, and some authors have gone so far as to accuse him of having betrayed the Weimar Republic. Certainly as a monarchist von Bock was not particularly sympathetic to that government.

In late 1928, at the age of nearly 48, Bock was promoted Major-General and appointed commander of the 1st Cavalry Division at Frankfurt-an-der-Oder; in 1930 of the 1st Infantry Division; and between 1931 and 1934 he commanded 2 Infantry Division and the 2nd Military District at Stettin, with the rank of Lieutenant-General. From 1935 to 1938 he was in charge of Gruppenkommando 3 at Dresden as a full General of Infantry. It was there that he got to know Kesselring, with whom he was to co-operate so fruitfully in the coming war. In 1939 von Bock, by then a Colonel-General, was commanding Heeresgruppe I from Berlin, and was regarded in the Service as a coming man in any future war. Not that he was universally popular. By many he was deemed to be too stiff, too aloof, too autocratic, too cynical, or too caustic. His boundless ambition was well known, and unlike von Brauchitsch or von Falkenhausen, cultured men with wide interests outside the Army, Bock had a closed mind outside soldiering. Even within it he was not notable for original ideas; he was a disciplinarian, well trained and experienced, but perhaps his greatest strength was his fire and zeal.

In 1938 Bock, with Reichenau, organised the invasion of Austria, as a result of which he received his promotion to Colonel-General and was made C-in-C of the German Army in Austria. The result of that experience seems to have increased Bock's contempt for anything Austrian, and put him on bad terms with Major-General Heinz Guderian, who led the mechanized troops.

In August 1939 Bock had charge of Army Group North for the invasion of Poland, in which he co-operated closely and successfully with his old acquaintance from Dresden days, Kesselring, whose Air Fleet I worked very well with Bock's 4th and 3rd Armies. Bock and Kesselring had studied army-air co-operation closely, and each relied upon the other with trust, though Kesselring put himself under Bock's guidance in all matters where ground tactics were concerned. The partnership was to be progressively successful in France and Russia. Some critics have affirmed that Bock's limitations were exposed in Poland, and W.E. Hart refers to his 'mediocre handling of the Northern Army Group', but I know of no justification for this. Moreover Bock was fortunate in having as his Chief of Staff in Poland one of the ablest of the younger generation of soldiers, Lieutenant-General Hans von Salmuth, who went on to become, after serving Bock in the same capacity in the Low Countries and France, a Corps and then Army commander in Russia and France.

For the campaign against the Low Countries and France Bock was, as we have seen, to have had under the original plans the lion's share.

His Army Group 'B' comprized thirty-seven divisions (eight panzer and two motorized included), and later forty-three divisions (including nine armoured and four motorized). The latter was the force allocated to him at the end of October 1939; but as things turned out after the Manstein Plan had been adopted, he wound up with only twenty-eight divisions, of which three were panzer ones, and lost his most powerful Army, the 4th under von Kluge, to von Rundstedt's Army Group 'A'. Nevertheless the forces remaining to him in von Küchler's 18th Army on the right flank looking at Holland and in von Reichenau's 6th Army on the left, destined for Belgium, were formidable ones, especially the latter. Holland was not to survive long, for she was quite unprepared to cope with the well-trained German troops, who included highly effective parachutists. In five days Holland was conquered, and on 14 May the Dutch commander ordered a ceasefire. That same day Reichenau's soldiers tried to capture Louvain, but were vigorously thrown back by Major-General B. L. Montgomery's British 3rd Division, which successfully resisted a series of attacks on the city during the next two days.

Bock had been told that it was extremely important to break through the enemy position between Louvain and Namur, to prevent the French and Belgian forces establishing a line there. Because of the German breach at Sedan, however, and their successful crossing of the Meuse, General Billotte on 16 May ordered the French 1st Army, the B.E.F., and the Belgian Army, to withdraw from the Dyle progressively to the Escaut. Bock's troops had failed to dent the Dyle front on 15 May, and when they attacked in force again on the 17th they found that most of the B.E.F. had gone back to the Senne.

Bock's superiors had it in mind that he should put his main strength towards the south in support of the breakthrough by Army Group 'A'. Bock had different ideas, and fancied his own breakthrough at the junction of the B.E.F. and the Belgian Army, in the general direction of Courtrai, and an advance thence to the coast. But by 20 May this last became unnecessary when Guderian's armoured troops from Army Group 'B' reached the sea themselves at Abbeville. That night and on 21 May Bock's troops were involved in heavy fighting against the British in the Audenarde-Petegem area of Belgium, but they did not manage to break the British front or capture Arras.

On 25 May Lord Gort, C-in-C the B.E.F., made his fateful and wise decision to retreat, rather than to prepare for a southwards attack with the French that was never practicable. By doing so he saved the B.E.F., and just in time closed the gap between Menin and Ypres, through which Bock's forces were poised to strike. Bock had already broken some of the Belgian positions on the Lys. General Halder had not approved of what he called a 'private battle in the area of Audenarde, which will probably cause losses without a return of operational advantage'. But it was this battle which finally broke the Belgian front and Belgian morale, so that by midnight on 27 May King Leopold ordered a ceasefire. But Bock may be criticized for not having properly exploited the gap on the left of the B.E.F. which occurred when the Belgian front was broken. As the battle unrolled and came to its final stages at Dunkirk, Bock's task was to break the British front from the east. His soldiers endured fiercer fighting on the east of the Dunkirk perimeter than did Rundstedt's on the west. Had Bock been given full authority to control the final operations, as von Brauchitsch ordered on 24 May, when he put Kluge's 4th Army under Bock, things might have worked out very differently from the actual course of events. Bock might have won his great triumph, which, in spite of his competent handling of his Army Group in Holland, Belgium, and France, so far evaded him.

In the second part of the French campaign, which started when the Germans renewed their attack across the Somme on 5 June, followed by pushes against the Lower Seine and Aisne fronts, Bock was finally given 4th Army. It ran into unexpectedly heavy French resistence, but the end was inevitable and it was hastened by a tank breakthrough led by Major-General Rommel's 7th Armoured Division, which broke through on the Somme front west of Amiens and on 8 June took Elbeuf on the Seine. Rundstedt's Army Group 'B' had joined the attack on 9th June, and by 14 June Bock had the satisfaction of seeing Paris surrendered to Küchler's 18th Army.

Bock's record in the campaign has been dismissed by W. E. Hart as 'not outstanding', and it is true that he was overshadowed by Rundstedt. Yet by any standards his advance had been spectacular, and the achievements of Küchler's Army in Holland and France and Reichenau's in Belgium and France had been great. The B.E.F. could testify especially to the toughness of Reichenau's men. Major Ellis in his official history sums up of Bock: 'Bock, the second army group commander principally concerned in the northern campaign, was a less distinguished soldier than either Brauchitsch or Rundstedt. Like them he was a Prussian and a regular soldier, but his rise had been due to zeal and industry rather than to natural talent, and there is nothing very striking in his handling of Army Group B.' This omits the masterly army-air co-operation achieved by Bock and Kesselring, even after Bock's Army Group had been depleted by the loss to Rundstedt on 13 May of von Richthofen's 8th Air Corps. As Galland has pointed out, the secret of these 'unbelievable successes' of the Germans was 'the co-operation between the fast-moving army and the Luftwaffe, where every move was carefully planned in advance and executed with precision'.

Field-Marshal von Bock, as he became in July 1940, and his Army Group 'B' were selected to occupy the French coast between Brest and Spain. This not very romantic job prompted Bock to observe that all he had to do was 'to watch out that the sea-shore wasn't carried away or the demarcation line stolen.' But on 31 August he was ordered to move his headquarters to East Prussia, and later to Poland, in preparation for the attack on Russia next year. List took over his occupation area in France.

When this attack came, Bock was given command of the strongest formation, Army Group Centre, which assembled in the Warsaw area. It consisted of von Kluge's 4th Army, the 9th Army of Colonel-General Rudolf Strauss, the 2nd Army of Colonel-General Maximilian Freiherr von Weichs (a new formation) and the 2nd and 3rd Panzer Groups of Colonel-Generals Guderian and Hoth, the whole again backed up by Field-Marshal Kesselring's 2nd Air Fleet, which contained numerous Stuka wings. All in all, Bock's ground forces amounted to something like three quarters of a million men in fifty-seven divisions, of which thirty-seven were infantry, nine panzer, seven motorized, three security, and one—the 1st Cavalry Division under Major-General Feldt—of horsed cavalry. This last was to operate most successfully in the Pripet marshes, where tanks could not go, and in protecting the flanks of Guderian's Armoured Group and maintaining important liaison between Bock and Rundstedt's Army Group South. It was one of the few and certainly one of the most successful horsed cavalry formations used extensively in the Second World War.

There seems no evidence that Bock had any great reservations about Hitler's attack on Russia. He did, on 31 January 1941, express some doubts to Halder about the invasion plans, asking him if he had any firm grounds for assuming that the Russians would stand and fight west of the Dvina-Dnieper line. Halder had to admit that he had not. Between late September and mid-November, 1940, Bock was ill and his command was taken over temporarily by List, before he went to the Balkans. On 3 December Hitler visited Bock to congratulate him on his sixtieth birthday, and to inform him that 'it will be necessary to eradicate the Soviet Union from the face of the earth'. Bock recorded of this daunting piece of news, his first intimation of Hitler's plans, 'I was somewhat surprised by the Führer's statement and remarked that Russia's enormous terrain and untested military strength would make this a difficult task, even for our powerful forces'. Not unnaturally his reaction did not please Hitler, who became cold, but before leaving he notified Bock that he would be expected to play a decisive role in the coming crusade.

Bock and von Salmuth, in January 1941, proposed that Leningrad and Kronstadt should be by-passed and that Army Group 'B' in the central area should destroy as many Russian forces as possible and capture Moscow as the predominant objective; but their study was turned down by the High Command. On 31 January Bock returned to duty and on 3 February reached Posen, now his headquarters. In May he lost von Salmuth, promoted to a corps command; he was replaced by Major-General Hans von Greiffenberg, who had taken part in the Balkans campaign.

Bock had always regarded Smolensk as his first major objective, rather than Minsk, the capital of Belorussia, and when Hoth's 3rd Panzer Group reached Vilna in the north and the outskirts of Novogrodek in the south he decided to bypass Minsk and ordered Hoth on to Vitebsk. This order was approved by Brauchitsch.

But not by Hitler. Afraid, with some reason, that Bock's infantry would get too strung out over vast expanses of land, he decided on 25 June to limit the advances of the armour until large pockets of Russians in the Minsk area were encircled and destroyed. Bock was angered, and complained to Brauchitsch, who had signed the order, when the latter visited him next day at Kobryn. But worse was to come, for the Commander-in-Chief of the Army revealed that Hitler had decided to take the two armoured groups of Hoth and Guderian away from Bock's direct control and put them under Kluge's 4th Army, now to be known as 4th Panzer Army. By 30 June elements of Kluge's troops and those of Strauss from 9th Army linked up in the Slonim area to close a trap around tens of thousands of Russians. By 3 July Guderian's tanks were across the Beresina, and Hoth's across the Duna between Polotsk and Vitebsk; and on 7 July Guderian's spearhead crossed the Dnieper, only to be pulled back by Kluge, who rated Guderian for making an 'unauthorised crossing'. Bock intervened and ordered a recrossing, taking the opportunity to protest again to O.K.H. about Kluge's control of the armoured groups. Nothing came of his protest. On a flying visit to the north he found things more congenial, for he got on comparatively well with Hoth and Strauss, compared with Kluge, whom he did not like, and Guderian, whom he did not think had enough personality to command fifteen divisions. But in general the battle was going well, and on 8 July Bock issued an Order of the Day which began: 'The multiple battles for Bialystok, Novogrodek, and Minsk are concluded... The enemy's losses are stupendous'. And he listed 287,704 prisoners, 2,585 tanks, 1,449 heavy guns, and 346 aircraft, besides 'colossal amounts' of small arms, munitions and transport. These figures give one some idea of the scale of warfare in Russia.

On 11 July Bock moved his headquarters forward to Borissov, on the Beresina river. On 16 July the 29th Motorized Infantry Division of Major-General von Boltenstern, known as 'the hawks', captured Smolensk and the railway bridge across the Dnieper. Guderian had crossed the river on 10 and 11 July and driven north while Hoth's tanks under General Rudolf Scmidt, commanding XXXIX Panzer Corps, struck west from Vitebsk and encircled Smolensk from the north. Thus between Orsha and Smolensk itself a huge pocket of Russian troops was encircled. By 5 August all resistance inside it had ceased, though Guderian's and Hoth's forces did not actually link up until 27 July.

Bock issued another triumphant Order of the Day, claiming 309,110 prisoners, 3,205 tanks, 3,005 heavy artillery pieces, and 341 aircraft.

And now an astonishing thing happened. Hitler had always foreseen and promised a short campaign in Russia. After Smolensk it seemed obvious to Brauchitsch, Bock, and all the senior commanders that Moscow must, logically, be the next target. But Hitler hesitated. He was still confident of winning the war but his thoughts kept turning away from Moscow and towards Leningrad and the Ukraine. At his headquarters Brauchitsch, Halder, and the O.K.H. argued for an immediate attack on Moscow, once tanks had been serviced, reserves brought up, and supplies established. At various conferences leading field commanders, including Colonel-General Guderian, with Colonel-General Höpner the leading panzer expert, supported their views on behalf of Bock and indeed themselves. On 4 August, for example, Guderian and Colonel-General Hoth, another senior panzer commander of great merit, reported to Hitler that they would be ready to strike against Moscow between 15 and 20 August, and were confident of taking the capital. But still Hitler was doubtful. Of one thing Guderian and Hoth were certain; their worst enemy was time—and time was rapidly running out.

Guderian's leading elements were now on the Yelnya bend of the Desna River, forty-seven miles east of Smolensk and 185 miles from Moscow. Hoth's tanks had effectively prevented General Yeremenko's forces from recapturing Smolensk, and had reached the Vop. Dust, bad roads, and the wear and tear of war took a hard toll of the German tanks. Hoth at one time had reported to Bock being 60–70 per cent under nominal strength, and in the Yelnya bend between the end of July and the beginning of September the Russians poured in attack after attack to nip off this strategic starting-place for a Moscow offensive, forcing Army Group Centre into its first large defensive battle. These considerations must have weighed with Hitler. Nevertheless, every German soldier on the central front still looked to Moscow as the next and perhaps the final step.

It was not beyond the capacity at this time of Colonel-General Friedrich Fromm, commander of the Replacement Army, to make up most of the deficiencies caused by casualties in the fighting divisions, but supplies of fuel were already beginning to be a problem, and in motor vehicles there was a shortage of some 30 per cent. Broken-down tanks could often be repaired or cannibalized, but there was a growing shortage, and replacements were not readily forthcoming if only because production in Germany was being geared to new models. Experienced and well-trained tank crews were at a premium, being more difficult to replace than infantrymen. All this suggests that, once having regrouped and brought themselves up to strength as far as possible, if the Germans were to strike at Moscow it were best done quickly, while good weather still held. With the *blitzkrieg* conquests of Poland and France, it is all too easy to think of the German army in Russia as being composed mainly of massive panzer and motorized, i.e. wheeled not tracked, formations. This was far from the case: the vast bulk of the German army was made up of infantry divisions, and while motorization had gone further than in the armies of their enemies, especially as regards anti-tank and anti-aircraft artillery, there were still the long columns of marching infantry and of marching horses to consider in the vast areas of Russian steppe, mountain, forest, river, and plain. Most of the invaders had marched rather than ridden their 400 or 500 miles.

On 23 August, after weeks of waiting, the Chief of the General Staff, Colonel-General Halder, held a conference at Bock's headquarters at Borissov. The army commanders von Kluge, Strauss, and von Weichs were present, as was Guderian. Halder was depressed, and the reason for his gloom was that Hitler had decided against Moscow, and indeed Leningrad, in the immediate future. Hitler would now direct the main weight of the attack not against Moscow but against the Ukraine and the Crimea. The generals were amazed and resentful. Wearily Halder told them how at headquarters he and Brauchitsch had wrangled for five weeks for the drive to Moscow. Their latest plan of attack, submitted on 18 August, had been turned down by Hitler as 'not in line with my intentions'.

Hitler's own directive, issued on 21 August, ran in part: 'The most important objective to be achieved before the onset of winter is not the capture of Moscow but the seizure of the Crimea and of the industrial and coal-mining region on the Donets, and the cutting off of Russian oil supplies from the Caucasus area. In the north it is the isolation of Leningrad and the link-up with the Finns'. This was a far cry from the supplement to Directive No. 33, issued nearly a month before, on 23 July which had contained the words: 'After mopping up operations around Smolensk and on the southern flank, Army Group Centre . . . will defeat such enemy forces as remain between Smolensk and Moscow, by an advance on the left flank if possible. It will then capture Moscow'.

Now Army Group Centre was to stay on the defensive for the time being opposite the road to Moscow, use its left flank to join up with Army Group North, and lend much of its strength, including Guderian's Panzer Group, to Army Group South for the coming battle of Kiev.

Hitler had long been worried about the vulnerability of Army Group Centre's flanks, and it was also true that the very nature of the German armoured advances frequently left large gaps between the forward troops and the pursuing infantry, which could be exploited by by-passed Russian units or by increasingly dangerous partisan groups. The Germans had suffered casualties, especially in tanks, that were heavy though not crippling; the Soviet armies were becoming better organized, harder to entrap, and had learned to give ground and fight another day; there were difficulties of fuel, supplies, railway transport, repairs, and awful roads. But a highly professional army like Germany's had learned to cope with many of these difficulties, to improvise, and to produce the extra effort so often needed. Its commanders, down to battalion level, were experienced, tough, and often surprisingly imaginative, and not at all the hidebound 'square-heads' of popular British imagination. The shortage of younger officers on whom the fighting successes most depended had not yet become intense. But there was one thing that the German could not improvise—and that was time. The fact was that Hitler, however sensible his reasons for relegating Moscow to a future drive (and they were by no means foolish) was now committed to a death struggle which he had to end quickly in order to be successful. The almost limitless resources of the Russians, the vast size of the country, the bad terrain, were far more easily exploitable by the natives of that country than by the invaders. Given time, Stalin could produce new, trained formations and new and better weapons. Germany's manpower barrel, however, was not inexhaustible, and she was fighting on more than one front.

Hitler had therefore to act, and act quickly, for already he had dithered far too long. By turning away from Moscow he committed a fatal mistake because he seemed to be accepting the fact that Army Group Centre's drive had lost its impetus, and he was now making it impossible for it to have favourable odds, in the face of time and weather, for an attack on Moscow when it did come. That is, unless he was prepared to go over to the defensive until good weather in 1942—and he was not. But in effect his August decision was for a strategy of safety, and it was now too late for that. Hesitation, if not caution, should have been thrown to the winds. But the peasant in Hitler would not allow him to be thus confident, either of himself or of his generals. The mere fact that they nearly all disagreed with him must have increased his certainty that he, who had been right all along so far, was right again.

Bock was as angry, if less heated, as anyone. He had always been for Moscow. After a discussion with Halder and Guderian it was decided to send them both back to Rastenberg in a last attempt to change the Führer's mind. Whether because of Hitler's powers of mesmerizing his audience, or whether Guderian botched his case, which seems unlikely, it failed.

Bock resented particularly the loss of substantial forces to Rundstedt's Army Group South. Curiously enough, he was inclined to blame the High Command rather than Hitler personally at this moment, but then he had always enjoyed a peculiar relationship, based upon mutual toleration and guardedness, with Hitler.

He rang up Brauchitsch to protest about the transfer, saying: 'I will tell you that all of this is, in my professional opinion, quite asinine.

It has come to my attention that your headquarters believes that my objective is the capture of Moscow. This is untrue! My first objective is, and has been, to destroy the enemy forces, after which Moscow will fall into our hands like a ripe cherry! There is, then, only one solution on my front. Attack the enemy! Defence is absolutely out of the question! How can you expect me to repel the enemy with weakened forces? . . . Every hour that we lose is irretrievable. We are permitting the enemy the time he needs to recover, to slip from the noose we have placed upon him'.

Brauchitsch could only reply that he understood, and that the decision had not been his.

Bock was angry also with Guderian for his failure, considering that he had been too easily persuaded by Hitler. All the same, he continued to press attacks, despite orders on 31 August that he was to make no further advances towards Moscow until authorized, and moved his headquarters to Smolensk early in September.

Some time at the beginning of September Hitler seems to have regained his full self-confidence. At any rate he now changed his mind: Moscow was, after all, to have priority when the Kiev battle was won. Hitler decided this at the latest by 5 September, when the Kiev encirclement was by no means well advanced. On 9 September O.K.H. requested Bock to prepare an operation order for continuing the attack on Moscow, to be called Operation 'Typhoon'. When this was approved, Bock was informed that for the attack he would dispose of not only his three original Armies but the 2nd, 3rd, and 4th Panzer Armies, as they had now become, under Guderian, Hoth, and Höpner. The infantry Army commanders remained von Weichs, Kluge, and Strauss.

On 29 September Bock summoned all these Army commanders, with Kesselring for the air command (8 Air Corps had now returned to command), and on this eve of his greatest attack reminded them that they were now equipped with stronger forces than when Army Group Centre had invaded from Poland. He had promised Hitler that Moscow would be taken before 7 November and the onset of winter. Bock also issued a new Order of the Day exhorting his troops to victory: 'Soldiers of Army Group Centre! After weeks of waiting, the army group renews the attack! Our objectives are none other than the destruction of remaining enemy forces to the east of us and the capture of the citadel of Bolshevism—Moscow!'

The attack on 30 September took the Russians by surprise. In the southern sector the 4th Panzer Division, commanded by Lieutenant-General Wilhelm Freiherr von Langermann und Erlenkamp, from von Geyr's XXIV Panzer Corps in Guderian's 2nd Panzer Army, took Orel, well east of Bryansk. Its tanks had covered eighty miles in one day beforehand. The Panzer Brigade which took the town was commanded by Colonel Hans Eberbach, later to become a General.

When Karachev was taken on 5 October by the 18th Panzer Division under Major-General Walter Nehring, in Lieutenant-General Joachim Lemelsen's XLVII Panzer Corps, the Bryansk-Orel road was cut and General Yeremenko was in serious danger. His situation was made even worse when the 18th's companion division, the 17th Panzer under Lieutenant-General Jürgen von Arnim, who had captured Minsk, took Bryansk itself on 6 October 'with unexpected ease'. Bryansk was a highly important railway junction. Guderian's tanks now linked up with men from Weich's 2nd Army coming up from the west, and also contacted Höpner's 4th Panzer Army to the north. The Bryansk pocket was closing around three Soviet Armies. Next day, however, the first snow fell, displacing rain. On Höpner's front on 7 October an equal success was gained when, after fierce and confused night fighting, Lieutenant-General Fischer's 10th Panzer Division entered Vyazma on Marshal Timoshenko's front. After cleaning up Russian resistance, it controlled the Smolensk-Moscow highway.

To the north General Hoth's two Panzer Corps—LVI and XLI—and VI Infantry Corps broke through west of Kholm in difficult, hilly ground. Despite fierce enemy resistance they managed to link up with Höpner in Vyazma on 7 October, thus closing yet another pocket, this time round six Soviet Armies (each nearer in size to a large British Corps). The same day Rommel's old division, 7th Panzer, now under Major-General Hasso von Manteuffel, cut the Moscow highway east of Vyazma, thus earning a special commendation from von Brauchitsch. It was now left to the infantry of Strauss's 9th Army and von Kluge's 4th Army, coming up *ventre à terre*, to finish off the encircled enemy, and by 14 October this was done. In the south the Bryansk pocket lasted until 17 October. Thus in little more than a fortnight, von Bock had won two great encircling battles. On 19 October he put the count of Russian prisoners at 673,098; and 1,277 tanks, 4,398 heavy artillery pieces, 1,009 anti-tank and anti-aircraft guns, and 187 aircraft were destroyed or captured.

All this was very satisfactory. On 8 October Bock had been instructed by Hitler to put the 3rd and 4th Panzer Armies astride the Smolensk-Moscow highway and encircle Moscow from north and south as soon as possible. It now appeared that Hitler's intention was not so much to capture the capital as to destroy it by artillery fire and bombing. There was now, however, one grave drawback to any plans—this was the weather. Since 9 October—and earlier in Guderian's sector—constant rain and mud had made progress extremely difficult, and now were added sleet and snow. Mud, more than the Russians, was slowing down Bock's complete front, and making opportunities for roving partisan bands as German units got stranded or left behind in the awful weather. Even Hitler and the High Command realised the dangers, and on 11 October Bock was asked if it was practical to continue the advance

He decided it was. So the Germans slogged on through the mud.

On 13 October Kaluga fell, only 100 miles from Moscow to the south-west. Next day Lieutenant-General Rudolf Kirchner's 1st Panzer Division took Kalinin and cut the Leningrad-Moscow railway. Kalinin was ninety-three miles from Moscow. An important bridge over the Volga was also taken. On the same day Fischer's 10th Panzer Division and S.S. Lieutenant-General Paul Hausser's 'Das Reich' Infantry Division began a savage battle at Borodino against Siberian troops equipped with the new Katyusha rocket mortars, known as 'Stalin's organ-pipes', and—for the first time—with the formidable T.34s in massed formations. At one time General of Panzer Troops Georg-Hans Reinhardt made available the whole of 3rd Panzer Army's artillery to his attack, under Colonel Karl Weidling, the gunner later to become famous as the last commander and surrenderer of Berlin. Reinhardt had recently succeeded Hoth, who had been transferred to Army Group South somewhat to Bock's distress, since the composed Hoth was one of the few senior commanders with whom Bock had never had a serious disagreement.

This was a bitter battle, with strong low-level bombing activity on both sides. Finally the Germans prevailed, and on 19 October pushed through to Mozhaysk and took it. The first line of defence had been breached, and Moscow now lay only sixty miles away. In this battle Hausser was seriously wounded.

In Moscow there was something like panic. The Government was moved to Kuibyshev in the Urals, and hundreds of thousands of Moscovites evacuated the city. But Stalin remained, and gave command of the defences to Marshal Zhukov, who replaced Timoshenko.

By the latter part of October the first line of defence of Moscow had been broken on a broad front between Kaluga and Kalinin. In the north, Kirchner's 1st Panzer Division from Thuringia and Hesse had forced a bridgehead over the Volga at Kalinin, but then ran into stiff Russian counter-attacks; so did Fischer's 10th Panzer Division; between 16 and 22 October the Nara River had been crossed, first by 19th Panzer Division under Lieutenant-General O. von Knobelsdorff north of Gorki, and then by 98th Infantry Division on 23 October at Trautino.

Guderian's troops in the south had been slowed down by mud more than anyone. Many of his vehicles were sunk up to their axles and he was out of fuel. Since 7 October his advance had been negligible, and Geyr's XXIV Panzer Corps was bogged down in front of Mtsensk. The town was finally taken, however, with heavy losses in tanks, on 24 October. Four days later Geyr's advanced troops under Colonel Eberbach got within a few miles of Tula, but an attempt to rush the city failed in the face of strong Russian defence. Tula was to hold out in most determined fashion again on 30 October. By 31 October Breith's 3rd Panzer Division had lost all but 40 of its 150 tanks as a result of the fierce resistance. The wheeled vehicles now had mostly to use hastily-made 'corduroy' roads of felled logs. The infantry, if unaffected by fuel, were feeling the pinch after scores of miles of foot-slogging through rain and mud, often without supplies. General Heinrici's leading infantry in XLIII Infantry Corps received no bread ration for eight days in a row. Everywhere Russian resistance seemed to be hardening, and the weather was getting colder with no winter clothes yet issued.

By the end of the month the weather had broken again after a short improvement, and the Red Army resisted more tenaciously than before. But it was the mud and terrain rather than resistance which stopped the Germans. As Colonel Albert Seaton has written in his comprehensive *The Russo-German War, 1941–1945* (p. 190): 'In the first fortnight of the *Typhoon* offensive Army Group Centre destroyed nearly 700,000 of the Soviet defenders at comparatively little cost to itself, and with another three weeks' dry, mild and clear weather, it would inevitably have been in Moscow'. He makes the point that once Bock's forces had lost their mobility 'the tactical concept of the *blitzkreig* foundered'. And the conditions became so almost unbelievably bad that all wheels and horses were halted, and tracked vehicles used so much fuel that they soon exhausted it.

Bock had believed all along in the Moscow offensive in August, and cannot be blamed for its too late start. At the end of the first week of November the frost came, and Army Group Centre spent most of the first half of the month refitting and nursing its wounds. 2nd Army did secure the Kursk-Orel highway, however; and on 8 November, when the Russians attacked Kalinin suddenly, the Germans repelled them, though with some difficulty. The general supply situation was still far from satisfactory, though Bock spared no efforts to improve it; and winter clothing was still lacking.

Bock should have seen by now that it was useless to continue, but he still chose to believe that one last effort could take Moscow. At Orsha on 13 November, with the temperature 20 degrees centigrade below zero, Halder held a conference of all Army Group representatives and Army Chiefs of Staff. This was to decide whether to dig in, withdraw, or continue the offensive. For Rundstedt, von Sodenstern was emphatic for going on to the defensive. So was Brennecke, for von Leeb who was already on the defensive in the Leningrad sector. Only von Greiffenberg, speaking against his own personal beliefs, gave Bock's view for continuing, on the grounds that the capture of Moscow was a military and also a psychological necessity.

This view was agreeable to Hitler, if not to Brauchitsch, for an atmosphere of euphoria had grown up at Hitler's headquarters on the mistaken assumption that the Russians were at the end of their tether; truly the whole rotten structure was about to come crashing down, it was thought. This was far from being the view of Bock's Chief of Staff, or of his Chief of Operations, Colonel von Tresckow. Nor indeed, to be fair, was it that of Bock. He knew there was little time left, but thought offence better than defence; there was a sporting chance. Halder agreed. Guderian thought the chances were slight; and von Kluge, typically, sat on the fence.

The attack was renewed on 19 November, though Bock had wished it to start earlier. Now the weather was relatively mild. By 24 November Lieutenant-General Ferdinand Schaal, the captor of Calais, had taken Klin, on the second line of Moscow's defence, with his LVI Panzer Corps, helped on its right by VII Infantry Corps under Lieutenant-General Wilhelm Fahrmbacher. Next Rogachevo fell, and then Schaal established a bridgehead over the Moskva-Volga Canal at Yakhroma, due to good work by Colonel von Manteuffel. But fierce Russian counter-attacks recaptured the canal bridge on 29 November, and the chance to strike quickly at Moscow from the north was lost.

Further south, however, elements of 2nd Panzer Division under Colonel Eberhard Rodt, fighting against dismounted Siberian cavalrymen and Moscow workers' militia, took Krasnaya Polyana, Pushki, and Katyushki. One rifle regiment reached Gorki, nineteen miles from the Kremlin; and an assault party of panzer engineers blew up the railway station at Lobnya, two miles closer. South-west, the Istra river was the scene of another coup by Lieutenant-Colonel Kurt von der Chevallerie, commanding the 86th Rifle Regiment of 10th Panzer Division (Fischer), who seized the bridge at Busharovo. After 10th Panzer had reached the northern outskirts of Istra itself on 26 November, 'Das Reich' S.S. Infantry Division stormed the town. On 28 November the S.S. took Vysokovo and advanced to within twenty miles of Moscow, until they were held up at the village of Lenino on 2 December.

To their south things were going less well. The IX Infantry Corps, under the senior Lieutenant-General Geyer, a pre-war commander of V Corps, and 'no Hitler enthusiast', in his old friend von Hassell's words, got stuck at Zvenigorod, due west of Moscow. The 4th Panzer Army, helped by Fahrmbacher's VII Corps, tried in vain to break through the Russian defences running from the Nara Lakes to the Moskva bend. Finally, in order to gain the Moscow highway, von Kluge launched a 4th Army attack near Naro-Forminsk on 1 December, led by Lieutenant-General Materna's XX Corps. 3rd Motorized Infantry Division from Brandenburg at last took Naro-Fominsk and advanced three miles eastwards along the high-road to Moscow, but they were in great difficulties in temperatures of 38 degrees centigrade below zero. Due to frostbite as much as to casualties, some battalions were down to eighty men. 258th Infantry Division pushed a mobile combat group further still, and one motorized column got as far as Yushkovo, another to neighbouring Burzevo, both some twenty-seven miles from Moscow, on 2 December. But next day Field-Marshal von Kluge ordered the withdrawal of the division, because he felt that he could not guarantee its safety, and his losses were already enormous.

From 23 November, when Guderian had reported that his troops were worn out, Bock had seen his prospects dwindling, and according to Guderian had actually asked permission to go over to the defensive Brauchitsch had not been able to authorize this, and Bock continued his last desperate attacks. On 29 November forward forces of 4th Panzer Army and 4th Army reached the outer suburbs of Moscow, some tanks getting as far as Tushino; and on 4 December units of 2nd Army struggled into Kuntsevo, a suburb in the city's south-east But when their ammunition ran out they had to withdraw.

At the beginning of the month Bock lost the support of Kesselring and two air corps of 2nd Air Fleet which were transferred to North Africa. In the south Guderian had failed to capture Tula, though on 2 December his 3rd and 4th Panzer Divisions made good the Tula-Moscow railway line, and next day the latter reached Kostrova on the Tula-Serpukhov road. But XLIII Corps could not quite link up with the tanks north of Tula, and on 6 December the attack had to be given up because of hard frost and temperatures ranging from 30 to 45 degrees centigrade below zero. On the same day Marshal Zhukov launched a counter-attack all along the front. Bock's soldiers were already, in his own words, 'totally exhausted'. Nor were his commanders in much better shape: Guderian was depressed, von Weichs so near collapse that Bock gave his command to General of Panzer Troops Rudolf Schmidt, and von Kluge had been dragging his feet in the Nara area despite repeated requests from Höpner to attack Moscow from the west.

On the night of 5–6 December, sitting in Tolstoy's manor house at Yasnaya Polyana, Guderian gave the order to his leading tanks to withdraw, and put his 2nd Panzer Army on the defensive. It would withdraw to the Don River. Kluge's 4th Army had already gone over to defence. The troops now had to fall back to the Nara to avoid encircle-ment. The Moscow offensive, which had got so near, was over as far as Bock was concerned by 5 December, and by 13 December his Army Group had retreated fifty miles or so all along the front in the face of Zhukov's well-prepared attacks. On 8 December Bock recorded in his war diary that the main causes had been the mud, the breakdown of the supply system, the primitive road and railway systems in Russia and underestimation of the strength of the enemy. He wrote with some bitterness, and much justification:

'My troops have given all they have; they can do no more. Their supreme efforts are reflected in the shockingly high losses among both commanders and men. . . .

'All along, I demanded of Army High Command the authority to strike down the enemy when he was wobbling. We could have finished the enemy last summer. We could have destroyed him completely. Last August, the road to Moscow was open; we could have entered the Bolshevik capital in triumph and in summery weather. The high military leadership of the Fatherland made a terrible mistake when it forced my army group to adopt a position of defence last August. Now all of us are paying for that mistake. . . .'

Yet, however true this was, Bock had committed a grave error by maintaining his offensive far too long—long after the time when the weather had broken, when it was no longer possible to outflank the enemy and all attacks had to be frontal, when winter clothing was needed desperately but was only available to a few, and when casualties on his front were well over a quarter of a million. Whether it was that Bock was too obstinate to give way, or whether his vanity clouded his good sense, he forbore to call the decisive showdown with Hitler that common sense must have dictated. After the battle for Moscow Army Group Centre was never the same again, and for its terrible casualties Bock must take a large part of the responsibility.

Brauchitsch went on 19 December, and that same day in 1941 Bock left his headquarters for the last time, officially on extended sick leave. Indeed his health had long been bad, as he suffered from a stomach ailment. Von Kluge took his place. Bock was officially placed at the Führer's disposal, and returned to Berlin.

It was not often under Hitler that erring generals received a second chance. In Bock's case it came about because of the sudden death of a colleague. Field-Marshal von Reichenau, who had taken over Army Group South from von Rundstedt, suffered a heart attack on 15 January 1942, and died two days later. Hitler called upon Bock, who flew to Poltava on 19 January and assumed command from the acting commander Hoth next day. From now on he was to be in telephone touch with Hitler every few days.

For the next two months and more Bock was mainly on the defensive, with the Russians making costly attacks in the Crimea and round Kharkov. At the beginning of April, however, Field-Marshal von Kleist's Army Group under Bock's direction attacked and cleared the area west of the Don, taking some 200,000 prisoners with the loss of under 50,000 Germans.

On 8 May Bock's Army Group began its long-prepared Crimean offensive, and by 18 May the Kerch Peninsula had been overrun and Kerch itself captured. The Russians lost 170,000 prisoners, 1,133 guns, and 258 tanks; the Germans only 7,000 men. At the same time Kleist's forces were pushing forward to the Donets River. On 3 June the attack on Sevastopol started, with intense artillery and air bombardment for several days. The siege was directed by Colonel-General von Manstein's 11th Army, working with von Richthofen's VIII Air Corps. On 1

July a special announcement from Hitler's headquarters proclaimed the fall of Sevastopol, which was clear in another two days, falling to infantry attacks combined with heavy shelling and Stuka raids. The Russians had lost 90,000 prisoners, 467 pieces of ordnance, 758 mortars, and 155 anti-tank and anti-aircraft guns.

Bock now turned his attention almost 1,000 miles north to the city of Voronezh, which he had always intended to take. On 5 July two German divisions entered Voronezh with unexpected ease, but when they moved out east and north-east came under strong Russian counter-attack. Bock, who had secured Hitler's approval, as he thought, for seizing Voronezh to secure his northern flank (though not for 'needless' effort there), committed two more divisions, both panzer, to the area. For some reason this infuriated Hitler, who demanded their withdrawal. Bock, who should by now have known better, ignored this, and for the next week while the battle continued in the Voronezh area there were unpleasant altercations between Bock and Hitler's headquarters, with the Führer openly criticizing Bock's conduct of operations and on one occasion actually moving Hoth's 4th Panzer Army Headquarters south without consulting Bock. On 7th July Army Group South was split into two groups, 'A' under List and 'B' under Bock; and on 13 July Hoth's Panzer Army was given to List. That same day Keitel informed Bock by telephone that he was directed to give up his command for health reasons and hand it over to von Weichs. Bock was completely taken aback, and argued in vain. On 15 July he handed over to Weichs and flew back to Berlin. He would never again command troops.

It was a measure of his prestige and reputation within Germany, however, that for months the pretence was kept up that Bock was still commanding on the southern front. Photographs from the previous summer appeared in German newspapers and magazines, and his name was constantly associated with Stalingrad and the Caucasus. Bock became embittered, and considered that he had been made a scapegoat. In 1943 some officers who knew him, including Beck, sounded Bock out as a prospective recruit to their campaign to get hostilities ended. Bock considered the matter, but decided that to join such a group would be treasonable. He had, of course, been approached before, for in June 1941 the headquarters of 'active operational conspiracy', in Wheeler-Bennett's words, had been right inside his own Army Group Centre headquarters. His G.1, or chief operations officer, Major-General Henning von Tresckow, was its leader, backed up by officers such as his A.D.C. Fabian von Schlabrendorff, Bock's two A.D.C.s, Graf Hans von Hardenberg and Graf Heinrich von Lehndorff, Colonel Freiherr von Gersdorff, Colonel Schultze-Boettger, and Lieutenant-Colonel Alexander von Voss. These officers had worked upon Bock, even to the extent of trying to persuade him to have Hitler arrested on one of his visits to Army Group, but without success. Wheeler-Bennett puts it thus: 'Though he despised National Socialism and found repellent its increasing blood-lust, he was consumed with vanity and egotism, and the insignificance of his character prevented him from lifting a finger to overthrow a system for which he felt nothing but contempt. He was among those many whose response to the approaches of the conspirators was: "If it succeeds, I'll support you, but I won't take the consequences of failure."'

Von Schlabrendorff summed up: 'Although Bock detested national socialism, he was never willing to lift a hand against Hitler. Much of his character was already mortgaged to vanity and egotism, and what remained was diminutive'. On one occasion he had threatened to have General Thomas arrested when the latter pushed him too far towards conspiring, and on another told him that he would only join in the plot if Himmler was a party to it. He did, however, give the conspirators one good piece of advice, which it is a pity that they did not ponder more—not to trust Colonel-General Fromm.

Bock was a disciplinarian, and not considered an easy man under whom to serve. At the same time he stuck up for his subordinates, as in the case of Generals Stumme and von Boineburg-Lengsfeld when a German plane carrying secret plans crashed inside Russian lines. The former was sentenced to five years' fortress detention at Hitler's instigation, though soon released and sent to Africa, where he died in action. The latter survived and was posted from the Russian front to Paris later on. Neither of them was in any way responsible for the accident. Bock prized highly the traditional virtues of the good soldier, and therefore would have nothing to do with Hitler's infamous 'Commissar order', which directed that all such political advisers with Russian formations be shot out of hand. Nor would he circulate any orders, whether from Hitler or not, which he felt detrimental to good discipline among his troops, such as those encouraging pillage and arson, if not worse, in Russia. Indeed on more than one occasion Bock suggested that it would be a good idea to treat the Soviet farmers and peasants better, that it would be easy to get them on the German side, especially in the Ukraine, if promises were kept. His whole attitude to the occupation of Russia was a good deal more sensible, and more liberal, than was official policy.

In comparing a commander like Bock with, say, Rommel, one has to remember that the former controlled as many armies as the latter German divisions. In his last command Bock had authority over some one-and-a-half million men—the German 2nd, 6th, 11th and 17th Armies and 1st and 4th Panzer Armies, and Hungarian, Rumanian and Italian armies. How highly should he be rated?

In Poland and the Low Countries, despite some accusations of slowness, his performances cannot seriously be faulted, given their imposed limitations. Criticism of his prolongation of the Moscow campaign has been stated; in the Army Group South affair he comes out of it unjustly, if explicably, treated. Bock won great victories, and suffered great losses. W.E. Hart, an unfriendly critic, is not altogether justified in saying 'Bock conquered territory but not the Russian armies', as a look at the Soviet casualty figures will show. He also says: 'The Hitler-Bock combination was just about the worst for Germany that could be found, and its existence contributed substantially to the shortening of the war and the certainty of Allied victory'. And 'Von Bock was far more the professional soldier than Generals Jodl, Warlimont and their kind. There is no doubt that in normal times von Bock would have made his name as a subordinate general. Given responsibility beyond his capacity, and even worse, called upon to advise a civilian with supreme political and military power, who overnight thought he had become a strategist, von Bock's leadership was disastrous for the armies under his command'.

The American historian Earl Ziemke refers to his 'passive philosophy of leadership', and suggests, rather puzzlingly, that most of his experience 'had been gained on a static front'. Surely not Poland, France, or the road to Moscow? Ziemke suggests that because he had not had a chance to prove himself as a tactician, von Bock was more compliant than some others as far as Hitler was concerned 'and tended to welcome the Führer's guidance'. I can see no evidence for this, indeed Bock's recorded comments in his war diary are often bitter. Ziemke does admit that Bock was 'a highly regarded army commander'. Colonel-General Halder, with whom Bock normally seems to have got on reasonably well, has one acid comment: 'It is characteristic of this officer that he should demand a written confirmation of an order from my headquarters, simply because he does not agree with it'. Characteristic, perhaps; wise for that time, certainly.

Perhaps Bock approaches that typecast pattern of a ruthless, rigid Prussian officer. He worked, as it were, in blinkers, and orders were sacred to him even when he disagreed with them. Because he had no flexibility and little inventiveness and because he failed, like Brauchitsch to stand up to foolish orders from Hitler, he cannot be accorded a place among the great commanders. But his several large, decisive victories and the sheer efficiency and drive with which he controlled huge bodies of highly able soldiers with apparently little trouble, and the respect which both his colleagues and, surprisingly, Hitler felt for him after his dismissal as well as before, all these suggest that Bock deserves a high place in the second class.

On 28 April 1945, as the war was drawing to its close, Bock received a telegram from Manstein, who had once served under him, suggesting that he go to Hamburg where Grand-Admiral Karl Dönitz was supposedly forming a new 'North German' government. Despite constan allied air raids he made his way by car to the Hamburg area where, on 2 May, he decided to drive round the city and head for Kiel. He never got there, for he was caught by one last air attack and died by the roadside, his 64-year-old body riddled with bullets.

It was thus that British troops found him several days later. At last death had met 'Der Sterber'.

If Hans Günther von Kluge had been a man of more impressive moral stature none would have exemplified better than he the tragedy of the German generals under Hitler. As it was, there was a sad futility about von Kluge's suicide, in his sixty-second year, in the summer of 1944 when his long career in high command was summarily ended. He had been summoned back to Berlin in disgrace by Hitler, which meant in effect a sentence of execution in the hysterical aftermath of the July Plot. Kluge told his driver to take him to Metz, but before that city was reached he was dead in the back of his car from poison.

Clouds had gathered over Kluge's head on three counts: first, Hitler believed that the Field-Marshal had been in sympathy with the conspirators of 20 July, although nothing could be proved against him. Second, he was in disfavour for the failure of the Avranches counteroffensive, in which he had not really believed and which he had not been permitted to stage as early as he thought right; nor was his conduct of the defence of the Falaise pocket pleasing to Hitler, who had forbidden him to let Army Group 'B' break out of it on 15 August 1944, although Kluge decided that he would ignore that order. And third, and the clinching black mark, on 15 August Kluge had 'gone missing' from his headquarters for twelve hours when he was supposedly on his way to confer at Nécy with General of Panzer Troops Heinrich Eberbach, commander of the so-called 5th Panzer Army. This absence aroused the darkest suspicions at Hitler's headquarters, where it was put about that Kluge had been negotiating a surrender with the Allies and had arranged a secret battlefield rendezvous with them. This was absurd enough, but Hitler was prepared to believe it, and Army Group headquarters was ordered to report back every hour on Kluge's whereabouts.

What had happened, in fact, was something liable to happen to any commander. Kluge's car and radio trucks had been caught in an air strike, shot up, and he himself trapped in the chaotic night traffic of a defeated army. Hitler refused to believe this, which was why, on 17 August, Field-Marshal Walter Model from the Russian front turned up unexpectedly at Kluge's headquarters with a personal note from Hitler and orders to take over command.

Kluge wrote a last letter to Hitler, which reads as a pathetic and undignified apologia.

'My Führer.

'When you receive these lines I shall be no more. I cannot bear the accusation of having brought about the fate of our armies in the West by mistaken measures, and I have no means of defending myself. I am therefore taking the only action I can, and shall go where thousands of my companions have preceded me . . .

'Both Rommel and I, and probably all the commanders here in the West with experience of battle against the Anglo-Americans with their preponderance of material, foresaw the present development. We were not listened to. Our appreciations were *not* dictated by pessimism but from the sole knowledge of the facts. I do not know whether Field-Marshal Model, who has been proved in every sphere, will still master the situation. From my heart I hope so. Should it not be so, however, and your new, greatly desired weapons, especially of the Air Force, not succeed, then, my Führer, make up your mind to end the war. The German people have borne such untold suffering that it is time to put an end to this frightfulness . . .

'My Führer, I have always admired your greatness, your conduct in the gigantic struggle, and your iron will to maintain yourself and National Socialism. If Fate is stronger than your will and your genius, so is Providence. You have fought an honourable and great fight. History will prove that for you. Show yourself now also great enough to put an end to a hopeless struggle when necessary'.

The man who could write this to Hitler, whom he knew well and with whom he had frequently discussed and sometimes argued military matters, shows an astonishing naïvete. For ten years at least, Kluge had been among the senior ranks of the German Army (in 1939, after the 1938 'purge', Kluge stood equal fifth with Blaskowitz in the Army List). Now here he was fawning upon the man who, most of all, was responsible for his subsequent misery.

Von Kluge ended: 'I depart from you, my Führer, as one who stood nearer to you than you perhaps realized, in the consciousness that I did my duty to the utmost.'

Hitler read this letter without comment, according to Jodl's evidence at Nuremberg, then passed it to him without saying a word. He denied Kluge military honours at his funeral.

Von Kluge was an artillery officer, like many of Germany's top generals. After serving in the Great War he went steadily up the ladder of promotion, and by 1935 was a Lieutenant-General commanding the VI Army Corps at Münster. The following year he became a full General of Artillery, and in 1939 was in command of *Heeresgruppe* 6 at Hanover. In the Polish campaign, and in France in 1940, von Kluge commanded 4th Army, first under von Bock in Army Group North, and secondly under von Rundstedt's Army Group 'A' as a Colonel-General. In these campaigns Kluge established his reputation as a sound and shrewd strategist and as an energetic front-line commander. In France his 4th Army contained no less than ten Army

Corps, four of them mechanized ones under great leaders such as Guderian, Reinhardt, Höpner and Rudolf Schmidt, with Hoth and von Kleist as Group commanders. With leaders such as this it would have been hard to go far wrong, but General Blumentritt, an acute observer, characterized Kluge as 'a very energetic and active commander who liked to be up among the fighting troops'. Kluge was 'impulsive', he writes, 'and, like Rommel, continuously at the front, never sparing himself'.

This extreme energy and considerable intelligence naturally brought Kluge to Hitler's attention. He was among the dozen new Field-Marshals appointed in July 1940, and commanded 4th Army again under von Bock in the war with Russia. When Bock was dismissed in December 1941, von Kluge acceded to the command of Army Group Centre. He was to hold this appointment until October 1943, when, as a result of a car accident, he was sent on sick leave and replaced by Colonel-General Busch. What was his record in Russia like?

Despite his energy, Kluge had a reputation for coolness and even, at times, caution. Paul Carell in *Hitler's War on Russia* tells a story of how, in July 1941, the dashing Guderian tricked von Kluge, who wanted Guderian to wait on the Dnieper for the infantry to come up, by giving false positions for his leading tanks. 'Your operations invariably hang by a silken thread,' Kluge told Guderian, but he let him have his way. But Carell calls Kluge's encirclement battle at Vyazma later in 1941 'the finest example of a battle of encirclement in military history'.

At the end of 1941 Kluge got rid of Guderian, whom he had found hard to control, if not insubordinate. Their quarrel was not the end of the affair, for in July 1943 Kluge actually challenged Guderian to a duel with pistols, with Hitler as his second, until wiser heads intervened.

Kluge did not get on very well with Bock either; he could do little about this in view of the latter's unbending temperament and ruthless way with dissenters. According to General Blumentritt, Kluge was not in favour, after Smolensk, of continuing the advance on Moscow. He much preferred his own idea that his 4th Army and Guderian's tank forces should encircle the Russians around Kiev. Not least weighty in Kluge's mind was the fact that he would then be serving under von Rundstedt rather than von Bock. On at least one occasion, on 30 October 1941, Kluge instead of Bock was called before Hitler to report on the general situation, since Hitler, while tolerating Bock, distrusted his staff. 'Der kluge Hans'—Clever Hans—was on his way to becoming the messenger boy between Hitler and the Army commanders.

Kluge's mistrust of the Moscow offensive may explain some otherwise inexplicable delays on his part. During November 1941 his 4th Army remained passive in the Nara River area, which had been reached on 24 October. There were, it is true, Soviet counter-attacks, and it had been agreed that Kluge should not join the main attack until the tanks of Guderian, Höpner, and Reinhardt had begun to draw off Soviet forces from the Nara, west of Moscow, to the northern and southern flanks. But towards the end of November, when Höpner and Reinhardt were in position north of the capital, Kluge should have moved. He did not, despite frantic telephone calls from Höpner daily requesting him to attack from the Nara and engage Russian forces west of Moscow. Eventually Höpner lost patience, and on 29 November ordered 78 Storm Division, which was only twenty-five miles from the capital, to attack, as 4th Panzer Army was going to press on regardless of what 4th Army did. In fact Kluge began his own attack on 1 December, but on a very small scale, and the Russians rightly regarded Höpner's thrust from the north as the dangerous one. On 3 December Kluge, whose only noteworthy success had been in the Naro-Fominsk area, called off his attack, and by then it was clear that Moscow would not fall.

Why Kluge did not attack much earlier, and in greater strength from the Nara positions, is unclear. By doing so he would have drawn off Soviet reserves which were committed against the Panzer formations, and given the tank commanders greater scope. As it was, Kluge's inactivity or fumbling were such that the Russians could actually withdraw some troops from the Nara front. It may be that the ultimate responsibility was von Bock's, but the episode was discreditable to Kluge. Höpner felt that he had been badly let down, and did not forbear to say so. On 3 December he told Kluge that if that was the best that 4th Army could do, then the offensive against Moscow should never have been resumed. Meanwhile his own 4th Panzer Army was at the end of its resources within twenty miles of the Kremlin, and he suggested that both he and Reinhardt should pull back thirty miles from their exposed positions to straighten the line.

Kluge did not take this rebuke well. Soon Höpner was to go, unsupported by Kluge, and so were some twenty other generals from Army Group Centre. It now seems extraordinary, and only due to Hitler's whim, that it was von Kluge who was chosen to succeed von Bock. But so it was.

It was thus mainly as a defensive commander that Kluge confirmed his reputation in the winter of 1941–2 and later. Indeed he was to engage in no great offensive until the Kursk-Orel battle of the summer of 1943. He had to get Hitler's permission, frequently refused, for any withdrawal, and became in effect the channel for requests to do so, usually for good tactical reasons, from his subordinates. The operations of Army Group Centre bore, after Moscow, no clear individual stamp of a powerful and commanding hand. The result was bad for the German Army and led to an unwillingness to take responsibility, and lack of confidence, in the junior commanders of Corps and divisions. On 15 January 1942 the able 9th Army Commander, Colonel-General

Rudolf Strauss, through whose front in the Rzhev area the Russians had made a dangerous break-through, asked to be relieved. Strauss was ill; he was succeeded by one of the 'new' generals, General of Panzer Troops Walther Model, the former commander of XLI Panzer Corps, known to the troops as a lucky general and correspondingly popular.

A convinced Nazi, Model had not attained divisional command at the outbreak of war, but had been Chief of Staff to Busch's 16th Army in France in 1940. He was a 'thruster' who was to have considerable influence on Kluge, who tended to be influenced by strong-minded men and by those who had most recently talked to him. In Halder's view Kluge lived from hand to mouth in the light of the crisis of the moment. He basically believed in Hitler's 'hold-on' strategy, but had not the strength to dispute fallacious orders hard enough.

A good example of how easily Kluge could be swayed is provided by Alfred Rosenberg. He recalled in his memoirs how Kluge, at whose Münster headquarters the Nazi philosopher had a speaking engagement in 1939, said to him afterwards: 'Permit me, Herr Reichsleiter, to say a frank word. You were depicted to us as a specially fanatical person and I admit having had some misgivings. But what you have said is so interesting and reasoned that I am very grateful to you'. Rosenberg became quite a friend of Kluge, and visited him in the summer of 1942 near Smolensk, when Kluge confided that he disapproved of the activities of Gauleiter Koch, the overlord of the Ukraine. But Kluge did little about them.

Although his army Group contributed half of the forces engaged in the great tank battles of Kursk and Orel in July and August 1943, it is surprising that Kluge's name is not more closely associated with those German failures. Kluge seems to have been sceptical about the plan for, like Manstein, the other Army Group commander involved, he thought it would have been better accomplished two months earlier. But he was not actually against it, as were Model, Jodl, and, most strongly of all, Guderian. The latter's opposition may well have inspired Kluge to disguise his misgivings, for he eventually supported 'Citadel', perhaps also because his Army Group had been so long on the defensive. In the event, however, Kluge was the first to call off the attack. Whereas by 12 July von Manstein in the southern sector rightly thought that victory was in sight, Kluge had suspended aggressive operations in the north because the Russians had made a deep penetration of 2nd Panzer Army in the rear of Model's 9th Army and were actively threatening Orel. Kluge decided that it would be useless to continue the battle and that his formations should be withdrawn to their starting lines. Rather surprisingly Hitler agreed with this, probably because the Allies had landed in Sicily on 10 July, and left Manstein in the southern sector to continue his effort alone. When Hitler ordered the withdrawal of the S.S. Panzer Corps for transfer to Italy—delayed, as it turned out—Manstein was unable to make further headway. 'Citadel' had failed for three main reasons: first and most important, it was too late; second, the Russians knew it was coming; and third, the new tanks and assault guns, the Panther, the Porsche and Henschel Tigers, and the Ferdinand, did not live up to Hitler's high hopes. This was not surprising, since none of them had passed their final acceptance trials, and they were not ready, in the view of Guderian and Albert Speer, the Armaments Minister, for wholesale committal to action. The Porsche Tigers and the Ferdinands were exceptionally vulnerable because of lack of machine-guns in their armament to deal with infantry. The Panthers and Ferdinands had not been given enough ammunition; and the Tigers' sophisticated engines required an exceptionally high standard of driving and maintenance to keep them in the field.

'Citadel' left von Kluge short of some 20,000 trained fighting men, and he became very concerned about casualties and thus hesitant about making counter-attacks. For the rest of the summer and autumn Army Group Centre was on the defensive, first at Orel, and later from the Kursk salient. In August Reinhardt's 3rd Panzer Army on the left and Heinrici's 4th Army in the centre were heavily attacked. Reinhardt made several complaints about his grave shortage of men, nearly every division being under strength. He was also sceptical of the efficiency of the 21 Luftwaffe Field Corps of four Air Force ground divisions under the parachute General Alfred Schlemm, who had been Student's Chief of Staff for the Crete operation.

Schlemm's ability was not in question, but Reinhardt thought his divisions under-trained, and their being under the Luftwaffe for administrative and certain command functions made his life difficult. He was proved right on 6 October when the 2nd Luftwaffe Field Division broke and ran, and the Russians were enabled to capture Nevel, in a critical area near Kluge's boundary with Army Group North. Reinhardt had to use Lieutenant-General Clössner's IX Corps to restore the situation, but was refused permission to counter-attack in conjunction with the 16th Army of Army Group North. This was yet another request which Kluge forbore to judge, but simply forwarded to O.K.H. Meanwhile, farther south, the Soviets under Generals Eremenko and Sokolovsky had made good advances between the Desna and Sozh rivers, and by 25 September had recaptured both Smolensk and Roslavl, the latter on the 4th Army front. By October Kluge had his hands full with the Russians pressing 4th Army west of the Sozh in the Orsha and Mogilev regions. On 14 October Kluge wrote to Hitler complaining of a deficiency of 200,000 men in his Army Goup, and of the poor standard of such replacements as did arrive. While his soldiers' morale remained good, he said, the Russians could always put together enough forces to attain local superiority, and in sum Army

Group Centre felt both isolated and neglected. Kluge was careful to stress his own faithfulness, but he received no answer, and in any case on 27 October he was invalided home because of his car accident. At least it can be said for Kluge that with limited resources he had made the best of a bad job.

On 3 September 1943, he and von Manstein had had an unpublicized meeting, at their request, with Hitler at Rastenberg. It was a final attempt at a showdown by two of the four most senior commanders on the eastern front, and the two most involved in danger. They went to demand reinforcements, but, most important of all, to ask for a single integrated command in the east under a single, fully responsible Chief of Staff. Hitler was to give up personally directing operations in Russia, and nominate a Commander-in-Chief, East, with complete and independent powers. Presumably either Kluge or Manstein were expecting to get this appointment with the support of the other, and though Kluge was senior (so for that matter were von Kleist and von Küchler), the weight of informed opinion in the Army would undoubtedly have favoured Manstein. In the words of Paul Carell:

'This move represented a legitimate attack by the most senior commanders in the field upon the dangerous concentration of power in the supreme leadership of the Reich—a move of historic importance but still insufficiently known and appreciated.'

Hitler remained foreseeably obdurate. Apart from allowing Kluge to withdraw his southern wing behind the Desna, and Manstein to give up the Kuban bridgehead and pull back 6th Army from the Mius, he conceded nothing. Least of all would he countenance the idea of a separate C-in-C, East.

It is thus surprising to read in Göbbels' diary for 23 September 1943 that Hitler 'spoke very favourably about Günther von Kluge, Georg von Küchler, and even Fritz Erich von Manstein, although he regards him as rather excessively ambitious'. Doubtless Hitler had other things on his mind with the invasion of Italy that had started as the two Field-Marshals saw him.

It is clear that Hitler regarded von Kluge as his man. Not only had he promoted him twice and awarded him high decorations, but on Kluge's sixtieth birthday he had made him a big financial gift and given him permission to spend a large amount on improving his estate. Far from rejecting the money, as some other generals such as List had done, Kluge accepted it with equanimity. This became known, first to von Schlabrendorff, and thus to von Tresckow, Kluge's Chief of Staff, who used the information to bring pressure upon Kluge in his dealings concerning the conspiracy against Hitler. It may have seemed that Kluge was a Nazi sympathizer, but he was not. Sir John Wheeler-Bennett has best summed up his character, that of the eternal fence-sitter, matched in this respect only by Fromm. Both of them came to unpleasant ends.

'Von Kluge proved in effect to be too malleable. He was *non*-Nazi rather than *anti*-Nazi, and by nature he was a man of indecision. For two-and-a-half years Henning von Tresckow battled for von Kluge's soul, waging an intensive, clever and wearisome campaign against the Field-Marshal's vacillation. He succeeded in establishing a degree of personal ascendancy over his quarry, but it was only personal. Once removed for a moment from von Tresckow's direct influence von Kluge lapsed again into compliant obedience to Hitler. Time and again von Tresckow thought he had won him over to a definite plan of action; time and again the elusive soldier backed out at the critical moment.'

With wry bitterness Tresckow used to refer to 'the Kluge clock'— 'only I could wind it up ... unfortunately it stopped rather often'. Thus Kluge's removal from Russia, and his subsequent transfer to France, was a serious blow to the conspirators. Von Tresckow, who was friendly with General of Infantry Rudolf Schmundt—Hitler's chief Army Adjutant, and holder of the vital post of Head of the Army Personnel Office—tried desperately to get himself posted as Kluge's Chief of Staff on the Western Front. Had he succeeded events in Paris after von Stauffenberg's assassination attempt might have been allowed to run their course. As it was General Blumentritt, who received the appointment, knew nothing of the conspiracy, although potentially sympathetic towards it.

Von Kluge cannot be blamed for losing the battle of Normandy. By the time he took over command from von Rundstedt in early July 1944, the Anglo-American invasion was already a success and the German defences were strained to the limit. He could do nothing about Allied air superiority. When he arrived at St Germain Kluge was cheerful and confident, and lost no time in giving a dressing-down to Rommel for having forwarded a pessimistic situation report to Hitler. 'Even you will have to get used to obeying orders!' he told Rommel. A few days in France, however, and talks with the senior ground commanders, soon altered Kluge's attitude. He realised how grim the situation was, and that Rommel had been perfectly correct in his assessments. He apologised. For the next week or so the two worked in harmony, but on 17 July Rommel was badly wounded by a British Typhoon attack near Ste Foy de Montgommery on the Livarot road. The man who might have persuaded Kluge to seek an armistice on 20 July was out of action.

Kluge himself took over Army Group 'B', but even his long experience of heading off disaster in the East was now fruitless. He urged on Jodl a withdrawal to the Seine, where a new defence line could be formed. Hitler countered with a demand for a full-scale attack on Mortain and Avranches, in which area the tanks of General George S. Patton's 3rd U.S. Army were already running riot. Kluge was aware of the need for urgent action, whereas Hitler wanted a round-up of the panzer divisions, which was impractical and would take a week. Kluge ordered the attack for the night 6 August but it was already too late. The so-called 5th Panzer Army of General Eberbach mustered one panzer division, the 2nd, under Lieutenant-General Smilo, Freiherr von Lüttwitz, and bits and pieces of the 1st S.S. 'Leibstandarte' Division under S.S. Major-General Wisch; 22nd S.S. 'Das Reich' Panzer Division under S.S. Lieutenant-General Hans Lammerding; a combat group from the 17th S.S. Panzer Grenadier Division 'Götz von Berlichingen'; and the pathetic remains of Lieutenant-General Fritz Bayerlein's prize Panzer Lehr Division, smashed beyond recall by the British in Normandy and the Americans at St Lo. The whole ramshackle force was under command of General of Panzer Troops Freiherr von Funck of XLVII Panzer Corps, and amounted to only 120 tanks. To him von Kluge stated that Avranches must be taken and held at all costs: 'On it hinges the decision in the West', he said.

On 7 August Allied fighter-bombers crippled the attacking force, which was mopped up on the ground by the American VIII Corps. There was no sign of the 300 German fighters optimistically promised to Kluge by General of Fliers Alfred Bülowius, who had told S.S. Colonel-General Paul Hausser, commander of 7th Army, 'In ceaseless sorties they will keep the skies clear above the area of operations'. In fact when these aircraft took off from their bases in the Paris area they were engaged by British and American fighters, and none of them reached the Mortain-Avranches area. After forty-eight hours the first Avranches counter-attack was back on its start-line. A second attempt never got off the ground, and by 12 August was impossible; only retreat across the Dives remained, and that had been left too late, for to the north-east the Falaise Pocket had been formed and fighting there was approaching its climax.

During the seven or so weeks that von Kluge was in command in France in 1944, he consistently followed Hitler's orders, where a tougher personality might have ignored or side-stepped them in the interest of his troops. After 20 July especially it seems that he was conducting the battle with one eye on Berlin. He was gloomy about the Avranches fiasco and told Blumentritt, 'That is where I lose my reputation as a soldier'. He was worried sick about possible involvement with the conspirators, as indeed were other generals.

Opinions among his contemporaries vary as to how much Kluge was in the know, how deeply involved. Certainly he did not have the strength of character to back up the action in Paris of General Heinrich von Stülpnagel, who had resolutely had all the S.S. and Gestapo arrested. When news of Hitler's survival came, the whole thing was over for Kluge. Stülpnagel, an officer whom he must have known and well respected, made a last appeal to him: 'Field-Marshal, everything is *not* over. It is still possible to take independent action in the West. You have pledged yourself to act, your word and your honour are at stake. Something must be *done*.' Von Kluge would have none of this. He replied: 'Gentlemen, nothing can be done. The Führer is still alive. Now let us go in to dinner.' He advised Stülpnagel to go into hiding. Earlier at La Roche Guyon where this scene took place, General Beck, the leading conspirator, had reached Kluge on the telephone and asked him to take the initiative in the West. This was not at all Kluge's cup of tea, and when Beck further demanded to know whether Kluge would place himself under his authority, he played for time and said he would ring back in half an hour. He never did. Instead he used that breathing space to contact Keitel and Warlimont by telephone at Rastenberg, from whom he learned the true state of affairs, and to whom, doubtless, he gave protestations of his own loyalty.

It was charitable of von Geyr, in his book *The Critical Years*, to conclude: 'Kluge vacillated both before and during July 20th. Those who best know his character and person say that this was due to his anxiety for the fate of his own family.'

It is not by Avranches that Kluge will best be remembered. It is as a high commander, promoted above his ceiling but still in authority, who by his own indecision at a critical moment in history let down both his soldiers and himself, and, having nothing to offer, in the end found nothing.

Of all Hitler's Field-Marshals, the one who seems to us most shadowy today is Georg von Küchler. Even in Germany his name was never known in the way that Rommel, Dietl, von Reichenau or von Bock were household words. Von Küchler was an artilleryman, and his pre-war command in that outpost of the Third Reich, East Prussia, was to influence his wartime career. For apart from his campaigns in the Low Countries and France in 1940, von Küchler was destined to serve entirely on the Northern Front. He was in Army Group North in Poland iń 1939, when he commanded 3rd Army under von Bock; and he was commander of the 18th Army through the Baltic States in the summer of 1941. Then he went on to the Leningrad front, where in January 1942 he succeeded von Leeb as C-in-C, Army Group North. This was a post that he held for the unusually long time—on the Russian front, in Hitler's Army—of two years, and in fact that two-year tenure constitutes a record for longevity in the East. One has the feeling that von Küchler was content to stay out of the limelight.

He was successful in the Polish campaign; brilliantly successful in Holland, where he linked up with the German parachutists; and competent enough in Belgium and France. His 18th Army was mainly an infantry one, which had to do a good deal of hard slogging. It was his troops who made the final ground assault on the Dunkirk perimeter, and a division from his command, the 8th Infantry under Lieutenant-General Rudolf Koch-Erpach, which had the honour of marching first down the Champs-Elysées on that memorable day, 14 June 1940.

In 1937 von Küchler, who was born in 1881, was already a full General of Artillery, and he commanded I Corps at Königsberg, first under von Rundstedt and by 1939 under von Bock. In between he had been retired in Hitler's 'purge' of 1938. Küchler had one distinction, if it may so be called, somewhat rare in a high-ranking regular officer. He had been a *Frei-Korps* officer, which commended him to Hitler.

In occupied Poland von Küchler, like his superior Blaskowitz, had had some violent disagreements with Gauleiter Koch over the scandalous behaviour of the S.S. and some Party functionaries in the areas taken over by the Reich. In France in 1940 his conduct aroused the admiration of a shrewd American foreign correspondent, Louis P. Lochner, head of the Berlin bureau of the Associated Press. Lochner wrote:

'Another military leader whom I learned to know on the western front was Field-Marshal Georg von Küchler [*sic*: Küchler was still then a General]. The men in his army speak in the most glowing terms of his fatherly care of his soldiers—how he would stand by a wounded man while shots were popping all around him, until first aid could arrive. They told me with pride how he ventured out to the front lines day after day sitting in the side-car of a motor-cycle'.

Von Küchler's experience as a Free Corps fighter in the Baltic States after the Great War was put to good use in his next assignment when, as a Colonel-General, he commanded his old 18th Army under von Leeb's Northern Army Group in 1941. It fell to him to lead his men over the old battle-grounds in Latvia, Estonia, and Lithuania. Army Group North always tended to be kept short of troops compared with the other Army Groups. In mid-August 1941, Küchler was given the unnecessary double task of destroying the Soviet 8th Army withdrawing through Narva from Estonia, and capturing the fortified coast along the southern part of the Gulf of Finland. It was unnecessary because there was no point in tying down large forces round Narva when every man was needed for the main objective, Leningrad. These operations took time, whereas if some of Küchler's troops had been diverted to help Höpner's 4th Panzer Army, which had been held up first at Luga, then at Krasnogvardeysk, there was a good chance that Höpner might have taken Leningrad. By autumn 18th Army was still deployed along the Luga River from Narva to Lake Ilmen, though Novgorod had fallen in late August and Estonia was cleared by 4 September; by mid-September Küchler had reached Lake Ladoga. But Leningrad still had not fallen by 15 January 1942, when von Küchler succeeded von Leeb as C-in-C Army Group North, turning over his own 18th Army to General of Cavalry Georg Lindemann. As Chief of Staff instead of

Major-General Brennecke, Küchler chose Major-General W. Hasse. What Leeb had failed to do, von Küchler could not accomplish either. Leningrad was never to fall.

Hitler again issued orders for its capture in August 1942, and at one time, Küchler apparently being in disfavour, brought up von Manstein to conduct operations against Leningrad. All in vain. It would have been better to seal off the city and by-pass it earlier on, instead of wasting numerous battalions in frontal assaults.

Von Küchler had been promoted Field-Marshal in 1942 and was to remain in command of Army Group North for two years until January 1944. For most of this time no significant successes were gained on his front, though there was constant bitter fighting all along the Volkhov and Lovat Rivers and round Lake Ilmen, and on two occasions the Russians sealed off German formations, one in large numbers in the Demyansk Pocket, and again at Kholm. In the latter pocket Major-General T. Scherer, a tall, bearded figure in spectacles, certainly earned his Knight's Cross. He held out against vicious Soviet attacks for over three months until May 1942, without any heavy artillery, his 5,000 or so troops living in ruined houses and filthy conditions in an area hardly amounting to a square mile, and resisting continual attacks from the Russian rifle divisions, and—in the end—the threat of typhus. They had to be supplied entirely by air, and were relieved by troops from Lieutenant-General Jürgen von Arnim's XXXIX Panzer Corps.

Demyansk was a much larger affair. Here in February, in the southern sector of Küchler's command, the Russians succeeded in encircling General Count Erich von Brockdorff-Ahlefeldt's II Corps from Busch's 16th Army. The siege was notable in that a major airlift to supply Ahlefeldt's six divisions, amounting to some 100,000 men, was used by the Luftwaffe for the first time in the war. This international precedent was, by its success, a credit to the Luftwaffe's Transport Command, under Colonel (later Major-General) F. Morzik, whose aircrews flew in blizzards, frost, storms, and fog to supply the trapped men, making 100–150 flights a day. But the precedent was to prove a fatal one, for Hitler was so impressed by it that it swayed his judgement in the matter of Stalingrad nine months later—a very different affair, for then a whole Army was involved. Thus was the doom of Paulus and Hitler born in the far distant Valday Hills.

Demyansk was relieved on 21 April 1942 by a combat group led by Lieutenant-General Walther von Seydlitz-Kurzbach, whose achievement was recognised by promotion to command of LI Corps, a move which was to take him to Stalingrad. Later, General of Artillery von Seydlitz was to become a notorious and rather pathetic figure in captivity who succumbed to the Communist line and headed Soviet-sponsored organizations such as the 'Association of German Officers' and the

'Free German National Committee'. His was the pre-eminent voice exhorting his former colleagues and soldiers to stop the war and surrender, after Stalingrad, and drew forth particularly virulent outbursts from Hitler. Years later he returned to Germany and lived in retirement, still defending his actions, which had cost him the respect of most of his fellows.

Demyansk was strongly reinforced, and thenceforward until 1944 von Küchler managed to hold the area south of Lake Ilmen.

In December 1942 von Küchler had to transfer three divisions from his northern front to reinforce the Demyansk corridor. This proved a correct if short-lived decision, for the corridor was severely threatened; but it weakened the German defences between Leningrad and the Volkhov, so that when early in 1943 the Russians started the second battle of Lake Ladoga the Germans could not prevent them relieving the blockade of Leningrad. On 15 February Lieutenant-General P. Laux, who had now taken over II Corps, told Field-Marshal Busch, commanding 16th Army, that in the face of the odds—five Soviet armies grouped round a dozen German divisions—the Demyansk corridor must now be abandoned. Hitler agreed, and the evacuation which Laux carried out between 17 and 27 February was a model of its kind. Not a gun was lost, and Laux got away 100,000 men. But the fourteen months of hard fighting in the corridor were witnessed by the further 10,000 Germans who lay now in tidy graves along it.

Busch put the troops to good use in rebuffing fresh Russian attacks along the Lovat, and made them suffer especially at Staraya Russa.

During the second half of 1943 von Küchler maintained an almost static front, but his requests for reinforcements fell on deaf ears. In November, when it was clear that the Russians were getting ready for a big new push, he asked for six infantry divisions. He did not get them. He also made preparations for a general withdrawal of his Army Group to the so-called 'Panther Line', roughly running down the 1940 frontier between the Baltic States and Russia, though a request on 20 November to pull back 16th Army to that line was refused. Far from getting reinforcements, Küchler over the months had lost several divisions to Manstein. On 30 December 1943 he protested to Hitler in person about this, and also proposed a withdrawal to the Panther Line before the Russians started their offensive. This eminently sensible suggestion was turned down by Hitler on the grounds that it would lead to Finland's abandonment of the war.

On 14 January 1944 the Soviet attack started, and soon Küchler became aware that the Russians were trying to encircle his 18th Army in the Novgorod area on both flanks. He therefore asked permission to withdraw two of its Corps, but this was not granted. By 22 January, when a third Corps was threatened with encirclement, he made a detailed explanation to Hitler of the facts of the situation. His only reward was the promise of a panzer division. On 27 January, at a conference at Königsberg, Hitler positively prohibited *any* withdrawals by 18th Army on the Leningrad front without his express orders. Küchler declared that 18th Army had already suffered 40,000 casualties and that it was fighting as hard as it could. Hitler replied that that was 'not quite' true. It was this interview that finished von Küchler's career, though Hitler seized on the pretext next day of Küchler's order to 18th Army off his own bat to retreat to the Luga River. Had it not done so it would have been encircled, but that made no difference to Hitler. On 29 January Field-Marshal von Küchler was dismissed and replaced by that favourite of the Führer, Colonel-General Model.

Because much of the fighting on Army Group North's front, after the heady initial advances, was limited by lake, forest and swamp, much of it turned into somewhat static trench warfare. There were few panzer battles and it was primarily an infantry and artillery war. Thus at the time of his dismissal Küchler commanded—on a 500-mile front mostly filled with woods and swamps—forty infantry divisions, two mountain, one panzer grenadier, one field training and three security divisions. The Nevel area on his front was one of the worst for partisan operations, and von Küchler, a tough character, did not deal with them lightly. West of the Nevel the countryside earned the reputation of being the most heavily-manned partisan area in Russia.

We know from Göbbels that, at least as late as September 1943, Hitler had held a good enough opinion of Küchler. But he was always suspicious of his leading generals, and when Nevel was lost in October 1943 he held it against him, calling it a 'Schweinerei'. Nor did Küchler always get full support from Busch and Lindemann, the commanders of 16th and 18th Armies, indeed he tried to get rid of the former.

Von Küchler sat out the remainder of the war in obscurity. He had been approached by Gördeler and Popitz in the cause of the resistance, but while he showed understanding of their aims he refused to be drawn. As a result of his 'cold-blooded and ruthless' dealings with partisans in Russia and the Baltic States, Küchler was given a sentence of twenty years' imprisonment at Nuremberg on 27 October 1948.

It is an oddity of history that the two men who were successive German Military Governors of France from 1940 to 1944 were both called von Stülpnagel. In fact they were cousins, members of a famed old military family. General of Infantry Otto von Stülpnagel exercised German military power in Paris and over most of occupied France from 1 November 1940 to 6 February 1942, and in doing so made himself—next to the S.S. and the Gestapo—the most hated man in France. It was over his name that the lists of the deported and those shot for resistance activities, or made hostage, were published. Otto von Stülpnagel had reached the rank of major in the Great War, in which, according to Curt Reiss, he was to blame even then for crimes committed against the civilian population.

In the late 'twenties Stülpnagel became head of the Motor Transport Staff of the Reichswehr, which dealt with the study of tank and motorized warfare. He divided his training formations into four groups—tanks, armoured cars, armed motor-cyclists (used later in warfare much more extensively by the Germans than by the Allies) and anti-tank companies —the latter the creation of Lieutenant-Colonel Guderian. Many of his staff went to Russia for training in the field on tanks. Stülpnagel was promoted Major-General on 1 February 1929, but not long after he left the Army and became one of a number of efficient, well-trained Army officers who helped to organize and train the new air force (which did not yet have the title of Luftwaffe). He was well regarded by his colleagues and became a General of Fliers (General der Flieger). In 1939, however, he returned to the Army as deputy commander of Wehrkreis XVII, and went back to France in 1940 as a full General.

Being too old to get a more active command, von Stülpnagel had an unenviable task. As a Prussian he was predictably severe. Although basically a fair-minded man he was not above terrorizing those sections of the French who got out of order and, to his eyes, threatened the German rule of law. He said himself that he did not resign only to 'prevent worse things happening', and this was probably true. Von Hassell, who noted in January 1942 that 'now he is more hated in France than almost anyone else', summed him up: 'He is intelligent, but somewhat overworked, deaf in one ear, of no great calibre . . . . He has a pretty clear understanding of things, but seems to lack decision.'

General Otto von Stülpnagel, born in 1878, died by his own hand, aged 69, in the Cherche-Midi Prison in Paris on 6 February 1948, in the eyes of the French a much-wanted war criminal. It was his second suicide attempt, the first having taken place in December 1946. Both he and his cousin were soldiers of distinction, and the elder von Stülpnagel had once been put forward by the Nationalist Party as a prospective Minister of Defence in place of von Schleicher. Both in their different ways lost their lives because of Hitler.

Had Hitler invaded England, the German forces landing between Brighton and the Isle of Wight would have been commanded by Colonel-General Rudolf Strauss, who was promoted to command 9th Army after the fall of France. In that campaign he had led II Corps in von Kluge's 4th Army, having commanded Wehrkreis II and II Corps at Stettin since before the war as a General of Infantry. At the outbreak of war Strauss was twenty-seventh in seniority on the Army list, having become a Major-General in 1935 when commanding 22nd Infantry Division at Bremen.

Instead of coming to England, Strauss's 9th Army went to Russia in 1941, as part of von Bock's Army Group Centre. It was successful in the battle of the Bialystok pocket, and captured Kalinin on 21 October; though earlier that month Bock fell out with Strauss when he thought the latter was not pressing hard enough to finish off the Vyazma encirclement. Strauss justified his slow progress by complaining about the bad weather and numerous partisan attacks. Bock replied with a fairly stiff letter expressing hope for 'a renewal of the comradely co-operation that I have enjoyed with you in the past' but stating: 'I am not unaware of the extremely difficult conditions regarding supply, transportation, and communications behind your front. I do not agree, however, with your analysis that it is impossible to move your infantry.'

Strauss's 9th Army was normally only twelve to fifteen divisions in size (one says 'only' because some Armies mustered larger numbers, but it is instructive to recall that such a total would have nearly equalled all the British divisions in Montgomery's 21st Army Group in 1944). But for the attack on Moscow Strauss had Hoth's 3rd Panzer Group under command, and a total of twenty-three divisions, three of which were panzer and two motorized. Strauss was, however, primarily an infantry commander.

By the end of 1941 the situation on the northern edge of Bock's area, which Strauss commanded, was grave. Kalinin was retaken by the Russians on 15 December, and then Staritsa; and Rzhev, at which was situated the headquarters of General Albrecht von Schubert's XXIII Corps, was seriously threatened. Hitler gave out the order, '9th Army will not retreat another step', for there was serious danger that 9th Army might be encircled by Colonel-General Konev's forces. Although Strauss's previous suggestions of retirement to a safer line had been turned down, on 12 January he was relieved of command at his own request on the grounds of ill-health.

In his place came Model, three months earlier only a divisional commander, and at 50 the youngest Army commander in the Wehrmacht. Halder recorded bleakly in his diary for 15 January 1942, 'Strauss is done for'. He was not re-employed in the field. Despite his prodigality with generals, Hitler could ill-afford to lose experienced commanders such as Strauss, who could only console himself with the fact that he had gone of his own volition without having committed any major mistake.

One senior general to be dismissed in Russia was Colonel-General Rudolf Schmidt, who lasted until 10 July 1943, just before the battle of Kursk. This was unfortunate, on the eve of the biggest tank battle in history, since Schmidt was a panzer expert who had risen to prominence by leading 1st Panzer Division in Holland and France and, later XXXIX Panzer Corps in Russia. In 1937 as a Major-General he commanded the former at Weimar, being promoted Lieutenant-General by January 1939. Schmidt's XXXIX Panzer Corps led the breakthrough in Holland in 1940 and he played a major part in forcing that country's surrender. At Rotterdam he tried to prevent the bombing of the city, but the red flares that he used to warn off the Luftwaffe were just five minutes too late.

Later his Corps came under the Hoth Panzer Group in France, and for some time he had Rommel under his command. In Belorussia in 1941 Schimidt's Corps was prominent in the fighting round Vitebsk, and took Smolensk. Both in France and during the early months of the Russian campaign Schmidt worked under Hoth. From mid-August his XXXIX Panzer Corps was transferred from the central front to the north to help von Leeb's operations against Leningrad, and by 8 November 1941, with I Corps, it had taken Tikhvin, well east of Leningrad and the Volkhov River. This so impressed Hitler's headquarters that Schmidt was asked if a drive to Volagda was possible. As Volagda was 250 miles further east, and it was already the beginning of winter, Schmidt's answer was a dusty one.

During some of the operations in September and October a 'Group Schmidt' had been formed which comprised XXVII Corps and XXXIX Panzer Corps.

In mid-November 1941, because von Weichs was ill, Schmidt assumed temporary command of 2nd Army on the central front. During this time there were Soviet successes at Yelets and Yefremov, and some hard fighting to protect Guderian's 2nd Panzer Army right flank. Guderian himself was dismissed on Boxing Day 1941, after von Kluge had accused him of creating a twenty-five-mile gap by giving up Chern on his own account, and Rudolf Schmidt became C-in-C 2nd Panzer Army in his place. Having previously been General of Panzer Troops he now rose to Colonel-General. For most of 1942 he fought a series of mainly defensive but successful battles on the Orel-Bryansk front.

Schmidt was another senior leader whom Hitler could ill afford to spare, but he was no Nazi. He was known as a sharp critic of the O.K.W. In the Bryansk area he had some success with the unusual experiment of appointing a Russian civilian, Kaminsky, as a sector governor, who was allowed to appoint officials free of interference by a German below the rank of Army Commander. Schmidt was far-seeing enough to realise by 1942 that final victory was not in the cards.

His dismissal came about in an unusual way. Although in private he freely criticized Hitler and the Nazi régime, such disloyalty failed to reach Hitler's ears. In a talk with General von Senger und Etterlin, for example, which he told the latter to forget all about afterwards, Schmidt 'took for granted our mutual abhorrence and criticism of the régime'. The crisis came when Schmidt's brother was arrested by the Gestapo in 1943. A number of letters from the General were found which, in Göbbels's words, 'spoke very disparagingly of the Führer'. Göbbels added in his diary entry for 10 May 1943: 'Yet he was one of the generals of whom the Führer thought especially well! So once again he suffered a great disappointment. As a class, the generals seem like total strangers to him and he will in future stay farther away from them than ever . . . .'

Colonel-General Friedrich Dollmann twice figures briefly in the mainstream of history and then is washed away to be forgotten. How many veterans of the Normandy landings today remember his name? Or how many Frenchmen?—yet his few days of importance were spent entirely in France.

Dollmann was born at Würzburg in 1882, and joined the artillery in 1899. At the outbreak of the Great War he was a captain, and saw service as both a regimental adjutant and as a staff officer; after that war he held a post on the administrative side of the Peace Commission. He was promoted colonel the day before his forty-eighth birthday, and having commanded at both battalion and regimental level, and been the equivalent of a British C.R.A., became Inspector of Artillery in 1933. Later that year he was made Major-General.

Dollmann became an expert in long-range artillery, and in the early years of Hitler was prominent in encouraging good relations between the Army and the Nazi Party. Possibly as a result he was made commander of Wehrkreis IX in 1935 and, in October of that year, commander of IX Army Corps with headquarters at Kassel, with the rank of Lieutenant-General. From 1936 to 1939 he held the same command but with the rank of General of Artillery, and on 1 March 1939 was appointed C-in-C 7th Army. He was then 57, and the eighth ranking officer in the German Army.

Dollmann was not a Nazi, but in a talk he gave in 1937 to the Catholic chaplains of his command (he was himself a Catholic) he deplored the introduction of political strife into the Wehrmacht and said of the ordinary soldier: 'The Oath which he has taken to the Führer and Supreme Commander of the Wehrmacht binds him unto the sacrifice of his own life to National-Socialism, the concept of the new Reich. It follows then that no doubts may be permitted to arise out of your attitudes towards National-Socialism. The Wehrmacht, as one of the bearers of the National-Socialist State, demands of you as chaplains at all times a clear and unreserved acknowledgement of the Führer, State and People'.

In January 1936 Dollmann, as Commander of Wehrkreis IX, had issued a directive (though it is not certain whether he wrote it or merely passed it on from the War Ministry) in which he stressed, 'We must share a common front with the Party'. Amongst other points made were the instruction that 'worthy' pictures of Hitler as well as of Hindenburg were to be displayed prominently in all officers' messes (the Kaiser being relegated to special 'tradition rooms'), and that 'talks may be given only by people without political bias, and who will speak in a National-Socialist sense' (!) A desire was expressed that officers' wives 'take an active part in the National-Socialist League of Women'. The directive stated that in conversations off-duty 'officers must always show a positive attitude towards National-Socialism', and that 'it lies in our own interests that as many members of the Party as possible come into more friendly contact with the Officer Corps, through their appointment to reserve commissions'. Finally Dollmann urged that all commanders should urgently ensure 'that the conduct of every single officer in every case becomes positively National-Socialist'.

There were doubtless many officers who found parts of this directive somewhat amusing, and others who found it distasteful, but to the majority it would be nothing strange. Similar orders were given throughout Germany in the mid-'thirties. What is rather ironic is the fact that Dollmann himself once remarked later that a National-Socialist had no business in an officers' mess.

Dollmann's Army remained under Leeb's Group in France while the Polish campaign was fought. Nor did it have a very spectacular role in the invasion of France, being at the southern end of the whole front, manning the Siegfried Line opposite the Maginot Line. Only towards the end of that war did 7th Army come into its own, attacking the Maginot Line and breaking through north of Belfort. On 19 June Dollmann linked up with Lieutenant-General Kirchner's 1st Panzer Division and trapped 400,000 French troops in the Vosges.

In the rash of promotions that followed the fall of France, Dollmann was made Colonel-General. Thereafter he had a quiet life for nearly four years, since he did not serve in Russia, Africa, or Italy, but held a comfortable, static command in France. This became anything but comfortable on 6 June 1944.

It so happened that on D-Day, when the German meteorologists thought that rough weather would continue in the Channel, Colonel-General Dollmann was away from his 7th Army headquarters in Le Mans. He was conducting a conference and map exercise for divisional and regimental commanders at Rennes. This cannot have made his initial responses to the invasion any quicker or easier.

Dollmann had no scope to make great decisions during the initial battle of Normandy. He was responsible for a huge stretch of France, from the Seine to the Loire, but subordinate to Rommel, and his own lack of operational experience did not incline him towards anything adventurous. Nor, to be fair, was there much he could do except try to hold, especially in the face of murderous air raids and naval bombardment. Dollmann was an experienced staff officer, he had commanded troops, and there is no reason to suppose that he was lacking in ability.

One definite mistake he made was to insist on Lieutenant-General Bayerlein's moving his Panzer Lehr Division in daylight when Bayerlein correctly wished to move it by night. This led to bad casualties which were unjustified by the urgency of the move to Caen.

Dollmann was, in fact, in poor health, and probably should never have been left in command. A big man, running to fat, he suffered from a bad heart. This condition was not improved when, after the fall of Cherbourg on 26 June 1944, Hitler wanted to have him court-martialled. Quite rightly von Rundstedt would have none of this nonsense. Hitler still went on demanding that at least Dollmann be dismissed, but Rommel stood up for him and refused. The situation was resolved when Dollmann had a heart attack and died on 29 June.

Lieutenant-General Hans Speidel, then Rommel's Chief of Staff, wrote an apt epitaph for Dollmann: 'The methods of Hitler had wounded him deeply, both as a soldier and as a man.'

The Luftwaffe Generals

The rise and fall of the Luftwaffe is linked inseparably with the career of Hermann Wilhelm Göring, its first Commander-in-Chief and part creator. Göring was undoubtedly one of the dominant personalities of the Third Reich, and basically one of the ablest, but he failed to keep pace with technical developments in aviation, had no scientific or staff training, and burdened himself with too wide a portfolio of jobs, let alone hobbies, to devote the complete concentration which his post required. Thus, after early and dramatic pre-war and wartime successes, he gradually lost his touch and his authority, so that by late 1942 he had become to some extent discredited and to a large extent frequently a step away from reality because of his chronic use of drugs. Although he attended less and less at Hitler's headquarters, and often delegated subordinates to attend important conferences, Göring was reluctant to give up any of his powers and until his downfall in 1945 maintained complete power over the Luftwaffe.

It is true that he, Milch, Kesselring, and the other Air Force leaders had programmed the final development of the Luftwaffe for 1942 rather than for 1939. Even so they were better off than their naval colleagues, and in 1939 the Luftwaffe was superbly equipped for blitzkrieg campaigns. The failure to develop four-engined bombers, and to produce enough long-range fighters, cost the Luftwaffe dear in the years when it was forced to face three enemy Air Forces—the R.A.F., the Red Air Force, and the United States Army Air Corps. To many in the Luftwaffe, including two Chiefs of Staff (one of whom was driven in despair to commit suicide), it seemed that Göring, in whom so much trust had been put and on whom so much loyalty and esteem lavished, had betrayed his comrades, squandered his own gifts, and frittered away Germany's lead in aerial warfare.

Hermann Göring was born in Bavaria in 1893, the son of a consular official by his second marriage, and at a very early age was separated from his parents for three years and brought up by friends. He had a happy boyhood, however, and when only 12 was sent to the military cadet school at Karlsruhe. At 16 he went on to a military training college at Lichterfelde, near Berlin. He was commissioned into the Prinz Wilhelm Infantry Regiment No. 112 in March 1912, when 19. The next year he became close friends with a fellow officer, Bruno Lörzer, who communicated to him his own love of flying. When the Great War broke out, Lörzer got himself seconded to a flying school but Göring continued as an infantry officer. In the latter part of 1914 he did creditably in the fighting, but after a spell in hospital he ignored the regulations and joined Lörzer, already a qualified pilot, as his observer. He got away with it and stayed in the fledgling Air Force.

Between 1916 and 1918 Göring built up a well-deserved reputation as a leading fighter pilot, being credited with 22 victories and winning many decorations for bravery, including the sought-after *Pour le Mérite.* He and Lörzer saved each other's lives in air combat. In 1918 after Baron von Richthofen had been shot down, and then his successor Captain Reinhard had been killed in a test flight, Göring succeeded to the command of the renowned 'Richthofen Circus', having previously commanded the 27th Fighter Squadron. Pilot casualties mounted in the last months of the war and Göring's squadron merged with that of Robert von Greim, who was to rise to high rank in the Luftwaffe and indeed to succeed Göring as its commander at Hitler's whim in the last days of the war. Göring's adjutant, Karl Bodenschatz, was another man destined to become prominent in Nazi aviation.

After the war Göring worked as an aircraft salesman in Denmark, and then as a civil pilot in Sweden. It was there that he met Karin von Kanzow, whom he married in 1922 after her divorce, and after whom he named his famous hunting lodge north-east of Berlin, 'Karin-hall', after her death in 1931.

Göring first met Hitler in 1922. Late that year he joined the Nazi Party, and was made the first commander of the 'Brownshirts' or S.A. In the 1923 debacle when Hitler, Ludendorff, and their party were fired on by the Bavarian police in Munich, Göring was severely wounded in the groin. In hospital at Innsbruck after being smuggled across the Austrian border by friends, he was given daily shots of morphia against the pain. This was the start of an addiction from which, though cured at least twice, he never really freed himself, though in later years he relied most upon paracodeine and pethadine.

In 1924 the Görings were in Italy, where they met Mussolini. In 1925, back in Sweden, Göring was certified as a dangerous and violent drug addict, and given a cure which by 1926 appeared successful.

In 1927, after the Nazi Party had been granted legality by President von Hindenburg, Göring returned to Berlin and picked up the threads of his aviation career and renewed old friendships among fliers. In 1928 he became a Reichstag deputy and gained the financial backing of Fritz Thyssen. He now began to be very close to Hitler, and with his impeccable war record was most useful as a 'front man' for the Nazis in entertaining foreign contacts. In the election of 1932 he was one of the chief speakers for the Nazi Party, and in August became President of the Reichstag. He became Minister of the Interior (and later Prime Minister) of Prussia, in which capacity he controlled the

Prussian police. Göring was discreditably connected with the events of the Reichstag Fire in February 1933, which he was reputed to have connived at as an anti-Communist stunt. When the Nazis came to power in March 1933 Göring was already Hitler's right-hand man, and owing to his bluff geniality and human foibles was probably the most popular man in Germany. His bonhomie concealed a ruthless intelligence and opportunism. When Hitler made Göring Reich Commissioner for Aviation in 1933, he delegated planning to Erhard Milch, an old acquaintance since Great War days, and General Wever, first Chief of Staff of the Luftwaffe, and an advocate of long-range bombers, who, unfortunately for that arm, was killed in an air crash in 1936. Ernst Udet, a top-scoring 'ace' of the Great War with 62 victories, did not rejoin the Luftwaffe until 1936, but as a well-known and well-liked stunt flier in America tried in vain to warn Göring of America's capacity for large-scale aircraft production in a future war.

In 1934 Göring's brutal side was revealed when he took a prominent part in the extermination of Röhm and the leaders of the S.A. who had wished to take over the Army. He also had Himmler appointed chief of the Prussian Gestapo, which until then he himself had controlled, and created a police force for his own use, the Landespolizeigruppe General Göring. For although only a retired captain who had not continued his military service, Göring had been made an Army General by Hindenburg. This had not sat well with the C-in-C, Kurt Freiherr von Hammerstein-Equord, a strong anti-Nazi who resigned in 1934. In March 1935 when the German Air Force, which had already been built up considerably under the cloak of Lufthansa and 'gliding clubs', was officially declared to exist, Göring was named as its C-in-C, with the rank of Colonel-General in the Luftwaffe.

This should have been job enough on its own for any one man. But Göring had his pudgy fingers in other pies as well. He was Hitler's deputy in fact if not in name—Hess held that position officially. (His position was recognized when he was designated the Führer's successor in September 1939, and appointed his deputy by decree in June 1941.) He was a Cabinet member, Minister-President of Prussia, Chief Reich Forester, and to become responsible for the Four Year Economic Plan.

The new Luftwaffe was essentially the most Nazi of the Services. It enjoyed one great advantage, that its chief was close in the counsels of Hitler and could easily bring influence to bear upon him in securing money, new aircraft, and promotions. It was, initially, a small service, but it had a nucleus of high-ranking officers, many of them veteran fliers from the Great War, others seconded from the Army, and it had above all a tremendous spirit. It prided itself on its superiority to the Army, who, in turn, looked upon it as containing too many brash and upstart young officers. In this respect Göring did not improve matters by his sometimes slighting references to the Army's leadership and his boasting about the bravery and confidence of his own officers. At one course in National Socialism for generals at the War Ministry Göring did not endear himself by starting: 'In this building lives the spirit of faintheartedness. This spirit must go!'

Von Fritsch and many of the old aristocrats of the German Army had no time for Göring, who had thrown in his hand with the Nazis and conspired to undermine their own influence. It was no secret that Göring wished to become C-in-C of the Armed Forces himself. To this Hitler would not agree, as he rightly thought Göring lacked concentration. But he was to be given the sop of promotion to Field-Marshal in February 1938, and thus became, von Blomberg having retired, the ranking officer of the Wehrmacht.

In 1935 Göring married again, his second wife being the actress Emmy Sonnemann, who was to bring him much happiness and always remained loyal to him. Hitler was Göring's best man.

The Spanish Civil War from 1936 to 1939 gave Göring the opportunity to try out his new aircraft in the Condor Legion. The Junkers 52 transport, the Heinkel III and Dornier 17 twin-engined bomber, the Junkers '7 'Stuka' dive-bomber, and the Messerschmitt 109 fighter, all made their bow in action over Spain. Various senior officers, such as Sperrle and von Richthofen, and junior ones such as Mölders and Galland, gained rich experience in Spain. The pre-war Luftwaffe, although so young, was used like a club threatingly brandished by Göring against the French, the Austrians, the Czechs, and the Poles. It was effectively propagandized by Göbbels, and its size and strength exaggerated. All the same, anyone who had travelled by air in pre-war Nazi Germany could not have failed to notice how much more airminded Germany was than England, and how many of her young men were training as pilots. Threats of bombing by the Luftwaffe, such as Göring used to good effect against the Czechs, were certainly taken seriously by her European neighbours. France's Air Force was in a comparatively poor state, and the R.A.F. only beginning to expand slowly from 1935.

What went wrong, then, finally? The fact that Göring built up a brilliant tactical air force, but not a strategic one. It was extremely effective in working in conjunction with a land *blitzkrieg*, but it had insufficient long-range fighters and bombers to win the Battle of Britain, and similar strategic contests. Yet in four-and-a-half years Göring and Milch had created the strongest air force in the world. It was no mean achievement. In his book *The First and the Last* Lieutenant-General Adolf Galland rightly points out that in the pre-war years the Luftwaffe had to share its appropriations with the heavy demands of the Army and the Navy, and also with the civilian sector, where the housing and roads programme swallowed up much money and labour. 'It was unquestionably thanks to Hermann Göring, the creator of the

Luftwaffe', writes Galland, 'that it was at all possible for the German air force to develop while such a vast programme of construction and enlargement was taking place at the same time in all fields. It was estimated that the reconstruction of the Luftwaffe represented 40 per cent of the total German rearmament capacity during those years. With great energy and a passionate love for his arm, Göring knew how to create for it the place which in his mind was its due in the structure of a Continental military power. In any case, the importance of the air force in a future war had been recognized in Germany in good time, accurately, and fundamentally'.

Galland goes on to point out that the Battle of Britain broke new strategic ground for the Luftwaffe, being an unlimited struggle for air supremacy independent of army operations; introducing strategic warfare by means of both daylight bombing with fighter escort, and night raids; air warfare against supply ships, and sending of fighter-bombers into action. As it turned out, the Luftwaffe, developed mainly as a close co-operation arm with the Army, was not suited to all these tasks.

Where had Göring gone wrong? Basically in production, of all things. Had he concentrated entirely upon the Luftwaffe and less upon his high offices, decorations, gorgeous uniforms (one designed in white), high living, and art collecting, he would have been able to supervise a more balanced and certainly a bigger air force. When war came he badly lacked the needed reserves in aircraft. Unfortunately Göring let his friendships overcome his common sense. It was an absurd mistake to put Udet, a fine flier and the life and soul of many a party, but no technical expert, in charge of the Technical Office of the Luftwaffe and then of aircraft production. Udet was an outgoing character who loathed desk-work. It would have been far better to give the technically-minded, studious, and hard-working Milch complete control, and, like Dönitz, Göring could have done with the services of Albert Speer at an earlier stage.

The facts were that production output from German aircraft factories between 1937 and 1941 were too inadequate to meet the demands of Hitler's strategy, especially after the invasion of Russia. From 1936 to 1938 production varied between only 5,100 and 5,600 planes a year. In 1939 this was increased to nearly 8,300, in 1940 to 10,250, and in 1941 to 12,400. But in 1940 British aircraft production was substantially greater than Germany's; and so, in 1941, was that of the Soviet Union. The entry of America into the war of course disturbed the balance even more severely, and it is hard to see why Göring had always chosen to scoff at American aircraft production capabilities.

The R.A.F. was to enjoy a decisive advantage over the Luftwaffe in radar, and in general its signals and Intelligence branches were far superior. Göring must bear a large share of the blame for the Luftwaffe's lack of stamina, as it were. He failed to strike an equitable balance with the Navy over naval aircraft production, nor did he have enough bombers or fighters to win the war and protect the Reich. Indeed his 1939 boast—'If an enemy bomber reaches German soil, you can call me Meier'—became a bad joke in time. And when Albert Speer did become involved with aircraft production, in 1944 alone—with all the damage from air raids and difficulties of production—he gave Germany five times as many planes as Udet had managed to do in 1939. Although Hitler and Göring preferred bombers to fighters, Milch by superhuman efforts in 1943 had managed to get 7,600 fighters produced in the first eight months of the year. Of these, however, very few went to the air defence of the Reich. Galland has well described the difficulties under which the fighter arm functioned, always short of planes, and—from 1942—of skilled pilots. There had been hardly any night fighters at the beginning of 1940, since Hitler and Göring had a mistaken belief that there would be few night raids and that those could easily be dealt with by anti-aircraft artillery. The round-the-clock bombing programme of the Anglo-American air forces put an excessive strain on the Luftwaffe's fighter arm, already too weak because of the incessant demands of the Russian front, of Italy, the Balkans, and North Africa. When the Allies began continually to attack German fuel supplies in 1944 (and Galland wondered rightly why they had left it so late) the Luftwaffe was in a serious position. It managed to put up only token resistance in the air to the invasion of Normandy, there being at most 350 aircraft available to Sperrle in the West, and the Ardennes adventure finally killed off the Luftwaffe.

Göring had been widely discredited by 1942, and after the failure of the air lift to Stalingrad lost his influence altogether with Hitler. The crippling bombing of Hamburg the following summer undermined even more what was left of his authority. It serves no purpose to write down Göring's undeniable achievements. He had built up a splendid attacking air force which worked superbly well with the ground forces, especially the armour, in Poland, the Low Countries, France, and Russia. But his Luftwaffe was overstretched and in fighter production and pilots could not keep pace with heavy losses in a two-front and even three-front war. With no radar equivalent to the British the air defence of Germany, which had never been organised adequately before hostilities, and tended to operate in a makeshift way, was powerless to prevent the enormous damage caused by Allied raids from 1942 onwards. By specialising in attack at the expense of defence while still not favouring the long-range bomber, Hitler and Göring had made it more than ever vital to win the Battle of Britain and destroy the R.A.F. This they signally failed to do, and the Battle of Britain marks the beginning of the end of the Luftwaffe's record of success.

Here, too, Göring has a large share of the blame, for by switching the attack to London and big city targets rather than maintaining pressure on air and detector stations he lost a battle which had, at one time, been so nearly won. It was his second big tactical mistake. The first had been his over-confident assertion to Hitler, who had believed him, that the Luftwaffe could destroy the British rearguard at Dunkirk when the armour facing them had been halted. It was the R.A.F., and not merely some days of bad weather, which refuted his claim, and of course a very large part of the B.E.F. got safely away.

It was typical of Göring, the bluff buccaneer, to be over-confident. He brushed aside the excellent qualities of the Spitfire and Hurricane, and thought that some 1,000 Messerschmitts would have no difficulty in dealing with 600-plus R.A.F. fighters. But the Messerschmitts, though faster, were less manoeuverable and had a limited time in the air over England.

Göring's next disastrous error was to assure Hitler that the Luftwaffe could supply the beleaguered 6th Army of Paulus in Stalingrad, though some of his senior commanders, including the talented and experienced von Richthofen, disputed this. Doubtless seeking the chance to restore his prestige, Göring brashly promised an airlift of 600 tons of supplies daily to the pocket, overriding the strong doubts expressed by Colonel-General Kurt Zeitzler, the Army Chief of Staff, and by intelligent field commanders such as Field-Marshal von Weichs. Because Göring and Hitler had been so influenced by the successful airlifts earlier to the Demyansk pocket, the Stalingrad airlift went ahead, and—inevitably—was a costly failure. As David Irving writes in his book, *The Rise and Fall of the Luftwaffe*: 'Had either Göring or Jeschonnek firmly challenged the proposal, Hitler would certainly have abandoned it and ordered Paulus to fight his way out of the encircling ring'. As it was Jeschonnek, a blindly trusting Nazi who had been promoted Chief of Staff of the Luftwaffe at an early age, grew hopelessly disillusioned with Göring, and, before he committed suicide in August 1943, composed a memorandum to Hitler in which he listed the numerous errors made by the Reichsmarschall.

Göring's personal leadership was that of a dilettante. He was not always well-advised to lean on his old comrades from the Great War, men such as Lörzer, Bodenschatz, and Sperrle; some of them followed their commander's example and took too much to the easy and luxurious life. There were dissensions within the upper ranks of the Luftwaffe, and the lower ones justifiably resented accusations of inefficiency and even cowardice that Göring was apt to fling about if things went wrong.

All the same, Göring was intensely proud of his Luftwaffe, and would brook no interference with his conduct of operations when he bothered personally to command. He disliked Raeder, so that there was perpetual friction between the Luftwaffe and the Navy, and he did not get on much better with von Brauchitsch. He was furious about not being consulted over the Norwegian venture, and was made by Hitler to

111

apologise to Raeder for a rude telegram he sent the Grand-Admiral about the Navy's performance in Norway. In his letter of apology, dated 8 August 1940, Göring asked, rather abjectly, that the offending telegram be destroyed. Handsomely, Raeder complied.

Göring disliked but had to tolerate Himmler, though he squashed Himmler's attempt to found a separate S.S. air force: and he loathed Bormann. This brought him into occasional alliance with Dr Göbbels, though the two were extremely suspicious of each other. He could not bear Ribbentrop or Rosenberg, and did not get on with Dr Schacht when the latter was President of the Reichsbank. Schacht saw that Göring's economic abilities as Commissioner for the Four Year Plan were hopelessly ill-qualified, and—being Schacht—said so. Yet in 1939 it was largely upon Göring that peace hopes rested, and he was certainly not in favour of war with England, as his machinations through the Swedish industrialist Birger Dahlerus and others prove. Even von Hassell and the conspirators at one time had the desperate idea that Göring might be rallied to their cause, but even if he had managed to replace Hitler he would probably have been almost as bad. In any case Göring, like most of the senior Nazis, was afraid of Hitler. Schacht's description of Göring at Nuremberg caused the Reichsmarschall to writhe:

'I have described Hitler as an amoral type, but I can only regard Göring as *im*moral and criminal. Gifted from the start with a certain *bonhomie*, which he knew well how to exploit in the interests of his own popularity, he was the most egocentric creature one could imagine. For him the attainment of political power was but a means to personal enrichment and personal luxury. He was consumed with jealousy over anyone else's success. His greed knew no bounds. His love of precious stones, gold and jewels was incredible. He was entirely lacking in *ésprit de corps*. So long as anyone was useful to him—and only so long—he could be pleasant enough, and even so, it was merely put on.

'Göring's knowledge of all the subjects which a member of the government should master was precisely nil, especially in the field of political economy. He hadn't the faintest idea of any of the economic details Hitler entrusted to him in the autumn of 1936, although he built up an enormous staff and abused his power as economic leader according to all the rules of the game. His personal appearance was so theatrical that one could only compare him with Nero.'

Von Weizsäcker in his memoirs was more sympathetic:

'He was more intelligent than he was usually held to be, and was by no means the "Iron Hermann" of popular legend. In 1938 he proved his mettle as a supporter of peace.'

In March 1942, in his first notable reference to Göring in his diary, Göbbels found himself, evidently to his surprise, in agreement with Göring on all important points. He referred to Göring's hard work and 'enormous successes'. A year later, however, Göbbels (who also noted that 'his dress is somewhat baroque and would, if one did not know him, strike one as almost laughable') found Göring rather jaded. Göbbels was clearly trying to revive his alliance so that the two might effectively combine to head off Bormann's and possibly Himmler's ambitions. At this time Göbbels still thought Göring's leadership vital, and was trying to galvanize him into something of his old self. They agreed that Hitler had aged 'fifteen years' since the war and led an unhealthy life, and while Göring undertook to try to 'win over' Himmler, Göbbels was already confident of Speer's support, and that of Funk and Dr Ley, the toping Labour leader.

Göbbels' assessment of Göring in mid-year is interesting: 'It seems to me that Göring has been standing aside too long from the political factors which supply the real driving force. As a result he has a number of wrong ideas. But that can be corrected easily. His advantage is his healthy common sense which always enables him to pick his way through confused situations. As he is no longer closely connected with our political leaders, he has probably become rather tired and apathetic. It is therefore all the more necessary to get his views straightened out. For he is a first-rate factor of authority. A determined leadership can't possibly be set up without him or even against him for long'. A year later Göbbels would not have held the same views, but this was before Hamburg and the devastation of much of Germany.

Even a week later the weathercock propaganda chief was writing: 'Unfortunately the utter failure of the Luftwaffe has reduced Göring's prestige with the Führer tremendously, not only in this [a reference to misinformation commonly given to Göring by his own generals] but also in other respects. That somewhat upsets my plans for making him more conspicuous.' Hitler, Göbbels noted, was 'thoroughly dissatisfied' with Göring's direction of the air war, and only thought well of Jeschonnek. 'He thought the influence of General Bodenschatz (Göring's representative at Hitler's headquarters, and an old crony) whom he regards as a cold cynic, was especially harmful. Field-Marshal General Sperrle, too, in France, was not equal to his tasks. Like all air-force generals, he had withdrawn to a castle and was there leading the life of a sybarite. Air warfare against England probably didn't interest him much more than, say, an excellent luncheon or dinner. The Führer wants to recall him.' Actually the corpulent but shrewd and tough Sperrle managed to survive in his post.

It is significant that there is no mention in Göbbels' reporting of Hitler of new efforts to improve *defence* in the face of enemy bombing, by way of increased fighter production, but only of countering terror with 'terror from our side'. There is, however, a reference to 'too much experimenting' in Luftwaffe production, which must be simplified, and to minimization of enemy bomb damage. Because Göring's cronies did not want to displease him they kept the truth from him.

By now Hitler was seriously displeased with the Luftwaffe; and, as was his custom when he took against anyone, nothing was too bad for them. Göbbels and Speer stood up for Göring, though not without misgivings. A month later, on 9 April 1943, Göbbels returned to the subject of Göring's limitations. This time they had come up in a talk he had had with Field-Marshal Milch, who had been extremely sharp in his criticism, possibly fairly but certainly disloyally. 'He blames him for having let technical research in the German Luftwaffe run down completely. The Marshal, he said, had gone to sleep on the laurels won by the Luftwaffe in 1939 and 1940. The worst factor of all had, in his opinion, been the part played by General Udet who, before his collapse, had committed sins of omission on a scale deserving to be commemorated by history. ... Milch regards our situation in the air as very serious.'

And a month later Göbbels is completely disillusioned with his one-time prospective partner. 'One can no longer really depend on Göring. He is tired and somewhat washed out.' (9 May 1943). Even a civilian often contemptuous of the generals, such as Göbbels, could see where much of the blame lay. 'Göring pushed his old comrades of World War I too much into the foreground. They were obviously not equal to the heavy tasks imposed by this war.' (22 May 1943.) In September he reports Göring as being rather more optimistic than before about air warfare, in fact 'somewhat too optimistic', but regards this as a good sign. And on 14 November 1943, his last entry of note dealing with the Reichsmarschall, he writes: 'Göring, thank God, is showing himself more often in public. He was evidently recovered from his recent period of stagnation. I am very happy that he is again in evidence and that his authority is gradually being strengthened as a result.'

In Africa, Rommel was highly suspicious of Göring, whom he regarded as 'my bitterest enemy'. In Rommel's view, Göring thought that there were easy laurels to be won in Africa, and to further his inordinate ambition was manoeuvring to get the Luftwaffe put in charge of the African front in 1942. He criticized all Rommel's warnings sent to Hitler's headquarters as pessimism, and spread rumours that Rommel was a 'fair weather' commander only. Later Göring tried to get a Luftwaffe general put in charge of Sicily, but Rommel managed to spike that gun and insisted on the excellent General Hube.

The fall of Tunis and the end in Africa in May 1943 shattered morale at Hitler's headquarters. In *The Rommel Papers* the Field-Marshal explains: 'This will be incomprehensible unless it is realized how certain people at these highest levels were waging their struggle for power on the backs of the fighting troops. Göring was particularly busy just then trying to get the better of the Army. His Luftwaffe field divisions were a beginning. He probably wanted to introduce his scheme with a great military victory, which would be placed to the credit of the Luftwaffe. As a suitable site for this victory he chose North Africa, thinking that victories came relatively easily there. With virtually no military experience behind him, it probably all looked terribly simple.

'It cannot be denied that Göring had considerable talent for organization and an intelligence above the average. But he was too fond of his comforts to put his whole strength behind the realization of his plans.'

The Luftwaffe field divisions, which began to be apparent about mid-1942, eventually amounted to some 22 divisions, but they cannot be counted to have been a great success. They were often inadequately trained, and their equipment was different from that of the Army, to whom they frequently proved an embarrassment. Many of them were incorporated in the Army or disbanded in the last eighteen months of the war. The anti-aircraft and parachute divisions were a different matter, often being excellent. Some of the latter attained the prestige of élite troops as infantry, though never seriously used in their proper role after the heavy casualties of Crete. Even so there were occasions, such as in Normandy before the invasion, when Göring intervened to prevent anti-aircraft batteries being moved to where Rommel wanted them.

Göring's constant jeering at or belittlement of the Army generals did little credit either to his common sense or to his generosity. Even with people who were not only useful to him, but invaluable, at least to the Luftwaffe, Göring would be suspicious and vent his pique. Thus because Hitler had once mentioned Speer as a possible successor, Göring tried to downgrade the Minister of Armaments, upon whom the Luftwaffe relied so greatly. And he told General Werner Kreipe, speaking of Milch, whom he could certainly not afford to lose, 'First he wanted to play the part of my crown prince, now he wants to be my usurper'. This was in 1943. The fact was that Göring's position had already been much eroded, and that for the last two years of the war he was more and more removed from central decisions until at the end he was discounted by Hitler. Only his last-minute attempts to negotiate with the enemy aroused Hitler's animosity and led to his arrest.

Göring had been against the Russian venture, mainly on the perfectly correct grounds that the Luftwaffe could not carry on effective war against both the Red Air Force and the R.A.F. Kesselring thought that it could, and Hitler accepted the latter's opinion. Instead of Russia, Göring favoured a three-pronged attack in the Mediterranean to knock Britain out of the war, something that also appealed to his enemy Raeder. This was to be aimed via Spain, Gibraltar, and Morocco; Italy-Tripolitania; and the Balkans, Greece, the Dardanelles, Syria, and Suez. In November 1941 Göring actually suggested to Hitler that he stop the war in Russia—hold the Ukraine but go no further. Nevertheless he ordered the maximum exploitation of the occupied eastern territories, even at the cost of their own subsistence, reasoning in April 1943, 'because the Russian people cannot be won over to the German cause in any case', they should be exploited to the utmost.

As for the invasion of England, there was a chance for Göring to dominate events had he adopted a wiser strategy and put all his energies into proper planning. As it was he kept boastfully aloof from the Army and Navy, and misplayed his hand. An imaginative suggestion from Milch on 18 June 1940 to drop all available parachutists and air landing forces on vital English airfields such as Manston and Hawkinge, then to hold them until follow-up Army troops could be airlifted to join them, was rejected out of hand as nonsense. Göring was apparently amazed by the idea. This was only a day or two after the end of the fighting in France, and Milch proposed that Luftflotte 2 and 3 transfer their whole effort to England, with the Navy ferrying across food, fuel, and ammunition. The authors of *The Narrow Margin*, Derek Wood and Derek Dempster, comment, 'One of the most unusual opportunities in German military history has been thrown away'.

Hectoring his own commanders rather than patiently listening to their views, failing to encourage excellent scientists to be first in the field (the German lag in radar was crucial), unable to agree on strategic types of aircraft, Göring frittered away the lead he had built up. His own vain and sybaritic way of life and greed proved ill-fitting distractions in an air commander. He failed to keep up with technical developments, knowing even less about radio than his Intelligence chief, Beppo Schmid. 'As a commander and strategist (Göring) had few qualifications', is the view of Wood and Dempster. 'His flying knowledge was out of date and his understanding of technical subjects non-existent. The correct application of the air force which Milch built up was more than he could grasp.... The Luftwaffe lacked any long-term directive on economic warfare or any real guidance from above.'

All this brought disillusion to the senior commanders and to even the younger men, such as Galland, who performed individually with such distinction. It is a sad record, that of Göring, made the sadder by the frequent gallantry of his air crews. The picture in Normandy and thence onwards to Berlin would have been inestimably changed had Göring managed to build up sufficient reserves and kept a large fighter force constantly renewed. As it was, a tank or armoured car troop leader in advance of his own division or corps was just as likely, sometimes more likely, to be *strafed* by his own side's aircraft than by the Luftwaffe in 1944 and 1945. An abundance of recognition signals from coloured smoke to shining panels of material only seemed to attract American and British fighters, not Messerschmitts or Focke-Wulfs. In Italy the air superiority of the Allies was not quite so blatant, but it was still evident.

Let one of his own pilots sum up the feelings about Göring that must have been rife throughout the younger ranks of the Luftwaffe in 1944 and 1945:

'Göring's prestige and influence had suffered continuously since the Battle of Britain and had weakened so greatly after the catastrophe of Hamburg that it was doubtful whether he could ever have recovered them again. The man who had been chosen to be Hitler's successor, "the Führer's most faithful paladin" as he called himself with pride, the creator of the Luftwaffe, perhaps the only one of the National-Socialist leaders who had ever enjoyed real popularity with the mass of the German people, now retired from leadership and public life. At the end of 1944 Göring made his last strenuous attempt to regain the confidence of the Führer, the Luftwaffe, and of the people. It was too late. Mistakes and omissions had started a chain reaction which could never be halted.

'As the central force that the Reichsmarschall had represented for the Luftwaffe since its birth weakened, other forces surged into the lead of the air force. Certain circles formed that fought for influence and position. Decisions were not made on a realistic plane but as a result of the tough struggle which had started between the overlapping circles. This grew more bitter from day to day.'

Captain Gerhard Boldt, who saw the last days of Hitler as a young member of Hitler's staff in Berlin, has described Göring's rather pathetic latter-day appearances in the bunker in March 1945, when the rotund Reichsmarschall took to appearing in a uniform without decorations—he whose rows of medals had once inspired endless jokes in Berlin's cabarets. On one occasion Hitler lost his temper completely, treated Göring like a schoolboy, insulted him viciously, and threatened to degrade him to the rank of private and send him to an infantry battalion at the front. He raged: 'Göring, your Luftwaffe is no longer worth keeping as an independent branch of the Armed Forces!' Göring withdrew to restore his shattered nerves with brandy. On another occasion he went to sleep with his head on the conference table.

Ironically it was at the Nuremberg Trial that Hermann Göring was to shine again. Unquestionably he dominated the dock, and frequently the courtroom. Once again weaned off drugs, and with his uniform flapping about him from his loss of weight, it was a bravura performance. The other defendants seemed to defer to him as he passed comments, often ribald, on the testimony or the remarks of judges or counsel. He seemed not to have a care in the world, and only lost his self-control when there was some particularly choice piece of character assassination directed against him from an expert like Dr Schacht. In the long duel with the American prosecutor, Mr Justice Jackson, Göring decidedly came off best and scored various telling points. Stripped of his rank and of all his offices as he might have been by Hitler, on the grounds

117

that he had treacherously tried to seize power illegally, and snubbed by Eisenhower, who had ignored the suggestion of talking as one Marshal to another, Göring nevertheless had his day at Nuremberg. Apologising for nothing, he shouldered the self-imposed burden of defending his Nazi faith. It was, in many ways, an unforgettable performance, though Göring must have known that he was doomed.

Yet he had the last laugh. By taking poison that he had concealed he evaded the hangman. Though there is as yet no sign of the statues that Göring promised himself would arise, he managed to rehabilitate himself somewhat in the eyes of the German people. When newsreels of Nuremberg were shown it was noticeable how Göring's still imposing figure always aroused ripples of friendly laughter or interest. 'Unser Hermann', the Reichsmarschall, had indeed been popular. Of all the leading Nazi figures, he was at once the most sympathetic and the most flawed. His own weaknesses and failings of character had destroyed the once handsome, heroic figure of charm and affability, his own vanity and laxness undone the great early achievement of the Luftwaffe. Here indeed was a lost leader.

The real architect of the Luftwaffe, within the limits of Göring's ability to intervene, was a stocky, plump-faced administrator called Erhard Milch, whose round, undistinguished features concealed a tough brain and great ability. Milch was born in 1892 at Wilhelmshaven, the son of a chemist who had reached senior rank on the Quartermaster-General's staff in the Great War, and, apparently, of a Jewish mother. When this came to light in 1933 she was forced to sign a declaration that her son was a bastard, and Göring forbade all further inquiries into Milch's background.

In 1910 Milch joined the 1st Heavy Artillery Regiment at Königsberg as an ensign, becoming a lieutenant in 1911; he was early to show a flair for technical matters and great talent for organization. In 1915 however, he transferred to the German Air Force and became a reconnaissance flier, then an air general staff officer; by 1918 he was a captain. After the Great War Milch left the Air Force, but not the aviation world. In 1920 he was managing director of Danziger Luftpost and in 1923 a technical director of the Junkers Air Traffiic Company In 1926 he was instrumental in the formation—as a result of a merger— of Lufthansa Ltd., of which Dr Adenauer many years later was to describe him as 'the real architect'. It was chiefly out of Lufthansa which acted as an excellent cover for various military and paramilitary air training activities, that the Luftwaffe was formed. During these years Milch became a close friend of Udet, who was not always in favour with Göring, although he was to become Quarter-Master-General of the Luftwaffe in 1935. Between 1924 and 1926 Milch enlarged his horizons by paying visits to the United States and to South America.

From 1933 onwards, when the Nazis came to power, the rise of Milch was spectacular. First he became State Secretary to Göring, then Reich Commissioner for Air in January 1933 and when the Air Ministry was formed in May with Göring as Minister, Milch was brought in as Under-Secretary. When the Luftwaffe became officially recognized on 1 March 1935 Milch, not without some reluctance since he had made a fine civilian career as one of the chief directors of Lufthansa, was recommissioned as a Colonel, and shortly afterwards promoted to Major-General. By February 1935 he was Secretary of State for Air and a Lieutenant-General; in 1936 a full General der Flieger; and, on 31 October 1938, a Colonel-General. He was thus the second man in rank as well as in power to Göring.

In 1936 Milch visited Italy, and again in 1939, to encourage collaboration with the Italian Air Force. But he had little opinion of it, and later regarded the Italian contingent in the Battle of Britain as more of a liability than an asset. He also paid pre-war visits to Japan and to France, where he was on cordial terms with General Vuillemin, Chief of the French Air Staff, perhaps because he had successfully 'hornswoggled' Vuillemin about the strength of the Luftwaffe when Vuillemin visited Germany. The French Air Force was, however, deplorably weak and out of date. In 1937 Milch visited England, where he was impressed by the R.A.F., which led him to warn Hitler not to underestimate the British.

Although he often asked Milch's opinion, Hitler chose to disregard him. Some time before the war, probably in 1937, Milch fell out of favour with Göring, presumably because the latter saw him as a potential rival, and was stripped of some of his powers. Thus control of the air staff, the personnel office, and technical development, passed to Udet and Kesselring. Milch thereupon asked, reasonably enough, to return to Lufthansa, but Göring, who realized that he could not do without him, refused this request. In 1939 Milch was back in favour, and as well as being State Secretary was also Inspector-General of the Luftwaffe. By 1943 he held five big jobs, the others being Deputy C-in-C, Director of Air Armament, and Chairman of Lufthansa. Milch was also a devout Nazi, and a Party member. Hitler once said of him, 'Nothing is impossible to him', and Milch in his turn once avowed, 'Even if he commanded me to walk across the waves to him, I would unhesitatingly obey.'

The air production programme which Milch initiated has already been described. What is most important to remember is that Milch, Udet, and Kesselring were thinking in terms of 1942 as the earliest date for war, and perhaps even as late as 1944. Although Göring agreed with them he was powerless to stop Hitler. However, as we have seen, he tried for peace in 1938 and 1939. Milch had envisaged fighters assuming priority over bomber production by 1937, but in fact this did not occur, mainly because at that point Milch's star was not in the ascendant. He had also feared that the four-engined bombers proposed by Wever would absorb too many rare metals and scarce raw materials. In this view he was supported early in 1936 by Kesselring, then Chief of the Air Staff, and in the autumn of that year the two of them with Udet arranged that further development of four-engined bombers should be halted. This turned out to be an expensive mistake, particularly since at that time the Americans, whom Göring constantly underrated, were testing their first B-17s. It was, of course, a great mistake to put the ebullient Udet, no administrator, in charge of the Technical Office in 1937, and later make him Director-General of Equipment and Head of Air Supply in the last peacetime and first wartime years. These were jobs that needed a ruthless administrator like Milch himself, and could have been well handled by senior generals like Stumpff or Keller. Milch of course was at the heart of things, but he was far too busy to do Udet's job for him. It is illuminating that as early as 10 April 1933 an intelligent woman journalist, Bella Fromm, recorded: 'Milch is the real creator of the German Luftwaffe. He supplied the initiative for the construction of underground plane factories. He is no boaster, and is extremely polite and well-behaved. But he is as tough as steel, and would trample on anyone who stood in his way.' Nor should it be forgotten that, starting from more or less scratch, Milch created the most powerful air force in the world by 1940. Fritz Thyssen's statement that Milch only bothered about airfields and nothing else is very wide of the mark.

Yet he had his failures. In 1936 he and Udet rejected the rocket-engined HE 176, which he may later well have regretted, and though seemingly convinced by Galland that the ME-262 could turn the tables in the air, he was unable to convince Hitler of this. Between September and November 1939 Milch pressed strongly for more bomb production but without result, and only after mid-October was he given by Hitler authority for a full-scale air force munitions programme. After Udet's suicide in November 1941 Milch was able really to get the air production programme into top gear, and between 1941 and 1944 he more than trebled aircraft production. But he was not successful enough in equipping Germany with adequate interceptor defence. As David Irving has written in his biography of Milch, 'By 1942 at the latest, the provision of adequate air defences for the Reich should have found first priority. The truth was that the Reichsmarschall lacked the courage to represent this to Hitler.'

Irving has also criticized Milch for his 'unconcealed prejudices against able officers like Kesselring (and even Jeschonnek) and his ready acceptance of indolent and harmful commanders like Sperrle'. Kesselring, for his part, though he referred to him as 'Baby-face', wrote of Milch: 'I appreciated Milch as an expert, a splendid organizer and an unflagging worker.' Irving's view is that 'Göring was characterized by a pathological vanity and hunger for power, while his deputy Milch was motivated by a more congenial alchemy of personal ambition and deep-rooted nationalism.' And he writes of Milch 'refusing to recognise his minister's qualities, Göring reluctant to trust his state secretary further than he could throw him'. But, as Irving also states, Milch saw very clearly from the time of Udet's death 'the need to defend German air-space above all else', which he championed in vain. Hitler and Göring were only to be convinced of this in 1944, when the disillusioned Milch had given up the unequal struggle, in Irving's view. Yet Hitler, according to the S.S. leader Sepp Dietrich, had once commented that it would probably have been far better to hand over the Luftwaffe long before to Milch: 'Then perhaps Udet would be alive now'. The last great service to the war effort that Milch managed to render was to restore Speer to his favoured position with Hitler, in April 1944.

Milch had only one spell of operational command. This was during the Norwegian venture, when as a Colonel-General he commanded Strumpff's 5th Air Fleet, including X Air Corps and all the transport aircraft between April and May 1940. His success brought him the Knight's Cross from Hitler. He was among the first to raise the question of invading England, and immediately after Dunkirk—on 5 June 1940—suggested as a matter of urgency massive parachutist drops on R.A,F. airfields after heavy bombing attacks on them in the south of England. He was still mindful of his English impressions gained in 1937, and foresaw trouble, but this annoyed Göring; and Hitler in any case ruled out the idea as being too risky. Milch laid much of the blame for the loss of the subsequent Battle of Britain on Sperrle, but he himself was under a cloud at the time.

Milch had originally wanted to spend eight to ten years in building up Germany's strategic air force, but Göring and Hitler were in a hurry. Not that, like other Nazi generals, Milch had not suffered from Hitler's frequent deceptions. As Derek Wood and Derek Dempster have pointed out, 'Milch had repeatedly tried to get bomb production a higher priority. On 1 July 1939, while Hitler was inspecting prototype aircraft at the Rechlin experimental station, he had broached the subject with the Führer, much to the annoyance of Göring. Hitler speciously commented that he had no intention of getting involved in a general war, and that bomb production could wait.' Göring's removal from reality is typical, just as he roared with laughter when Milch, who had already in 1942 doubled fighter production over Udet's figures, offered him a monthly output at the end of the year of 1,000 fighter planes. It was not until 28 July 1943, after the second disastrous R.A.F. night raid on Hamburg, that Göring told Milch to concentrate on defensive production. This was too late in the game, though Milch did order accelerated production of a non-jammable airborne radar set.

On 15 January 1943 Milch was called in, far too late, to direct the air supply of Paulus's 6th Army at Stalingrad, an operation that had in fact never been feasible, but which owed its inception to Göring's euphoria. Next day he joined Colonel-General von Richthofen's staff train at Taganrog with special powers from Hitler to reorganise the airlift. Von Richthofen put the maximum possible at 200 tons a day, which was far under Göring's 600 tons, but even Milch's organisational genius could not achieve the impossible. On 9 April 1943 Milch discussed his efforts with Dr Göbbels, who had a high opinion of him, and recorded: 'One cannot call Milch a pessimist. While he sees the tremendous danger threatening us in Tunis, nevertheless he does not consider the situation there as lost. He claims that our Sixth Army in Stalingrad could have been extricated and that, had he been in command, he would have retreated even in the face of the Führer's orders to the contrary'. This last was, of course, plain common sense.

Milch at one time in 1943 wanted Göbbels to take over the whole civilian air defence programme, but Göbbels was too busy, though flattered by the approach. As a dedicated Nazi, Milch had no difficulties with the Party leaders, but his relations with his own colleagues and the other Services were not always pleasant. He had been one of the Air Force generals who initially opposed giving aircraft to the Navy, and he certainly did not get on with the Army Chief of Staff, Halder, who even in captivity refused to shake Milch's proffered hand. According to Ernst Englander, 'Göring and Milch hated each other, and we have it in their own words—there can't be any question about that'. Certainly relations between the two had cooled ever since 1936, but Milch, the brain behind the organisation of the Luftwaffe, could not be dispensed with. Milch was essentially a product of the Nazi era, and as the Nazis lost credence he seemed to develop more enemies than friends. No one could complain of his loyalty, however, either to the régime or to his friends. His qualities of optimism and buoyancy were invaluable in good times and bad, but as the war progressed he became increasingly domineering and subject to his hot temper. Irving writes: 'In later years he ruled the ministry by bluster and fear, by threats of court-martial and firing squad'. Telford Taylor thinks him 'egocentric to a degree that his colleagues and subordinates found painful and often intolerable', though he admits that he was 'an able, ruthless administrator'.

Due to Göring's veering favouritism and the intrigues in the higher ranks of the Luftwaffe mentioned by Galland, Milch was dismissed on 20 June 1944. He retained his title as Inspector-General of the Luftwaffe until January 1945, when that too was removed by Göring. Milch, who had always been the advocate of massive reinforcement of Germany's fighter defences, was arrested in Sierhagen Castle at Neustadt, on the Baltic Coast, in May 1945, having declined Speer's invitation to join Dönitz at Flensburg. But at no time had he been a likely candidate to join any resistance group against Hitler, indeed at Nuremberg he was to state of his dismissal date: 'Will you please note it was 20 June, not 20 July! I attach great importance to not being associated with those vermin!' In his farewell address to his staff on 30 June 1944, Milch said: 'I do not believe I have been an easy-going leader. I have had to use some rough language and some harsh methods. Nor am I sorry for having done so, however wrong I may occasionally have been.'

As deputy to Göring, Milch had not trod an easy path. His achievements were very substantial, his abilities great. Not one of the famous fliers himself, he lacked the easy cameraderie of the typical fighter pilot. But as an organiser and administrator he was in the first rank.

Field-Marshal Erhard Milch (he had been given the baton on 19 July 1940) gave evidence for Göring at Nuremberg. He was later himself sentenced to life imprisonment after being convicted on two out of three charges relating to the deportation of foreigners (including Russians), for forced labour, and the torture and deportation of Hungarian and Rumanian slave labourers. This was on 17 April 1947. Early in 1951 his sentence was reduced to 15 years, and in mid-1955 he was released on parole after ten years' captivity. Thereafter he lived quietly at Ratingen.

In 1972 there appeared a brief announcement in the German press which recalled the wording of the signal that the last Luftwaffe units trapped in Stalingrad had radioed to him in 1943:

'Erhard Milch, Field Marshal: born 30 March 1892, died 25 January 1972, signs over and out.'

Next to General Kesselring, who appears in another chapter, the ranking Luftwaffe officer in the summer of 1939 was General der Flak Artillerie (anti-aircraft) Günther Ruedel. He had dropped to tenth in seniority by August 1940, but was still Chief of Air Defence in 1941. He was succeeded in 1942 by General Helmut Förster, who had been Director of Operations to Göring, had commanded an instructional air division before the war, and commanded I Air Corps in Russia in 1941. Förster, whom Kesselring describes as 'gifted', was a comparatively junior officer; but next in seniority to Rüdel in 1939 was General der Flieger Hugo Sperrle, who was to maintain high commands throughout the war.

Born in 1885, Sperrle had been a flier in the Great War, and was one of those former Reichswehr officers under the Weimar Republic who exchanged the Army for the Luftwaffe in 1933. His rise was rapid thereafter. In 1935 and 1936 he was commander of a 'Luftkreis', and from 1936 to 1937 as a Major-General he led the Condor Legion in Spain, which at that time consisted mostly of Junkers 52 bombers, Heinkel 31 fighters, and six 88 mm. anti-aircraft batteries. This was valuable operational experience with modern arms. Sperrle was promoted Lieutenant-General and then General der Flieger in the same year, 1937; and in 1938 became G.O.C. 3rd Gruppe (South) with headquarters at Munich.

With his air units based in Bavaria he was in a good position to threaten Austria, but he was called to the Berchtesgaden meeting of 12 February 1938 by Hitler less for that reason than for his formidable appearance. A huge, solid, ferocious-looking man with an eyeglass, Sperrle qualified with von Reichenau for inclusion in Hitler's category 'my two most brutal-looking generals', which, if not exactly a compliment to either, apparently had the desired effect upon the frightened Dr Schuschnigg. In March 1939 aircraft from the 3rd Air Fleet of Sperrle and the 4th Air Fleet of Löhr took part in the occupation of Czechoslovakia. Sperrle did not participate in the invasion of Poland, his 3rd Air Fleet being kept on the southern wing of the German defences facing France, which were flimsy enough at that time. His aircraft, by Hitler's orders, were not to cross the French frontier until 10 September. In the invasion of France Sperrle worked with Rundstedt's Army Group 'A', while Kesselring's 2nd Air Fleet was with von Bock's Army Group 'B'; between them the two generals controlled some 3,400 aircraft at the start of operations, and the devastating effects of the Stukas and the close co-operation of bombers, fighter-bombers and fighters with the advancing German ground forces, never an easy task when the front is fluid, was almost invariably executed with precision and great efficiency. Sperrle and Kesselring were rewarded on 19 July when both became Field-Marshals, with Milch, thus bringing the Luftwaffe's total of Marshals to four.

After the fall of France Sperrle was to spend the rest of the war in that country, with his main headquarters in Paris; a locale which aroused misgivings in Hitler, as synonymous with idleness and debauchery. His Luftflotte 3 was based in north and north-west France. Sperrle was not too sanguine about the role of the Luftwaffe in 'Sea-Lion', being by nature rather the reverse of the over-optimistic Kesselring. In late July 1940 Sperrle's opinion was that the maximum effort should be directed against British ports and supply bases. Kesselring was first in favour of concentrating on the British periphery, and of smashing Gibraltar, or of using maximum strength against a few such given targets. As far as England was concerned he rightly thought that R.A.F. airfields, not London, should be attacked. By 6 August differences of opinion had been sorted out and small raids over a wide area began on 14 August. But Göring did not direct his two top leaders wisely or steadily enough during the Battle of Britain. He was too confident, and though the Luftwaffe had numerical superiority this was not enough when their losses in experienced pilots mounted up faster than those of the R.A.F. The trouble was, as Derek Wood and Derek Dempster have pointed out, that Sperrle and Kesselring 'lacked a positive strategic plan of action' and not only underestimated their enemy but showed inflexibility in their thinking. In September Sperrle had heated disagreements with Kesselring over the strength of the R.A.F., which Sperrle now over-estimated, thinking it still had 1,000 aircraft, while Kesselring and Göring underestimated it. The fatal mistake of turning away from the airfields to the bombing of cities, particularly London, must be placed at Göring's door.

On 21 May 1941 Sperrle became the sole air commander in the West, but out of 44 bomber Gruppen which had been operating for the past ten months against Britain, there were now only four left. The rest, apart from a few diverted to the Balkans, had been taken back to Germany to rest and refit before the Russian campaign. For the rest of the war Sperrle was to suffer from a shortage of aircraft, and though he supervised a great deal more bombing of Britain, and fighter protective activities over France, he never again controlled a victorious Air Fleet. He became more cynical, and though a tough-minded man, disillusioned with Göring and Hitler. So we find Göbbels estimating on 9 March 1943, as he parrots the venomous remarks of the Führer: 'Field-Marshal General Sperrle, too, in France, was not equal to his tasks. Like all air force generals, he had withdrawn to a castle and was there leading the life of a sybarite. . . . The Führer wants to recall him.' But despite Hitler's plan to replace Sperrle with a young general given full powers over a new bombing programme from France, à la Dönitz in the submarine field, Sperrle remained as the head of Western Air Command for more than another year. He had, after all, been around a long time and knew his way about in Services in-fighting.

Sperrle's last command was his most depressing one. His 3rd Air Fleet was grotesquely under strength to repulse the invaders on its own. On paper according to his operational log he had a strength of only 496 aircraft, of which but 319 were operational—88 bombers, 172 fighters, and 59 reconnaissance planes. Most of the rest of his aircraft, which were not ready for front-line work, were twin-engined bombers. Another source gives Sperrle's total aircraft strength in France as 890, of which about 150 planes were transport or reconnaissance; on 31 May 1944, according to these figures, only 497 were serviceable, and the figure of 319 operational on D-Day is agreed.* By 10 June Sperrle's strength had been augmented by some 300 more fighters, 45 torpedo-carrying planes, and 90 long-range bombers, and by 13 June his paper strength was about 1,000 aircraft of all types. In the face of the combined American and British air effort this was still not nearly enough, especially as many of Sperrle's planes were obsolescent. Göring had once said: 'I can't keep my fighters in France waiting for an invasion.

* Cajus Bekker gives his strength on D-Day as 198 bombers and 125 fighters, operational.

I need them for the defence of the Reich'. Sperrle must have pondered such remarks sourly on D-Day and thereafter, for on 6 June his fighters flew only 12 sorties, and soon II Air Corps was reporting that it had 'no aircraft at all available in the West'.

A desperate situation had been made even worse by the lack of fuel supplies from 11 August 1944, and from that date restricted missions were the order of the day—and they had already been fairly restricted! As one who fought in an armoured car reconnaissance regiment from Normandy until the end in Germany, I may remark that there were more occasions when I was attacked by the U.S. Army Air Corps or, occasionally, the Royal Air Force, than when I was the target of a Luftwaffe fighter attack. That is not to include the constant German bombing of the Caen region and its 'factory area', from which we all suffered at night, but to specify fighter operations. Nor is it meant as a criticism of the Allied fliers, for an armoured car regiment out in front must often be difficult to identify. I may add that on two of the various occasions when Focke-Wulf 190s attacked me, in one case the German pilot misjudged his dive and went straight into a ploughed field, in the other we brought the plane down with a concentration of Vickers 'K-gun' and small arms fire. Apart from various attacks in Normandy and Northern France, we were generally not worried by the Luftwaffe until 1 January 1945 and occasionally thereafter, during the Ardennes offensive and in the last fight for the homeland.

In the early days Sperrle had been a Nazi sympathiser. Later he changed his views. Lieutenant-General Hans Speidel, who knew him in France in 1944, wrote that Sperrle was 'a man of unusual vitality; but the more clearly he saw the unholy disorder in Hitler's leadership, the more he expended his energies in bitter sarcasm. He tried to work with us in a comradely manner, whenever he could, especially since he shared the political views of Rommel. Sperrle was made the scapegoat for the shortcomings of Göring and dismissed by Hitler on 18 August 1944'. Given his head earlier on, Sperrle might have made a satisfactory commander of the Luftwaffe instead of Göring. So, for that matter, might either Kesselring or Stumpff. Milch was more the technician whom any of these would have needed to run things behind them and back them up.

Sperrle at any rate showed good sense in 1940, and was not lulled into complacency. When he, Göring, and Kesselring conferred at the Hague on 3 September 1940, Göring pressed his view that large-scale attacks on England should be continued, but wanted to know if this could be done without undue risk to the bomber force. Were the British sufficiently weakened? Kesselring said 'Yes', but Sperrle, 'No'. He wanted the offensive to be continued against the fighter bases, whereas Kesselring thought them expendable, in the sense that R.A.F. fighters could be withdrawn to other bases north of London beyond the range of the

Luftwaffe. In the event Sperrle was right. What would have happened if the concentrated strength of the Luftwaffe had continued to pound the fighter bases, we shall never know. It is likely that the R.A.F. had already gained the upper hand, but it was a very near thing.

Sperrle's task in June 1944 was an impossible one with his limited resources. His dismissal solved nothing. The official British historian, Major L.F. Ellis, is rather hard on him.

'The commander of the Third Air Fleet, Field-Marshal Hugo Sperrle, had held that appointment during the whole of the German occupation of France, "living soft" in Paris. He does not seem to have had any lively reaction when the Allies landed and none of his subordinates is distinguishable in the air fighting in Normandy. The war diaries of the army commands in the West have few references to the *Luftwaffe* that are not critical and they give no indication that Sperrle had any voice in shaping the conduct of operations. He was, in fact, relieved of his command at the end of August and placed on the retired list.'

Field-Marshal Hugo Sperrle was officially 'denazified' on 9 June 1949, having been acquitted of war crimes at Nuremberg on 27 October 1948. He died in 1953.

General der Flieger Helmuth Felmy, another Great War flier and subsequently an able staff officer in the Reichswehr, was sixth on the Luftwaffe list of mid-1939, having been promoted to that position in February 1938. He commanded Air Fleet 2 or 'North' from then until 10 January 1940, when he was the victim of one of those totally un-deserved and capricious dismissals in which Hitler increasingly indulged. The occasion for Felmy's fall was the famous plane incident at Malines when a German aircraft carrying the German attack plans crash-landed in Belgium and the plans were captured more or less intact, though the German staff officer carrying them tried to burn them in a stove. Felmy and his Chief of Staff, Colonel Kammhuber, suffered as a result, though both were able to work their passage after a time in disgrace. Here was one occasion when Göring should certainly have intervened, as he could have done, to protect his own. The fact was, however, that Felmy had been out of favour with the Reichsmarschall for some time.

As a trained staff officer Felmy was apprehensive about a long war and on 17 September 1938, as G.O.C. 'Sonderstab England', he reported in a staff study that the Luftwaffe was incapable of effectively attacking Britain. In May 1939 he conducted large-scale exercises from his Bruns-wick headquarters with 2nd Air Fleet over three days and nights, as a result of which he concluded that the Luftwaffe could not possibly be ready for a full-scale war that year. He agreed with Milch, who in 1933 had asked for a ten-year production and armaments programme. Not unnaturally, this sort of conclusion did not sit well with Göring or Hitler.

In the spring of 1941 General Felmy was restored to duty for special assignments in the Balkans and the East. He was put at the head of 'Sonderstab F' which was due to intervene in Iraq in 1941, but did not do so because of the failure of Rashid Ali's revolt. He then served in Greece and Yugoslavia. At Nuremberg, where he accepted responsibility on four charges of taking reprisals, Felmy was sentenced to 15 years' imprisonment.

Colonel-General Hans-Jürgen Stumpff was one of the few top-ranking Luftwaffe officers to emerge from the war with a completely clean sheet both as far as Hitler and the Allies' records were concerned. He was tried for no crime and his reputation was unscathed. Stumpff will go down to history as one of the three main signatories of the final act of capitulation to the Allies in Berlin on 8 May 1945, he signing for the Luftwaffe.

Stumpff was originally a Grenadier officer, and between the wars served in the Army and at the Ministry of Defence in Weimar Republic days, like Sperrle. Transferring to the Luftwaffe, he became chief of personnel in 1935, a job in which he was successful, for Kesselring refers to him as the man 'who had built up the officers' corps of the Luftwaffe with a most tactful hand and had become a real father to the N.C.O.s and men under his care'. In October 1937 he visited England with Milch and Udet, in that year having succeeded Kesselring as Chief of Staff of the Luftwaffe (who had taken over between 1936 and 1937 on Wever's death). Stumpff became a General of Fliers in 1938, and on 1 February 1939 handed over as Chief of Staff to the younger Major-General Jeschonnek.

Stumpff was the field air commander for the invasions of Norway and Denmark, and between 1940 and 1943 was in command of Luftflotte 5, having previously served as head of Air Defence. He became an excellent Air Fleet commander, and was to stay in the North for a long time. After Norway, 5th Air Fleet participated in the Battle of Britain, though on a much smaller scale than Kesselring's 2nd and Sperrle's 3rd Air Fleets, having only 123 bombers and 34 twin-engined ME-110 fighters to contribute, compared with the other two's 929 fighters, 875 bombers, and 315 dive-bombers. This was partly because Stumpff's air bases were at a great distance from England and thus he was obviously operating at a disadvantage; indeed many of his units had been transferred to France, and thus away from his command, in May 1940. All the same, Stumpff played his full part in the discussions about 'Adlertag'—13 August 1940—and contributed what he could. In Norway the Colonel-General's headquarters were at Kristiansand and later Oslo, and in the autumn of 1941 he moved for a time to Kemi, Finland. From June 1941 to November 1943 Stumpff was primarily concerned with the northern front, attacks on enemy convoys and shipping, supporting Finnish and German troops against the Russians, and reconnaissance. In the winter of 1941 he directed from Kemi the main bombing effort against Murmansk and the Russian railways. As Earl Ziemke has noted, 'the uninterrupted darkness of the arctic winter made air operations against shipping targets at sea unprofitable in any case'.

Stumpff's appearance—'fat, round, provocative-looking' as he has been described—concealed an 'ingenious brain', as Kesselring noticed. From December 1943 until the end of the war he was Commander, Air Fleet Reich (formerly Air Arm Command Central) and thus primarily responsible for Germany's air defence in the skies. From September 1944 this command included what had previously been Sperrle's 3rd Air Fleet in Normandy. In the Autumn of 1944, due mainly to the efforts of Milch and Speer, production of single-engine interceptors and jets reached its peak, but it had meant a corresponding drop in bomber production. Stumpff was handicapped in his task by the fuel shortage, by lack of trained pilots, and by the loss of the early warning system when the Allies advanced. Even so his night-fighter force created by General Kammhuber was formidable, and Stumpff and his pilots cannot be blamed for losing their battle against superior odds. Stumpff also maintained overall control of anti-aircraft defences and Luftwaffe ground crews. But in the summer of 1944 the Luftwaffe was losing 300 aircraft a week, and by February 1945 Berlin alone had endured 40 heavy raids. Stumpff's problems were not lessened by the poor relations which existed between his flying commanders and the Air Force General Staff.

Stumpff was one of the ablest commanders of the Luftwaffe. His greatest success was Norway, but some of the attacks mounted by 5th Air Fleet in the northern theatre were rewarding, notably that on Convoy PQ-17, in which, out of the 24 vessels lost, eight were sunk directly by German planes and seven more damaged and slowed down.

Colonel-General Alfred Keller, who was equal fifteenth in seniority in mid-1939, had risen to sixth on the Luftwaffe list by August 1940. Born in 1882, he joined the Army in 1902 and did his pilot training in 1913, thus becoming one of the earliest air aces. In the Great War he led Kampfgeschwader I and acquired the nickname 'Bomben-Keller'. Between the wars he worked in civil aviation, but was back in military aviation in the underground Luftwaffe by 1931 as a lieutenant-colonel. Keller was a bomber specialist; he was also an ardent Nazi. In 1939, when Air Commander, East Prussia, he became General der Flieger. In the Battle of France he commanded IV Air Corps, and at the somewhat advanced age of 58 personally led his wing into action against the B.E.F. at Dunkirk. Thereafter he was stationed in France with headquarters near St Malo, but was chosen to be one of the air leaders in the invasion of Russia. He took command of Luftflotte

I, whose 400 aircraft were delegated to support von Leeb's Army Group North. Keller maintained his headquarters at Norkitten/Insterburg, and later at Ostrov in 1942. In 1943 he retired from active duty and became head of the NSFK, the National Socialist Flying Corps.

Keller's near contemporary, Ulrich Grauert, who was his equal in seniority in mid-1939 and eighth on the Luftwaffe list in August 1940, had also flown in the Great War. Thereafter he had been an artillery officer, and transferred to the Luftwaffe in 1935. An officer who was professionally highly competent, he led 1st Air Division in the Polish campaign in 1939 from headquarters at Crössinsee, Pomerania, with great success, and then I Air Corps in the French and Low Countries campaign which, from August 1940, had its headquarters in Brussels. Before the war Grauert had commanded a fighter division which helped in the takeover of the Sudetenland. He was killed over the Channel coast in May 1941, when a transport plane was shot down.

The Luftwaffe was unlucky to lose several of its outstanding senior officers in mishaps or accidents. General of Fliers Otto Hoffman von Waldau, born in 1898 and a pre-war Air attaché in Rome, who had been Chief of the Operations branch of the Luftwaffe in 1940 and 1941, was killed in an air accident in Africa. At the end of 1940 he had directed the formation and grouping of Luftwaffe units for Italy, and had been Air Officer, C-in-C Africa in 1942. General of Fliers Helmuth Wilberg, who had been Milch's commanding officer in the Great War, and while still a captain in the 'twenties had been an air adviser to the Army, was killed in an air crash in November 1941. Major-General Werner Mölders, the famous ace and first general of fighters (promoted thus after his hundredth kill) was killed in an air crash in Russia in November 1941. Mölders had won a name famous throughout Germany, even before the war being well known as the youngest wing commander in the Luftwaffe.

Hubert Weise, who had been a lieutenant-general in April 1938 in command of the 1st Flak Corps, was an anti-aircraft expert who rose to the rank of Colonel-General. He was seventh in seniority in 1940 when commanding Flakkorps I, and until 23 December 1943, when he was succeeded by Stumpff, was Head of Air Defence and Luftwaffe Commander, Central. According to Göbbels he made a most unhappy decision when removing the heavy anti-aircraft guns from Hamburg to Italy only two days before the first heavy R.A.F. raid on the city.

Ernst Udet is both one of the most attractive and saddest figures in Luftwaffe history. Universally popular, he had gained fame as an outstanding air ace in the Great War, in which he was credited with

62 victories, second only to Manfred von Richthofen's score of 80. He became a stunt flier in peacetime and travelled widely, being especially popular in America. He was a friend of Milch, whom he taught to fly; of Göring, until he fell out of favour; and of von Greim, who had been a wartime comrade. A highly talented airman, Udet was not a man who should have been tied down to a desk. He would have been far more successful as an Air Fleet commander. Gregarious, humorous, and a great party-goer (and giver), he was perhaps over-fond of drink and women, and in the closing stages of his life apparently turned to drugs. As a test pilot he was superb, and he deserves the largest share of the credit for developing the Stuka dive-bomber, which was partly his brain-child. He visited England in 1937 and was on good terms with senior R.A.F. officers, never thinking that war against England would come. Udet had joined the Luftwaffe in January 1936, and was immediately appointed Inspector of Fighter and Stuka pilots, with the rank of lieutenant-colonel. By 1937 he was Director of the Technical Department, which he took over from Colonel Wimmer, and in charge of aircraft production, as a Major-General. He was not successful enough in getting either adequate superiority of aircraft or bomb production before the war. Nevertheless his promotion was accelerated, and he rose from Lieutenant-General in 1939 to General der Flieger and then Colonel-General in 1940. On 10 October 1939 he was appointed Quartermaster-General of the Luftwaffe and was Chief of Air Supply, though not a born organizer.

Udet was against a long-range bomber force, and was one of those who rejected the Heinkel 176 rocket plane. Naturally enough, when things began to go badly for the Luftwaffe, Udet was given more than his share of the blame, and even his buoyant and charming personality cracked under the strain. There are similarities to his career in the magnificent play (and film), *Der Teufel's General*, by Carl Zuckmayer. Udet had been strongly against the Russian war. His Chief of Staff, Major-General Ploch, from 1936 to 1941 was a close friend whom Göring and Milch dismissed from that job in September 1941 and posted to Russia.

On 15 November 1941 Ploch visited his old chief, and hinted to him that Milch might be planning to dismiss him. He also told Udet about the massacres of the Jews in the East. Two days later Udet was found shot dead, a suicide, though the Nazi propaganda machine announced that he had died testing a new plane. On the headboard of his bed Udet had written in red lettering, 'Reichsmarschall, why have you deserted me?'

Udet had run into constant difficulties with Göring, and as Bekker relates: 'After spring 1941 Ernst Udet became a mere shadow of his former self. Though he drove himself to the limit, as chief of supply, he became the scapegoat for every failure, and the weight of responsibility broke him'. His sad end reminds one of that of the younger Colonel-General Jeschonnek, also burdened with cares greater than he could endure and verbally tortured by Göring and Hitler in 1943.

A third prospective suicide, but not until after the war, was Robert, Ritter von Greim, whose title was not inherited but came from his winning the Militär-Max-Joseph Order for bravery in the Great War. Von Greim was a senior pilot then, and won 28 victories. After the war he joined Udet in stunt flying, trained Chinese pilots at Canton, and went into German civil aviation. Udet had met Hitler in 1927, but never became an enthusiastic dialectical Nazi. Greim on the other hand did, and was one of the many Bavarians to find quick promotion. In 1939 he was a Lieutenant-General and Chief of Personnel. In 1940 he commanded V Air Corps in France under Sperrle, and took it to Russia in 1941, where he was under Löhr in the Ukraine at first. Most of his wartime service was spent on the Russian front; he commanded some of the air forces supporting Army Group South in 1941 and 1942, the 6th Air Fleet in 1943 when he was promoted Colonel-General, and the 4th Air Fleet on the Russian front from 1944 to 1945.

He was present at the conference on 9 July 1944 when Hitler discussed the deteriorating Russian front, and in April 1945 flew to Berlin and was ordered by Hitler to organize air support for General Wenck's 'offensive' to relieve Berlin. When Göring fell into his final disgrace and was dismissed by Hitler, von Greim was promoted to be the second, and last, C-in-C of the Luftwaffe, on 26 April 1945. Dönitz intended to retain him in that post, describing von Greim as 'this fine man and officer'. On 2 May 1945, at Plön, von Greim 'spoke bitterly of the fact that the idealism and devotion to duty of soldiers who believed they had been serving a noble cause should have ended in so dire a catastrophe: He did not wish, he said, to go on living, and we parted, deeply moved'.

Von Greim, the commander of Luftflotte 6, had made a hair-raising flight from Munich to Berlin in the closing days of the war to be at Hitler's side, as ordered, during the course of which he had been shot in the foot. His second pilot was the well-known woman aviator, Hannah Reitsch, who took over and managed to land the small Fieseler-Storch plane in the Tiergarten on the road that runs through the Brandenburg Gate, despite Russian small arms fire. A few days later, after Hitler had promoted von Greim, the Field-Marshal—as he now was—and Fraülein Reitsch took off from the East-West Axis in an Arado, again through a hail of shots, and reached Rechlin.

Field-Marshal Robert Ritter von Greim, true to what he had told Dönitz, committed suicide in a Salzburg hospital in late May 1945. His reign over the Luftwaffe had lasted less than a fortnight.

General of Fliers Hans Ferdinand Geissler was a recruit to the Luftwaffe from the Navy, a fact which was to shape his future career. In the summer of 1939, as a Lieutenant-General, he was head of German's Coastal Command and responsible for naval co-operation with flying-boats, with headquarters at Hamburg. In September he was head of the Hamburg Air Administrative Command and commander of 10th Air Division, in charge of anti-seaborne forces, but he had virtually no bombers at his disposal. In October 1939 his command was raised to that of X Air Corps, which he took to Norway and which he commanded thence in the Battle of Britain. With this Corps he also ran the anti-shipping campaign in the Atlantic. Geissler was, in Kesselring's words, 'a most competent officer'. At one time he had served as Special Duties General with 2nd Air Fleet, where he was responsible for planning aerial operations and objectives for the war against England. The higher reaches of the Luftwaffe chose to ignore his conclusions, which were, broadly, that only partial success could be achieved against Britain in 1940 and that victory in the air would be won by 1941 only if 'available forces were strictly concentrated, operations were conducted flexibly and *for a considerable length of time* with gradually increased forces'.

Geissler got into some trouble when two of his aircraft, on 22 February 1940, by mistake sank two German destroyers in the Dogger Bank area of the North Sea. There was a painful court of enquiry about the disaster. In January 1941 he took his X Air Corps to Sicily with headquarters at Taormina, and was responsible for many of the attacks on Malta. He also worked with the Afrika Korps and at Rommel's request attacked Benghazi.

We have already met Bruno Lörzer, Göring's old comrade and squadron commander in the Great War. He was to rise to the rank of Colonel-General, but was one of those appointed to important commands without the real qualifications to run them successfully. He depended very largely on Göring's good-will and his resultant influence in high places. All the same he refused to give evidence on Göring's behalf at Nuremberg. Irving calls him 'incompetent and corrupt', and there is a story that while serving in Italy he sent back trainloads of oranges and silk stockings to Germany. He was also capable of making fatuous reports to Berlin such as: 'In the course of the period from 20 March to 28 April 1942, Malta had been completely eliminated as a base for the enemy's navy and air force'.

However, Lörzer was not without dash and initiative, as his score of 44 victories in the Great War proved. Between the wars he worked in commercial aviation and kept up his friendship with Göring. He became head of the NSFK in 1935, and by 1939 was a Lieutenant-General commanding II Air Corps.

Lörzer had the professional interest to engage in long discussions with Guderian on air co-operation with panzer forces, and these indeed paid off fruitfully in France in 1940. He was responsible for the successful bombing of the Sedan area which helped the German breakthrough, despite the fact that he had ignored orders from his superior, Sperrle, to the contrary. His aircraft flew from the Pas de Calais and over the Dover Straits in 1940, and if 'Sea-Lion' had been attempted Lörzer would have been responsible for the air cover of the embarkations, crossings, and landings, and for bombing inland targets and communications in Britain.

II Air Corps took part in the invasion of Belorussia in the summer of 1941 under Kesselring's 2nd Air Fleet, but in October was transferred to Sicily, where Lörzer's headquarters were at Messina. Later he was in Italy.

Bekker has an interesting story about the Stalingrad airlift: 'The most reliable evidence as to how the Reichsmarschall ever came to give his assurance to Hitler against all informed opinion comes from his friend and World War I comrade, Colonel-General Bruno Lörzer. Göring, Lörzer reported later, often discussed the tragedy of Stalingrad with him, and repudiated the notion that he should be saddled with the blame. "Hitler took me by my sword-knot and said: 'Listen, Göring, if the Luftwaffe cannot supply the 6th Army, then the whole Army is lost!' There was thus nothing I could do but agree, otherwise I and the Luftwaffe would be blamed from the start. I could only say, 'Certainly, my Führer, we will do the job!'"'

Colonel-General Friedrich Christiansen was one of the very few Luftwaffe officers who became a theatre or country commander. From 1940 until 1945 he was Wehrmacht Commander for the occupied Netherlands, with Seyss-Inquhart as his political mentor.

A bluff, jovial character known as 'Krischan', liked by nearly everyone, he was on excellent terms with Göring. Christiansen had originally been a naval officer, and during the Great War had commanded the naval base at Zeebrugge. He held the coveted *Pour le Mérite.* After the war he worked for Dornier as an expert on naval aviation at Friedrichshafen, but in 1933 became a Major-General in the Luftwaffe. One, of his chief pre-war jobs was to head the Aviation and Sports Department of the Air Ministry, and in 1939 as a General of Fliers he was in charge of the National Socialist Air Corps.

Christiansen's job in Holland was mainly one of administration and internal security, and though C-in-C on paper he did not exert much influence on events in 1944 and 1945. Speidel has summed him up: 'He was a bluff, simple seaman and did not have the experience, education, and mental qualities to lead an army; he knew very little of land warfare. This made his appointment as commander all the more unusual—there was no regard for military qualifications.' In fact the defence of Holland was largely handled by Colonel-General Blaskowitz.

Of all the Luftwaffe operational commanders, the ablest after Kesselring was Wolfram, Freiherr (Baron) von Richthofen, a younger cousin of the famous Great War leader, in whose squadron he had served. Von Richthofen worked in engineering after the war and then rejoined the Army in 1923, and for a time served as a military attaché in Rome. Transferring to the Luftwaffe, he worked in the Air Ministry from 1933, and in 1936 was assistant to the head of the Technical Department, Colonel Wimmer. In 1936 he became Chief of Staff to Sperrle as a Lieutenant-Colonel in the Condor Legion in Spain, and later commanded it. In 1938 he was a Major-General.

Richthofen was known as a close-support specialist, and made a careful study of co-operation with the Army, and it was in this role that he was to make his name. In personality he was aggressive and dashing to the point of flamboyance, and, like Kesselring, an habitual optimist. Despite or perhaps because of his close relations with the ground forces, especially tanks, he was often very critical of the Army, but he never let this interfere with his performance. Göring for once showed good judgement in rating Richthofen and Kesselring his best operational commanders; and his long experience in Russia, where his VIII Air Corps and later 2nd Air Fleet flew on every front with marked success, did not fault this opinion. Richthofen commanded VIII Air Corps (which he had led since 1938 as a Major-General) in France in 1940 under Sperrle, and it was there that his Stuka dive-bombers perfected their technique and put the gloss on their terrifying reputation earned in Poland. Ironically, as a colonel in 1936, Richthofen had been sceptical about dive-bombing. In an invasion of England, the Folkestone area would have been his main target, as he was to support the landings made by Colonel-General Busch's Army. Richthofen had doubts about a wide-front landing, and indeed proposed that initially only one Corps should be landed, because of the lack of supporting aircraft available.

In 1941 his VIII Air Corps was transferred to Russia with Lörzer's II Air Corps and Lieutenant-General Walter Axthelm's I Flak Corps to make up Kesselring's 2nd Air Fleet supporting von Bock's Army Group Centre. At Kalinin in October 1941 von Richthofen several times saved the day with fierce attacks by his Stukas against Russian armour and mortar batteries when XLI Panzer Corps was in serious difficulties. At Sevastopol in June 1942 he commanded seven bomber, three Stuka, and four fighter groups, and 17 Flak batteries, to support von Manstein's siege. VIII Air Corps flew between 1,000 and 2,000 missions a day.

135

In the summer of 1942 von Richthofen was promoted to command 4th Air Fleet with the rank of Colonel-General, and for Bock's Army Group South campaign against the Don area he had under his command IV and VIII Air Corps and I Flak Corps, amounting to ten single-engined fighter and 8 long-range fighter groups, sixteen bomber, and 5 Stuka groups.

Richthofen's original VIII Air Corps was probably the most famous such formation in the Luftwaffe. As well as Poland and France and the Low Countries, it had flown in Greece and spearheaded the invasion of Crete in May 1941, where Student and Richthofen were the operational air commanders of the invasion under General Löhr. In the German attack on Greece Richthofen had commanded nearly 500 aircraft against the R.A.F.'s seven squadrons with some 80 planes.

Von Richthofen was rightly dead against trying to supply Paulus's 6th Army at Stalingrad by air (he reckoned a maximum of 200 tons per day possible, with luck), and was very much in favour of a breakout. Unfortunately he held no high opinion of Paulus. On 3 October 1942 Richthofen, Jeschonnek, Paulus, and von Seydlitz held a meeting, at which Richthofen told Jeschonnek: 'What we lack is some clear thinking and a well-defined primary objective. It's quite useless to muck about around here, there, and everywhere as we are doing. And it's doubly futile, with the inadequate forces at our disposal. One thing at a time, and then all will go well—that's obvious. But we must finish off what we've started, especially at Stalingrad. . . .' (Craig, *Enemy at the Gates*, p. 132). By 16 November he was telephoning to Zeitzler, 'Both the command and the troops are so listless . . . we shall get ourselves nowhere —let us either fight or abandon the attack altogether. If we can't clean up the situation now, when the Volga is blocked and the Russians are in real difficulty, we shall never be able to. The days are getting shorter and the weather worse!' Zeitzler agreed with him. Richthofen's successor as commander of VIII Air Corps was Lieutenant-General Martin Fiebig. After a conversation on 21 November 1942 with Lieutenant-General Arthur Schmidt, Paulus's Chief of Staff, in which Schmidt demanded air supply, Fiebig telephoned von Richthofen and told him: 'You've got to stop it! In this filthy weather we have here there's not a hope of supplying an Army of 250,000 men from the air. It's stark staring madness!' (ib.) Richthofen made his protest to the Chief of Staff of the Army, but Zeitzler was bound by Hitler's unbending orders.

Richthofen was promoted to be the Luftwaffe's fourth Field-Marshal on 17 February 1943. At a conference with Hitler on 23 July 1943 he gave his opinion that Marschal Badoglio would not continue to fight on the German side. Here he was right, but he had erred earlier in thinking that Sardinia, not Sicily, would be the Allied target after Tunis. Richthofen had been transferred to the Mediterranean front from Russia in 1943 to strengthen the German resistance, and had most of his squadrons in Sicily at first. He moved the bulk of them to Sardinia as a result of his wrong appraisal. By now he was weaker numerically than his Allied opposition, and for the brief time that Italy remained in the war co-operation with the Italian Air Force was poor.

Field-Marshal von Richthofen had almost unparalleled experience on various fronts as an air commander. He remained loyal to Hitler and to Göring, though after the Stalingrad fiasco, when Hitler had ignored Seydlitz—all in favour of a Paulus breakout—he raged that he himself and other senior commanders were treated as 'nothing more than highly paid N.C.O.s!'

Alexander Löhr, C-in-C of the small Austrian Air Force, and a friend of Göring, was one of the few senior Austrian officers incorporated into the Wehrmacht after the Anschluss in 1938. Though himself an Austrian, Hitler had always been opposed to, and suspicious of, the Austrian ruling class, and few Austrians were promoted to positions of consequence. Not one became a field-marshal.

In the summer of 1939 Löhr was commander of the 4th Air Fleet as a general of fliers, and this was one of the two major air formations used in the Polish campaign. On 15 April 1941 Löhr submitted the original plan for an airborne attack on Crete, which appealed strongly to Göring. For this operation in May General Löhr was the overall commander of air and ground forces, with Student below him.

In the early part of the Russian campaign, Löhr provided the air support for von Rundstedt's Army Group South, with a strength of some 600 aircraft.

In 1942 Löhr became C-in-C Balkans, as a Colonel-General, and between January and August 1943 was Air Commander in Italy. For the last two years of the war he was the commander of Greece and the Aegean area under Von Weichs, and of Yugoslavia, his commands being known as Army Group 'E' and Army Group South-East. In the former he controlled 300,000 men. About 90,000 of them were stationed on islands, which Hitler authorised to be evacuated on 15 September 1944.

Colonel-General Löhr was the only Luftwaffe officer except Kesselring, and the only Austrian officer except Rendulic, to become a theatre commander. He was an efficient and experienced air leader, but had little knowledge of ground operations. It was his misfortune to be held responsible after the war for the bombing of Belgrade. He was captured by Tito's partisans, against whom much of his air activity had been directed, and—found guilty of the mass murder of Yugoslav civilians— was executed on 27 February at the age of 62.

Another of Göring's old cronies from Great War days was General of Fliers Karl Heinrich Bodenschatz, who was to spend the entire Second World War as Göring's chief air assistant and personal representative at Hitler's headquarters. In this capacity he wielded influence beyond his merits, for often Göring would not turn up to important conferences, especially in the latter half of the war.

Bodenschatz, born in 1890, had been von Richthofen's adjutant and then Göring's, in 1918, and a fellow-flier of Göring. He became an officer in the peacetime Reichswehr, and in 1933 adjutant to Göring again. He remained faithful to his chief, though he had many an uneasy passage at Führer headquarters, and testified on his behalf at Nuremberg. The saturnine Bodenschatz did not display any military genius and functioned mostly as a liaison man and deliverer of messages. As personal Chief of Staff to Göring, however, he was in a position to influence appointments and promotions. Bodenschatz worked in the Air Ministry before the war as a Major-General, and became a Lieutenant-General in 1940. He attended every major pre-war and wartime conference on operations and future plans, and thereby accumulated a vast fund of both political and military knowledge, but his influence on events was more in the field of personalities than of operations. Göbbels thought that this influence 'was especially harmful' and regarded Bodenschatz as 'a cold cynic'. (Diaries, 9 March 1943.) Bodenschatz was severely wounded in the legs in the bomb explosion of 20 July 1944 at Rastenburg.

At Nuremberg he told the court that the big night raids of the R.A.F., especially that on Cologne in May 1942, had first resulted in Göring's loss of influence with Hitler. 'From that moment, there were differences of opinion between Hitler and Göring which became more serious as time went on. The outward symptoms of this waning influence were as follows: first, the Führer criticized Göring most severely; secondly, the endless conversations between Adolf Hitler and Hermann Göring became shorter, less frequent, and finally ceased altogether.'

Bodenschatz also testified: 'The air defence of Germany was very difficult, as the entire defence did not depend on the air crews alone, but it was also a radio technical war, and in this radio technical war, it must be admitted frankly, the enemy was eventually better than we were'. He confirmed that Göring had tried hard to dissuade Hitler from the Russian venture, and that by 1939 the Luftwaffe was not ready for war as far as leadership, training and equipment were concerned.

Colonel-General Hans Jeschonnek was easily the youngest officer to attain that high rank, having been born in 1900. Even so, he managed to fly a few missions in the Great War. Afterwards he served in the cavalry in the Reichswehr, then became a staff officer, transferring to the RLM (Luftwaffe) in 1933. By 1937 he was still only a major; by 1939 a colonel on the staff, having been one of Udet's assistants in the Technical Branch and then principal staff officer to Milch. The latter has described him as a 'plucky, intelligent officer but narrow-minded and headstrong, and contemptuous of other walks of life'.

Jeschonnek was certainly an ardent Nazi who worshipped Hitler. He was picked out from the ruck of staff officers—and the Luftwaffe was short of first-class ones—by Göring, and much to everyone's surprise made Chief of Staff of the Luftwaffe in succession to Stumpff in February 1939, when still only a colonel. He was soon promoted Major-General.

Jeschonnek had served in Russia in the 'twenties, and for whatever reason was one of those definitely in favour of 'Barbarossa'. Indeed he was originally one of its most enthusiastic supporters. In the spring of 1942 he was convinced that the Russian war would soon be won, which led him—swayed by Hitler—to strip the West of aircraft, where in fact the Luftwaffe faced its most serious enemy in the air. He even denuded the Luftwaffe of its fighter reserves to pour them into the Russian battles. Galland has testified that Jeschonnek was 'an able and lively Chief of General Staff', and has written of 'his high intelligence and his absolute integrity'; but well makes the point that he was 'no magician, as thought at the Führer's H.Q.', and that, despite his virtues, Jeschonnek had fallen 'more and more unconditionally under the spell of Hitler'.

The British air historian Asher Lee thinks that Göring made 'a cardinal mistake' when he picked Jeschonnek for his high office, since he rather needed men with Jeschonnek's undoubted qualities who were also highly critical, which Jeschonnek was not. In this context he was hampered by his youth and lack of seniority (he was still a Lieutenant-General in January 1941). Although he had served under Milch both in the latter's squadron briefly in the Great War, and later as a staff officer, he was not always on good terms with him. As Chief of Staff for over four years he bears responsibility for both successes and failures, and the job undoubtedly took its toll of him, and even unbalanced him.

Jeschonnek was a keen exponent of the close support theory of aerial warfare, and vigorously backed the high-speed medium bombers and Stukas which operated so well in Poland, the West, Greece, the Desert, and the Balkans. But he neglected fighter defence. When much argument had arisen about the 'stop-line' imposed before Dunkirk, Jeschonnek—who was in a position to know—told von Richthofen at the end of July 1940 that Hitler 'wants to spare the British a humiliating defeat'.

He also thought at that time that the Navy would not be needed to defeat England, according to Rear-Admiral Mössel, and boasted: 'The Luftwaffe will conquer England in a matter of months'.

What really finished Jeschonnek were the disasters at Stalingrad (he had been against the attempt to supply Paulus by air) and the heavy bombing raids on Germany in 1943 which the Luftwaffe could not prevent. By then his master Göring had lost most of his influence and nearly all of his concentration, and a terrible burden was thrown on Jeschonnek's shoulders. So this 'sound and sensible man', in Paul Carell's words, lost his balance. On 1 August 1943 he even suggested to Hitler the Führer assume personal command of the Luftwaffe as he had of the Army, because thus alone could its prestige be restored. He complained that 'the Reichsmarschall is never available for consultation' and later composed a memorandum to Hitler in which he cited the numerous errors of Göring.

On 9 March 1943 Göbbels had recorded that Hitler now thought well only of Jeschonnek among his Luftwaffe generals. 'Jeschonnek was an absolute fanatic for truth, he said; he saw the situation very clearly and had no illusions.' Unfortunately one illusion that possessed Jeschonnek was admiration for his Führer, who, like Göbbels, was always blowing hot and cold. Hitler may be held almost directly responsible for Jeschonnek's death, since in August he insulted and upbraided him in his typical fashion and almost spelled out that there was only one course left for him. Jeschonnek took it, and on 19 August 1943 shot himself.

Colonel-General Otto Dessloch, an ex-cavalryman who had flown in the Great War, had one of the longest records of operational command in the Luftwaffe, which testifies to his stamina and ability, since most of his service was in the East under demanding conditions. He was widely respected. As a Lieutenant-General Dessloch commanded the II Flak Corps, working under von Kleist in France and Russia in 1940 and 1941. He then became second-in-command of 4th Air Fleet under von Richthofen in the East. Between August and September 1944—the period from Falaise to Arnhem—he took over 3rd Air Fleet in the West from Sperrle. From 27 September 1944 to 6 April 1945 he commanded 4th Air Fleet in the Balkans, Hungary, and Slovakia. For the last eleven days of the war he took over from von Greim the 6th Air Fleet covering the East and South-east. He distinguished himself in the supply of the Tarnapol pocket in 1944, and in air support of Army Group South Ukraine in August 1944. He was both an experienced anti-aircraft commander and skilled at using his aircraft.

General of Fliers Paul Deichmann, whom Kesselring thought 'distinguished and resourceful', had as a major been chief of the operations section in the General Staff under Kesselring in 1937, and was one of the advocates of the long-range bomber. In France in 1940 he was Chief of Staff of Fligerkorps II as a colonel, and then successively of 2nd Air Fleet and to the C-in-C South (Kesselring). At Orel in 1943 he commanded the 1st Air Division with 700 aircraft (Dessloch's 4th Air *Fleet* in 1944 was reduced to 300!) and later the I Air Corps, again with 700 aircraft, as major-general and later lieutenant-general. He did very well in the operations for evacuating the Kherson Peninsula in May 1944, and had for long supported 17th Army in the Black Sea area, over which his aircraft kept control. In the Simferopol area in April 1944 his planes knocked out over 50 Russian tanks. His last command was of Luftwaffe Command 4 (formerly 4th Air Fleet) for the last twelve days of the war in the Balkans, Hungary, and Slovakia.

General of Fliers Martin Fiebig, who took over von Richthofen's VIII Air Corps in 1942, had to bear the brunt of the Stalingrad airlift operations. In the course of this hazardous operation there were only two occasions on which even the minimum target of 300 tons daily was reached, and the experienced Fiebig lost 550 aircraft.

As a colonel in 1939 and 1940 Fiebig had commanded the 'General Wever' KG 4 squadron of 88 Heinkel bombers in Poland and the French and Low Countries campaigns. It was these planes taking off from bases at Delmenhorst, Fassberg, and Gütersloh on 14 May 1940 that bombed Rotterdam. In Russia Fiebig commanded II Air Corps, which specialised in close combat, under Kesselring, before taking over from Richthofen in VIII Air Corps as a Lieutenant-General.

Fiebig was to give repeated warnings that the Stalingrad airlift was 'not on'—in vain. On 21 November 1942 he had a telephone conversation with Major-General Arthur Schmidt, Paulus's Chief of Staff; Paulus himself was listening in. After Fiebig had asked what were 6th Army's plans, the conversation went like this:

'The C-in-C proposes to defend himself at Stalingrad'. F: 'And how do you intend to keep the Army supplied?' S: 'That will have to be done from the air.' F: 'A whole Army? But it's quite impossible! Just now our transport planes are heavily committed in North Africa. I advise you not to be so optimistic!'

Fiebig then telephoned to protest to von Richthofen, who agreed with him. On the first two days of the airlift, 25 and 26 November, the weather was atrocious, and Fiebig reported: 'We are trying to fly, but it is impossible . . . situation desperate'. On 11 December Paulus bitterly reproached Fiebig with the failure of the airlift, despite Fiebig's previous warnings. On 24 December Fiebig left his temporary headquarters at Tatsinskaya for Rostov, in the last JU-52 to leave. Göring had issued absurd orders that the airfield was not to be left until it was under fire, with the result that the Luftwaffe lost 60 JU-52 aircraft (one-third of their total) and all the spare parts and ground equipment. Fiebig had previously asked Paulus to build a landing ground for VIII Air Corps, but this was never done. According to Bekker, 'Paulus even declined Fiebig's offer to send into the pocket an air force general to take charge of the air lift at the receiving end—an expert who would be responsible not only for airfield construction and the unloading system, but all the other technical and tactical problems that the air-lift posed'. This was idiocy on Paulus's part.

When von Waldau was killed, Fiebig was promoted to take over Luftwaffe Command South-east, comprising the air force components in Greece and part of the Balkans. He held this post from March 1943 until September 1944. His final command was Luftwaffe Command North-east, formed on 2 April 1945, to carry out defensive operations on the Eastern front and under Air Fleet Reich.

Despite the unfortunate impression Fiebig made upon Milton Shulman (he 'looked and talked like a Park Lane playboy'), he was a brave and competent commander. He went with Richthofen to implore Hitler to evacuate the aircraft from Tatsinskaya before it was too late, on 24 December 1942. They were told to hang on.

For his part in the bombing of Belgrade early in the war, General Fiebig was executed after the war by the Yugoslavs.

Lieutenant-General Adolf Galland, a Westphalian, was one of the generation of young fighter aces which included his friend and rival, Werner Mölders, who became household names and rose to high rank because of the war. Dark, dashing, easily recognisable from his moustache below which jutted very often a cigar, Galland bore a remarkable similarity to Hollywood screen stars like the young Warner Baxter or George Brent.

As a youth he started flying gliders, entered a flying training school in 1932, and next year in the still unofficial Luftwaffe was trained in Italy. In 1937 he volunteered for the Condor Legion, and between 1937 and 1938 flew over 300 sorties in Heinkel HE-51s and Messerschmitt 109s in Spain. He then worked in the Air Ministry, became a captain in October 1939, and joined the 27th Fighter Wing at Krefeld. In the Polish campaign he commanded a squadron of fighters, as he did over France in 1940. By July 1940 he was a Group leader with the rank of major, and he was so successful that he had risen to lieutenant-colonel by September.

In November 1941 Galland was put in charge of fighters, with the rank of Major-General, and kept this post until January 1945. By this time he had fallen into disgrace with the Nazis, though he still went on flying and was wounded in April.

Galland was one of the comparatively rare Luftwaffe officers who was both a highly distinguished fighter pilot and a thoughtful commander with new ideas of his own. His book *The First and the Last* is interesting reading and gives a very clear insight into some of the causes of what went wrong with the Luftwaffe. Galland himself always wanted to strengthen the fighter arm, particularly in jet planes and night-fighters, and with the agreement of both Speer and Milch advocated three to four times as many as were allocated in plans. But his efforts to urge

Göring to concentrate on a 'Reich defence force' were only partly successful. His personal record was impeccable—his total of 103 enemy aircraft shot down put him in the same class as Mölders and Marseille—and he had the confidence of his pilots. He acted as commander of fighters in Sicily in 1943.

It was about that time, in May, that Hitler told him that the Luftwaffe without Milch 'just did not bear thinking about'. As a popular hero Galland for long stood high in Hitler's favour, but he could not persuade the Führer that the development, increased production, and deployment in fighting squadrons of the ME-262 jet fighter was vital. Galland, who first flew the plane in May 1943 nearly a year after Wendel, chief test pilot of Messerschmitts, had first tried it out, recorded that until the 262 was available the Luftwaffe was virtually powerless against Mosquito raids, so fast and manoeuvrable was the wooden British plane.

Galland reported to the Air Ministry in 1944: 'Between January and April 1944 our daytime fighters lost over 1,000 pilots. They included our best squadron, Gruppe and Geschwader commanders. Each incursion of the enemy is costing us some fifty aircrew. The time has come when our weapon is in sight of collapse'.

In the final weeks of the war Galland led Jagdverband 44 Squadron flying ME-262s with success. Had this plane been widely available earlier it would have posed some problems to the Americans and British.

The modern Federal German Air Force owes much to the enthusiasm and experience of Lieutenant-General Adolf Galland, and it is pleasant to record that he has for many years been a popular figure with British aviation circles.

Colonel-General Günther Korten succeeded Jeschonnek as Chief of Staff of the Luftwaffe on 25 August 1943, and held the post until he died two days after being wounded in the 20 July 1944 explosion at Rastenburg.

Korten, a Prussian, was a believer both in long-range strategic bombing and in strong fighter defences. He was an ardent Nazi, but against the invasion of Russia. In 1940 he had been Chief of Staff of 3rd Air Fleet. From June 1941 to 23 August 1943 he commanded 1st Air Fleet on the Russian front, with the additional command—between October 1942 and April 1943 when it was disbanded—of Luftwaffe Command Don. This was formed by Göring to co-operate with Army Group Don. Korten was at one time a close friend of Göring, but by 1943 their relations had become very strained. Before he died, Korten told Milch that he wanted to resign by August 1944 at the latest, as with the best will in the world he could not get on with Göring. Milch thought very highly of Korten, who had worked for him as a staff officer, and Korten managed to gain Hitler's confidence. He even managed to take away six fighter squadrons, a small enough number,

143

from the Eastern front to strengthen the Reich's defences. He promised Hitler 400 long-range bombers by mid-February 1944, though their entry into operational service was delayed until late March because of training.

Von Richthofen noted in his diary for 22 May 1944: 'Korten is very optimistic. I.e. in this connection he exactly follows the views of the Führer's headquarters. He has far-reaching plans for the re-organization of Luftwaffe command. Conflicts with Milch and his organization, but of a concrete nature and fully justified. Plans to expand the Luftwaffe; what Korten wants is quite sensible. But he is no fighter, so we must wait and see whether he manages to avoid all the pitfalls.'

Stauffenberg's bomb took the decision out of Korten's hands.

Korten was succeeded on 1 August 1944 by General of Fliers Werner Kreipe, a one-time A.D.C. of Milch, and an enthusiast for the ME-262. Kreipe was young and comparatively junior in the Luftwaffe hierarchy. He had been a major in 1940, had commanded a bomber squadron at the beginning of the war, and then been Chief Operations Officer of 3rd Air Fleet. He came to his job with energy and enthusiasm, but by October 1944 had resigned in disgust. In 1951 General Kreipe was appointed adviser in civil aviation in the West German Traffic Ministry.

Kreipe was succeeded by General of Fliers Karl Koller, who lasted from 2 November 1944 to the end of the war. Koller was a sound but uninspiring staff officer who had been Korten's deputy in 1943 and 1944. He had been a colonel on the staff of Sperrle's 3rd Air Fleet in the Battle of Britain, and then became Chief of Staff to Sperrle. He was given to plaintive outbursts in his diary, having discovered when he took over that things were even worse than he thought. Thus he wrote on 24 July 1944: 'Was General Korten, who repeatedly emphasized in his speeches that he and I were the closest personal friends, really so faithless? Or is there a lack of moral courage somewhere else, is somebody taking cover behind the dead general?' And two days later: 'The Jeschonnek and Milch episodes are common knowledge. Brauchitsch [Hitler's Air Force A.D.C., not the Field-Marshal] and Diesing once told me they were sick of the game and wouldn't ever intrigue again, but "cats can't stop mousing"!'

He also wrote later: 'Not counting 1940, Hitler conducted every operation and almost every battle without reserves. One cannot improvise wars with only half-prepared forces, unless one risks everything, and this is actually what has been done'. On 25 April 1945 he told Field-Marshal von Greim, in the context of trying to explain away Göring's attempt at peace talks, 'It's not for me to defend the Reichsmarschall. He has too many faults for that. He has made my life unbearable— he has treated me abominably, telling me he'd have me court-martialled and killed, for no reason at all, and threatening to shoot General Staff officers in front of the assembled General Staff. I know that the Reichsmarschall did nothing on the twenty-second and twenty-third of April that could be called treason'. Greim unrelentingly disagreed with Koller.

Casualties in dismissal were not as high in the Luftwaffe as they were in the Army, but Göring relied over much on his old Great War fliers and did not promote enough younger men to important jobs. When he did, as in the case of Jeschonnek and Galland, he gave them insufficient support and freedom. Casualties by accident or enemy action were higher than among equivalent ranks in the R.A.F. Two divisional commanders of Luftwaffe Field Divisions, the 4th and 6th, for example, were killed in action in Russia—Lieutenant-Generals Pistorius and Peschel. As a result of the inquiry set up by Göring after Udet's suicide, Engineer-Generals Reidenbaum and Tschersich were arrested, and were dismissed by Milch whose close technical and planning advisers they had been. Major-General Ploch, who had been Chief of Staff to Udet from 1936 to 1941, was dismissed shortly before Udet's death and sent to Russia.

The German airborne forces, which had some spectacular successes in the earlier part of the war, never realized their full potential, largely due to Hitler's fear of excessive casualties after the costly invasion of Crete. In the latter half of the war they were mainly used as infantry in a normal ground role. They were, however, crack troops, and their performance in Africa, Russia, Italy, and north-west Europe was invariably first-class. They had a high morale and were usually imbued with Nazi spirit.

Their commander throughout the war was Colonel-General Kurt Student, who had formed the airborne and parachute divisions. Göring was at pains to explain to Hitler that Student's distinctive, unusually slow form of speech was only a mannerism and did not mean that he was foolish.

As early as 1924, when he was head of the air technical branch of the Reichswehr, Captain Student was running glider instruction courses. He became a colonel in 1934, and a Major-General in 1938 when he formed the first, secret battalions of paratroops. In 1939, Lieutenant-General Student's 7th Air Division was not used in Poland, but only because Hitler did not want to give away his new weapon. As VII Air Corps it was used with high success in operations in the Low Countries and in Norway, at Rotterdam, Moerdijk, Dordrecht, Eben Emael, Oslo, and Stavanger, to mention a few airborne actions. Of these the most spectacular was the capture of the Belgian fort of Eben Emael, when gliders actually landed on the roof.

Student was unlucky to be wounded by a stray S.S. bullet in the fighting in Rotterdam, and was out of action for some time. He returned to take control of the airborne operation against Crete in May 1941, in which his XI Air Corps were the principal participants, backed up by the whole of 5th Mountain Division; parts of 6th Mountain Division; an armoured regiment; an engineer battalion; and two light anti-aircraft units. The air cover was provided by the whole of von Richthofen's VIII Air Corps. Even so, Crete was no pushover for the Germans, and the fate of the parachutists hung in the balance for the first two days. Every single air landing and drop had been opposed, and the casualties—particularly among senior officers—were very heavy. One crack battalion was nearly wiped out.

There were those in the Wehrmacht in favour of cutting losses and calling the whole thing off. Milton Shulman has written that Student's rise 'was due primarily to his undoubted loyalty and close personal association with Hitler', but Alan Clark is on surer ground when he describes him as 'a commander of the highest calibre. He had two attributes that are seldom found together. He had a fresh and unconventional approach to problems together with a calm and thoughtful manner'.

Student thus thought things through, and decided to concentrate everything against Maleme. Despite the fact that his battle plan was captured by the New Zealanders, he was in the end successful. (Student had not been allowed by Löhr, co-ordinating the whole operation, to go to Crete himself.) But it was an expensive victory. Student lost nearly 6,500 men, and the Luftwaffe 272 Junkers 52s. Allied casualties were about 5,000. Among the first Germans to die was the commander of the 7th Air Division, Lieutenant-General Wilhelm Süssman, whose glider containing many of the divisional staff crashed on Aegina with fatal results to all. Süssman had been destined to lead the centre assault on the Canea-Suda area. His place was taken by Colonel Richard Heidrich (later Lieutenant-General), of the 3rd Air Regiment. Equally bad news for the operation was that Major-General Eugen Meindl, in charge of the western attack, was badly wounded soon after landing near Maleme. Colonel (later Lieutenant-General) Hermann Bernhard 'Papa' Ramcke, one of the great characters of the German fighting men, took over. The leadership of Heidrich and Ramcke rose to the occasion, and the Maleme crisis was overcome.

In 1942 Student prepared for months for the invasion of Malta, upon which he was very keen. Like Raeder and Korten he was a firm believer in more action in the Mediterranean. But it was not to be. In June 1942 Hitler called Student to Rastenburg, called off the proposed invasion, and told him: 'I forbid you to return to Italy. You will stay in Berlin'.

The rest of Student's war was, therefore, a frustrating experience, since his airborne troops were never used properly on a large scale again. He himself, however, held high command in 1944 as G.O.C.

146

1st Parachute Army, which by mid-September held a front from east of Hasselt to Antwerp, and caused no little trouble to the British and Canadians. Student led them forcefully, and, as the official British war history relates, 'had shown great energy in building up a coherent defence of the country for which he was responsible, using his own troops and any others he could get hold of'. He was partly responsible, under Model, for organising the defence of Arnhem, and from midnight on 29 October 1944 assumed command of all operations in north-west Holland. In early November his Army Group 'H', consisting of eleven divisions from 1st Parachute Army and 25th Army, took over the front from Roermond to the Dutch coast. Student was relieved by Colonel-General Blaskowitz in February 1945, but maintained control of 1st Parachute Army. Anyone who fought against this formation will remember how tough, well-trained, and ruthless were the parachutists. They fought to the last, and some of the credit over the years must undoubtedly go to the man who was, in Kesselring's words, 'a guiding, clear-sighted leader'.

Student picked his parachute leaders well. Meindl rose to be a General of Parachutists, and as a Lieutenant-General commanded the II Parachute Corps brilliantly both in Normandy and later. He also commanded an assault parachute regiment and the 'Meindl Division', later 21st Luftwaffe Field Division, in Russia and played an important part in the relief of Kholm in 1942. Although II Parachute Corps lost heavily in the Falaise Gap battle, Meindl succeeded in extricating 3rd Parachute Division, parts of 12th S.S. Panzer Division, and the headquarters of 7th Army, from the trap. When visited by von Kluge's son near St Lo in Normandy in late July 1944, Meindl told him: 'The time has come when Normandy can no longer be held. It cannot be held because the troops are exhausted. .... If your father knew what it means to operate against an enemy with a downright fabulous command of the air, then he would know that our only chance of doing anything useful at all is by attacking at night. Tomorrow's tank attack is going to be a failure, because it is scheduled on too broad a front and because it isn't going to start until dawn, which means it will take place in daylight. Those tanks are going to be smashed. And all that's left for the grenadiers to do is to lie down and sacrifice their lives. It's heart-breaking to have to stand by and watch'.

Meindl, however, was no great admirer of Student, of whom he said, 'Student had big ideas but not the faintest conception as to how they were to be carried out'. Student himself was only informed of the Ardennes attack eight days before it started. He pressed for a share in the glory (only one parachute battalion was used in the Ardennes) and was allotted three infantry divisions, two parachute divisions, and 150 armoured vehicles for a push to Antwerp on 27 December, depending however on Model's success in the Ardennes. This never came off, and Student told Shulman: 'My troops were scheduled to cross the Maas the moment that either one of Dietrich's (S.S.) or Manteuffel's armies reached the Meuse River in the Ardennes. Since this was not reached by the New Year I was forced to abandon my plans'. General Eugen-Felix Schwalbe, commanding LXXXVIII Corps, who had directed the evacuation across the Scheldt of Colonel-General Gustav von Zangen's 15th Army in the autumn, saving some 65,000 men and 225 guns, was to be the assault leader. But he was not told how his troops were to be supplied when they reached the south bank of the Maas and complained that 'General Student was very vague about such details'.

General Alfred Schlemm had an outstanding fighting record. He had had an embarrassing experience when the Russians captured Nevel in 1943, and 2nd Luftwaffe Field Division from his II Luftwaffe Field Corps had broken and run—a débâcle which caused Göring to send 600 aircraft and extra Flak batteries to the area. But after being Chief of Staff to Student in the Crete operation he had taken over I Parachute Corps in Italy, and had done well at the containment of the Anzio bridgehead. On the Albano Road, in the defence of Rome, on the Caesar Line, at Lanurio and Campoleone, he had increased his reputation, and in 1944 and 1945 he fought a series of excellent defensive actions with 1st Parachute Army. Schlemm did not at all look the part of a typical Prussian general, being shortish, stocky, and having a large nose, a rather broad, Slavic face, and a dark skin, as Shulman relates.

Whatever his appearance, he had fought skilful defensive actions at Smolensk and Vitebsk, and at Anzio. He was transferred from Italy in November 1944 to the West to take over 1st Parachute Army, holding a front from Roermond to Wesel and the Rhine. In February 1945, when the weather was foul, Schlemm expected an attack through the Reichswald, though Blaskowitz and Rundstedt thought that the Americans would attack south of Roermond, and the British in the Venlo area. Schlemm was proved right when the Canadians attacked on 8 February in the Reichswald. Schlemm disposed of three parachute, three infantry, and three panzer divisions, which engaged the Canadians, British, and Americans between the Maas and Rhine rivers in what General Eisenhower described as 'some of the fiercest fighting of the whole war'. Schlemm maintained an unbroken front, though with heavy losses, until the advance of the American 9th Army over the Roer from 23 February onwards threatened his rear, since they breached the lines of 15th Army; by 2 March München-Gladbach, Krefeld, Roermond, and Venlo had fallen, and Schlemm had to make a fighting withdrawal out of encirclement. He was then ordered by Hitler not to allow any Rhine bridge to fall into enemy hands, on penalty of a court-martial and possible death sentence. 'Since I had nine bridges in my army sector, I could see my hopes for a long life rapidly dwindling', said Schlemm. At last Schlemm's defensive area round Wesel shrank to an area of some fifteen square miles crowded with troops, whose only escape route was across the bridge at Wesel. By 9 March Schlemm had got away the best part of three Corps, and II Parachute Corps caused 52nd Lowland Division a good many casualties in defending the Rhine. But on 10 March Schlemm pulled back his last troops and blew the Wesel bridges. In the past month's bitter fighting the Americans, Canadians, and British had lost some 23,000 men, but the Germans over 90,000 men.

In conducting his delaying action under very difficult conditions, not the least of which was direct interference from Hitler, Schlemm had proved his worth as a general.

The Luftwaffe was generally a thoroughly indoctrinated Nazi force, but Schlemm admitted after the war to Shulman that had he known on 20 July 1944 what he discovered subsequently about the true state of affairs, he would have had 'every sympathy with the assassins'.

The Luftwaffe, often working under very hard conditions, was just too widely stretched over too many fronts during the war to be able to cope with the demands made upon it in all of them. Its early successes were remarkable, and for a time there is no doubt that it ruled the skies. Later on, its replacements in aircraft could not keep up with its losses, and many of its members found themselves taking part in infantry and armoured battles on the ground for which they had not been properly trained. The backing given to it by the aircraft factories and the Quartermaster-General's staff, under General Hans-Georg von Seidel, was remarkably resilient in view of the grave problems from enemy bombing, weather, and rough conditions on the ground and in transport. Thus General von Seidel at one time reported, 'Of 100,000 Luftwaffe vehicles in the East, only 15 per cent still functioning early in January 1942'. The great work done by the Luftwaffe's transport command, also over-stretched, under General of Fliers Joachim Coeler from October 1941 to January 1945, should not go unremarked.

In all, the Luftwaffe lost 96,917 men killed, wounded, or missing during the war. It lost 19,923 bombers, more than the total produced during the war, and 52,042 fighters—staggering totals.

The Waffen S.S. Generals

The Waffen S.S. posed problems to the Army in some ways similar to, in others greater than, those presented by the Luftwaffe's Field Divisions. They were trained differently, they had their own equipment and uniforms, they were not under Army discipline and often conducted feuds with the Army, and they were bound only to their own officers, and to Himmler and Hitler. In actual practice, of course, it soon became impossible for an Army or Corps commander to control S.S. formations unless their commanders were willing to obey and co-operate, and the more level-headed and responsible of them soon did. But the old rivalry between Army and S.S. continued. Thus the latter were used strictly in their own formations, and by the end of the war had even reached Army strength. By then, however, the élite, separatist character of the Waffen S.S. had largely disappeared, due to casualties, and for the last two years at least of the war it became less and less different from the Army, except in certain cases. (This élite character in no way applied to the Allgemeine S.S., the S.D., the Gestapo, and concentration camp guards, who usually had all of the viciousness of the Waffen S.S. but little of their courage or skill at arms.)

Heinrich Himmler fought for years to get the Waffen S.S. properly recognized, and in the end succeeded. In 1939 and 1940 they made up comparatively little of the armed forces, but as time went by he succeeded in getting them the best equipment, and their fanatical bravery and ruthlessness on many fronts earned them a fearsome if unenviable reputation. A large number of the S.S. divisions became panzer ones, and whereas the B.E.F. in 1940 encountered only two (infantry) S.S. divisions, by Normandy in 1944 there were two good S.S. Panzer Corps under Rommel, plus four S.S. infantry corps; in the Ardennes there was the complete 6th S.S. Panzer Army. In Russia six S.S. Corps were used, including a Mountain S.S. corps, four S.S. Panzer divisions, two S.S. Cavalry divisions (including the Florian Geyer), an S.S. Police Panzer Grenadier division, an S.S. Panzer Grenadier division, and several S.S. brigades and battalions. Even so, the Army managed to keep the S.S. ratio down to an acceptable one, and the S.S. never reached the great numbers that Himmler would have liked. A great number of its personnel were, of course, kept busy as extermination squads, concentration camp guards, and security forces of one sort or another.

Anyone who fought against Waffen S.S. troops was unwise not to have a very healthy respect for them. They were tough, ruthless, well-trained, and sometimes savage. Various atrocities were committed by them, such as the massacre at Oradour, but in general they were well-disciplined; and if they stood out from their fellow Germans in captivity it was because of their arrogance. They considered themselves the Nazi élite, and in many cases they were feared by Germans as well as by the occupied countries.

It is perhaps surprising that the Waffen S.S. did not produce more outstanding leaders than it did. In fact there were only four or five, and at least three of these had the advantage of having served for years in the regular Army. It may well be that intellect was not an essential quality for success in the S.S., and the fact that it considered itself apart from, even above, the Army did not help when it came to fighting battles.

Unquestionably the ablest military commander in the S.S. was Colonel-General Paul Hausser, who was 65 in 1945. He had been at a Prussian Cadet College and fought in the old Imperial Army. He retired in 1932 having reached the rank of lieutenant-general. He was an officer of the old school, experienced in staff work. When the S.S. Verfügungstruppe were formed in 1933, the forerunners of the Waffen S.S., Hausser joined Himmler's new organisation and set up a training school for them at Brunswick in late 1934. Between 1935 and 1939 Hausser was in charge of the training of the Waffen S.S., and he made a good job of it.

In Russia in 1941 Lieutenant-General Hausser commanded the S.S. 'Das Reich' Motorized Division, which operated in the Yelnya Bend and in the advance to Moscow. It suffered heavy casualties at Borodino —where the T.34 Stalin tanks appeared for the first time *en masse*— and one of them was Hausser himself, who lost an eye and part of his jaw. He was out of action for a time, and was to be wounded again in Normandy. In the great Kursk tank battle Hausser commanded the S.S. Panzer Corps in Hoth's 4th Panzer Army, and had 300 tanks, 120 assault guns, and a complete brigade of Nebelwerfer mortars. His Corps made excellent progress at first, gaining 20 miles, but was finally stopped in the tremendous tank battle at Prokhorovka, in which 1,500 tanks took part.

Rattled by the Allied landing in Sicily, Hitler ordered Hausser's tanks to be withdrawn from the Kursk battle on 17 July, because he was going to send the whole Corps to Italy. In fact most of it remained in Russia for several months.

Hausser had requested tanks for the S.S. Leibstandarte Adolf Hitler and Das Reich divisions in August 1941, and these formations were not sent east until early 1943. In February Kharkov, a city that changed hands several times during the war, was held by the Germans but heavily threatened and almost encircled by two Russian armies. Hitler

151

gave orders that it was not to be evacuated. It fell to Hausser to try to conduct a hopeless defence, for Manstein's efforts to get Hitler to rescind his order failed. On 14 February 1943 Hausser noted that he had not enough forces to seal off enemy penetrations north-west of the city, and that the Russians were greatly strengthened. Kharkov had been dynamited, and his war diary continued: 'City burning. Systematic withdrawal increasingly improbable each day. Assumptions underlying Kharkov's strategic importance no longer valid. Request renewed Führer decision whether Kharkov to be defended to the last man'.

Hausser rang up General of Mountain Troops Hubert Lanz, his superior and the commander of Army Detachment Lanz, to beg that he be allowed to disengage and break out. Lanz stuck to Hitler's cast-iron order to defend the city, though he sympathized with Hausser, and stuck to it more than once. Hausser disobeyed, and ordered a fighting evacuation of the S.S. Panzer Corps and of Lieutenant-General Erhard Raus's XI Corps. Even after the break-out had been ordered, Hausser received another order from Lanz to defend the city, but ignored it.

When the news reached Hitler he was naturally furious, the more so because it was his beloved S.S. that had disobeyed him. But it became clear that Hausser's action had saved two vital Panzer divisions and the 'Grossdeutschland' Panzer Grenadier Division; their break-out through the single remaining gap in the Udy sector of Kharkov was a fine performance, and enabled Major-General G. Postel's 320th Infantry Division to link up again with Army Detachment Lanz.

Four weeks later Hausser's troops with the same divisions, which included the S.S. Totenkopf, retook Kharkov. Hausser was under Hoth's orders, who did not want the troops to get involved in street fighting, and there is some question whether Hausser obeyed Hoth's orders strictly enough. On the whole it seems that he did largely do what Hoth ordered. At any rate it was a triumph for the S.S., but Hitler forebore to give Hausser any honour for several months, while immediately decorating Major-Generals Hörnlein and Postel, of the 'Grossdeutschland' and 320th Infantry Divisions, with the Oak Leaves to the Knight's Cross.

In Normandy Hausser, now General of S.S., commanded II S.S. Panzer Corps, which had grown out of his original S.S. Panzer Corps. On 29 June he attacked the British 2nd Army front from the Evrecy area with 250 tanks and 100 guns to break through the Caen-Bayeux road. Although his tank crews were mostly veterans, that attack was a failure. Hausser told Shulman why after the war: 'It was scheduled to begin at seven o'clock in the morning, but hardly had the tanks assembled when they were attacked by fighter-bombers. This disrupted the troops so much that the attack did not start again until two-thirty in the afternoon. But even then it could not get going. The murderous

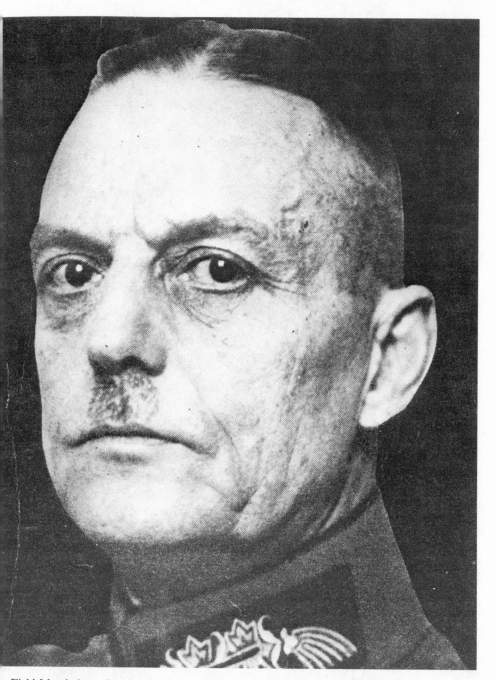

Field-Marshal von Rundstedt

2. Hitler with Field-Marshal von Brauchitsch

3. Colonel-General Blaskowitz

4. Field-Marshal von Leeb

5. Field-Marshal List

6. Field-Marshal von Bock

7. Field-Marshal von Kluge

8. Field-Marshal von Küchler

9. Field-Marshal Göring

10. Field-Marshal Milch

11. Field-Marshal Sperrle

12. General Christiansen

13. Lieutenant-General Galland

14. Colonel-General Student

15. Field-Marshal von Greim

16. Colonel-General Dietrich

17. General Bach-Zelewski

18. General Gille

19. General Steiner

20. Field-Marshal von Kleist   21. Field-Marshal von Weichs

22. Field-Marshals von Reichenau and von Brauchitsch with Hitler

23. Colonel-Generals von Reichenau and Keitel with Hitler

24. Lieutenant-General Dietl

25. Field-Marshal Busch

26. Field-Marshal Model

27. Field-Marshal von Reichenau

28. Field-Marshal von Witzleben

29. General of Infantry von Stülpnagel

30. Colonel-General Halder

31. Colonel-General Halder with Field-Marshal von Brauchitsch

32. Colonel-General Zeitzler

33. Field-Marshal von Manstein

34. Field-Marshal Kesselring

35. Colonel-General Hoth with Field-Marshal Rommel

36. Colonel-General Guderian

fire from naval guns in the Channel and the terrible British artillery destroyed the bulk of our attacking force in its assembly area. The few tanks that did manage to go forward were easily stopped by the English anti-tank guns. In my opinion the attack was prepared too quickly. I wanted to wait another two days, but Hitler insisted that it be launched on 29 June'.

In early July 1944 Hausser was appointed directly by Hitler, who did not bother to consult Rommel, to take Dollmann's place as Commander of 7th Army. He thus became the first S.S. officer ever to command an Army, and reached the rank of S.S. Colonel-General. His next big task was the German counter-attack in early August at Mortain against the Americans. Von Kluge was directing the operation, while General of Panzer Troops Baron von Funck was the actual ground commander of the panzer formations. In an Order of the Day Hausser told his troops, 'On the successful execution of the operation the Führer has ordered depends the decision of the war in the West and with it perhaps the decision of the war itself. Commanders of all ranks must be absolutely clear as to the enormous significance of this fact'.

The Mortain counter-offensive was a failure, but it had been overtaken by events, for the American 3rd Army captured Le Mans on 9 August. On 10 August Hausser asked Kluge to call off the attack, but Kluge was bound by Hitler's orders, and could not. The Americans and Canadians attacked too strongly themselves for the Germans to continue, and finally on 13 August the German forces were allowed to retreat behind the Seine. It was far too late.

Next came the hell of the Falaise Gap. Hausser, responsible for the withdrawal of all the fighting formations left, gave the order for a general break-out on the night of 19–20 August. Caught in the cauldron himself, Hausser was marching with his men when he was badly hit in the face by shrapnel. He managed to escape on the back of a tank of 1st S.S. Panzer Division.

Hausser temporarily commanded Army Group B after Kluge's death, but was succeeded by Model. Hausser was a fearless and competent commander, who understood his Army colleagues and, unlike most of his S.S. colleagues, fitted to command an Army. He was highly respected by his men. Guderian called him 'one of the most outstanding wartime commanders', and Kesselring 'the most popular and ablest of the S.S. generals'. The German military historian Paul Carell calls him 'a man of common sense, strategic skill, and with the courage to stand up to his superiors'.

Hitler had ambivalent feelings about Hausser. 'He looks like a fox . . . with his crafty little eyes,' the Führer once said; while Guderian added, 'He's smart as a whip,' and Keitel, 'Very quick on the trigger'.

For a man of his age, nearly 60 when the war began, Hausser

showed remarkable stamina and fitness. He caustically described his chief Himmler, of whom he was not in awe, as 'a fantastic idealist with both feet planted firmly several inches above the ground—a mighty queer bird'.

Hausser after the war sought to re-establish the reputation of the S.S., and claimed that 'the S.S. was really the NATO army in prototype, in ideal', a judgement that rings either sourly or humorously to those who encountered that pitiless organization.

The prime favourite of the S.S. generals with Hitler was Josef 'Sepp' Dietrich, who rose to the rank of S.S. colonel-general. Here was one of the original Nazi storm-troopers, an old-time rowdy, bully-boy and Party wheel-horse, who for many years was Hitler's chauffeur and body-guard. Dietrich had been in the regular Army between 1911 and 1918, and ended as a senior N.C.O. This short, burly tough who looked like a butcher (which he had been) or a chucker-out, was a veteran of the Free Corps and of street fighting against the Communists. He joined the S.S. in its very early days in 1928; by 1933 he was major-general and by 1934 a lieutenant-general. In 1932 he commanded the S.S. Stabswache, and in 1933 the personal bodyguard of Hitler, the S.S. Leibstandarte Adolf Hitler. As such, he was one of the few men who had Hitler's implicit trust, and this typical Nazi rowdy, an ex-sergeant-major with four years of fighting in the Great War behind him but no success in civilian life, warranted it through his loyalty and zeal. As a strong-arm boy Dietrich had few rivals.

He played a leading and unsavoury part in the 'Night of the Long Knives'—the suppression of Röhm and other S.A. leaders on 30 June 1934. He commanded the S.S. execution squad at the Stadelheim Prison near Munich. One of the senior S.A. leaders arrested, August Schneid-huber, police prefect of Munich, appealed to him, 'Comrade Sepp, this is madness! We are innocent!' But Dietrich repeated to him, 'You have been condemned to death by the Führer for high treason. Heil Hitler!'

Even Dietrich was affected by the numerous executions, however, and recalled later, 'Just before Schneidhuber's turn I grew sick of it, and left'. He reported back to Hitler at the Brown House when the executions had been completed. Years later, in May 1957 at Munich, Dietrich was convicted of 'aiding and abetting manslaughter during the Röhm purge', and sentenced to—18 months! Yet even before the war he was guilty, according to Curt Riess, of 'every crime from murder to petty theft'. The L.A.H. at Stadelheim with Theodor Eicke's Toten-kopfverbände were the murderers of Munich, and Dietrich was at their head.

Sepp Dietrich commanded the Adolf Hitler regiment (not yet a division) in France in 1940. Near Watten in late May he ignored the 'stop order' and allowed a scheduled S.S. attack to go forward, breaching the Canal Line temporarily and securing a height near Watten. In the Esquebeck area on 28 May 1940 Dietrich was nearly killed when his car was shot up by the British. It caught fire, and to treat his burns Dietrich had to cover himself with mud from head to foot. A complete battalion helped by tanks had to be used by the Germans to take Esquebeck from the rear and rescue Dietrich.

In Greece and Russia Dietrich first commanded the L.A.H. Division (the 1st S.S. Panzer Grenadier, later Panzer Division), though at first it was still only a brigade in strength. It was, however, magnificently equipped, with its own heavy weapons, self-propelled ack-ack guns, self-propelled assault guns, armoured cars, and carriers. It gave a good account of itself at Rostov, Stalingrad, and the third battle of Kharkov. According to Dietrich, by 1943 only 30 of his original 23,000 men were alive and uncaptured—but this was an exaggeration.

By 1944 Dietrich was in charge of 1 S.S. Panzer Corps in Belgium and France, with headquarters at Brussels. He was directly under the orders of von Rundstedt, who was to describe Dietrich in biting terms: 'He is decent, but stupid'. General of Panzer Troops von Geyr thought him 'complaisant and comradely'.

Dietrich was ordered to drive the British into the sea on 6 June 1944 by attacking from Caen, using 12th S.S. Panzer Division 'Hitler Jugend', 21st Panzer, and Panzer Lehr Divisions. His attack was to start on 7 June: unfortunately the Panzer Lehr Division was many miles away and never got to the front on time, and bitter British artillery, naval and air barrages, backed up by good work from British tanks and anti-tank guns, completely halted Dietrich's attack before it made any significant progress. Apparently Dietrich, who had a well-earned reputation for making inaccurate reports to higher commands, did not pass on to Rommel the news of this reverse, for Rommel certainly knew nothing of it on 8 June. After three weeks of Normandy fighting Dietrich's troops, some of the toughest in the German forces, were gravely weakened and no longer capable of concerted attacks. 'I'm being bled white and I'm getting nowhere!' he complained to Rommel.

After the July plot Dietrich was promoted to command the newly formed 5th Panzer Army on the Caen front, but this was rapidly weakened when von Kluge took away from him three panzer divisions for the Avranches counter-attack. This left Dietrich unable to hold Falaise. He protested, but again it was a Hitler order. Dietrich, as General Speidel has related, normally co-operated in a 'soldierly' manner with the Army commanders. By now he was thoroughly disillusioned with Hitler, at any rate as a military genius. Adding to his troubles were disputes with the Luftwaffe, which disposed of a large number of 88 mm. dual-purpose and anti-aircraft guns. Major-General Hermann Plocher, a parachutist who had succeeded Keller as Sperrle's Chief of Staff in the West, told Shulman how 96 of these were sent to Normandy immediately the invasion was known. Early in August another 40 were sent to Dietrich's area, but the guns, like their predecessors, were not under his command or the Army's, but directly under the experienced Luftwaffe Ack-Ack General Pickert. Endless arguments raged about where they should be sited, but von Rundstedt finally allowed Pickert to choose the sites. Dietrich told Shulman: 'I constantly ordered these guns to stay forward and act in an anti-tank role against Allied armour. My orders were just as often countermanded by Pickert, who moved them back into the rear areas to protect administrative sites. I asked time and again that these guns be put under my command, but I was always told by the High Command that it was impossible'. Here one cannot but sympathize with Dietrich.

On 10 August Kluge announced that the Avranches counter-attack, which had bogged down, would be continued. This was against his own better judgement and the warnings of Hausser, General of Panzer Troops Heinz Eberbach, and Dietrich himself. The latter recalled: 'But the Field-Marshal had received a new order from Berlin insisting that he go ahead. There was only one person to blame for this stupid, impossible operation. That madman Adolf Hitler. It was a Führer order. What else could we do?'

Dietrich was rightly afraid for Falaise, and after that battle his Army was never again the same. He became responsible for defending the Seine line, but that too had to be abandoned soon. Then the Somme fell. After that, Dietrich busied himself with trying to rebuild his shattered divisions. His next task was to command 6th S.S. Panzer Army in the Ardennes, using the S.S. divisions, reconstituted, that he had had in Normandy, and a number of scratch, hastily formed infantry divisions plus a parachute division. Dietrich's task—to bridge the Meuse between Liege and Huy and advance north-west towards, or even to, Antwerp— proved an impossible one. Hitler decided that the S.S. must be given the greatest strength, and even when Dietrich was bogged down he sent the main reinforcements to him rather than to General of Panzer Troops Hasso von Manteuffel and his 5th Panzer Army, which had made some progress and had a chance of success. Rundstedt was to blame Dietrich for making a mess of the offensive—though he admitted from the beginning that he saw no chance of its success— but Dietrich had never been included in the planning and did not really believe in the attack. His right wing was halted by the Americans at Monschau, and though his left penetrated 30 miles, beyond Stavelot after by-passing Malmedy, it too was held fast by the Americans after a few days.

At the end of January 1945 Dietrich was given his last assignment— to halt the Russians pouring into Hungary. With his now badly battered 6th S.S. Panzer Army he did his best, but he was driven back to

Vienna, where he was ordered to make a stand in front of the city and on no account to withdraw into it. But in the face of superior numbers and equipment, Dietrich had to fall back into Vienna, losing touch with General of Panzer Troops Hermann Balck's 6th Army on his right flank as he did so. Balck was angered by having his flank completely exposed, and said to General of Infantry Otto Wöhler, commanding Army Group South, 'If the Leibstandarte can't hold their ground, what do you expect us to do?' This remark, typical of Army-S.S. rivalry, but uttered in the heat of the moment, found its way back to Hitler, though not through Wöhler, who was anti-Nazi.

Hitler was incensed, and sent the following message via Keitel to Dietrich: 'The Führer believes that the troops have not fought as the situation demanded and orders that the S.S. divisions Adolf Hitler, Das Reich, Totenkopf, and Hohenstauffen be stripped of their armbands'. This was equivalent to removing, say, the Desert Rat or the HD sign for members of the British 7th Armoured or Highland Divisions. Dietrich was incredulous. He summoned his divisional commanders, showed them the signal, and said, 'There's your reward for all that you've done these past five years'. He then ignored the order, and wrote a stiff message back to Hitler's headquarters. The story is, aprocyphal though it may be, that he packed all his decorations up in a chamber pot and sent that off to Hitler too. Whether true or not, it catches the right spirit of Dietrich's feelings.

For all his brutal background, Dietrich emerges as a much more human figure than Himmler. He was at least a fighting man, and showed considerable common sense in his assessments. But it is questionable whether he was qualified to command an Army. No such doubts at one time had bothered Hitler about his qualifications.

Sepp Dietrich, who had a certain swaggering bravado and good nature, had been pumped up in the Nazi Press to become almost a national hero. Göbbels, in his diary for 27 January 1942 writes: 'Sepp Dietrich is a real comrade and makes one think of a Napoleonic general. If we had twenty men like that as divisional commanders we wouldn't have to worry about the Eastern Front'. On 9 March 1943 the little doctor becomes more specific: 'Sepp Dietrich enjoys his (Hitler's) unlimited confidence. He considers him one of our best troop commanders and expects miracles from him. He is, so to speak, the Blücher of the National Socialist movement.' At another time Dietrich is compared with Marshal Ney.

One should not forget the sinister side of Sepp Dietrich's character. In Russia, when it had been discovered at GPU headquarters at Taganrog that the Russians had butchered six of his S.S. men, Dietrich ordered all Soviet prisoners taken in three days to be shot in reprisal. These amounted to some 4,000 men.

In 1946 Dietrich was given life imprisonment by an Allied Military

Court for his part in the shooting of American soldiers and Belgian civilians in the Malmédy massacre. In 1951 this sentence was reduced to twenty-five years, but in 1955 he was a free man again, released on parole. His life had been so closely bound up with Hitler's that the Führer should, perhaps, be allowed the last word on Dietrich: 'unique . . . a man who's simultaneously cunning, energetic, and brutal. Under his swashbuckling appearance, Dietrich is a serious, conscientious, scrupulous character. And what care he takes of his troops! He's a phenomenon in the class of people like Frundsburg, Zeithen and Seydlitz. He's a Bavarian Wrangel, someone irreplaceable. For the German people Sepp Dietrich is a national institution. For me personally there is also the fact that he is one of my oldest companions in the struggle'.

Yet during his last decade Dietrich often abused Hitler for his treatment of himself and the Waffen S.S. He died in 1966 at Ludwigsburg, aged 74.

S.S. Obergruppenführer (General) Felix Steiner was an ex-Army officer who resigned from the Reichswehr in 1933 as a major and joined the S.S. He commanded the S.S. motorised Regiment 'Grossdeutschland' in France in 1940, which fought against the B.E.F. withdrawing into the Dunkirk perimeter in the last days of May and the first of June. In Russia he led the S.S. 5th 'Viking' Division, composed of German, Scandinavian and Baltic volunteers, at Rostov in 1942 and at Tuapse, and in the penetration of the Maykop oil-fields. As a Panzer Grenadier division, again very well-equipped, this formation fought in 1943 at Krasnoarmeyskoye on the Voronezh front. In January 1944 he was commanding III S.S. Panzer Corps in the Oranienbaum bridgehead south-west of Leningrad, where he was forced back by strong Soviet attacks; but in February 1945, by desperate attacks from Pomerania, he won a measure of success by slowing down Marshal Zhukov's advance. By this time Steiner had been given command of a newly-formed 11th Army, but this was a misnomer, and its fighting troops amounted to hardly more than the strength of one full division. It was upon this so-called 11th Army that Hitler was to pin his last desperate hopes for the relief of Berlin, and his despairing cries of 'Where is Steiner?' were to echo through the condemned corridors of the bunker.

Despite Steiner's success in the Stargard area, in April there was not the slightest hope of his 15,000 men fighting their way to the relief of Berlin. His was a phantom army, and in any case Steiner had decided to seize the earliest opportunity to get away from the Russians and surrender to Eisenhower. He ignored or refused orders from Jodl, Keitel, and General Heinrici to attack to relieve Berlin. By 24 April even Hitler had realized that Steiner was a broken reed, and when General Burgdorf made some remark about Steiner's leading an attack north of Oranienburg, Hitler lost all control and shouted, 'Those arrogant, boring, indecisive S.S. leaders are no good to me any more. I do not wish Steiner to continue in command there under any circumstances'. Hitler now pinned his hopes on the Army and General Wenck, who had an equally fantastic and impossible task with his so-called 12th Army.

Steiner had been happier in command of III S.S. Corps, which was really an élite formation, in Curland. In former days he had been a particular protégé of Hitler. His reputation was high in the S.S. It was not enough to save Hitler or Berlin.

It is a terrible commentary on Hitler's Reich that a man of upper class background and good education like Erich von dem Bach-Zelewski should have misused his rank of General of S.S., even in Himmler's organization, in the way that he did, and been responsible not only for numerous reigns of terror and reprisal, but for actual massacres. Bach-Zelewski had not the excuse of being an unintelligent or boorish man— he was neither. What he was, in effect, was the ruthless and unscrupulous hatchet-man of the S.S., given special powers both by Himmler and, one regrets to say, by military commanders, to clean up partisans, dissidents, and trouble-makers in their areas. And the back areas in Russia and the Balkans could stretch very far.

On 31 January 1941 Himmler told Bach-Zelewski that the German master plan for the East necessitated the elimination of 30 million Slavs. Zelewski was later to become Higher S.S. and Police Chief of Russia Centre, and also Special Representative of the Reichsführer S.S. in charge of operations against partisan bands. He became responsible for large-scale massacres of the Jews, especially in the Minsk area where he had his headquarters. In 1942, not surprisingly perhaps, he had a nervous breakdown, hallucinations, and congestion of the liver. Bach-Zelewski was responsible for the 'pacification' of White Ruthenia, which led to further outrages. Although basically operating as a Police Chief with S.S. Police units he also frequently had Waffen S.S. under his command, such as the 1st S.S. Motorized Infantry Brigade and the Denmark Volunteer Corps. He was in charge of anti-partisan warfare in the Belorussian civil administrative area, and on 1 November 1943 used two divisional-sized units against uprisings in the Rossono area on Hitler's orders in 'Operation Heinrich', which was not completed. Back-Zelewski was a Pomeranian and former Army officer, who had had to resign from his infantry regiment on account of his Nazi intrigues; in 1931 he had been S.S. organizer on the Austrian frontier.

Such a man had obvious appeal for Hitler, who ranked him—with S.S. General Heinz Reinefarth and Colonel Otto Skorzeny—at the top of his list of favourite S.S. officers. Hitler used to say, 'Von dem

Bach is so clever, he can do anything, get round anything,' and 'this Bach-Zelewski is one of the cleverest of men'.

In the aftermath of the Warsaw uprising of August 1944 by General Bor, which the Russians failed to support, Bach-Zelewski was entrusted by Himmler with the job of quelling the insurrectionists. Using 12 S.S. Police companies and two of the most vicious formations in history —the S.S. Sonderkommando, which was made up of ex-convicts and concentration camp inmates of Oskar Dirlewanger, a pervert, sadist, convicted child rapist and gaolbird; and the White Russian brigade of Kaminski, composed chiefly of Russian prisoners of war—Bach-Zelewski left a trail of horror. Indescribable atrocities were committed by these formations, so much so that, according to Guderian, 'Von dem Bach took the precaution of having Kaminski shot and thus disposed of a possibly dangerous witness'.

This was not the first time that this repulsive man had turned on his own colleagues. In 1934 he had arranged for the murder of the S.S. leader Anton Freiherr von Hoberg und Buchwald, who was in no way implicated in any of Röhm's plans or S.A. activities. Bach-Zelewski simply wanted his post.

His conduct in Warsaw, as at Cracow, Budapest, and numerous other places, was indescribably savage. Von dem Bach was a disgrace to his aristocratic background, to his country, and even to the S.S. uniform. Yet he was the man nominated to negotiate with a hero like General Bor!

Bach-Zelewski was not tried until 1951, and then was awarded by his fellow-Germans—a 10-year suspended sentence. This for a man described by Heinz Hohne as 'Himmler's most aggressive Eastern minnion'. He should have been shot years before.

Von dem Bach gave evidence at Nuremberg, and a sorry sight he was. The best excuse that he could find for himself, apart from the universally adopted 'Orders are orders', was that everyone else knew what was going on and should bear equal responsibility. In his own words later: 'Coming out of prison after several years, I note that people are still asking who knew about these things. Nobody admits to having seen anything. Regardless of whether it is damaging to me or not, I am anxious to establish the truth. ... In view of my task, which was to wage total war against the partisans, I was probably the most travelled of the German generals during the war. I talked with hundreds of generals and thousands of officers of all ranks. ... Anybody who travelled knew from the first day that the Jews were being exterminated, by methods which, at the beginning, were not systematic. Later, when the Russian campaign was launched, the killing was explicitly prescribed, with the object of exterminating Judaism.'

Of the remaining S.S. generals, one of the nastiest pieces of work was Theodor Eicke, a notorious butcher, who commanded the S.S. Motorized Division Totenkopf in France in 1940. It saw comparatively little action and did not distinguish itself, some of its members running away during the British counter-attack at Arras. 'Papa' Eicke had a grisly past. He had been sprung by Himmler from a Würzburg psychiatric clinic to which Gauleiter Bürckel had had him committed as a dangerous lunatic. He became the first commandant of Dachau and inspector of concentration camps, and in 1934 reputedly was one of the two men who shot Ernst Röhm (the other being Lippert). Eicke, who combined ruthlessness with joviality, worked his way up the ladder to become head of the concentration camps system by 1939. As Dr Henry V. Dicks puts it: 'Dachau became the *alma mater* in which Eicke played his sinister, norm-setting role for numerous KZ (concentration camp) officers, drawing on his own record of brutality and chicanery derived from Free Corps and Feme days, combined with an old grudge against the regular army. Eicke also introduced the infamous skull-and-crossbones badge for "Death's Head" S.S. units.'

In 1940 men from his division under Captain Fritz Knochlein were responsible for the massacre of some 20 men of the Norfolk Regiment at Le Paradis, but Eicke managed to stall the official investigation. In November 1941 he told the S.S. recruiting authorities that his was an élite division which had no use for 'undisciplined and dishonest scoundrels and criminals'! In Russia Eicke commanded the Totenkopf Division and the 'Group Eicke' at Fedorovka in the Demyansk Pocket in 1942, and was killed in action in 1943.

S.S. (Lieutenant-General) Wilhelm Bittrich had flown as a lieutenant in the Great War, and been wounded twice. He stayed on in the Army after the war, with an interval during which he taught flying to the Russians for eight years. In the S.S. he was a colonel in Russia in 1941, and in 1943 and 1944 commanded the II S.S. Panzer Corps, first in Hungary and then in Normandy. He attempted to help 7th Army break out from the Falaise Pocket without much success. Bittrich had once been an ardent Nazi, but grew disillusioned—'sick and tired of Berlin's orders and the sycophants around Hitler'. He was a courageous, able, leader, whose best performance was his organization of the successful defence of Arnhem. In the regular Army he had served under Colonel-General Höpner, and when he heard of Höpner's arrest and death sentence after the July Plot Bittrich said: 'This is the blackest day for the German Army.' He himself spent eight years in prison after the war and was released on 22 June 1953.

Another ex-regular Army officer who rose to high rank in the Waffen S.S. was General Herbert Gille, renowned as a morale builder. He was Steiner's artillery commander in the third battle of Kharkov in

1943, previously having commanded an armoured group with success at Rostov. At Krasnoarmeyskoye in 1943 he was responsible, through skilful use of his guns, for deluding the Russians into much overestimating the strength of the German forces—'a masterly tactical manoeuvre', as Carell calls it. As a lieutenant-general Gille took over the Viking Division from Steiner, and later IV S.S. Panzer Corps, which engaged in the defence of Warsaw and Budapest. In March and April 1944 he had conducted a successful defence of Kovel until that garrison was relieved.

He fought at Cherkassy in 1944 and in the Korsun Pocket with III Panzer Corps in February 1945, where in the retreat to Lysanka he lost many of his men and tanks in a dangerous river crossing. Ziemke has described him as 'a well-meaning bumbler who spent most of his time at the front'.

S.S. Major-General Kurt 'Panzer' Meyer deserves mention not so much as the fanatical roughneck Nazi that he was, but for becoming at the age of 33 the youngest divisional commander in the German forces in 1944. He commanded the reconnaissance detachment of the L.A.H. in the Crimea and the Perekop Isthmus in 1941 and 1942 as a major; and as a colonel he commanded the 25th S.S. Panzer Grenadier Regiment in Normandy at Caen. Finally he commanded the 12th S.S. Panzer Division between Caen and St Lo. Meyer was in the thick of the bitterest fighting, and whatever else may be said of him he was certainly very brave. At one time on 27 June 1944 when the 2nd Army crossed the Odon at Caen, Meyer's headquarters at Verson was nearly overrun by the 11th Armoured Division. When the British finally got into Caen on 9 July Hitler ordered the town to be held to the last man. Meyer, who had witnessed terrible casualties in a month's bitter fighting, for once ignored higher orders, saying, 'We were meant to die in Caen, but one just couldn't watch those youngsters being sacrificed to a senseless order.' Meyer's crack division, 'Hitler Jugend', was virtually destroyed in the battle for Falaise, though he himself managed to escape from the Falaise Gap killing ground. Even before Falaise, Meyer's tank strength was down from 214 to about 40 tanks in 12th S.S. Panzer Division.

Meyer, tall, good-looking, with a moustache, was dedicated to Hitler. When Milton Shulman interrogated him after the war, Meyer's first words were, 'You will hear a lot against Adolf Hitler in this camp, but you will never hear it from me. As far as I am concerned he was and still is the greatest thing that ever happened to Germany'.

Meyer was condemned to death on 28 December 1945—the first German war criminal so sentenced—for his part in the massacre at Ancienne Abbaye of Canadian prisoners-of-war in the Ardennes. He was subsequently reprieved. In 1957 he was still the Nazi fanatic, and told a rally of former comrades: 'S.S. troops committed no crime except the massacre at Oradour, and that was the action of a single man. He was scheduled to go before a court-martial, but he died a hero's death before he could be tried.'

Meyer is interesting as an archetype. Bold, tough, arrogant figures like him did indeed exist—and flourish—in Hitler's Germany, and especially in the Waffen S.S.

It is in character that Ribbentrop's son was a major in the Waffen S.S.

Even the pasty-faced Himmler, with no useful military training, was inspired by ambition to take command of Army Group Vistula from January to March 1945. His Stargard offensive in February, which he believed would win the war, was a hopeless failure, and Himmler, who spent much of his time receiving massage or issuing useless orders, was relieved by Colonel-General Heinrici, a professional. Himmler remained commander of the Replacement Army which he had taken over from Colonel-General Fromm on the latter's arrest after 20 July. Himmler had no idea how to control an Army Group, and would have been equally at a loss with a regiment. Only the fact that he had as Chief of Staff a brave and experienced soldier, though one without any Staff training, S.S. Lieutenant-General Hans Lammerding, prevented him from making more of a fool of himself than he did. Lammerding, whose name was linked with massacres in the East and with the Oradour massacre, commanded the 2nd S.S. 'Das Reich' Panzer Division in Normandy and during the Mortain offensive in 1944.

The S.S. were feared and hated with good reason all over Europe. Yet at one time they had represented the flower and hopes of German youth. In battle they were brave, not always subtly led, ruthless, and often fought to the bitter end.

The Cavalry Generals

The German cavalry produced many of the finest leaders in armoured warfare. Hitler could not abide horses, but was not above using the ancient Field-Marshal von Mackensen to add dignity and colour to ceremonial Nazi parades, when the old man was trotted out in his Death's Head Hussars uniform. The rank of general of cavalry survived the Nazi advent and, as in Britain, the cavalry were considered something of an élite. It is pleasant to be able to say that—with only one or two exceptions—its generals represented all that was best in the German Army, and very few of them emerged with anything but credit from the war.

The senior cavalry general was Paul Ludwig Ewald Baron von Kleist, who became a field-marshal on 1 February 1943, the same day as another cavalryman, Maximilian Baron von Weichs zur Glon. Von Kleist commanded the 2nd Cavalry Division at Breslau as a lieutenant-general in 1934, then the VIII Army Corps from 1935 to 1938, becoming a general of cavalry in 1936. He was one of the officers retired in 1938 but brought back in 1939. He was far from being a Nazi, and told Liddell Hart after the war, 'The German mistake was to think that a military success could solve political problems. Indeed, under the Nazis we tended to reverse Clausewitz's dictum and to regard peace as an interruption of war'.

In 1934, on the basis of long talks with Edmund Haines, the S.A. leader in Silesia, Kleist was convinced that the S.A. had not got any firm plan to overthrow the Army. He came to the conclusion that rumours to this effect were part of an S.S. plan against the S.A., and tried to convince von Fritsch of this. But by then things had gone too far to be stopped. This was partly due to the influence and machinations of von Reichenau, a close friend of von Kleist, who was at that time an ardent Nazi.

In Poland in 1939 von Kleist commanded XXII Panzer Corps, and in France in 1940 his Panzer Group consisted of Guderian's XIX Corps and Reinhardt's XLI Corps, five tank divisions with three motorized ones. In both these campaigns von Kleist won spectacular victories, though he may fairly be judged to have been over-cautious in France. It emerges from Guderian's memoirs that he did not think very highly of Kleist, who had not originally been an advocate of tanks—indeed, he had even spoken against them. But Guderian was not an easy man to command, and Kleist at least seems to have handled him better than von Kluge did. Kleist's tanks reached Lyons on 20 June 1940, a very long way from their starting-point. If an invasion of England had occurred they would have landed on the south coast and been directed cross-country at Bristol.

It was Kleist's tanks that were primarily affected by Hitler's and Rundstedt's 'stop' order in France. On 22 May 1940 Reinhardt's leading elements had reached the Aire-St Omer Canal, and it was there that they were ordered to halt. Kleist told Liddell Hart, 'I decided to ignore it, and to push on across the canal. My armoured cars actually entered Hazebrouck, and cut across the British lines of retreat. I heard later that the British Commander-in-Chief, Lord Gort, had been in Hazebrouck at the time. But then came a more emphatic order that I was to withdraw behind the canal. My tanks were kept halted there for three days'.

In the second part of the French campaign Kleist had Höpner's XVI Panzer Corps instead of Guderian's XIX Panzer Corps. He also controlled General of Infantry Gustav von Wietersheim's XIV Motorized Corps, which attacked from Amiens on the Somme, gained a bridgehead over the Oise, and finally finished in the Bordeaux area and down by the Spanish frontier.

Writing about Kleist's handling of the armour in the first part of the campaign, W.E. Hart says he made 'clumsy dispositions' and that he 'was recognized as a complete failure, both as a general and as a disciplinarian', but I can find no evidence to substantiate this assertion.

In Russia as in the latter part of the battle in France, Colonel-General von Kleist was under command of his friend von Reichenau and 6th Army, in Rundstedt's Army Group South. Now Kleist commanded the 1st Panzer Group, whose vehicles bore a white 'K' on them. In July 1941 this Group won a handsome victory in the encirclement battle of Uman, when Kleist got round twenty-five Russian divisions and forced them against formations from 6th, 17th and 11th German Armies. Kleist's tanks, driving south-east, took Belaya Tserkov, Novo Arkhangelsk and Pervomaysk before closing the ring. More than 100,000 Russian prisoners were taken, and Kleist was able to push on to the lower Dnieper. Uman was a prelude to the battle of Kiev, in which the Panzer Group again distinguished itself. From 1 October 1941 1st Panzer Group became 1st Panzer Army, and on 6 October Kleist linked up with the 11th Army on the Black Sea coast. Together the two armies took another 106,000 prisoners.

Kleist's next objective was Rostov on Don, but here he was to take, in his own words, 'a bad knock'. He reached the Mius River on 28 October, but then his army was held up for nearly three weeks by mud. With the Russians frantically organising new armies, von Kleist could not get moving again until 17 November. But by 20

November Rostov, the 'gateway to the Caucasus' had fallen, mainly to another cavalry general, Eberhard von Mackensen, commanding III Panzer Corps. But now Marshal Timoshenko, spotting a gap between 17th Army and Kleist's Panzer Army, counter-attacked in strength, and burst through to strike at the rear of Mackensen's III Panzer Corps. Mackensen could not hold his seventy mile front with the strength at his disposal, and von Rundstedt therefore asked permission to abandon Rostov. Hitler refused this, relieved Rundstedt of his command of Army Group South, and replaced him with Reichenau.

On 1 December he too had to tell Hitler that the front must be taken back behind the Mius, and this time Hitler agreed to surrender Rostov. Kleist, meanwhile, had received an unpleasant telegram from the Führer stating that 'further cowardly retreats are forbidden'. This message did not take account, apparently, of the fact that the Russians had broken through the positions of the S.S. Leibstandarte!

Kleist undoubtedly suffered a reverse at Rostov, but it was more significant in being the first of the war than important in its own right. Several German commanders had thought that Rostov would be hard to hold.

On 12 May 1942 Timoshenko struck again south of Kharkov, against General Paulus's 6th Army, forestalling a German attack about to start further south. Von Kleist, now commanding 'Group Kleist' with his own army added to by units of 17th Army, attacked on 17 May from south of Izyum and reached the Donets the same evening. Timoshenko was now forced on to the defensive in the south. After a series of battles, in which Mackensen again distinguished himself, Kleist tore great gaps in the Soviet front, took the pressure off Paulus, and by 29 May destroyed the bulk of two Russian armies—the 6th and 57th—with help from 6th Army, and mauled parts of 9th and 38th Soviet Armies.

All these operations took their toll on the armour, and by late July 1942 von Kleist had only 400 tanks fit for operations. The next drive was southwards from the Don towards the Caucasus, but things were not so easy in this area for the Red Air Force held superiority and the Germans were often running short of fuel. As Kleist was to point out to Liddell Hart, the German airfields were often very far back, and such air superiority as was enjoyed in the opening months of the Russian campaign was 'local rather than general', and a tribute to the superior skill of the Luftwaffe pilots.

Hitler had told Kleist that the Baku, Groznyy, Tiflis and Maykop oil-fields must be captured by the autumn. When Kleist pointed out the great dangers of a long exposed flank that a drive to the Caucasus would involve, Hitler said that he would cover it with Rumanian, Hungarian, and Italian troops. Kleist warned him that it would be rash to rely upon these allies, but Hitler would not listen. Kleist got to

Maykop by 9 August, but by the end of the month he was still 350 miles from Baku. Groznyy, only sixty miles distant, was not to fall. Kleist was short of troops, having only eight divisions with which to attack the Russians, who were strongly entrenched on the Terek with some forty divisions to call upon. General von Schweppenburg with only three panzer divisions in his XL Panzer Corps, could not get to Groznyy and switched south towards Malgobek. But Russian resistance was tough and towards the end of September Kleist's offensive bogged down; he had to go on the defensive while awaiting reinforcements. On 25 September von Mackensen attacked towards Ordzhonikidze with his III Panzer Corps, and reached the road to Tiflis, but he too had to stop and await fuel and manpower reserves. Late in October he attacked again, and on 5 November 1942 Major-General Traugott Herr's 13th Panzer Division got to within three miles of Ordzhonikidze; but they could do no more. Except for isolated patrols that got to the Caspian, this was to be the farthest east that the Germans ever reached in Russia. Von Mackensen claimed to have taken 16,000 prisoners and 249 guns, and to have destroyed 188 tanks, between 25 October and 12 November 1942.

Lack of petrol and the diversion of forces to Stalingrad, were Kleist's biggest problems. Hitler was trying to take two places at once— Stalingrad, and the oil areas of the Caucasus. By attempting both he failed to win either. Kleist gave lack of petrol as his primary setback, but added to Liddell Hart: 'But that was not the ultimate cause of the failure. We could still have reached our goal if my forces had not been drawn away bit by bit to help the attack at Stalingrad. Besides part of my motorized troops, I had to give up the whole of my flak corps and all my air force except the reconnaissance squadrons.' As a result, when the Russians started using 800 bombers based near Grozny, they were able to slow his advance.

Between 21 November 1942 and 31 March 1944 von Kleist was C-in-C Army Group 'A'. In January 1943 he was seriously threatened by a Russian attack from Lake Elista, 175 miles south of Stalingrad, and, even worse, by an attack from Stalingrad down the Don towards Rostov in his rear. But Hitler would not abandon his dreams of oil, and Kleist was ordered to remain in his exposed positions. On 2 February 1943, when Stalingrad finally fell to the Russians, Kleist's Army Group was still in the Caucasus, and therefore in considerable danger.

Kleist has related how, when the Russians were less than forty-five miles from Rostov and his armies were 400 miles east of it, Hitler sent him an order not to withdraw under any circumstances. 'That looked like a sentence of doom', he said. But next day Hitler changed his mind and told Kleist to retreat with all his equipment, with his flank protected by Marshal Antonescu's Rumanians, in whom

Kleist had little faith. Fortunately for him von Manstein took over control, and with his help Kleist was able to get through the Rostov bottleneck before being cut off by the Russians.

Kleist's withdrawal from the Caucasus and the Crimea between January and March 1943 was one of his greatest achievements. By the end of February 1943 Kleist had got most of his Army Group back to the Dnieper River without heavy loss, and by March he was able to counter-attack and win a breathing-space which lasted until after mid-summer.

In March 1944 Kleist agreed with General Wöhler, the commander of 8th Army, that they must retire behind the Dniester River. He was aware that this decision would not be popular with Hitler, but said, 'Someone must lay his head on the block'. Sure enough, Hitler seized on this withdrawal as an excuse to get rid of Kleist. With Manstein he was summoned to the Führer's headquarters on 30 March where they were both decorated with Swords to the Knight's Cross, and then dismissed on the grounds that they were tired out. Hitler told them: 'The time for operating is over. What I need now is men who stand firm. . . .' Such men, in Hitler's view, were Model and Schörner, both rabid Nazis, who now took over from Manstein and Kleist.

Kleist noted that Russian military equipment was good, even in 1941, and that from 1943 it got better and better. He agreed with many other commanders that the Soviet artillery was first-class, and the T.34 the best tank in the world. He also thought that the Russians were considerably helped by Allied equipment deliveries, especially transport.

Field-Marshal von Kleist was a solid, unflappable commander rather than a brilliant one, who showed his worth in retreat as well as in victory. A gentleman of the old school, he was much admired and well liked in the German Army. On 23 September 1943 Göbbels wrote: 'Ewald von Kleist has made a very close approach to the Führer and to the National Socialist movement'. But this seems doubtful.

How much he may be blamed for not pushing on with his tanks in France in 1940 is very questionable. The German Army insisted on obedience, and though Kleist ignored the first order to stop, he could not ignore the second, stronger one. Gregory Blaxland, in his excellent account of the campaign, *Destination Dunkirk*, writes: 'It was extremely fortunate for the Allies that von Kleist in particular lacked the imagination to conceive the deadly thrust that it was well within his power to make, namely a concentrated drive on Cassel, which at forty-four miles was very much nearer his leading troops than Abbeville had been at sunrise on the 20th [of May].'

It is certainly true that Cassel—a small hill rising out of the surrounding, placid plain—was far more important to the defenders of Dunkirk than Calais or anywhere else. Blaxland holds that, 'If Kleist, or for that matter von Rundstedt, had appreciated the importance of

Cassel and had had the daring to go for it at full throttle, it would have been his on 22 May, and it could be argued that his country would have won the war. . . .' I think this is overstated, and that the responsibility lay more with Rundstedt than with von Kleist.

An illuminating exchange between von Kleist and one of his Army commanders, Colonel-General Erwin Jänecke, is given in Earl Ziemke's *Stalingrad to Berlin: The German Defeat in the East.* Jänecke had commanded a Corps at Stalingrad, and had made his name by a skilful evacuation of the Kuban. On 28 October 1943, as G.O.C. 17th Army, he told Kleist that he was going to evacuate the Crimea, since he would not take responsibility for another Stalingrad. Kleist told him that he was to hang on to the Crimea at all costs, and promised reinforcements in a fortnight, but Jänecke refused to accept this order. The following telephone conversation took place:

K. *You are to defend the Crimea.*

J. *I cannot execute that order. No one else will execute it either; the Corps commanders believe the same as I do.*

K. *So, collusion, conspiracy to disobey an order! If you cannot, someone else* will *command the Army.*

J. *I repeat again that in the light of my responsibility for the Army I cannot execute the order.*

K. *As a soldier, I have often had to struggle with myself, in similar situations. You will not save a single man. What is to come will come one way or another. This attitude only undermines the confidence of the troops. If I get one more division everything will be all right.*

J. *That is building castles in the air. One must deal with realities here.*

K. *To retreat under pressure of the enemy is well and good; to retreat this way is something else.*

J. *I cannot wait until Army Group South has gone that far. [A reference to the threatened Russian breakthrough to the west on Army Group South's right flank.]*

K. *The Army has not yet been attacked. A little reinforcement on the isthmus and everything will be in order. The enemy will prefer to strike west and north into the flank of 1st Panzer Army rather than into the Perekop narrows.*

J. *The Crimea must be defended on its entire perimeter. If the Russians attack the catastrophe is at hand. I must recall once more the example of Generalfeldmarschall Paulus at Stalingrad.*

K. *The details of events there are not known. The accounts of what happened vary. Do you believe that the Führer will let himself be influenced by you? He has already said once that he will not allow any general to subject him to blackmail. If the Commanding*

General, Seventeenth Army, does not execute the order he will break every rule of soldierly deportment. Will you execute the order or not?

Jänecke thereupon requested time in which to consult his Chief of Staff. An hour later he gave in. Kleist recounted the incident to Zeitzler, saying he did not wish to court-martial Jänecke, but could not keep him as an Army commander. However, Jänecke stayed on for the time being, presumably because neither Kleist nor Zeitzler wanted to tell Hitler. After Hitler had imposed a virtual death sentence on the troops at Sevastopol by ordering the city to be held to the last, Jänecke flew to protest to the Führer in two stormy meetings. He was removed from command and replaced by General of Infantry Karl Allmendinger. When Sevastopol fell in the days following 7 May Allmendinger lost 26,700 out of 64,700 men, the casualties being left stranded on the beach.

The dialogue between Kleist and Jänecke shows the straits to which senior generals were reduced. Even Kleist, generally regarded as an enlightened man, was afraid to challenge Hitler's orders.

Maximilian, Freiherr von Weichs was a Bavarian Catholic born in 1881 (the same year as von Kleist) at Dessau, Anhalt. In 1900 he became a fahnenjunker in the 2nd Bavarian Heavy Cavalry Regiment, of which he became adjutant in 1906. After attending the War Academy he was a Rittmeister (captain) at the outbreak of the Great War, in which he fought with the Bavarian Cavalry Division and later served as a staff officer. As a lieutenant-colonel in 1928 he commanded the 18th Cavalry Regiment and became major-general in 1933. He was one of those officers who at first looked fairly kindly upon Hitler, but was much against the introduction of politics into the army. In December 1933 he assumed command of the 3rd Cavalry Division at Weimar, and in 1935, as a lieutenant-general of the 1st Panzer Division, a plum appointment under Lieutenant-General Lutz, at that time head of armoured troops. In 1936 he became general of cavalry; in 1937 G.O.C. XIII Army Corps, with headquarters at Nuremberg. This post meant that he was heavily involved with the preparation and conduct of the Nuremberg rallies. He has described himself in those days as 'a cross between a film producer and a drill sergeant. . . .'

In Poland General von Weichs commanded a corps under Blaskowitz. In the Battle of France in 1940 he commanded the 2nd Army of three infantry corps, which Rundstedt used mainly in a follow-up role.

In April 1940 Theodor Eicke, the ruffianly commander of the S.S. 'Totenkopf' Motorized Division, was offended because von Weichs had been 'cold and hostile' when he inspected that formation. Some weeks later, however, von Weichs had become 'very friendly' and had nothing but praise for the S.S. men, particularly of their fine physical condition.

His first completely independent command was that of the ground forces in the invasion of Yugoslavia in 1941, which he managed very successfully. Von Weichs took his 2nd Army to Russia, and in 1941 was engaged with his eight divisions in battles in Belorussia, the Ukraine, on the Bryansk front, and towards the Desna River. He was part of von Bock's Army Group Centre. In November and December 1941 von Weichs was away ill, and his place was taken by General Rudolf Schmidt. In mid-January 1942 he was back again, but this time in Army Group South, although his 2nd Army was still stretched between Orel and Kursk. He turned back one Russian attack in January.

In the summer of 1942 Colonel-General von Weichs commanded a Group consisting of his own 2nd Army, Hoth's 4th Panzer Army, and 2nd Hungarian Army, and on 28 June on the northern edge of 'Operation Blue' attacked in the Kursk area with Voronezh as his objective. Richthofen's famous VIII Air Corps was in support, and the spearhead of Hoth's Army was the 24th Panzer Division led by Major-General Ritter von Hauenschild. This division was the former East Prussian 1st Cavalry Division, which had given up its horses for tanks in the winter of 1941–2. By 2 July troops from General of Panzer Troops Kempf's XLVIII Panzer Corps had linked up with men from Paulus's 6th Army at Staryy Oskol, and four days later Hoth's men were over the Don and had captured Voronezh, evacuated by the Red Army.

Von Weichs commanded Army Group 'B' from July 1942 until February 1943, when it was disbanded. As such he was closely involved with the Stalingrad fiasco. Some German sources have criticized Weichs' Army Group for attempting piecemeal solutions. On 24 November 1942 Weichs ordered Stalingrad and the Volga front to be held 'in all circumstances' and for Paulus to prepare for a breakout. Next day, however, Paulus was told by O.K.H. to hold on and await further orders. On 23 November Paulus radioed urgently for permission to break out, but Hitler told him to stay where he was; he would be supplied by air. Weichs should then have made a determined stand against this idea, particularly as all Paulus's Corps commanders were then in favour of breaking out. Paulus forwarded on 23 November a message to O.K.H. stating that only a tenth of what was needed could be supplied by air. However, even if Weichs had made a protest he would almost certainly have been overruled by Hitler.

Von Weichs may be held partly responsible for Stalingrad. Indeed, he must be, since he was the operative Army Group commander. Hitler had publicly committed himself to staying on the Volga; his mind was not to be changed.

In February 1943, von Weich's Army Group was disbanded, the troops being shared out between Army Groups South and Centre.

From August 1943 von Weichs, now a field-marshal, was C-in-C Yugoslavia, Albania, and Thrace, with headquarters first in Belgrade and —from 5 October 1944—at Vukovar. He commanded Army Group 'F' and was variously known as C-in-C South-East and C-in-C Balkans. He had under him 600,000 men in thirty-eight divisions and brigades, of which seven divisions were Bulgarian and nine made up of foreign collaborators. He had fifteen German divisions, seven fortress brigades, and large numbers of Wehrmacht, air, police and naval units. In September 1943 von Weichs advised Hitler to evacuate the Balkans quickly, since some of his troops were of poor quality, mightily over-stretched on the ground, and much beset by partisans. He did not think, rightly as it turned out, that he could hold the Balkans against a strong attack. Hitler did not agree, and the later retreat north which von Weichs had to conduct became in many cases a shambles. Ziemke comments on his performance: 'Weichs, as Commanding General, Army Group F, had tried to create a front on the east; but, as Commanding General, South-East, he had failed to make the decision that would have enabled him to do so; he had therefore fought the battle piecemeal, always several steps behind the enemy. Nevertheless, after he had lost Belgrade and as the month [October 1944] wore on, it \began to look, in the north as well as in the south, as if he had displayed a genuine feeling for timing and a talent for sure-footed retrograde manoeuvre. . . .'

Von Weichs, tall, rather bald, with horn-rimmed spectacles, looked more like a university professor than a general. Yet he was one of the ablest and most experienced commanders, who at one time had directed six Armies, and a Group in Army Group B. Guderian proposed him in January 1945 as C-in-C Army Group Vistula, but Hitler thought Weichs too old. 'The Field Marshal seems to me a tired man. I doubt if he's still capable of performing such a task. . . .' Jodl put paid to Weichs's chances by mentioning his strong religious feelings, and Hitler gave the appointment to—Himmler! Weichs was put on the reserve on 22 March 1945.

Colonel-General Eberhard von Mackensen came of a highly dis-tinguished military and diplomatic family. He was the son of the famous Field-Marshal August von Mackensen, and his brother Hans-Georg, was Ambassador in Rome during the war and a State Secretary at the Foreign Office.

As a major-general in 1939 he was Chief of Staff to List's Heeres-gruppe 5 in Vienna, and continued in that post with List's 12th Army in France. He was given command of III Panzer Corps as a lieutenant-general for the invasion of Russia, and his seizure of the bridgeheads at Dniepropetrovsk across the Dnieper and Samro Rivers enabled von Kleist to break through. It was troops from his Corps who took Rostov briefly in November 1941, and in the summer of 1942 Mackensen was promoted General of Cavalry.

III Corps took part in the great battles south of Kharkov and reached Bayrak on the northern Donets. In this prelude to Stalingrad Mackensen, according to Carell, showed 'brilliant tactical skill' and routed the Russians in what was for them a very expensive action. In June 1942 he fought another successful action in the Kupyansk area. Later his troops penetrated into Asia and the Caucasus approaches, where he took Salsk. It was his III Corps which crossed the Terek and attacked to within the outskirts of Ordzhonikidze in early November.

Von Mackensen took over 1st Panzer Army from von Kleist during Stalingrad, and in February 1943 destroyed parts of General Popov's Tank Group between Krasnoarmeiskoye and Barvenkovo. In August and September 1st Panzer Army was forced back from the Donets Basin towards the Dnieper, and in October he was pushed back again by Chuikov and Danilov. Shortly after he was replaced by the outstanding General Hube, and transferred to Italy.

In Italy Mackensen commanded 14th Army, where his first big task was to liquidate the Anzio bridgehead. But in spite of repeated attacks upon it, he was not successful, and in the end failed to prevent the American General Lucius Truscott breaking out of Anzio. Mackensen and Kesselring did not get on well, and on at least one occasion the latter rebuked Mackensen for not obeying orders. Kesselring thought him too parochial in his conduct of operations, and in spite of his successes in Russia, he was replaced in June 1944 by General of Panzer Troops Joachim Lemelsen.

Von Mackensen was accused of responsibility for the massacre in the Ardeatine Caves. He was given the death sentence on 30 November 1945, which was later commuted to a sentence of life imprisonment.

Colonel-General Georg Lindemann started the war as the commander of 36th Division at Kaiserlautern in von Witzleben's Heeresgruppe 2, with which he went to France in 1940. He was then a lieutenant-general and one of the senior cavalry officers. In Russia he commanded first L Corps and, from 17 January 1942, 18th Army on the Leningrad front in place of von Küchler, when the latter relieved von Leeb as C-in-C Army Group North. Lindemann faced savage Russian attacks on his front, but his troops held fast, and by 20 May 1942, he was able to announce in an order of the day, 'The Russians are pulling out of the Volkhov pocket.'

Now a General of Cavalry, Lindemann won a considerable defensive success in the first battle of Lake Ladoga in late August and September 1942, destroying 244 Russian tanks. He also fought actions at Oranienbaum, Krasnoye Selo, and Staritza, and in 1943 in the Sinyavino Hills, on the Leningrad front.

During the summer of 1942 Lindemann filed a complaint with S.S.

Headquarters in Berlin, listing specific occasions on which members of the 2nd S.S. Infantry Brigade had shot prisoners-of-war in Russia. Lindemann is described by Carell as 'a realist who knew his job', and I can find no evidence to substantiate Charles Whiting's claim that he was 'a fervent Nazi'. Short of troops as everyone else, Lindemann fought a particularly tough series of defensive battles in the north, realizing that the crucial point was the Sinyavino Hills between the Volkhov and Neva. On 1 March 1944, Colonel-General Lindemann replaced Model as C-in-C Army Group North. This was despite the fact that he had admitted making mistakes in his estimate of Soviet reserves in January 1944; and that on 23 January 1944 he had ordered the evacuation of Pushkin and Slutsk on the Leningrad front, and had reported to O.K.H. that it could either accept his decision or send a general to replace him.

On 3 July 1944 when his Army Group North was under considerable pressure in Belorussia, Hitler wanted him to attack in the Polotsk region. Lindemann insisted that his troops were not strong enough to do so, and was dismissed. He was succeeded by the infantryman, Colonel-General Johannes Friessner.

Lindemann was appointed C-in-C Occupied Denmark, in place of Lieutenant-General Herman von Hannecken, where he surrendered to the British in 1945.

Colonel-General Erich Höpner was one of the finest commanders of armour in the German Army, thought by some to be even better than Guderian or Hoth.

In 1938 Höpner was commanding the 1st Light Division in Thuringia, and undertook—in the event of Hitler's arrest then being planned by Beck, Halder, Witzleben and others—to cut off the S.S. troops in Munich if they tried to march on Berlin. In 1939, as a lieutenant-general, Höpner had command of XVI Motorized Corps, containing 1st and 4th Panzer Divisions, which he used to great effect in the attack on Warsaw. In France in 1940 this Corps was part of the Hoth Group. Höpner can be bracketed with von Reichenau and Guderian as a real thruster, with drive and talent, as opposed to the more cautious Paulus and von Kluge.

At first Höpner's Corps was part of von Reichenau's 6th Army, and after crossing the Meuse it won the battle of the Gembloux Gap, where Höpner's tanks outmanoeuvred the French. Then, despite protests from Reichenau, XVI Motorized Corps was transferred to 4th Army to help exploit the Ardennes breakthrough.

After Charleroi and Maubeuge it fought on the Escaut, then on the Lys. In the latter part of the Battle of France Höpner came under von Kleist, advancing across the Somme from Peronne and fighting a heavy action near Noyon before the Aisne. Höpner's crack divisions were the 3rd and 4th Panzer. It was he who ordered an enquiry into the massacre at Le Paradis of men of the Royal Norfolk Regiment; and he also had a brush with Sepp Dietrich, who said that human life mattered very little to the S.S. and would not interfere with his fulfilment of a mission. Höpner became very angry and said that no decent officer with a sense of responsibility would talk like that.

In the early part of the Russian campaign Colonel-General Höpner commanded 4th Panzer Group under von Leeb's Army Group North, and led the push across the Baltic states towards Leningrad. Unfortunately for him, Leeb did not have enough infantry to support the flanks of the armoured columns. Both Reinhardt and Manstein, under Höpner, became dangerously exposed with a gap between XLI and LVI Panzer Corps. The areas round Lake Peipus and Lake Ilmen, being marshy and wooded, were not suitable for fast tank operations, and Höpner was all for going between the two lakes and making a direct thrust to Leningrad. Because of the lack of infantry and the bad going, Leeb's first advance on Leningrad came to nothing, and on 8 July 1941 Hitler decided to leave that city to be merely contained, and concentrate on Moscow. Höpner's Group was therefore transferred to Army Group Centre in September.

On 7 October his tanks joined Hoth's at Vyazma, and closed a huge pocket around fifty-five Soviet divisions. We have seen how tough was the fighting in the advance to Moscow, but even by mid-November Höpner was convinced that the capital could be taken. He had been thwarted on the Leningrad front, where Hitler's removal of his Panzer Group and all the bombers on 17 September had come at a time when one last effort might well have taken the city. Now, with four panzer, one motorized, and seven infantry divisions, he urged his men forward in one last effort to take Moscow. He made progress in his attacks north of the capital, as did Reinhardt with III Panzer Corps; but for some unknown reason their superior, von Kluge, G.O.C. 4th Army, did not begin his infantry attack from the west until 1 December, despite repeated requests from Höpner to do so. Meanwhile the Russians piled in more divisions against Höpner and Reinhardt, and by 5 December —against superior odds and in freezing cold—Höpner's Group was on the defensive and soon began to withdraw. Höpner's motor-cycle patrols had got to within five miles of Moscow, but he had not had the strength to make the final push.

On 1 January 1942 4th Panzer Group was elevated to become 4th Panzer Army, and Höpner became an Army commander. But then he was suddenly and unjustifiably dismissed in ignominy. Höpner's dismissal was the direct result of Hitler's anger at being thwarted at Moscow, and indirectly the result of his superior, von Kluge's doctoring of fact. What happened was this: Höpner quite rightly decided to withdraw the right wing of his Army to avoid encirclement, as there was a gap between it and 4th Army. Soon after Kluge's Chief of Staff was informed of this, Kluge himself discussed the matter with Höpner on the telephone.

When Kluge expressed some reservations, Höpner replied, 'Very well, then, Herr Feldmarschall, we'll only withdraw the heavy artillery and baggage train to begin with, to make sure we don't lose them. You will explain to the Führer the need for this measure and request his authorization. . . .' He then told his chief of Staff, Colonel (later Lieutenant-General) Châles de Beaulieu, to make the necessary preparations. But clearly Kluge did not do as Höpner requested; he told Hitler simply that the withdrawal was an accomplished fact. Consequently Höpner lost his job, without any enquiry or court-martial, and was never restored to it. He was even forbidden by Hitler to wear uniform.

Naturally this shocking piece of work had serious repercussions among senior commanders. Hassell noted that Höpner had been 'kicked out in the meanest and most dishonourable way, the official notice speaking of the "former" Colonel-General'. Hitler had even wanted him cashiered. Nevertheless Ruoff, who took Höpner's place, could not hold the line, and on 13 January Hitler perforce had to accept what had already happened—withdrawal.

Höpner was an outspoken, honest, no-nonsense character, not one to appeal to a leader whose military abilities were lower than his own.

In his retirement, Höpner became one of the leading plotters against Hitler. Field-Marshal von Witzleben selected him first as Commander of the Home Army in the event of the plot succeeding, and then as the C-in-C of the German Army, where he would have been acceptable to most of the more far-seeing generals. But it was not to be, and with the failure of the Stauffenberg plot he was arrested. In a scandalous trial Judge Roland Friesler, a man not fit to lick Höpner's boots, held him up to public ridicule. He had refused to commit suicide, and was executed by hanging. His fellow-cavalryman, Geyr von Schweppenburg, also an experienced commander of tanks, described Höpner and Henrich von Stülpnagel, another leading conspirator who was executed, as 'typical of the best in the older German Army set. They had both distinguished themselves as successful, responsible, leaders on the battlefield. As soldiers, as men, and in the strength of their character they greatly surpassed the typical Nazi generals, such as Reichenau, Busch, Model and others.'

General of Panzer Troops Leo Baron Geyr von Schweppenburg was a Catholic, born in 1886, who as a youth was page to Wilhelm II of Württemburg. He was an educated and cultivated man, the friend and protégé of Beck and of von Fritsch, a good linguist in Russian, French and English. He became German military attaché in London, Brussels, and The Hague between 1933 and 1937. He held a low opinion of von Blomberg and of Ribbentrop.

Geyr commanded 3rd Panzer Division as a major-general and then lieutenant-general from 1937 to 1939, and took part in the entry into the Sudetenland in 1938.

In the early days in Russia he commanded XXIV Panzer Corps and made a name as a shrewd and brave leader, narrowly escaping death on more than one occasion. He fought successful actions at Roslavl and in the Krichev area, under Guderian to whom in fact he was senior in rank. The C-in-C of the Army, von Brauchitsch, was, according to Geyr, 'not very well-disposed' to him, and as far back as 1928, when Chief of the Army Training Department, had not shown himself particularly appreciative to Geyr's ideas on Army-Air Force co-operation.

From July 1942 Geyr von Schweppenburg took over Stumme's XL Panzer Corps operating under Hoth in the drive towards the Caucasus, after fighting successfully in the Staryy Oskol area on the Voronezh front.

From Russia Geyr was recalled to become Inspector of Armour at G.H.Q. and in 1944 he was appointed G.O.C. Panzer Troops West, with headquarters at Paris. He was responsible directly to Colonel-General Guderian for organization and training, and to Field-Marshal von Rundstedt operationally. Geyr supported Rundstedt's views in the controversy about the disposal of the German tank forces against an enemy landing, and did not subscribe to Rommel's theory of pushing them right up to the beaches. He favoured holding them in reserve for counter-attacks, partly because he was afraid of massive airborne landings deep in the interior of France. Rommel refers to violent disagreements with Geyr, 'with whom I recently had to be very rough because he would not give way to my plans'. Nevertheless the two managed to get on, probably because Geyr—a generous man—did not find in Rommel the 'narrow, inflexible spirit' that he had deprecated in von Brauchitsch.

In the Normandy battle General Geyr had little chance as Commander, Panzer Group West, to show his undoubted skill. He prepared one counter-attack against the British on 8 June 1944 after Rommel had summoned him from Paris to take over the entire sector east of the Dives to Tilly-sur-Seulles. But the very next day Geyr's headquarters in a château at La Caine, some four miles from Thury-Harcourt, was wiped out by R.A.F. bombing, and though Geyr himself and the Chief of Staff of 7th Army, Major-General Max Pemsel, a future C-in-C of the Federal German Army, had lucky escapes, his own Chief of Staff, Major-General Rittler und Edler von Dawans, and most of his senior officers, were killed. On 5 July Rommel met Geyr in a forest near St Pierre-sur-Dives to tell him that he had been dismissed. 'I come to tell you that you have been relieved. Rundstedt has been too; I'm the next on the list,' said the Field-Marshal.

General von Geyr survived the war to become an accomplished military historian and commentator.

General Dr Hans Speidel had this to say of him: 'Schweppenburg was an unusual personality, capable in both military and political fields and able to make deductions from experience gathered in the conduct of modern warfare. He had been unswerving and fearless, as military attaché in London, in reporting the increasing isolation of Germany, and those warnings led to his recall'.

General of Panzer Troops Georg Stumme, born in 1886, commanded the 2nd Light Division at Gera as Lieutenant-General in 1939. In Russia in 1941 he commanded XL Panzer Corps in the assault on Moscow, in which his tanks were halted more by the mud than by the enemy. He got to within fifty miles of Moscow on the highway, but was continually counter-attacked by T.34s which could manoeuvre in the mud. It was during this advance that Stumme made the memorable remark to Major-General Fischer, G.O.C. 10th Panzer Division, 'Good, God, this is no more than a reinforced reconnaissance patrol!'

Stumme was short, very energetic, always wore an eyeglass, and suffered from high blood pressure which gave him a permanent flush. He was nicknamed 'Fireball' by his troops. In the Velikije Luki battle of 1941 his Corps took 30,000 prisoners.

Carell has described Stumme thus: 'Stumme was no scholarly General Staff officer, but a practical man with a genuine flair for spotting and grasping tactical opportunities. He was one of the best German tank commanders, clever in planning operations and resolute in executing them. He was a front-line officer, idolized by his soldiers, whose welfare was his constant concern. But he was also respected by his officers, who admired his energy and operational instinct. . . .'

Stumme lost his command in the same way General Felmy lost his—the chief of operations of 23rd Panzer Division, carrying plans for an impending attack, had been shot down in an aircraft by the Russians, into whose hands the plans fell. Stumme was held responsible, and given five years' fortress detention by the Reich Military Court. Because of his excellent record the sentence was remitted, and instead Stumme was sent to Africa.

He arrived at Rommel's headquarters on 19 September 1942 and on 22 September took over command of the Afrika Army. Kesselring wrote, 'Being a man of a more even and genial temperament than Rommel, he did much to relax the tension among officers and men, besides managing to create tolerable relations with the Italian Command.' But he was not quite physically fit. Rommel doubted whether a man with his blood pressure should ever have been sent to the desert. In the event, Stumme inherited Rommel's plan for the defence at El Alamein, and spared no effort to improve the defences despite (in

Rommel's words) 'the full extent of the supply deficiencies, on which the whole Africa problem turned'.

On 24 October, while driving at the front, Stumme's car was fired on by British troops and one of his N.C.Os was killed. The car turned round and drove off at high speed, with Stumme clinging to the side of it, but he dropped off and was later found to be dead, presumably from a heart attack. As Rommel wrote of Stumme, 'He had spared no pains to command the Army well and had been day and night at the front'.

Every army throws up its share of colourful eccentrics, even in the ranks of the generals, and there can have been few more idiosyncratic personalities during the last war than Lieutenant-General Ernst Baade. The son of a Brandenburg landowner, he farmed his own estate in Holstein where he bred horses. Before the war he and his wife were well-known international show-jumpers. In 1939 he was a squadron leader in Cavalry Regiment No. 3, which von Senger commanded. Senger found him 'an original character', and his disregard for pomp and circumstance would have found common cause with far more British officers than German ones. He fought in Poland, France, Russia, North Africa, and Italy.

As a colonel in 1942 he commanded the Combat Group of the Afrika Korps which forced a way into Bir Hakeim; and in 1943 he commanded the 90th Panzer Grenadier Division in Sardinia and Italy, under von Senger. Before becoming a general he had been known to lead patrols in Africa wearing a kilt, and to have signalled the end of a night raid by telling the British over their own radio network, 'Stop firing. On my way back. Baade'. At Cassino, where he was a general, it was rumoured that he had accepted an invitation to dine with the enemy at Christmas, and O.K.W. demanded in some agitation of von Senger if this was true. Von Senger denied it, but forebore to admit that Baade had signalled New Year Greetings to the enemy in English!

Baade gave Major-General Ryder's 34th U.S. Division a very bloody nose above Cassino in February 1944. His defence of Cassino and of the Hitler Line earned him a high reputation, and the 10th Army Commander, Colonel-General von Vietinghoff, thought Baade and Heidrich 'in a class by themselves' as divisional commanders. This very front-line General was promoted to command a Panzer Corps on the western front in 1945, but was to die from wounds received on the last day of the war in an air raid.

Predictably, perhaps, the cavalry did not produce many Staff generals, (though von Mackensen had served on the Staff) but one whom they did, of the very first class, was General of Cavalry Siegfried Westphal.

He was born in Leipzig in 1902, the son of a major, and from 1932 to 1935 served at the War Academy in Berlin. By 1941 he was G.I. Ops to Rommel in the desert as a colonel, and was wounded in late May 1942. In 1942 he became Chief of Staff to the German-Italian Panzer forces in Africa, and thus to Rommel, and in this post in December supervised the building of the Buerat position. In 1943 Westphal went as Chief of Staff to Field-Marshal Kesselring in Italy (C-in-C South-West and Army Group 'C'), and in 1944 he moved on to become von Rundstedt's Chief of Staff in the West. He was by then a lieutenant-general.

Rommel referred to Westphal's being wounded as 'a bitter blow' and said: 'For me his assistance had always been of outstanding value, because of his extraordinary knowledge and experience and readiness to take decisions. . . .' Kesselring said, 'I could not have wished for a better Chief of Staff than Westphal, with whom I had worked harmoniously in Italy. . . .' (Kesselring got him again in the spring of 1945 when he was brought back to Germany.) Rommel also refers to 'the splendid leadership of Kesselring and Westphal' in Italy. Von Senger, who got on well with Westphal, had personally recommended him for command in Sicily, and described him as, 'One of the best horses in the stable. Highly intelligent, very energetic and a quick worker, Westphal never strayed from the point; his attitude towards incompetent officers could sometimes be very cool, and this did not add to his popularity. . . .'

With good officers and his superiors and equals, however, Westphal was very highly rated. He would not have been chosen by three such commanders as Rundstedt, Kesselring and Rommel if he had not been in the front rank.

General of Panzer Troops Dietrich von Saucken fought in Poland in 1939 with the cavalry, and won the Knight's Cross with Oak Leaves and Swords. In 1943 he was lieutenant-general commanding the 4th Panzer Division under Model, and in the latter stages of the war fought a series of delaying actions against the advancing Russians. In late 1944 he was G.O.C. Group von Saucken north of Minsk. He commanded a Panzer Group on the Oder in 1945, and a Corps in East Prussia and in South Poland consisting of the Grossdeutschland and Hermann Göring Divisions. In February 1945 von Saucken successfully smashed a way through the Russians, who were behind him when the Vistula front crumpled, and led his tank Corps back to the Oder near Steinau.

In March 1945 he was G.O.C. 2nd Army in the Sopot, Gdynia and Danzig areas. His fellow-cavalryman Gerhard Boldt has left a brilliant description of a meeting between Hitler and von Saucken in the Chancellory in March 1945. 'Slim, elegant, his left hand resting casually on his cavalry sabre, von Saucken saluted and gave a slight bow. This was three outrages at once. He had not given the Nazi salute with raised arm and the words "Heil Hitler", as had been regulation since 20 July 1944; he had not surrendered his weapon on entering the operations room; and he had kept his monocle in his eye when saluting Hitler. . . .' Guderian and Bormann, who were present, seemed turned to stone, but Hitler merely asked Guderian to brief von Saucken on conditions in East Prussia and the Danzig area, where he was to take over 2nd Army Group. Hitler then told the General that in the Danzig area he would have to accept the authority of Gauleiter Forster. Von Saucken stiffened and, still with his eyeglass in place, struck the marble table with the flat of his hand and said: 'I have no intention, Herr Hitler, of placing myself under the orders of a *Gauleiter*!' Boldt adds: 'One could have heard a pin drop on the carpet. It seemed to me that Hitler shrank physically from the General's words. His face looked even more waxen, his body more bowed than ever. . . .'

Guderian and Bormann then tried to persuade von Saucken to be reasonable, but he would only reply, 'I have no intention whatsoever of doing so. . . .' Hitler, who seemed at last to have met his match in the matter of gazes, finally said in a weak voice: 'All right, Saucken, keep the command to yourself.' After a few more minutes of discussion von Saucken left 'with the merest hint of a bow'. Hitler did not shake his hand.

Guderian had a high opinion of von Saucken, whose abilities he thought 'outstanding'. He records that in eastern Germany in 1945 'Generals Nehring and von Saucken performed tasks of military virtuosity during those days that only the pen of a new Xenophon could adequately describe.'

No soldier had more miraculous good luck in surviving the war than the Thuringian Lieutenant-General Hans Wilhelm Freiherr von Boineburg-Lengsfeld. The thin, monocled von Boineburg commanded 23rd Panzer Division under Stumme in Russia in 1941 and 1942, but he was run over by a tank in Russia and was lucky to survive with countless broken bones. After Stalingrad he was sent to Paris as Commandant in 1943. He was deeply involved in the plot against Hitler and on 20 July acted upon Heinrich von Stülpnagel's orders to arrest General Oberg and all the S.S. and Security Police and Gestapo in Paris. Later, when things went wrong, he had them all released, and drank champagne with Oberg. Somehow or other he managed to charm or bluff the S.S. leader into forgiving the whole affair.

Early in August von Boineburg, who had miraculously escaped all censure so far, was ordered by Hitler to defend Paris to the last and blow all bridges over the Seine. He refused to do this, and ten days before the Allies entered Paris von Boineburg was relieved of his post. He begged his successor, General Dietrich von Choltitz, to save the city, which could not be defended. Von Choltitz agreed to do so, and kept his word.

In April 1945 von Boineburg was brought before a military court inquiring into the circumstances of the surrender of Paris without a fight. The trial was postponed, and Lieutenant-General von Boineburg-Lengsfeld travelled to Erfurt and was there taken prisoner by the Americans. He was, remarkably, safe—one of the very few anti-Hitler generals who 'got away with it'.

The Nazi Generals

Party-Army relations in the 'thirties were a constant see-saw, and it was primarily due to the influence of two men that the Army was steered along the Nazi course. These two men were Werner von Blomberg and Walther von Reichenau.

Von Blomberg was a Pomeranian infantryman who, though serving chiefly on the General Staff in the Great War, had won the *Pour le Mérite* for gallantry. He became *Chef des Truppenamts*, equivalent to Chief of Staff, in 1927 at the remarkably early age of 48, when still only a major-general, and in 1932 led the German military delegation to the Geneva Disarmament Conference. One of Hitler's first acts when he became Chancellor was to promote von Blomberg General of Infantry and make him Minister of Defence, and later in the same year he was promoted again to be Colonel-General.

Von Blomberg embraced Nazism with enthusiasm for he saw, rightly, that if Hitler remained in power the Army would be re-created and expanded. He was so ardent in introducing Nazi ideals into the Army, especially those of physical fitness, loyalty, the training of youth, and 'Aryanization', that he became known as 'Hitler-Boy Quex', after a movie serial popular in Germany which concerned the adventures of a lad in the Hitler Youth. His other nickname, 'the Rubber Lion', was equally unflattering.

Blomberg had proved his courage, had a thorough Staff training and much experience in the field, and was very widely travelled. He was also an intelligent and strikingly handsome man, with a fine military presence. Even the Jewish Bella Fromm recorded in November 1933, 'Blomberg, a reasonable man, except for his blind adoration of Hitler, apparently grasped what I wanted to make clear about myself. A Prussian soldier all his life, he is nevertheless amazingly well-bred. He has a good critical sense, and mental agility. Yet now he started to praise Hitler. His eyes shone with genuine rapture. "He is one of the greatest men of all time."'

Such blind devotion may have put Blomberg in a false relation with most of his colleagues, but it certainly put him in tune with the German youth of the day

In 1936 he became a field-marshal, the only one in Germany, and as Minister of Defence led the German delegation to the coronation of King George VI. It was during his visit to Russia in the late 'twenties, where the armed services seemed to prosper outstandingly under a totalitarian régime, that von Blomberg became convinced that a man like Hitler was needed to give the Army its due. He was less an ideological Nazi than an admirer of Hitler personally.

While encouraging good relations, he was careful to insist that there should be no Party interference with the Army. It was, perhaps, only this proviso which enabled von Blomberg to carry the majority of the generals with him, since his own C-in-C's Chief of Staff, Beck, and outstanding men like General of Infantry Wilhelm Adam, the first Commandant of the Wehrmacht Academy from 1935, were dead against the Nazis.

Unfortunately for von Blomberg, he got himself into stupid personal trouble in 1938, which led to his premature retirement at the age of 59. His first wife having died, he married a typist in the War Ministry. Both Hitler and Göring had dignified the wedding by their presence. But it later turned out that she had been a Berlin prostitute. Hitler was resentful at having been let down, as he saw it, by Blomberg and with the whole Officer Corps appalled at what had been revealed, Blomberg had to go. Go Blomberg did—but not before, in a moment of unconscious irony, suggesting that Göring should take his place.

Hitler would not accept Göring, and nor would he accept as Minister of Defence the Army Commander-in-Chief, Colonel-General von Fritsch, who was the Army's choice. Himmler, whose S.S. von Fritsch particularly hated, ganged up with Göring to block this appointment. And now another scandal broke out, which led to a charge of homosexuality being made against von Fritsch, based on mistaken identification. This was probably cooked up by the Gestapo, but the whole business was wretchedly handled by the Army, and von Fritsch was so upset by the charge, that he quite failed to establish a proper defence. So he too resigned, though cleared by the Court of Enquiry headed by Göring, and was fobbed off with an honorary colonelcy of his regiment.

The Army was now in some trouble. It had greatly lost face, and Hitler was to take advantage of its disturbed equilibrium. In 1938 he dismissed some of the generals whom he distrusted, most of them being supporters of von Fritsch.

Colonel-General von Fritsch was exonerated and reinstated in his rank, but he was a broken and embittered man, who later sought and found death with the rank and file on the Polish front. He wrote to a lady friend of his: 'Herr Hitler has lightly turned aside the word of honour of the then Commander-in-Chief of his Army, in favour of the word of an honourless scoundrel. Nor has he found a single word of apology for me. It is this, above all, that I cannot countenance.' In fact Hitler and his Nazi cronies were only too glad to be rid of von Fritsch, who had always been a potential threat to Nazi domination of the Services.

Von Blomberg went into exile with his new wife, for a year, and then returned to Bavaria where he lived quietly. He gave evidence at the Nuremberg Trials, and died in 1946. Shortly before his death he stated; 'Before 1938–9 the German generals were not opposed to Hitler. There was no reason to oppose him since he produced the results which they desired. After this time some generals began to condemn his methods and lost confidence in the power of his judgement. However, they failed as a group to take any definite stand against him, although a few of them tried to do so and, as a result, had to pay for this with their lives or their positions.'

With the departure of von Blomberg and von Fritsch, Hitler now saw his chance to put a real Nazi sympathiser at the head of the Army. This was General of Artillery Walther von Reichenau, who in the vital years of 1933 and 1934 had worked closely under Blomberg as Head of the Ministerial Office in the Reichswehr Ministry, and then as Head of the Armed Forces Office. But the consecutive leadership of the Army, under von Rundstedt, blocked von Reichenau's appointment again, as it had in 1934: Reichenau was too 'radical' for them. Von Rundstedt now proposed Beck, whom Hitler would not accept. Thus von Brauchitsch became the new C-in-C as a compromise candidate acceptable on all sides.

Von Reichenau was born at Karlsruhe in 1884. His father was a Prussian general, his mother came from Silesia. He joined the 1st Guards Field Artillery Regiment in 1903, and in the Great War he was first a regimental adjutant and than a Staff officer. In 1929 he studied English in Britain, and developed a high regard for the British. Reichenau commanded VII Army Corps and Wehrkreis VII at Munich from 1935 to 1938, first as a lieutenant-general, then as general of artillery. In 1938 he took over Heeresgruppe IV at Leipzig. He did not, however, become C-in-C of the Army, his appointment being blocked by von Rundstedt and by President Hindenburg himself. Von Reichenau had had a great deal to do with the development of unification of command and the creation of O.K.W. In Walter Görlitz's view, he had been 'the first military expert of real importance who placed himself entirely without reservation at the dictatorship's disposal'.

Reichenau was undoubtedly a gifted man, and also an ambitious one. He was a colourful character, and though in appearance typically Prussian, with his stern features and eyeglass, he was in fact somewhat unconventional, and enjoyed meeting people outside his own sphere. He was also a dedicated sportsman and athlete, who ran a racing car, played tennis and swam well, boxed, and took part in cross-country runs. He was a member of the German Olympic Committee. He had also studied science and was responsible for various technical innovations

185

in the Army. Reichenau had met Hitler in 1932, and impressed him by his far from stand-offish attitude. Reichenau was popular among the troops, being in favour of more comradeship and less inaccessibility among officers towards men, and he was not arrogant.

He played a covert but shady part in the Night of the Long Knives, being privy to the plans of Hitler, Himmler, and the S.S. against Röhm and other S.A. leaders. It has been said that he helped compose the lists of those to be shot. There is no proof of this, but it is quite likely that he drafted the statement by Blomberg that appeared in the *Völkischer Beobachter* on 29 June 1934, the day before the massacre. This read:

'The Reichswehr considers itself in close harmony with the Reich of Adolf Hitler. The time has passed when people from various camps could pose as spokesmen of the Reichswehr. The role of the Army is clearly determined: it must serve the National Socialist State, which it recognizes. The hearts of the Reich and the Army beat in unison. . . . The Reichswehr wears with pride the symbols of Germany. It stands, disciplined and faithful, behind the leaders of the State, behind the Marshal of the Great War, President von Hindenburg, its supreme leader, and behind the Führer of the Reich, Adolf Hitler, who, coming from the ranks of the Army, is and always will be one of us.'

When Hitler became Chancellor it was Reichenau who had drafted the oath of allegiance for the Army. Less of a personal admirer of Hitler than von Blomberg, he had a more far-sighted political prescience, and was considered by many to be an opportunist. He had travelled widely, and in 1936 was appointed military adviser to General Chiang Kai-chek in China.

Görlitz has variously described him as 'the most progressive thinker among the Army Commanders-in-Chief', as 'a man devoid of all sentiment, at times, indeed, a cold-blooded, brutal man', and as 'not an attractive personality, but he was certainly a bold and self-willed man, as ruthless towards himself as he was towards others'.

As the Corps commander in Munich in 1937 and 1938 von Reichenau played a leading part both in the invasion of the Sudetenland and in the terrorizing of Austria and the subsequent Anschluss. He was promoted to colonel-general to command 10th Army in the Polish campaign of 1939, in which he swam the Vistula River at the head of his troops.

10th Army consisted of five Corps, IV, XI, XIV, XV and XVI, and was used as the main aggressive force, outdistancing 8th Army. On 8 September 1939 von Reichenau had the satisfaction of ordering the open city of Warsaw to be taken by a coup de main.

In the next campaign Reichenau led the same Army (though its designation had been changed to 6th Army and it now consisted of only three Corps, IV, XI and XXVII, plus Höpner's XVI Motorized

Corps) in the advance into Belgium, as part of von Bock's Army Group 'B'. The American journalist William Shirer was highly impressed by a briefing von Reichenau gave to the Press on 21 May at his headquarters near Enghien. It was clear, thorough, and surprisingly frank. 'A few more questions and answers. The general is in an almost jovial mood. He is not tense. He is not worried. He is not rushed. You wonder: "Have these German generals no nerves?" Because, after all, he is directing a large army in an important battle.'

Shirer was surprised that von Reichenau could take an hour off from the war 'to explain to amateurs his particular job'. But Reichenau was a shrewd man, who, in von Hassell's words, 'always hears the grass grow'. The propaganda value to Germany of the press reports of his advance into Belgium was worth more than one hour of his time.

Reichenau was promoted Field-Marshal on 19 July 1940. He had vigorously opposed the withdrawal of Höpner's armour from his Army, but had had to yield them to Rundstedt's Army Group. This was particularly bitter to Reichenau, who had been a much keener supporter of tanks than many of his contemporaries, and who had, indeed, translated some of Liddell Hart's works into German.

In the vital early days in France his 6th Army destroyed the Belgian Army and pinned down the Allied mobile forces on the left wing. Von Reichenau personally accepted King Leopold's surrender. For the second part of the French campaign Reichenau had Colonel-General von Kleist's Panzer Group, with Höpner's Corps in place of Guderian's, under him. He used it to good effect in a two-pronged drive from the Marne to the Cher, taking Orleans.

Reichenau was a tough commander, who during the winter of 1939–40 had threatened to have men shot who went absent without leave. All the same, in Poland he had protested about S.S. atrocities. From now on he seems to have become somewhat disenchanted with Hitler and the Nazi leaders.

In the proposed invasion of England Reichenau's 6th Army would have played a prominent part. On 21 May 1940 Reichenau had first suggested the possibility of an amphibious invasion, but by August he was against it.

In Russia von Reichenau again commanded 6th Army, with a strength of five panzer, three motorized infantry, and 12 infantry divisions, under von Rundstedt's Army Group South. He ordered every junior commander to write on his mapboard 'Pursuit without rest' in the drive to Belgorod and Kharkov. In December 1941 Field-Marshal von Reichenau took over Army Group South from von Rundstedt but had to fall back to the Mius River, as Rundstedt had decided to do before his dismissal. Reichenau's command was short-lived, for on 17 January 1942 he died of a heart attack. He had had a successful career, though he had not reached the very top, as he had so ardently wished. He emerges as a gifted, ambitious, rather dangerous man, who had certainly done a great deal to smooth Hitler's path with the Army, had kept the S.A. at arm's length, and had differed from Hitler more from personal disaffection or disappointment than from any real quarrel with what Hitler stood for. Kesselring described him as 'temperamental', and Görlitz as 'one of the most unusual, most brilliant, and most controversial figures among the leaders of the last German Wehrmacht'. Undoubtedly Field-Marshal von Reichenau stood head and shoulders above a great many run-of-the-mill commanders, and until his death at the age of 57 he had never lost a major battle.

As one regarded Field-Marshal Wilhelm Keitel in the dock at Nuremberg, one wondered how this heavily-built, tall, fleshy-faced, rather ponderous man could ever have risen to high position. Keitel, in his uniform stripped of decorations and baton, looked more like the head gardener on a country estate than a general—even a desk general. In fact he owed his rise partly to happy chance, partly to nepotism, and partly to his own undoubted industry.

He was born in 1882 near Brunswick, not a Prussian, the son of a small estate farmer. He joined the artillery in 1901, was a captain at the outbreak of the Great War, and served first as a battery commander, being wounded, and then as a Staff officer. In 1925 he got his first job in the Reichswehr Ministry, leaving it after 20 months to command an artillery battalion. By 1931 he was a colonel, having been head of the Organisations Department of the Truppenamt since late 1929. He became a major-general in 1934, Head of the Wehrmachtsamt, a lieutenant-general in 1936, and general of artillery in 1937. He never commanded a division.

Keitel owed his vital promotion mainly to the fact that he was von Blomberg's son-in-law, having married his daughter in 1937. In 1938 he was made head of the O.K.W., by Hitler, who, having asked Blomberg once who Keitel was, had been told, 'Oh, that's merely the fellow who runs my office'. But Blomberg had given Keitel a good reference as an efficient *chef de bureau*. Keitel's brother Lieutenant-General Bodewin Keitel, was Head of the Army Personnel Office from 1938 to 1942, which gave Keitel a useful handle in appointments, but Bodewin was never a man of great influence.

Nor, in spite of his high position and rank, was Wilhelm Keitel. Despite having risen to be one of Hitler's most prominent military assistants, he displayed throughout his career the mediocrity which should have ensured that he never reached general rank. His basic stock-in-trade was his loyalty to Hitler, under which he seemed prepared to accept cruel indignities and insults. He was a man of little imagination or intellectual power, but by his very seniority—he was made a colonel-general in November 1938—he could exercise influence. He soon earned the nickname 'Lackeitel' (Lackey Keitel) for his sycophancy towards the Nazis. He did more than anyone except, perhaps, Jodl to bring about the domination of the Reichswehr by the Nazis. In the process he was thoroughly disloyal to his chief, General von Fritsch, in 1938, to whom he was 'that jack-ass'. To Dr Schacht he was Hitler's 'unthinking and irresponsible yes-man'.

Keitel would undoubtedly have been far happier running his small estate in the country. As it was, as Chief of Staff of the combined Services (O.K.W.) he was the funnel through which Hitler's orders passed and which received reports, complaints, and questions. Seldom did Keitel take a decision on his own, readily accepting the distasteful role of the Führer's mouthpiece, though he was not above bullying Army Group and Army commanders when he felt he could get away with it. Rarely did he intercede for them when they appealed for help in a crisis, as at Stalingrad. Admittedly Russia was, in theory, outside the O.K.W. sphere of influence but Keitel could have made his influence felt had he shown any persistence or flair. As it was, he became a sort of postman for the military and for Hitler, the front man who issued the Führer's orders. He also supervised matters like manpower replacement, the use of slave labour in the occupied countries and Germany, and relations between the Party and the military. In this capacity he became friendly with men like Himmler, Ribbentrop, and Bormann, but none of them really respected him— not surprisingly, when Hitler once said that he had the brain of a cinema doorman, and on at least one occasion rebuked him so vehemently that Keitel talked of committing suicide.

By his fervent Nazi attitude and admiration for the Party Keitel betrayed the Army, for he neglected to make use of his titular power as head of the O.K.W. and allowed the strategic direction of the war to pass unquestioned into Hitler's hands.

From 1938 to the end of the war this man was constantly at Hitler's side. Even by 1937, in fact, he had become known as 'the chambermaid of the Reich Chancellory' through his almost daily visits to Hitler. Then from 1938 one finds Keitel at every big conference and international meeting. He was at Berchtesgaden for the Schuschnigg meetings, visited Rome with Hitler in May 1938, held Staff talks with the Italians in 1939, conducted the French Armistice negotiations in 1940 at Compiegne, was with Hitler in Vienna, Poland, France, Russia, Finland—and so on, endlessly.

Keitel's signature appears at the foot of a number of very important documents, some of which were to help send him to the gallows. On 22 June 1939 he signed the orders for 'Fall Weiss', the invasion of Poland. On 16 December 1943 he signed an anti-partisan order for the Balkans: 'If the fight against the Partisans in the East, as well as in the Balkans, is not waged with the most brutal means, we shall shortly reach the point where the available forces are insufficient to control this area.'

Occasionally, even Keitel had glimmerings of strategic common sense. Early in 1941 he recommended the use of paratroops to take—not Crete—but Malta, which would have been far more use to the German African campaign; but Hitler chose Crete. In 1943 he was sceptical about the possibility of defending Sicily—but Hitler ordered it defended. Yet Keitel seldom volunteered a constructive opinion, and when he did believe in something was not tough enough in his advocacy. As one of the so-called 'Three Wise Men'—the committee which included Dr Hans Lammers, head of Hitler's chancellory for political affairs, and Martin Bormann, head of Nazi Party affairs—Keitel was partly responsible for laying down guidelines for foreign and domestic policy. In fact this committee was unpopular and at loggerheads with Göring, Göbbels, Dr Ley, Dr Funk, and Albert Speer. Göring thought that Lammers was trying to get power back into the old Civil Service bureaucracy, Bormann was trying to get it into his own hands, but that Keitel was 'an absolute zero who need not be taken seriously'.

Hitler kept Keitel because he was doggedly loyal and gave him no trouble, but he was not above telling Göbbels on 9 March 1943 that he had nothing but contempt for his generals; and 'about Keitel the Führer can only laugh'. On 23 September 1943 Keitel comes off rather better: 'The Führer has great regard for the personality of Keitel, but doesn't think much of his ability.'

When one reads Keitel's *Memoirs*, composed in his cell at Nuremberg, one comes to have slightly more respect for this unfortunate and second-rate man. He emerges at least with some dignity, and strikes one as a basically decent person who took the wrong road.

After failing pathetically even to get his orders obeyed in the field at the end of the war, when trying to persuade S.S. General Steiner to attack and relieve Berlin, Keitel was to sign the final instrument of the surrender of Germany in Berlin on 8 May 1945. He was sentenced to death for war crimes at Nuremberg, and hanged on 16 October 1946. Before he died he claimed that since 1938 none of the really important decisions had been taken as the result of joint counsel. 'It was the issuing of an order . . . but not a conference.' But he could not evade his own responsibility, even if he had often failed to exercise it. By his encouragement of Hitler's optimism he let down his fellows, and by his readiness to believe evil of them cost many of them their jobs and contributed to the loss of not a few of their lives.

Colonel-General Alfred Jodl was a very different man to Keitel. Here was a really intelligent Staff officer, an able man who would have been an asset to any Army headquarters. Born in Bavaria 1890, Jodl came from a middle-class background, and was something of an intellectual. He fought as an artillery officer in the Great War and thereafter served mostly on the Staff. By 1935 he was a lieutenant-colonel and head of the Home Defence Department of the Reichswehr Ministry. He had been introduced to Hitler by Röhm in 1923, and from early days decided that Hitler was the man to follow. An ambitious man, he furthered his own career in so doing. Of Hitler's success at Munich he wrote in his diary on 29 September 1938: 'The genius of the Führer and his determination not to shun even a world war have again achieved victory without the use of force. One hopes that the incredulous, the weak and the doubters have been converted, and will remain so.'

For a short time the Chief of Operations to the newly established O.K.W. in 1938 was Lieutenant-General Max von Viebahn, but he was not sufficiently pro-Nazi for Hitler's purposes, and the job went to Major-General Jodl. He was to hold it until the end of the war, as Chief of Operations of the Wehrmacht, rising to the rank of Colonel-General. Jodl was a technician, an expert. Hitler, who had long resented and envied the General Staff, found Jodl much more valuable than Keitel, for he was equally dedicated without being unintelligent and he tended to use him as a substitute for the General Staff. In the military sphere he thus became indispensable.

Although Jodl normally enjoyed the Führer's favour, there were occasions when he fell into bad grace, and one such was when Hitler decided to get rid of Halder, Chief of Staff of the Army, in 1942. Jodl was rash enough to try to persuade Hitler to let Halder stay on.

Jodl was Hitler's chief military planner. He had had a hand in the Czechoslovakian and Rhineland occupations, and he was to become primarily responsible for the Italian and Finnish-Scandinavian theatres of operations. Single-handedly he planned the invasion of Yugoslavia in a single night.

Jodl was against the battle of Kursk, 'Operation Citadel', in 1943 because he thought there were already prospective dangers in the Mediterranean. Neither he nor Keitel officially had any say in strategic planning for the Russian theatre, but each was able to—and did—back up Hitler's own ideas. What constantly baffles one about Jodl is how he fell completely under Hitler's influence and genuinely believed in his military genius. Even as late as 1944 he said to Guderian, 'Do you know of a better supreme commander than Adolf Hitler?' Guderian could probably have named several. But Jodl was not a stupid man. He had foreseen the danger of unlimited expansion of the S.S., which he thought 'disturbing' in 1940, and took steps to prevent expansion of the Waffen S.S. by getting the O.K.W. to investigate S.S. recruiting operations. He stood up to Hitler on various occasions, treating each problem coolly and academically, and refusing to be rattled. He defended List, and got into trouble for doing so. It was Jodl who removed Keitel's pistol from his desk when the Field-Marshal was contemplating suicide, after Hitler had verbally thrashed him for daring to suggest that it might be wiser after all to retreat during the winter of 1941–2 in Russia.

Jodl was loyal to his chief, but not to his Corps. Although he claimed to feel the moral pride and prestige of being a member of the General Staff, he had deliberately intrigued against the upright von Fritsch when still a comparatively junior officer. After the Rastenburg explosion of 20 July 1944, in which he was wounded in the head, Jodl endorsed a memorandum from O.K.H. that 'the whole General Staff should be abolished', which was an absurd idea.

Jodl was outspoken about many things. In 1939 he described the much vaunted Siegfried Line as being 'little better than a large building site', and he surprised Mannerheim by telling him that the Italians would never be a source of strength to the Germans in the war. He argued fiercely with Zeitzler about the demerits of the Kursk offensive; and he pushed hard his own and Raeder's sensible plans for the capture of Malta though without effect. In spite of Jodl's position as O.K.W. Chief of Operations, in matters such as Malta, Africa, and the northern front, he did not do anything contrary to Hitler's wishes.

Although he summed up the dilemma of the Generals as 'How to conduct a war they did not want under a Supreme Commander whose trust they did not enjoy and whom they themselves trusted only to a limited extent', he clearly believed that the fault lay with the generals, not with Hitler. 'His knowledge and intellect, his rhetoric and his will-power triumphed in the end in every spiritual conflict over everyone. As early as 1938 Jodl had confided to his diary that the General Staff lacked 'vigour of soul, because in the end they do not believe in the genius of the Führer'.

Göbbels, rather interestingly, had no high regard for Jodl's abilities, perhaps because they so nearly approached his own. They were the two intellectuals of Nazi Germany, one in the military, the other in the political field. Of Jodl's operations in Italy, Göbbels remarked on 4 December 1943: 'Jodl does not seem to me any too competent at evaluating a critical military situation. He has so often been wrong in his prognoses that personally I am unable to drop my worries about the southern Italian front'.

The greatest drawback from which Jodl, like Keitel, suffered, was lack of first-hand experience of the war. Though they made various trips to different fronts, they seldom stayed long enough to learn very much, and neither of them had ever commanded even a moderately large formation in peacetime, let alone wartime. They were desk soldiers.

After the war Jodl wrote of his relationship with Hitler:

'I cannot recall being so divided in my feelings towards any other man as I was towards Hitler. My emotions ranged from reverence and admiration to hatred. His destructive and caustic criticism of so much I held dear—the General Staff, the middle class, the nobility, the Reichswehr, our sense of right and justice—all this repelled me more and more, especially during the second half of the war.... Towards the end of the war, Hitler grew increasingly cruel, unjust and suspicious, and rounded on everybody.'

Jodl's conduct at Nuremberg was dignified enough, but it was almost pathetic to see an obviously intelligent man having to admit so many compromises in his way of life. He did not strike one as a typical German general; perhaps the chief characteristic of his that one carried away was a sort of intellectual obstinacy. Mentally he seemed very tough.

Colonel-General Jodl was hanged at Nuremberg for war crimes. He was 56 years old.

The one Army general on Hitler's staff who succeeded in keeping the goodwill and trust of both the Army and the Nazis was General of Infantry Rudolf Schmundt. In 1937 while still a major, he became a military adjutant to Hitler, succeeding Colonel Hossbach as chief adjutant in January 1938, when he became a lieutenant-colonel. Even in July 1940 he was still only a colonel.

Schmundt was an avowed Nazi, and because of his enthusiasm for Hitler was known in the Officer Corps as 'John the Disciple'. He kept the military diary at Hitler's headquarters, but in 1942 was given the important job of Head of the Army Personnel Office (formerly held by General Bodewin Keitel), in which capacity he dealt with promotions and appointments. This elevation was responsible for his elevation to the rank of general. He has been described variously as 'polite and gentlemanly' (Guderian); 'a suave, discreet, obedient soldier' (Ian Colvin); and 'very good-looking, very intelligent, very ambitious and very "smooth"' (Desmond Young).

Schmundt may well have been ambitious, but he was also somewhat ingenuous. Von Senger relates how, on a visit to Italy, Schmundt appeared to him and his staff 'completely forthcoming and apparently without guile; for hours he held forth to us about his good fortune in being allowed to work with so great a man in these great times'. He got on well with people—he was a friend of Rommel, of the conspirator von Tresckow (whose activities he did not in the least suspect), and, particularly, of Zeitzler. Despite his avowed Nazi sympathies he remained in touch with Canaris until the latter's dismissal. With his close contact with Hitler he wielded more influence than his rank or position warranted; even so, when he suggested that S.S. Colonel-General Hausser should succeed Rommel in Normandy, and Sepp Dietrich succeed Hausser, von Kluge got these appointments turned down.

Dr Göbbels recorded on 21 March 1943 how 'General Schmundt complained bitterly about the indolence of a number of senior officers who either do not want, or in some cases are unable, to understand the Führer. They are thereby robbing themselves, as General Schmundt put it, of the greatest happiness any of our contemporaries can experience —that of serving a genius.' Later that year Göring told Göbbels that he considered Schmundt 'the only honest and trustworthy personality at G.H.Q.', and Göbbels also refers to Schmundt's making 'a clean sweep of officers', like Dönitz in the Navy, to get new and presumably Nazi blood in high positions. Thus Generals such as Zeitzler, Model, and Schörner, probably owed their rapid rise partially to Schmundt. He remained a firm believer in Hitler until his dying day, which came after he was severely wounded in the 20 July bomb explosion. He was succeeded in the Army Personnel Office by General Burgdorf.

General of Infantry Wilhelm Burgdorf spent most of the war as chief Wehrmacht adjutant to Hitler, a position in which he acquired considerable influence. From July 1944 as Chief of the Army Personnel Bureau, he consolidated his position and finished as one of the inner circle around Hitler, and an ally of Bormann. It was Burgdorf who got General Krebs moved up to take Guderian's place as Chief of Staff in 1945.

Burgdorf was a thickset, stocky, florid man, who drank heavily, and whose portraits show a brutal and unprepossessing personality. According to Manfred Rommel, son of the Field-Marshal, he was 'hated for his brutality by 99 per cent of the officer corps', and Jürgen Thorwald describes him as the 'gravedigger of the German officer corps . . . who had done so much to make the German Army Hitler's obedient tool'. Apart from his slavish devotion to Hitler and the Nazi cause Burgdorf had few qualifications for high position. He earned his promotion to general from colonel without commanding troops. It was he who drove to Rommel's home after the July Plot, and forced him to choose between suicide and arrest, taking the poison with him. He was one of the witnesses to the Führer's will and political testament. He shot himself in the Chancellory after Hitler's suicide. He emerges as one of the least attractive of the unprepossessing bunch round Hitler and his self-justifying regrets expressed during a drinking session in the bunker with Bormann and Krebs in the last days of the war do not persuade us otherwise. Boldt records in *Hitler's Last Days* how Burgdorf on 28 April 1945 told Krebs: 'Ever since I took on this job, nearly a year ago, I've put all my energy and idealism into it: I've tried every way I know to bring the Army and the Party closer together . . . In the end they accused me in the Forces of being a traitor to the German officer class, and now I can see that those recriminations were justified, that my work was in vain, my idealism wrong—not only wrong, but naive and stupid. . . .

Our young officers went to war with great faith and idealism. Hundreds of thousands of them have gone to their deaths. And for what? For their fatherland, for our greatness and our future? For a decent, clean Germany? In their hearts, yes; but not in reality. They have died for you, for your good living and your megalomania. The youth of a nation of eighty million has shed its blood on the battlefields of Europe, millions of innocent people have been sacrificed, whilst you, the leaders of the Party [pointing to Bormann], have lined your pockets from the wealth of the nation. . . . You have destroyed our culture with its hundreds of years of history, you have destroyed the German people. That is the terrible burden of the guilt you bear!'

Of all the generals dear to Hitler, Colonel-General Eduard Dietl came close for a time to rivalling Rommel in national popularity.

Dietl was a Bavarian from Styria, a mountaineer who after the Great War joined the Epp Freikorps in 1919. In 1920 he became a member of the Nazi Party; as a captain on the Bavarian General Staff in the early twenties he became one of Hitler's chief informants in the Reichswehr; and he took part in the Hitler *putsch* of 1923. Later he commanded Alpine Regiment 99 at Kempten, and by 1939 he was a major-general and G.O.C. 3rd Mountain Division at Graz, Austria, having taken part in the occupation of Austria. He took this division to Poland in 1939.

Dietl's great reputation was gained in the Norwegian campaign, where he was nominally under the command of von Falkenhorst. His Mountain division was enlarged to a Mountain Corps, in which there was a large proportion of Austrians, on 16 June 1940, and less than four months after becoming a lieutenant-general on 1 April he was promoted General of Mountain Troops on 19 July. On 21 April 1941 Hitler received Dietl at the Chancellory and outlined to him the tasks that would fall to the Mountain troops during the invasion of Russia. The primary one remained the protection of Norway, but Mountain Corps Norway was also to secure the Petsamo area with its iron ore mines and the Arctic highway, and then in conjunction with Finnish forces to advance against the Murmansk railway and cut off overland supplies to the Murmansk area.

To Hitler the distance from Petsamo to Murmansk was only 'those ridiculous sixty miles' but to Dietl it was more or less impenetrable tundra. He urged Hitler to drop the idea of a direct attack on Murmansk, and to concentrate on defending the Petsamo area, cutting the Murmansk railway further south. Hitler promised to consider the matter, but in May Dietl was told that the Murmansk attack must go in. By mid-July his troops got to within twenty-eight miles of Murmansk, but neither of his formations—those of General of Cavalry Feige's XXXVI Corps to his south, and the Finns—got further.

Operating in the Arctic tundra was a very different matter from Western Europe, and even from Norway, and the Russians had the advantage of experience. In the swampland and myriad lakes outside Murmansk they defended so successfully that by 19 September Dietl had to authorize a withdrawal behind the river Litsa. Dietl's fears about an attack on Murmansk had been proved right.

His 'failure' did not affect Hitler's good opinion of him, however, and he was the subject of an intensive propaganda campaign by Göbbels during and after the Norwegian campaign. His face was constantly in the Nazi papers and magazines. Göbbels wrote in his diary on 13 February 1942: 'He is a true people's general. He is constantly with the troops and has achieved a popularity that is indescribable.'

The tall, slightly stooping Dietl, with his foxy, sharp face and frequent grin was also popular among the men of his 20th Mountain Army. He had a youthful zest, and being himself of comparatively humble origin mixed easily with the troops.

In January 1942 Dietl was made colonel-general and appointed C-in-C German Troops in Lapland. The Finnish front, unlike the Russian one, was an O.K.W. rather than an O.K.H. preserve, and Dietl had his fellow Bavarian, Jodl, mainly to deal with in Berlin.

He also got on well with the Finns, from whom in mid-November 1942 he took over the Utra sector of the front.

Mannerheim recorded in his memoirs that Dietl was 'a likeable person who had regard for our points of view and wishes'. His dashing and chivalrous personality gained him many friends in Finland and he became very popular among the population of Lapland.

Colonel-General Dietl, the first man in the Army to receive the Oak Leaves to the Knight's Cross, was killed in a plane crash in the summer of 1944.

Of the senior generals at the outbreak of war, only von Reichenau and Keitel were more devoted Nazis than Ernst Busch. He was born in 1885. As a major-general Busch commanded the 23rd Division at Potsdam between 1935 and 1937, and from 1938 to 1939 the VIII Corps at Breslau as Lieutenant-General and General of Infantry. In the campaign in France in 1940 he commanded the 16th Army of four Corps which he later took to Russia under von Rundstedt. It would have provided the main assault force for an invasion of Britain.

Busch was primarily an infantryman. After the fall of France, he was promoted colonel-general, and commanded the 16th Army under von Leeb in the first part of the Russian campaign in the North. Promoted Field-Marshal on 1 February 1943, he took over command of Army Group Centre on 28 October 1943 when von Kluge was injured in a car accident. In the Russian offensive of June 1944 his three Armies with only 34 divisions held a front stretching 450 miles.

They were attacked by nearly 200 Russian divisions with a strength of 6,000 tanks and assault guns, backed up by 7,000 aircraft. Busch's Army Group Centre was broken, and the bulk of 4th and 9th Armies were trapped between Minsk and the Gerezina River. In the disastrous fighting Busch lost about 25 divisions in 12 days. Von Tippelskirch's 4th Army lost 130,000 men of its original strength of 165,000, despite the fact that Tippelskirch, a highly experienced commander, on 25 June took matters into his own hands and ordered a withdrawal to behind the Dnieper. Busch tried to countermand this order, and to compel Tippelskirch's Army to retake its old front. Only on 28 June did Tippelskirch at Beresino receive an order from Busch to get 4th Army behind the Beresino front. He noted in his diary, 'This order has come too late!' And in his last conversation with the Army Group commander Tippelskirch on 28 June 'could not resist expressing his bitterness over the developments which had resulted from the way the Army Group had been led'. 3rd Panzer Army lost 10 divisions; and 9th Army—commanded first by General of Infantry Hans Jordan, and then, after Jordan was dismissed for irresolute leadership, by General of Panzer Troops Nikolaus von Vormann—lost several divisions, though it held the Bobruysk pocket open long enough for some 10,000 to 15,000 of its troops to escape.

After these disasters Busch was relieved on 28 June, and it looked as though his career was over. By September 1944 Hitler had already put him on the select list of generals who were not to be considered for future Army Group or Army commands. However, Hitler changed his mind. Busch was chosen to give the funeral address for General Schmundt after 20 July, and—doubtless by those protestations of loyalty and faith in the Führer which he was apt to make whenever subjected to Hitler's presence—he managed to work his passage back. In April 1945 Busch was appointed C-in-C North-West, commanding the front from Bremen to Magdeburg, and the Netherlands—or what remained of them—against the Allies.

But he could do nothing to prevent the inevitable. In Russia he had lost the confidence of men like Jordan because of his lack of moral courage, and his total dependence upon O.K.H. or Hitler orders. Now in the closing stages of the war the German troops and junior officers were thoroughly cynical and demoralized, and toughly as in many cases they still fought, they were not to be moved to impossible tasks by a commander like Busch giving out obviously impossible directives.

Field-Marshal Ernst Busch's final task as C-in-C North-West Europe was to implement the German surrender to Montgomery at Luneberg Heath. A soldier promoted above his ceiling, Busch lies buried in waste ground in an unmarked grave at Aldershot, where he died as a prisoner of war.

One of the most outstanding younger generals under Hitler was Walter Model. Born in 1891 in comparatively humble circumstances, Model worked in the Training Department of the War Ministry, and later became head of the inventions department. He established close relations with the Nazi leaders, and was taken up by Göbbels, who introduced him to Hitler. He made a good impression upon the Führer, who treated him as one of his favourites.

In the Polish campaign Model was Chief of Staff to IV Corps. In France he occupied the same position in Busch's 16th Army as a major-general. Model then left the Staff to command 3rd Panzer Division in the invasion of Russia, serving under Generals Geyr von Schweppenburg and Guderian. Despite his monocle there was nothing stuffy about Model. He was remarkably successful as a divisional commander, being a thruster with immense energy and popular with his troops. His division seized a very important bridge across the Desna at Novgorod which opened the way to the corn-belt of the Ukraine for Guderian's tanks. On 7 September Model established a bridgehead across the Seym River, swept past Konotop towards Romny, and on 15 September linked up with 9th Panzer Division at the bridge at Sencha thus closing a huge pocket round Kiev. As a result of these successes he was promoted Lieutenant-General in October 1941 to command XLI Panzer Corps on the Upper Volga. In January 1942 General of Panzer Troops Model took over 9th Army from the ailing Colonel-General Strauss, an impressive rise for a man who a few months earlier had been only a divisional commander.

He took over at a critical time, when the Russians were attacking Rzhev, a vital point in the Central front, and trying to outflank and encircle his Army. From the moment Model took command, the regiments of the 9th Army seemed to gain strength. He was always popping up at unexpected places and times, very much a front-line general; and the troops believed him to be lucky. His tactics were aggressive, and towards the end of January he turned 9th Army over to the attack, and won back the initiative from Sychevka to Rzhev without having lost either city despite the strength of the Russian attacks. By mid-February the battle of Rzhev and the Volga Bend had been won, though at heavy cost. One day Model asked one of his S.S. regimental commanders the strength of his regiment, which had been in bitter fighting, to be told it was down to 35 men. Model was promoted colonel-general on 1 February, an even more astonishing rise for a man who had been a colonel three years before. For the remainder of 1942 Model had to cope with various Russian counter-attacks, which, as a born improvisor, he managed to do despite his shortage of men.

In 1943, against Model's will, 9th Army was given a leading part to play in 'Operation Citadel', the Kursk-Orel offensive. Model made repeated objections on the grounds of the comparative strengths of the German attack and the Russian defence. These objections should have been taken seriously, for Model was not the man to complain idly; but they did not prevail. Model was given five Corps, consisting of six panzer, 14 infantry and one Panzer Grenadier divisions, and more than 900 tanks. Luftflotte 6 provided 1st Air Division in the north with 730 aircraft, and VIII Air Corps, 1,100 aircraft in the south, to support the whole Citadel operation.

Model's attack in the northern part of the front met initial success. On 5 July 1943 he breached the Russian first line of defence and advanced some six miles on a 20-mile front. But on the next two days he ran into fierce opposition in wooded country and lost over 10,000 men. He also began to run short of tank ammunition, and was badly slowed up by Soviet minefields. Soon his advance came to a standstill. Hitler called off the operation shortly thereafter, but it is easier to start a battle than to halt one, and the fighting round Orel continued for five weeks. From 13 July to 5 August Model commanded 2nd Panzer Army as well as his own 9th Army.

For the next six months or so Model was to add to his reputation by a series of defensive battles against the Russians on the Central front. In January 1944 he succeeded Field-Marshal von Küchler as C-in-C Army Group North, and in March was promoted field-marshal himself, at 53 the youngest such in the Wehrmacht. After some defensive successes in the north the great 'firm-stander' was transferred again, on the dismissal of von Manstein and von Kleist at the end of March 1944. He took over Army Group North Ukraine, and Manstein's lapsed Army Group South. In June 1944 he replaced Busch as C-in-C Army Group Centre, but still retained Army Group North Ukraine, where Colonel-General Harpe of 4th Panzer Army acted for him in his absence. Model thus became the most powerful German commander on the Eastern front.

In early July Model and Colonel-General Friessner, the newly appointed C-in-C Army Group North, asked Hitler to give up Estonia and provide them with badly needed reinforcements. They got no assent and their Army Groups' situations worsened. Army Group North Ukraine, consisting of 31 German divisions, four of which were panzer, and 12 light Hungarian divisions or brigades, had by this time been forced back into South Poland and parts of Czechoslovakia and Galicia. In July and August 1944 this Army Group was defeated by Marshals Konev and Rokossovsky. Model still darted here, there and everywhere, but by now his frequent interventions in matters which he should have left alone were causing resentment among his juniors. He was also having difficulties with Guderian, who had succeeded Zeitzler as Army Chief of Staff. It was therefore with some relief that he went on transfer to the Western front on 16 August 1944 to take over Army Group 'B' from von Kluge.

Model soon made his presence felt. Running into Lieut-General Fritz Bayerlein, the commander of Panzer Lehr Division, who told him that the remnants of his division were going to be pulled out of the line for a rest, Model said sharply: 'My dear Bayerlein, in the East our divisions take their rest in the front line. And that's how things are going to be done here in the future. You will stay with your formations where you are.'

Model had sent a message of loyalty to Hitler after the July Plot, and loyal to Hitler he undoubtedly was. But he also dared to disagree with him, and proved that by standing up to Hitler one could occasionally influence him. He was not generally liked by his fellow-generals, for he could be difficult both as a subordinate and as a superior. Von Manteuffel told Liddell Hart, 'Model was a very good tactician, and better in defence than in attack. He had a knack of gauging what troops could do, and what they could not do. His manner was rough, and his methods were not always acceptable in the higher quarters of the German Army, but they were both to Hitler's liking. Model stood up to Hitler in a way that hardly anyone else dared, and even refused to carry out orders with which he did not agree'.

Model's headquarters in mid-September 1944, when the Arnhem operation was executed, were at Oosterbeëk, only a mile away from the first British airdrop. He was thus able quickly to order the refitting 9th and 10th S.S. Panzer Divisions of II S.S. Panzer Corps to contain the threat and organize the defence of the area.

By December Model had about 25 divisions in Army Group 'B' manning the central defensive front against the Allies. Although he agreed with von Rundstedt, his superior, about the over-ambitious objectives of the Ardennes offensive, Model was obliged to carry it out. As he expected, it did not succeed; and it left the German Army, which suffered bitter casualties, in a state of lower morale than before. Model had used all his energies in stabilizing a very rocky front in the early autumn, drumming up scratch formations and using youths of fifteen and sixteen to fight. But he could not, despite his stirring Orders of the Day, perform miracles. On 8 January 1945 he was finally permitted to withdraw, and by 16 January the German forces were back on their startline. They had suffered estimated losses of between 80,000 and 120,000 men; 50,000, an unusually large figure, had gone into captivity. They also lost 600 tanks and assault guns and 1,600 aircraft. American losses had been heavy too, but the Americans could replace their deficiencies while the Germans could not.

Model cannot be blamed for the Ardennes, nor for the decision to stand and fight west of the Rhine, which he strongly deprecated. Time and again he asked Hitler to withdraw the order that the Siegfried Line must be held at all costs, and he recommended that at least 20 divisions be withdrawn to prepare the defences of the Rhine. But Hitler refused all such requests and Model was forced to fight on where he stood. By the end of March he could no longer prevent the advance of three American Armies, the 1st, 9th and 15th, and he was backed relentlessly into the Ruhr. When 9th and 1st U.S. Armies linked up at Lippstadt on 1 April Model's fate was sealed. His 15th and 5th Panzer Armies, consisting of 21 divisions, were encircled in the smoky ruins of industrial Germany.

Despite all his requests to abandon the Ruhr being turned down by Hitler, Model nevertheless made desperate attempts to break out—in the Hamm area in the north, and in the Siegen area in the south. Kesselring, then C-in-C West, has criticized the direction of Model's counter attacks—too far west—but in fact it was now too late to make much difference. Although isolated groups offered spirited resistance to the Americans, in general the morale of Model's troops was broken. There were widespread desertions and surrenders from 10 April onwards, and on 14 April the Ruhr pocket was split in two when American columns from north and south met on the Ruhr River near Hagen. On 18 April all organized resistance ended, with some 320,000 German soldiers captured, including thirty generals. It was a disaster comparable with Stalingrad or the end in Tunisia, and the number of prisoners taken was indeed greater than at either.

But Field-Marshal Model was not one of them. He had shot himself on 21 April in a wood near Duisberg, because he was convinced that the Allies would hand him over to the Russians, who regarded him as a war criminal. He had not carried out Hitler's order to destroy all factories and plant in the Ruhr. Some officers thought that he should have surrendered earlier, and indeed Bayerlein organized the surrender of his LIII Corps before the general capitulation, without consulting Model, on the grounds that further resistance was a waste of life.

For a short time in the summer Model had been C-in-C West, but it became obvious that he was not the man for this job. But as a field commander of an Army Model had few superiors, and he was certainly one of the best of the younger generation of generals, adept at swiftly organized defence, with an understanding of tank warfare. Ziemke may be over-praising him to suggest that by June 1944 Model was 'the best tactical mind the Germans still had in active command', next to Rundstedt, but he must certainly rank high. Paul Carell calls him 'one of the major defensive strategists of the last war', refers to his 'exceptional successes' in the Orel bulge in 1943, and makes the point that at the end of June 1944 Model's combined commands covered more than half of the Eastern front. 'Never before in the war had Hitler entrusted so much military responsibility to one man. This was very nearly Manstein's old dream of a Commander-in-Chief, East. But this measure, too, came too late'.

Field-Marshal Ferdinand Schörner (a product, like Dietl, of the Mountain Troops), ranks second only to Model among the pro-Nazi generals. As a young lieutenant in the Bavarian Infantry Regiment of the German Alpine Corps, he had won the *Pour le Mérite* at Caporetto in the Great War by storming the controlling mountain fortress of Monte Kolonrat and taking Hill 1114 far behind the Isonzo front.

Coming like Model from a lower middle-class background, Schörner was one of those officers who embraced Nazism and used it to foster his own career. In 1938, as a colonel, he was chosen to be the first German officer to greet the Italian troops at the Brenner Pass. Between 1940 and 1942 he commanded the 6th Mountain Division from Innsbruck as a major-general. This good division fought in Greece, where it broke the Metaxas Line, advanced through the Mount Olympus hills, and took Larissa, helped by the Viennese 2nd Panzer Division, and finally Athens. It then fought in Crete, and in 1941 was posted to the far north of the German front against Russia, in the Murmansk sector in the Arctic.

In January 1942 Schörner became a lieutenant-general and took over the German Mountain Corps, later XIX Mountain Corps, with which he stopped the Russian offensive against Kirkenes, and counter-attacked. But he was unable to reach Murmansk and the German far northern front froze up for want of strength and mobility. He then became G.O.C. German troops in northern Norway. Schörner became General of Mountain Troops on 1 June 1942 and at the beginning of October 1943, although untrained in tank warfare, took over XL Panzer Corps from General Siegfried Heinrici on the Dnieper front. He was soon entrusted with a group of three Corps in the Dnieper bend and bridgehead. This was called 'Group Schörner' or 'Army Detachment Nikopol', Schörner organized the defence of Nikopol against greatly superior forces, including large bands of partisans in the swamps, over a front of 75 miles. His defence and evacuation of the Nikopol pocket in January and February 1944 remains one of the outstanding examples of good German generalship in the war. Despite misgivings he had agreed to Hitler's order that the salient be held, but when Marshal Chuikov penetrated the rear of his bridgehead from the north on 31 January and 1 February, Schörner gave orders for the positions across the Dnieper to be abandoned, without waiting for further instructions. The withdrawal went by the delightful name of 'Operation Ladies' Excuse Me'. By holding Apostolovo and Maryinskoye despite repeated Soviet attacks, Schörner got most of his force away over a small bridge at Grushevka, repeatedly beating off attempts to break the corridor, using combat groups of infantry and Jägers. Schörner himself was usually in the line with his men, and though a great deal of equipment and vehicles were lost in the Nikopol pocket, he did not leave behind a single wounded soldier. The Intelligence Officer of XL Panzer Corps wrote in mid-February, as Carell records, 'The pocket is burst open. Schörner has been to say goodbye. Without him and his chief of staff (Colonel von Kahlden) we should probably all be marching towards Siberia at this moment. No one who fought at Nikopol will ever forget what he owes Schörner.'

On 18 February 1944 Schörner was appointed Chief of the National Socialist Leadership Corps, a post in which he was to strengthen the Nazi hold on the Army, where political officers somewhat like Commissars were now commonplace. But at the end of March he was promoted Colonel-General and succeeded Kleist, the retiring C-in-C Army Group 'A', though with the title C-in-C Army Group South Ukraine.

On 12 April Hitler decided that Sevastopol was to be held indefinitely, because to abandon the Crimea would mean the loss of Turkish chrome ore and Rumanian oil, and adversely affect the morale of the Rumanians and Bulgarians fighting with the Germans. Schörner flew to the Berghof on 21 April to get the decision reversed, but was held to a promise to hold Sevastopol if 17th Army was reinforced. The reinforcement never arrived, except for two battalions and some guns. On 5 May the Russians attacked in force, and three days later captured the Sapun Hills. Schörner signalled Hitler that further defence of Sevastopol was impossible, and requested evacuation. For once Hitler agreed. But by the time evacuation was complete on 13 May the Germans had lost something like 50,000 men, and the Rumanians another 25,000. It was a very serious reverse which could have been avoided if Schörner's advice had been accepted.

On 24 July Schörner exchanged places with Colonel-General Friessner, Army Group North. However, he did no better in the north than Friessner and Lindemann had done, and, like them, was reduced to recommending the immediate evacuation of Estonia. But Hitler insisted on hanging on to all the Baltic States, and Schörner was hard pressed by Russian attacks trying to split his Army Group. In September his front stretched from the Gulf of Finland to south-west of Riga, and later was extended to include Memel and the East Prussian frontier when 3rd Panzer Army, commanded by Colonel-General Raus, came under his command.

By late September most of Estonia had been taken by the Russians. In early October Memel was surrounded and Riga was evacuated a few days later. Everywhere the Germans fell back, though Memel was not to fall until January 1945. Hitler would not authorize the evacuation of Courland, despite urgent recommendations from Guderian and the Navy, and Courland was to remain a surrounded but undefeated theatre until the end of the war, with 16th and 18th Armies, consisting of 26 divisions, uselessly locked up in it.

Schörner was moved again in January to take over Army Group 'A' from Colonel-General Harpe, holding a line from north of Warsaw to the Carpathians in Czechoslovakia with four Armies—the 1st and 4th Panzer and 9th and 17th Armies. By the time Army Group 'A' had been driven back to the Oder in late January its title was changed to Army Group Centre, of which Schörner became the last commander. With 18 weak infantry divisions and parts of six Panzer and Panzer Grenadier divisions, he covered a 300-mile front, and was responsible for the Silesian industrial region which was by now the last big armaments-producing area left to Germany. All was now very nearly lost in the face of overbearing attacks from Konev, and Schörner's attempt to destroy his bridgehead over the Oder at Steinau was a failure. By the end of March all of Upper Silesia had been lost; by 18 April Konev had reached Cottbus, south-east of Berlin, and Schörner's Army Group was separated from Heinrici's Army Group Vistula. Schörner was promoted Field-Marshal on 5 April, the last officer to reach that rank, but promotions could do nothing to stem the Russians.

Hitler maintained his high regard for Schörner to the end, and in his will of 29 April 1945 named him his successor as C-in-C of the German Army. But in May Schörner ordered his Army Group in Czechoslovakia to escape from the advancing Russians and make for the American lines, and flew off to the Tyrol in a light plane to take command of the supposed Alpenfestung—the Alpine redoubt, which in fact did not exist. A week after the end of the war Schörner surrendered to the Americans, but was sent to the Soviet Union. There he was tried for war crimes and sentenced to 25 years' imprisonment. After serving nine years he was released and returned to Munich, where ——much to his surprise—he found that his name was abominated as a commander who had deserted his men to save his own skin. This charge had been made by his former Chief of Staff, Lieutenant-General Oldwig von Natzmer, and by others. But such behaviour is not in line with Schörner's previous character, and many officers came forward to defend him.

He was also wanted by the Belgians for supposed war crimes in 1940. There is no doubt that Schörner was a ruthless and sometimes brutal commander. In Hungary he had issued an order for the execution of all soldiers found behind the front without authority; and in August 1944 he had demanded of the commander of the 18th Army 'Draconian intervention' and 'ruthlessness to the point of brutality' to stop retreats. Ziemke suggests that, because of his known ruthlessness, 'Hitler would sanction retreats by Schörner which he would have forbidden to any other general'. But other commanders, such as Heinrici, achieved equally good if not better results without resorting to Schörner's brutality. Cornelius Ryan considers Schörner 'one of the least talented of the German generals', but Ziemke's estimate puts him more in proportion: 'Schörner was one of the "new" generals, a convinced Nazi whose military reputation thus far (October 1943) was founded on two qualities —energy and determination. He had a knack for cultivating cameraderie with the troops, which to some extent concealed a strong tendency toward ruthlessness and severity in his treatment of subordinates.'

Colonel-General Hans Krebs was the last Chief of Staff of the Army, succeeding Guderian, from 28 March to 8 May 1945. He also conducted the surrender negotiations with the Russians in Berlin, after which he returned to the Bunker and is believed to have committed suicide. Krebs was a small, plump, well-trained Staff Officer who had been deputy military attaché in Moscow in 1940 and 1941. He was a cheerful, gregarious man, smooth, and somewhat of an intriguer. Ziemke tells us that he was 'known for his unquenchable optimism and his chameleon-like ability to adapt to the views of his superiors', but Colonel-General Heinrici, with the benefit of personal knowledge, described Krebs as 'a man who refused to believe the truth, who could change black to white so as to minimize the true situation to Hitler'. By such devious means did Krebs establish himself within the Hitler circle, having become a crony and drinking companion of the unspeakable Burgdorf, Bormann, and others. However, he was not widely popular among his colleagues.

Krebs was Chief of Staff to Model in 9th Army in 1941 and 1942 as a colonel and major-general, and in 1943 and 1944 Chief of Staff to Busch in Army Group Centre. When Speidel was arrested in 1944 he succeeded him, in September, as Chief of Staff, Army Group 'B', and in 1945 was operational assistant to Guderian. Despite his considerable field experience Krebs in no way measured up to the job of Hitler's chief military adviser.

There were, of course, many other active Nazis among the generals, notably Guderian, but as the war went on their numbers dwindled, and enthusiasm for National Socialism became the exception rather than the rule. The S.S. could be classed as Nazi through and through, but even Dietrich, Hausser and Steiner became disillusioned. So did many of the leaders of the Luftwaffe, originally a notably Nazi Service. The closer generals were to the scene of battle, the less time they tended to have for Hitler and the Party leaders.

The Anti-Nazi Generals

It should not be thought that many generals were either strongly Nazi or anti-Nazi. Both the active Nazi supporters and the active anti-Nazis were in a minority. The great majority kept their real opinions to themselves. Few of the anti-Nazis were willing to risk their careers and even their lives in public antagonism; and nor should it be forgotten that these men had been brought up to be loyal public servants and not to meddle in politics. For a long time the interests of the Party and of the Army seemed to have coincided, and when war came the staggering early victories did nothing to encourage Hitler's critics. Up to 1942, and even after Stalingrad and Tunis in early 1943, it must have been hard to choose to oppose, even secretly, their country's leaders, for the generals were patriots, they had been brought up to wage war, and they were fully engaged on the task. They had taken an oath of loyalty, and were reared in the strict German Army tradition. Moreover, the war against Russia (always the major front until Normandy) was regarded as something of a crusade. Finally, the attitude that an honourable officer was non-political had long been advocated by the General Staff. But the crucial moral question arose, how long were the orders of an unbalanced and unpredictable dictator to be obeyed without questioning both his and one's own motives?

A few brave spirits did listen to their consciences, and decided that Hitler was an evil genius to Germany who must be removed. For doing so they were generally reviled during their lifetime and for some years after their death, but one gets the impression that the young Germans of today see the heroic and tragic side of their actions.

Chief among these men was Colonel-General Ludwig Beck. He was born near Wiesbaden in 1880 and joined the 15th Prussian Field Artillery Regiment in 1908. Most of Beck's career was spent on the Staff, in which he had wide experience in the Great War, but he was not a mere office soldier. Between the wars he commanded an artillery battalion and then a regiment, and in 1932, as a major-general, the 1st Cavalry Division. But he was unexcelled as a Staff Officer, and won the respect of the whole Army for his ability, approachability, and clear expression of his ideas. In 1933 he became Head of the Truppenamt, and in July 1935, as a general of artillery, Chief of Staff of the Army, holding this all-important post for over three years. But they were extremely difficult years for Beck. There was the conflict between Hitler and von Blomberg, on the one hand, and von Fritsch and many of the senior officers on the other; and there was Beck's wish to keep the peace while he saw, and to an extent naturally welcomed, the rearming of Germany and the strengthening of the Army.

Beck was one of the first to see through Hitler, though he seldom had any contact with him and was in fact an isolated man. He felt that his main task was to reconstitute the General Staff which had crumbled away in 1918, and this he did with some success. But the intrigues of Reichenau, Keitel, and Jodl impeded him, since they fostered the 'Führerprinzep' school of thought which relegated the General Staff to being the mere executor of the Leader's will, instead of his responsible adviser on equal terms.

In May 1938 Hitler announced in private to various senior officers his unshakable determination to crush Czechoslovakia. Beck foresaw a general war breaking out if this happened, and demanded specific guarantees from Hitler that he did not intend to start war. Hitler refused, and told Beck his function was to carry out the tasks that a statesman gave him. Beck now instructed one of his friends and colleagues, Major-General Karl-Heinrich von Stülpnagel, to canvas the generals about the prospects of collective military action against Hitler. Nothing seems to have come of this.

He also issued a paper to show what would be the results of an attack against Czechoslovakia, which was subscribed to by all heads of department in the General Staff. But the real power on the military side lay not with Beck but with von Brauchitsch, the Commander-in-Chief of the Army. Beck wrote to him: 'The leaders of the Wehrmacht will incur the guilt of shedding human blood unless they are guided both by their expert knowledge and their conscience. The limit to their soldierly duty of obedience is set at that point, where their conscience and sense of responsibility forbids them to carry out their orders. . . .' Brauchitsch, while sympathetic, was reluctant to take action, probably because he had not long been in office. When he called a meeting of all Corps and Army commanders on 4 August 1938 he described the situation as serious but did not back up Beck's demand that Hitler be forced to abandon his preparations for war. Nor did he read out a passage in Beck's memorandum which might have rallied the doubters. The unread words were: 'In order to safeguard our position before history and to keep the repute of the Supreme Command of the Army unstained, I hereby place on record that I have refused to approve any warlike adventures of the National Socialists. . . .'

Beck now felt that he had little choice but to resign, which he did on 18 August 1938. He briefly commanded an Army on the West Wall in September, but on 31 October was retired as a colonel-general and never held another appointment.

All through the war Beck was the unquestioned leader of the anti-

Hitler generals, but he was largely ineffective because he had no Army command with which to exercise power. It was a mistake for him to have resigned in 1938.

One man who for a time did hold a power base of a sort was Field-Marshal Erwin Job von Witzleben. Witzleben was born at Breslau in 1881, and joined the 7th Grenadier Regiment in 1901. He had been a brigade adjutant at the start of the Great War, in which he fought as both a company and a battalion commander, and also served on the Staff. In 1934 he was promoted major-general and given command of the 3rd Infantry Division at Berlin. In the same year he became a lieutenant-general, although his anti-Nazi views were suspected. In 1935 he was appointed to command III Corps in Berlin; and in 1936 he became a general of infantry. On 28 September 1938 he went to Halder's office to receive orders that would have set in motion the coup. But while they were conferring it was announced that Chamberlain and Daladier were to meet Hitler, and Halder, unwisely as may now be thought, called everything off. 'Therefore I took back the order of execution', Halder said later, 'because the entire basis for the action had been taken away.' In November 1938 he was appointed to command the 2nd Army Group at Frankfurt-am-Main.

In November 1939, by then a senior commander in the Siegfried Line, Witzleben was made colonel-general, and though he did not play any important role in the first stage of the Battle of France, he was an Army commander in the second half of the campaign. When France fell he was given the post of C-in-C France and Military Governor, and lived at the Ritz Hotel in Paris. He was promoted field-marshal on 19 July 1940. Unfortunately his health was not always good (he suffered from piles), and in March 1942 Hitler seized on this pretext to retire him from his important post in the West, where he had been gathering about him a staff of anti-Nazis. Thereafter he lacked a power base, for he was not employed again.

Witzleben was one of the soldiers trusted by von Hassell, who describes him as 'a man of clear purpose and good perception'. While he made no attempt to usurp Beck's place as prospective Head of State after a successful coup, he was always considered the best man to head the Armed Services in such an eventuality.

The most important conspirator left in France when Witzleben was removed was General of Infantry Count Karl-Heinrich von Stülpnagel, a cousin of General Otto Stülpnagel. Like Witzleben he was an East Prussian Junker, but of a more outgoing disposition. One of the finest looking men in the German Army, von Stülpnagel's abilities were highly thought of, and he was in the front rank both of field commanders and Staff officers. He was a confidante both of Beck and of Halder.

In 1935 Colonel von Stülpnagel was head of the Foreign Armies Branch of the General Staff, and in 1936 he commanded the 30th Division at Lübeck as a major-general. From 1938 to 1940 he was *Oberquartiermeister I* or Head of the Army Operations Staff, a post from which he could well observe all the struggles for power within the Wehrmacht and the Nazi Party.

Towards the end of 1939 he told his friend Geyr von Schweppenburg, 'The people in the Reich Government are all criminals. It's high time to put an end to their activities. In this connection you and the 3rd Panzer Division have been thought of. . . .' Geyr, himself an able soldier, tells us von Stülpnagel was convinced that 'no war against the Anglo-Saxons could possibly be successful', and that he wanted to put the German Army on a strong footing, which in his opinion could not be achieved before 1942 or 1943. Geyr sums up Stülpnagel as 'one of the finest men of the old German Army'. Another fine soldier, von Senger und Etterlin, refers to him as 'this highly gifted man'. Ambassador von Hassell, not uncritical of the weaknesses of the professional soldier in wider spheres, found that Stülpnagel 'makes an excellent impression, intelligent, clear-sighted, a fine type of Prussian officer'.

Von Stülpnagel became one of the few conspirators to attain an Army Command in 1940, and took the 17th Army to Russia in von Rundstedt's Army Group in 1941. There it was engaged at Lvov, Przemysl, Vinnitsa, Uman, and on the Donets River. But before 1942 von Stülpnagel had been replaced by Hoth and was appointed Military Governor of Occupied France, a position he held until the July Plot in 1944.

Why Stülpnagel was removed from the Russian front is not clear. He may have had an argument with von Brauchitsch, or he may have become ill. He was considered by the French an improvement on his cousin, Otto, who had shot dozens of civilians in reprisals. The younger von Stülpnagel also had to sign death sentences, but he never made himself so hated as his cousin. As the active leader of the plot in Paris, Stülpnagel had all the Gestapo and S.S. senior officers arrested, but then, when the plot collapsed, had to release them. He could not persuade his superior, von Kluge, to act against Hitler; instead Kluge suggested Stülpnagel should go into civilian clothes and hide himself. But von Stülpnagel was not made of that sort of stuff. Instead, he drove across some of the old French battlefields upon which he had fought as a young man in the Great War. Then leaving the car, he put a pistol to his head. Unfortunately, he only succeeded in blinding himself, and was taken to hospital. There in his delirium he mentioned Rommel by name. Thence he was removed to Berlin, and hanged on 30 August 1944. A brave man, and one of the few to take decisive action, it was a tragedy that he had not been in Berlin leading the conspiracy instead of those who dithered when all was still not lost.

A wholehearted supporter of the conspiracy was General of Infantry Alexander von Falkenhausen, German Military Commander in North-West France and Occupied Belgium from 1940 to 1944.

Von Falkenhausen was born in 1878, and won the *Pour le Mérite* in the Great War. He was cultured and unconventional, an old friend both of von Stülpnagel and of Rommel, having been Commandant of the School of Infantry when they were instructors there. One of the very few who were deeply implicated to survive 20 July, 1944.

In 1923 von Falkenhausen was Chief of Staff of an Infantry division. From 1934 to 1938 he was military adviser to the Chinese Nationalist Government, and became a friend of Chiang Kai-Shek. He won a notable victory with a Chinese Army Group over the Japanese in Shantung in 1938, which led to demands from the Japanese Government for his recall to Germany. Considered too old for an active command in the war, he was given the important post of C-in-C Belgium and northern France, which he held for four years from June 1940 to July 1944.

In 1941 he was already deep in the conspiracy, and tried to win von Brauchitsch over to it, but with no success. Falkenhausen unwittingly became a source of disagreement within the plot, for there was a faction headed by Dr Johannes Popitz which preferred him as C-in-C to von Witzleben. But the left-wingers and trade unionists were against Falkenhausen, as being tarred with the brush of reprisals and war crimes in Belgium. In fact it seems that von Falkenhausen's rule was in general fairly civilized, but in Belgium as in France there were executions of hostages and deportations of workers. Ernst von Weizsäcker of the Foreign Office found von Falkenhausen 'cultured'. General Eggert Reeder, who was head of the civil administrative staff in Occupied Belgium, told von Hassell in July 1943 that the main complaint against von Falkenhausen was that he was too soft with the Belgians, allegedly under the influence of his mistress, Elisabeth Ruspoli. Hassell on 4 July 1943, stated, 'the highly intelligent, far-sighted Falkenhausen is indispensable', and notes on 1 November 1941, 'Falkenhausen, who opposes the hangman's method . . . only escaped being kicked out by a hairbreadth, but seems to have been saved by Brauchitsch'. It was probably Falkenhausen's fortune that he was dismissed five days before the July explosion, for it may have saved his life.

A friend of Schacht, he was imprisoned with him, Halder, and others, at Dachau. He was lucky to be liberated by the American advance in late April 1945, but was re-arrested by the Americans as a war criminal and in 1947 handed over to the Belgians. Although the Belgians claimed to want von Falkenhausen as a war criminal, and eventually tried him as such, they certainly took their time about it—some four years. He was at length sentenced to twelve years' penal servitude for the execution of hostages and the deportation of Jews and Belgian workers. Eighteen days later he was released, and returned to Germany.

General of Infantry Georg Thomas was the very gifted head of the Economics and Armaments Branch of the O.K.W., and a disciple of von Seeckt. Sickened by the murder of von Schleicher in 1934, he broke completely with the Nazis after the von Fritsch affair in 1938. Thenceforth he was to be one of the most loyal and able of the conspirators. He was threatened with arrest by von Brauchitsch when he presented a memorandum in 1939 recommending the abandonment of any Western offensive and the removal of Hitler and the Nazi régime. In April 1940 Thomas failed again in trying to persuade Halder to have the attack on Scandinavia called off. Brauchitsch had taken the view that action against Hitler was impossible, since the great majority of the German people believed in him unfalteringly. 'If you persist in seeing me', he told Thomas, 'I shall have to place you under arrest. . . .'

In the midst of his anti-Nazi activities Thomas always worked hard at his job, and in a letter to his wife in 1945 explained that because there had been no objections to Hitler's reintroduction of conscription, or the occupation of the Rhineland, 'so every intelligent German came to the conclusion that the Western powers saw in Germany a bulwark against Bolshevism and welcomed German rearmament'.

Keitel refused to show Hitler a report written by Thomas after Stalingrad which mentioned the rapidly declining morale of the German people, and often kept from the Führer the more unpalatable parts of Thomas's reports on the war economy. From 1943 onwards, after various unsuccessful attempts or preparations to assassinate Hitler had failed, Thomas came to the conclusion that an assassination might do more harm than good. It could make a martyr of Hitler and be attributed in the public mind to the ambitions of dissident generals. He was arrested and imprisoned by the Gestapo after 20 July 1944, but miraculously emerged as one of the few conspiring generals to survive the war.

Major-General Henning von Tresckow was one of the most attractive personalities among the conspirators, and one of the bravest. By background he was a Pomeranian gentleman-farmer, who had been brought up in the old Prussian style. Originally an enthusiastic supporter of the Nazis, he was so sickened by what he saw of their atrocities in Poland, where he commanded a regiment, that he utterly broke with them.

In 1943, when Hitler was paying a visit to von Kluge's headquarters in Russia, von Tresckow gave one of the Führer's adjutants two bottles for his friend Major-General Stieff at headquarters in Berlin, supposed to contain cognac. They were in fact bombs to blow up Hitler's plane —but they failed to go off. Tresckow had been first von Bock's and then von Kluge's G.S.O.I. or Chief of Operations in Russia. Later he was promoted to be von Kluge's Chief of Staff. He tried to persuade both these commanders, especially von Kluge, the more vulnerable, to take action against Hitler, but was in despair when von Kluge was transferred to the West and he could not follow.

He tried to persuade Schmundt, with whom he was friendly, to make him Chief of Staff to von Manstein, so that he could convert him. But Manstein refused to have him, writing to Schmundt that Tresckow, while peerless as a Staff Officer, showed a negative attitude to National Socialism. This effectively hamstrung von Tresckow who was forced to await events on the sidelines. When the July Plot failed, he committed suicide in the front line. He had opposed Hitler from revulsion rather than from reasoning, but, as Wheeler-Bennett writes, 'Of the many who suffered a similar sense of moral outrage he was one of the few who was prepared to translate it into terms of action. . . .' Shortly before his death von Tresckow, a Christian gentleman, said, 'God once promised Abraham to spare Sodom should there be found ten just men in the city. He will, I trust, spare Germany because of what we have done, and not destroy her'.

His friend and co-conspirator, Fabian von Schlabrendorff, wrote of him: 'Tresckow possessed three qualities often found separately but seldom together: he was upright, able and industrious. His noble spirit, the acuteness of his understanding and his capacity for intensive work compelled the admiration of those who knew him. His outstanding quality was his ability to inspire those who surrounded him, to raise them up to his own lofty standard . . . . He threw every atom of his personality into our struggle, and he stands among the most eminent figures in the history of German resistance. . . .'

The chief engineer, as it were, of the conspiracy, the man who acted as sounding-board and clearing-house for all information, was Canaris's deputy, Colonel (later Major-General) Hans Oster. He was born in 1887, and served in the cavalry during the Great War. He was also at one time attached to the artillery. A sophisticated, good-looking, cool and witty man, Oster would have risen higher in the Service but for the fact that, owing to a love affair with the wife of a senior officer, he had been forced to leave the Army for a time in 1932. Von Senger has described Oster as the 'spiritual core' of the resistance for years, and von Schlabrendorff, who knew him well, wrote: 'Oster was a man such as God meant men to be, lucid and serene in mind, imperturbable in danger. He was, so to speak, the managing director and clearing agency of the resistance movement.'

Even before the war Oster had taken considerable risks. On terms of intimacy with the Dutch Military Attaché, Colonel Sas, he had warned him narrowly in advance of the coming invasion date of the Low Countries—accurately—in 1940. He was friendly with other foreign representatives, including the Swiss. Officially head of counter-espionage, Oster provided papers, pretexts and contacts for conspirators visiting the front or foreign countries, or travelling about the Reich. When the conspiracy looked like flagging, he worked tirelessly to keep it going. Through the arrest of three other leading anti-Nazi figures in April 1943 he lost his 'cover' job, a most serious blow to the resistance.

Von Tresckow took Oster's place for a time while on sick-leave; and with the appearance of Colonel von Stauffenberg the conspiracy began to show possibilities of real revival. But without the constant inspiration and hard work, often in excruciatingly dangerous circumstances, of Hans Oster in the earlier years, the conspiracy would never have remained alive at all. As Wheeler-Bennett has rightly said, 'To deny that Canaris and Oster constituted the intellect and the sword-arm of the conspiracy in its early stages would be to deny truth'.

General Oster was arrested after 20 July, and imprisoned by the Gestapo at Flossenburg concentration camp with Canaris. There they were both executed on 9 April 1945. Oster will go down to history as a realist, an unselfish hero, and a very gallant man.

One of the most fortunate, and most astute, of the conspirators was Lieutenant-General Dr Hans Speidel. He was born at Metzingen in Württemburg in 1897, and fought in the Great War in the same brigade as Rommel, of whom he became a friend. In 1932 he was working as a Staff Officer in the Truppenamt, but he had interrupted his professional soldiering career to become a Doctor of Philosophy and then a teacher and Professor at Göttingen University. In 1933 he was assistant military attaché in Paris. Speidel was a Lieutenant-Colonel and 1A Operations in IX Corps in 1940, and then on von Küchler's staff in 18th Army in the invasion of the Low Countries. He became Chief of Staff to Otto von Stülpnagel in Paris from 1940 to 1941, then on the 5th Army Staff in 1942, and Chief of Staff, General Wöhler's 8th Army in Russia in 1943, as a major-general.

In April 1944 Speidel was appointed Chief of Staff to Rommel in Army Group 'B' in France, with the rank of lieutenant-general. The two men worked in close harmony, and Speidel was able to persuade Rommel to take much closer notice of the conspiracy than before. Speidel even thought that the S.S. commanders Sepp Dietrich and Hausser might be persuaded to act against Hitler, or at least to refrain from acting against those who did.

Rommel would have no part in any assassination plan, but he thought Hitler should be arrested and brought to account for his actions. Rommel never sought himself leadership of the conspiracy; he was more interested in discussing with Speidel how best to secure an armistice from General Eisenhower. Nevertheless, the immense prestige and popularity of Rommel would have been an invaluable asset to the conspirators, and Speidel did not cease from working upon the Field-Marshal. Rommel was then wounded before the July Plot. For a time Speidel kept his job, and was not relieved until 5 September 1944. Two days later he was arrested, and brought before a Court of Honour on 4 October. But Speidel had covered his tracks well, and was fully equal to baffling the most searching Gestapo interrogation. He protested his innocence, betrayed no one and nothing, and despite Keitel's interjection that the Führer believed Speidel to be guilty, the Court found him innocent and he was released.

General Dr Speidel survived the war to distinguish himself in the Federal German Army, and in N.A.T.O. as Allied Commander Land Forces, Central Europe.

How many military men and civilians died as a result of the July Plot is uncertain, but at least thirty-five generals paid with their lives, and probably several hundred other officers. Hitler's vengeance was horrible and barbaric. Beck had shot himself in the Bendlerstrasse, but not fatally, and was helped on his way to a grim death by one of Fromm's soldiers. Goerdeler was executed after a farcical trial under the infamous Freisler, as were von Witzleben, Höpner, and many others. Not content with making a public spectacle of distinguished men like von Witzleben, who had to appear in court with no support for his trousers and without his false teeth, Hitler insisted on having the executions of the victims filmed, and gloated as he watched the torture of the naked bodies.

The Chiefs of Staff Officers

The outstanding Staff officer for the first three years of the war was Colonel-General Franz Halder, who succeeded Beck as Chief of the Army General Staff in September 1938. Halder has been regarded as one of the early conspirators but, as time went on, influenced no doubt by his constant proximity to Hitler, he became Laodicean, and finally refused to act at all. He was an intelligent, precise, slightly pedantic man who might well have been a university professor in a different age. Actually he came from a long line of soldiers. After General Adam, he was the first Bavarian to become head of the General Staff. But he was not a man of action, and suffered from the mental and no doubt spiritual conflict that his working relationship with Hitler and the Nazis imposed upon him. He was generally acknowledged before the war to be the brains behind the Army, and he worked closely with—though not always with scrupulous loyalty to—von Brauchitsch. The two undoubtedly made a formidable team, as was shown in Poland and France.

Halder was born in 1884 at Würzburg, and joined the 3rd Bavarian Field Artillery Regiment in 1902. Having passed through the War Academy in Munich before the Great War began, he spent most of the war serving on the General Staff. He became a colonel in 1931, a major-general in 1934, Commander of the 7th Division in 1935, and a lieutenant-general in 1936, when he headed the manoeuvres staff in the general Army manoeuvres held that year. In November 1936 he moved to the General Staff in Berlin, and in 1937 became Director of Operations, and on 1 September Chief of the General Staff, a position he held for four arduous years with few thanks except his promotion to colonel-general after the fall of France.

Halder had worked on the Bavarian General Staff under General von Lossow, and also with Röhm, and had served under von Reichenau on the General Staff. He early became acquainted with Hitler, whose personality struck him as extraordinary, part genius and part fool, but which he could never fully work out. All the same he kept in touch with Hitler even after the ill-fated putsch of 1923. Hitler, while not hesitating to avail himself of Halder's wide military and political knowledge, had him fully summed up—'*ein ewiger Besserwisser*' he called Halder, 'a chronic know-it-all'. Owlish, bespectacled, rather saturnine and cynical, Halder did sometimes provoke that image. He was not above talking sharply to Hitler and arguing with him, for he could be obstinate, and this did not increase his popularity. It was always Hitler's habit to take all the credit for successes, and spread it abroad that he personally had worked out strategy and tactics—a boast given publicity by von Reichenau in the early days. But without Halder's meticulous planning Hitler would have been unable to frame the simplest military operation effectively. Halder was a Christian, who saw that there was something diabolical in Hitler. On the other hand he took very seriously his oath of loyalty. It must have taken some keeping, since he was to become an Aunt Sally for Hitler's abuse. Halder would doubtless have been much happier occupying himself with botany or mathematics, two of his favourite pursuits, rather than listening to the rantings of the Führer.

He confided to his diary on 13 July 1940: 'The Führer is obsessed with the question why England does not want to take the road to peace. . . .' Halder had recommended that 'Sea-Lion' be launched against England immediately after the fall of France, but his advice went unheeded.

Halder supervised the planning of the Russian invasion, just as he had done the invasion of France. Like Brauchitsch, he wanted to go straight for Moscow in the first place, which led to endless wrangles with Hitler. Halder gives the impression of having been a cold man, at least in manner, and his laconic, icy logic was certainly capable of reducing Hitler to fury. Thus on 16 May 1940 Halder noted that Hitler 'rages and screams that we [he and von Brauchitsch] are on the way to ruining the whole campaign'.

But the real break between Halder and Hitler did not occur until things began to go wrong in Russia. On 3 July 1941, twelve days after the start of the invasion, things were going very well, and Halder wrote in his diary: 'Generally speaking, it is therefore already possible to say that the task of smashing the Soviet armies in front of the Western Dvina and Dnieper has been accomplished. It would probably be no exaggeration to say that the campaign against Russia has been won within the first fortnight. Naturally, this does not mean that it has been concluded. The vastness of the country and the stubborn resistance offered us in every possible way will keep our forces busy for many more weeks. . . .' Later Halder must have wondered how he could have been so optimistic.

Even within weeks of the start of the Russian venture Halder was driven to complain that Hitler's constant interferences on matters of which he had no expert knowledge was damaging. O.K.H. had nominal control over the Russian front, with the exception of the Finnish area, which was an O.K.W. preserve. O.K.W. was responsible for all other theatres of war, including France, Italy, Africa, the Balkans, Greece, Yugoslavia, the Mediterranean Islands, and Norway. This had the effect of reducing the Army Chief of Staff's authority to that of chief executive of the Russian war. Quite apart from Hitler's orders, there was additional interference from Keitel and Jodl in what was strictly none of their business. They had taken over from the Chief of Staff such matters as manpower, munitions, armaments and troop movements.

The furious arguments with Hitler continued, not only about Moscow but also Leningrad. In July 1941 he begged Hitler not to divide his forces, but to leave the Caucasus until Stalingrad had been taken and the Don made secure. But Hitler ignored him and from the beginning of 1942 Halder was in almost perpetual disfavour. After Brauchitsch's departure in December 1941 he probably urged Halder (despite the coolness between them) to stay on as the last representative of the General Staff authority.

It took only six months of the Russian campaign to make Halder realize how much he and others had underestimated Russian resources. He told Shulman after the war that when he had discovered in June 1942 the strength of Soviet manpower and armaments with which the Germans would have to deal, and tried to explain these matters to Hitler, he flew into a rage. 'When I presented him with the figures of Russian tank production he went off the deep end. He was no longer a rational human being. I don't know whether he didn't want to understand or whether he really didn't believe it. In any event, it was quite impossible to discuss such matters with him. He would foam at the mouth, threaten me with his fists and scream at the top of his lungs. Any logical discussion was out of the question. . . .'

In January 1942 his opposite number in the Finnish Army, General Heinrichs, had thought Halder 'over-tired and depressed. According to his opinion, the Russian campaign had been too costly for the Germans'.

When Field-Marshal Mannerheim paid a visit to Hitler in late June —'I had the impression that the courtesy visit was not altogether pleasing to Hitler and those closest to him. From what happened later, I concluded that General Halder, who at the beginning of 1943 had to relinquish his post, had already at the time of my visit fallen into disfavour. . . .' The shrewd eye of the old Finnish leader had not betrayed him, though actually Halder was dismissed on 24 September 1942. In September 1942 Hitler justified Halder's dismissal by stating that he had been 'no longer equal to the psychic demands of his position'. Yet, after Halder's departure, the German Army was never again to enjoy great success.

Although he had long ceased to have active contacts with the conspiracy, Halder was arrested the day after the July Plot in 1944, and in January 1945 was dismissed from the Army which he had served so well. He was imprisoned in Flossenburg and Dachau concentration camps, but survived the war, and died in retirement at an advanced age. It is a pity that his pamphlet, *Hitler als Feldherr*, overstated the case against Hitler as a war leader, and sought always to justify

217

his own part. Colonel-General Franz Halder was surely one of the best brains and ablest Staff officers of his time, but not even he could cope with the strain and uncertainty of working under a psychopath.

Hitler further diminished the stature of the General Staff by choosing a comparatively junior officer, Lieutenant-General Kurt Zeitzler, as Halder's successor.

Zeitzler was born in 1895, one of the younger generals. He was the son of a Protestant pastor, had been an infantry subaltern in the Great War, and had transferred to the tank arm in 1934. He had by no means a typical General Staff background, but had struck Göring as a sound Nazi, was very energetic, and was undoubtedly able.

In 1938 as a lieutenant-colonel on the O.K.W. planning staff under Warlimont, Zeitzler prepared the draft of '*Fall Grun*', the invasion of Czechoslovakia. In 1939–40, promoted colonel, he commanded an infantry regiment and then performed excellently as Chief of Staff to XXII Corps and to von Kleist's Panzer Group. In this capacity, as Liddell Hart noted, 'It was he who found a way to solve the problems of supplying armoured forces during long-range advances and rapid switches. . . . Zeitzler was an outstandingly resourceful organizer of strategic moves, with an exceptional grasp of what could be done with mechanized forces'. Later, in Russia, 'His brilliant staffwork in organizing and maintaining the panzer drive through the Ardennes and on through France, in 1940, had been excelled in the complex series of manoeuvres called for in 1941—when Kleist's panzer forces had first swerved down through the Ukraine towards the Black Sea, to block Budenny's retreat across the Bug and the Dnieper; then turned about and dashed north to meet Guderian and complete the vast encirclement round Kiev; then been switched south again, on to the rear of the fresh Russian forces that were attacking the German bridgehead over the Dnieper at Dneipropetrovsk; and, after producing a Russian collapse here, had driven down through the Donets Basin to cut off the Russian forces near the Sea of Azov. As Kleist emphasized to me, in paying unstinted tribute to his Chief of Staff, the biggest problem in "throwing armies about in this way" was that of maintaining supplies. . . .'

From early 1942 he was Chief of Staff, Army Group 'D', covering the Channel Coast and the Low Countries. In this admittedly rather tame backwater he showed his customary enthusiasm and vigour, so that he was nicknamed 'General Fireball'. He spent a lot of time organizing the defences of the West for von Witzleben and von Rundstedt, but he was necessarily losing touch with the war in Russia by the time he took over Halder's post with the rank of general of infantry.

For some time Zeitzler trod carefully. Hitler had thought to overawe a man who at the beginning of 1942 was still only a major-general. Göbbels noted in his diary for 20 December 1942: 'The appointment of Zeitzler has done a lot of good. Zeitzler has introduced a new method of work at G.H.Q., clearing away everything except essentials. This has relieved the Führer of a lot of detail, and everything doesn't depend upon his decision. . . .' But gradually Zeitzler proved to be less pliable.

In January 1943, he tried, without success at first, to persuade Hitler to evacuate the 100,000 men who looked like being trapped at Demyansk. Eventually Hitler gave in and in February a successful evacuation was carried out. On 14 February 1943 Hassell recorded: 'Even Herr Zeitzler, Hitler's new Chief of the General Staff, now sees what is going on and has summoned up enough courage to resist idiotic orders. For two days he did not appear at the staff meetings and in this way put across his own ideas. . . .' And on 28 March 1943: 'It is tragi-comic that Zeitzler, of all people, should show the most courage, that is, of course, in purely military matters; otherwise he is obedient. . . .'

Zeitzler had his first major difference of opinion with Hitler over Stalingrad. When the Russians started to counter-attack, he thought Paulus's 6th Army should be withdrawn immediately. This led to the start of frequent friction with Hitler. In November 1942 Zeitzler was behind Jeschonnek in trying to get the Stalingrad airlift called off. Jeschonnek did not believe the Luftwaffe could airlift the 700 tons of material per day necessary to maintain the defence of Stalingrad. Nor did Zeitzler. Zeitzler told Hitler and Göring, on 24 November, 'The Luftwaffe just can't do it'. This of course put Göring's back up, who retorted, 'I can manage that. . . .' Zeitzler then lost control and shouted, 'It's a lie!' Hitler intervened, and said that he was obliged to believe Göring. As General Blumentritt observed later, 'When the outcome proved the truth of his warnings, the Führer became increasingly hostile to Zeitzler. He did not dismiss him, but he kept him at arm's length'.

Zeitzler tried to reorganize the system of command in the East, when he saw what evil effects Hitler's direction of the Russian campaign was having. Under his plan the C-in-C Eastern Front would have complete independence of action—doubtless he envisaged von Manstein or von Kluge in that position. Keitel was to be dropped, with some respected general of strong character put in his place. The O.K.H. and O.K.W. Staffs were to be fused into one combined Staff for the whole Wehrmacht, with the S.S. also under its control. Naturally such proposals aroused opposition, not least from Hitler, who would have become little more than a military figurehead; and they did not, in fact, get very far. Even so, Göbbels recorded on 9 March 1943: 'The Führer continues to be very well satisfied with Zeitzler, who is at present his most effective assistant in the conduct of the eastern campaign. Keitel plays only a very subordinate role. . . .' Yet it was the opinion of Colonel-General Heinrici that Zeitzler 'had only a very slight influence' on Hitler, and of General Westphal that he was Chief of the General Staff 'in name only'.

Zeitzler was by nature an impulsive and hot-tempered man. In his later days he often lost his temper with Hitler, and on several occasions offered his resignation, but had it refused.

Zeitzler was no great strategist, but he was a very gifted organizer, and given a free hand he might have made a respectable job of his high position. As things were, it was virtually meaningless. He showed great enthusiasm for Operation Citadel, the 1943 Kursk tank offensive, which led to some angry arguments with Jodl. While he managed to get Hitler's agreement to tactical withdrawals from dangerous salients on the Moscow and Leningrad fronts, he could never get general permission for a strategic withdrawal. He did not, of course, get any help from Keitel or Jodl. He failed in April 1944 to get Hitler to countenance the evacuation of Sevastopol, where Schörner was in trouble. In July 1944 after the collapse of the German Armies on the Upper Dnieper, he urged the withdrawal of Army Group North in the Baltic States before it was encircled. Hitler's refusal led to another flare-up and another rejected resignation. Finally, in the bitter atmosphere of the July Plot, Zeitzler went sick and was succeeded on 21 July by Guderian.

Zeitzler was deprived of various privileges of his rank by Hitler, and then discharged from the Army without the normal right to wear uniform, a victim of the universal suspicion after the Plot—with which he had had absolutely no connection. One cannot help feeling that Zeitzler would have been far happier—and far more successful—had he been given an Army to command.

Two Great Commanders

World War II produced many good generals, the German Army more than any other. But the adjective 'great' must be used with reserve; and after a thorough appraisal of a dozen generals who at first glance merit the description, one is forced to select only two.

A great general must have tactical and strategic skill, a cool judgement, the trust and admiration of his troops. He must be a leader, but with the temperament to listen to advice and to delegate responsibility. He must probably be a specialist in at least one area. Finally, of course, he must be successful.

Of the very good generals who cannot be classed among the greatest, one would put von Rundstedt at the head, along with Guderian. Despite Guderian's spectacular successes and his brilliant development of the use of armour, he lacked the fine intelligence of the greatest Commanders. He was an arbitrary and difficult man; and there is no reason to insist that Höpner or Reinhardt should not equally share the credit for the development of the armoured arms. For reasons of temperament, one must put Model in this second class also.

Of all the candidates for greatness, to my mind one man stands out, and that is Field-Marshal Erich von Manstein. He would have been acceptable to every general on the Eastern front as commander-in-chief with total responsibility, and he was well liked and thought of by the men who served under him. Further, von Manstein was that *rara avis*, a man who combined the genuine intellectual equipment and precision of the good staff officer with the authority, decisiveness and imaginative flair of the good field commander. He proved himself to the hilt in both capacities; and if he made some mistakes, they were few and not irretrievable ones. Von Manstein was the greatest German general of the war, and probably the greatest of any participating nation.

Fritz Erich Lewinski was born in Berlin in 1887, but was adopted by the von Manstein family and thereafter always known by their name. He entered the 3rd Guards Regiment of Foot in 1906, and served in the Great War as an Oberleutnant and regimental adjutant. After some fighting he was trained at the War Academy, and spent most of the war in various Staff positions. After the war he made something of a reputation as a Staff officer with General von Lossberg. He became a major in 1927; a lieutenant-colonel in 1931, when he

221

had already served eighteen months in the Operations Department of Truppenamt; and a battalion commander in 1932. He became a colonel in 1933; and in 1935 Head of the Operations Department of the General Staff. In 1937 he was promoted Major-General, and the same year became *Oberquartiermeister I* or Deputy Chief of the General Staff. In 1938 he was switched to command the 18th Division at Liegnitz, and had some difficulty in returning to a General Staff position; but in August 1939 he was appointed Chief of Staff to the C-in-C East, and in October to Army Group 'A' (von Rundstedt).

As von Rundstedt's Chief of Staff in Poland and during the 'Phoney War' Manstein excelled, chiefly because of his brilliant Ardennes plan which won the war in France. Manstein was removed from von Rundstedt's side in February 1940 before the attack, and given command of the back-up XXXVIII Infantry Corps, consisting of the 26th and 34th Divisions. He nevertheless handled it so well that it almost caught up with the advancing panzers. At that time he was under General von Weichs in 2nd Army. Having thus proved himself in both staff and field work he was promoted General of Infantry in June 1940 and given command of LVI Motorized Corps under Höpner for the invasion of Russia. Manstein had been strongly in favour of 'Sea-Lion', and had been one of the commanders earmarked to take part in the assault landings, in the Bexhill-Eastbourne-Ramsgate-Hastings area.

In five days at the end of June 1941, and before the Russians really recovered their balance, Manstein pushed his Corps 150 miles from the Momel to Dvinsk in the northern sector. He ignored his flanks and was certain that a bold push should be made to take Leningrad. He was taking a risk, but he justified it by maintaining his advance. It was one of Manstein's tenets that the safety of an armoured formation in the enemy's rear depends on its continued movement. Manstein reached the Daugava on his own, with Reinhardt's XLI Panzer Corps and the left wing of Busch's 16th Army some sixty miles in his rear, but was then ordered by Hitler to halt. 'Daugavpils bridgehead will be defended. Arrival of Sixteenth Army's left wing will be awaited.' As in France, Hitler mistrusted his own success and would not take the vital risk. Manstein's Corps stood still for six crucial days, which gave the Soviet High Command time to prepare the Stalin Line.

In August 1941 Manstein's Corps was removed from Höpner's sector in the Leningrad area, and transferred to Busch's 16th Army which was in difficulties in the Novgorod–Lake Ilman–Staraya Russa area. This move was not popular, for it had seemed that Leningrad was bound to fall. Now Leeb had stopped the attack on it, being weakened, and Manstein's Corps was not to return, as it hoped, to that front. Manstein's task was to rescue General Hansen's X Corps from the heavy pressure it was resisting in the Staraya Russa sector. By skilful attacks with his 3rd Motorized Infantry Division and the S.S. 'Totenkopf' Division he rolled up the flank of the Soviet 34th Army and disrupted the Russian communications. The Russians were forced back across the Lovat, and X Corps was able to attack; between them Manstein and Hansen smashed the 34th Red Army. Manstein found that the officers and N.C.O.s of the 'Totenkopf' lacked experience and leadership ability, but 'as far as its discipline and soldierly bearing went, the division in question undoubtedly made a good impression', and struck him as 'probably the best Waffen S.S. division' that he had seen.

When General Ritter von Schobert was killed in a forced landing on 2 September 1941 his 11th Army, on von Rundstedt's southern front, was given to von Manstein next day. Manstein had proved himself a brilliant Corps commander, and was sorry to lose his Corps, but promotion to command an Army was the dream of every general. Manstein was ordered to capture the Crimea, and with the bulk of his forces to drive on Rostov. This was too ambitious an objective, and Manstein had virtually no armour, in excellent country for it. His first attempt failed, and due to Russian penetration of part of the Rumanian 3rd Army and of General von Salmuth's XXX Corps, he found himself in danger of being cut off in the Nogay Steppe. A timely intervention from the north by von Kleist's 1st Panzer Group came to his aid, however, and the Russians in turn found themselves surrounded between Mariupol and Bardyansk, on the Sea of Azov, in early October. The Germans won a clear-cut victory.

Three weeks later than it should have come, Manstein received an order to concentrate on the Crimea only, but this battle, which might have been much easier had he not had to dissipate his forces, was to be expensive. On 1 November the Germans took Simferopol, but by mid-November Russian resistance had stiffened, and Manstein was short of troops. By December he had only one division in the Kerch Peninsula, and on Christmas Day and thereafter the Russians put ashore massive reinforcements at Kerch and then Feodosiya. The G.O.C. XLII Corps, General Graf von Sponeck, had detached two of his three divisions to the Sevastopol front, and therefore ordered the remaining one, the 46th to evacuate the Kerch Peninsula, though Manstein had already rejected that very suggestion. Manstein countermanded Sponeck's order but it was too late; the 46th Division reached the Parpach Isthmus in good order, though abandoning many guns, only to find that the Russians had got there before them. In a gallant attack the 46th Division, under Lieutenant-General Kurt Himer, the former German C.-in-C. Denmark, beat back the Russians at Vladislavovka and then held the line against a possible breakthrough.

Von Sponeck was dismissed by Manstein, and then court-martialled and condemned to death by a board sitting under Göring. The sentence was commuted to seven years' fortress detention. Equally bad for the morale of the common soldier was the decision of von Reichenau to strip 46th Division of all its honours, a decision later reversed by von Bock. Manstein's dismissal of von Sponeck, a distinguished officer, may have been justified on the grounds of discipline, but it was a harsh one. And on 3 December 1941, in view of the situation on the Parpach Isthmus and at Feodosiya, von Manstein called off the Sevastopol attack and went over to the defensive. In this situation he was to remain for four months, and in January 1942 the Russians recaptured the Kerch Peninsula.

The regaining of Kerch was not an easy task for von Manstein, who was heavily outnumbered. The Russians deployed some twenty divisions behind an anti-tank ditch across the Isthmus of Parpach, the Crimea's gateway to Kerch, a distance of only eleven miles, with a pronounced bulge in the northern part of their line. This was the obvious target and Manstein, by clever use of dummies, false radio signals, and deceptive reconnaissance and troop movements, tricked the Russians into thinking that he was going to attack it. Instead he mounted his main attack in the south, using five infantry divisions, and one panzer one, helped by the Stukas of VIII Air Corps. He also used assault troops in boats which landed where the anti-tank ditch ran into the sea and seized it. The attack went in on 8 May, the infantry under von Sponeck's successor Lieutenant-General Maximilian Fretter-Pico, and the armour under Lieutenant-General Wilhelm von Apell. By 11 May Apell had taken Ak-Monay on the sea and cut off ten Russian divisions, and on 16 May Kerch itself fell. Manstein had been reinforced by a panzer division and numerous heavy assault guns, which he used to good effect, but it was a brilliant victory with only six German and three Rumanian divisions against greatly superior numbers. The Germans had 7,500 casualties; the Russians lost 170,000 prisoners, 1,133 guns, 258 tanks, 3,800 motor vehicles, and 300 aircraft.

Early in June 1942, while making a reconnaissance of Sevastopol from the Black Sea in an Italian torpedo-boat, Manstein was attacked by Russian fighters. Much to his grief he lost his sergeant driver, who had been with him from 1938 and had been wounded several times when Manstein himself had been unscathed; and a captain sitting next to Manstein was also killed.

Two days later Manstein launched the prelude to his attack on Sevastopol, a massive artillery bombardment from 1,300 guns, and scores of sorties by VIII Air Corps. This largest use of an artillery barrage by the Germans during the whole war went on for five days. Particularly effective were the massed mortars, used for the first time, and the 88 mm. flak guns employed most successfully against pillboxes and gun emplacements. Manstein also used the Gamma mortar, with a barrel twenty-two feet long, which could send its 16·8 in. projectiles nearly nine miles; the Karl or Thor 24·2 in. mortar, whose $2\frac{1}{4}$-ton bombs were designed to shatter concrete; and the heaviest gun of the war, the Dora, or Heavy Gustav: this monster had a calibre of 31·5 in., a barrel 107 feet long, and threw projectiles, weighing nearly five tons, twenty-nine miles, or seven-ton armour-piercing missiles, twenty-four miles. Each missile with its cartridge measured almost twenty-six feet, and sixty railway trucks were needed to carry all the parts of Dora. It stood on two double rails, fired three rounds an hour, was guarded by two flak battalions, and came under the control of an artillery major-general who disposed of 4,120 men.

The attack proper began on 7 June, against a Russian garrison of some ten divisions with much artillery, many mortars and naval coastal defence guns, housed in a series of forts. The Germans managed to crack the first line of forts but their casualties were heavy, and at one time it looked as though Manstein might have to call the attack off. On 17 June, however, he launched a new attack, and gradually the forts fell. By 20 June the Germans controlled the harbour, and on the night of 27–28 June assault parties in boats and dinghies attacked the town itself. By 3 July Sevastopol had fallen, with 90,000 Russian prisoners taken, 467 pieces of artillery, 758 mortars, and 155 anti-tank and anti-aircraft guns. It was a notable victory against the strongest fortress in Russia. Without superior numbers, against a determined enemy and in difficult terrain, he had pulled off a remarkable success. Manstein had been promoted Colonel-General on 1 January 1942, and was now promoted Field-Marshal on 1 July.

Hitler was so impressed and delighted by the capture of Sevastopol that he abandoned his previous plan to use 11th Army in the Kuban, and decided to send it north to stage a repeat performance at Leningrad. This was a mistake, and one which Halder strongly opposed, on the grounds that one could not attack Leningrad at the same time as attacking the Ukraine and the Caucasus. In the event, the siege train and heavy artillery of 11th Army was sent to Leningrad, but only half of the infantry divisions. Thus the 11th Army was needlessly broken up, and its close ties with the Rumanians, who had fought with and under it, needlessly severed.

In the north in September the Russians were on the offensive, and on the Volkhov front Manstein had to repel heavy attacks in the Lake Ladoga area. The attack on Leningrad was shelved. On 27 November Manstein was entrusted with command of the newly formed Army Group Don. This consisted of Paulus's encircled 6th Army at Stalingrad; Colonel-General Hoth's Combat Group Hoth, consisting of an enlarged Panzer Corps and two Rumanian Corps from 4th Rumanian Army; General Hollidt's Combat Group Hollidt, a mixed German-Rumanian force on the Chir River; and 3rd Rumanian Army. Many of Manstein's divisions, especially the panzer ones, were under strength, and his Rumanian forces and some recently formed Luftwaffe Field Divisions were unsuitable for aggressive operations. Paulus's 6th Army was only nominally under Manstein's command, since it had a direct radio link to O.K.H. and Hitler's headquarters. The Army Group could not stand comparison with any of those that had invaded in 1941.

Manstein had to hold the Don–Chir front at all costs, and prevent further Russian breakthroughs towards Rostov. On 24 November he signalled to Paulus, 'Shall do everything in my power to relieve you. . . . In the meantime it is imperative that 6th Army, while holding Volga and north front in compliance with Führer's orders, forms up forces in order, if necessary, to clear a supply channel towards the south-west.' Three days later he told Colonel Wenck, the new Chief of Staff, 3rd Rumanian Army: 'Wenck, you'll answer to me with your head that the Russians won't break through to Rostov. The Don–Chir front must hold. Otherwise not only the 6th Army in Stalingrad, but the whole of Army Group 'A' in the Caucasus, will be lost.'

Manstein entrusted to Hoth the breakthrough to Stalingrad, using LVII Panzer Corps; but assembly delays postponed the start of the advance from 3 December to 12 December. Hoth's tank divisions were under strength, and for some reason Hitler refused to release a generous number of formations from other areas, such as the Caucasus, to help Hoth in his vital task. Hoth had to cover sixty miles to Stalingrad. By 20 December his leading division reached the Mishkova, some thirty-five miles from the city, to encounter stiff Russian opposition. On the Chir front the situation was such that Manstein could not move any forces west of the Don towards Stalingrad. Worse still, on 16 December the Russians had launched an attack beyond Manstein's left flank (Group Hollidt) against the 8th Italian Army on the Don, broken through it, and within a week put it entirely to flight. This meant the loss of many supplies and dumps, and on Christmas Eve the Russians actually attacked the airfield at Tatsinskaya, the main airlift base for Stalingrad, some fifty miles in Hollidt's rear. Hollidt tried desperately to protect his left flank with Rumanian troops, but in vain. He therefore moved Lieutenant-General O. von Knobelsdorff's XLVIII Panzer Corps from his right front backed up by a panzer division from Hoth's Group which Hoth could very ill afford to lose, to seal off the gap. The situation was extremely serious, for if the Russians broke through to Rostov Manstein's Army Group would be cut off and Kleist's Army Corps in the Caucasus would have its communications cut.

Hitler, Paulus, and his Chief of Staff, Schmidt, were against an attempted breakout by 6th Army. But on 23 December Manstein had to tell Hitler that the situation on his left wing necessitated immediate switching of forces, and therefore meant 'dropping for an indefinite period the relief of Sixth Army, which in turn means that this Army would now have to be adequately supplied on a long-term basis. . . . The only remaining alternative is the earliest possible breakout of 6th Army at the cost of a considerable risk along the left wing of Army Group'. Hitler agreed to the diversion of some of Hoth's forces to the Chir—he could hardly do otherwise—but ordered that the relief attack must be resumed as soon as possible. He did not authorize a break-out by Paulus, because Paulus had reported that his tanks had fuel enough for only twelve miles.

On 24 December the Russians attacked again west of the Don. The Rumanians on Hoth's right gave way, and during the next three days Hoth's forces were driven back from the Myshkova, and finally to their starting-point in the Kotelnikovo area. By 27 December the tank and motorized forces of Marshals Vatutin in the north and Eremenko in the south threatened to surround Army Group Don and to cut Army Group 'A's lines of communciation. The next day Hitler had to agree to a general withdrawal by both to a new line some 150 miles west of Stalingrad, maintaining that Paulus would still be relieved. But by mid-January his situation was hopeless. Paulus refused to surrender; and by tying down no less than seven Russian Armies—sixty major formations—until the beginning of February 1943 he prevented a Russian move against Rostov. Some 42,000 wounded and sick were evacuated by air.

Mainstein was to write: 'The situation of the two Army Groups Don and Caucasus ('A') would have taken a disastrous turn if Paulus had surrendered at the beginning of January.' Paul Carell comments: 'The salvation of First Panzer Army, and indeed of the whole of Army Group 'A' and parts of Army Group Don, was due not only to Manstein's generalship and the gallantry of the troops, but very largely also to Sixth Army which had been holding out in Stalingrad throughout January.' All the same, when Paulus finally surrendered, some 200,000 men had been lost in a colossal defeat that was the turning-point of the war in Russia.

Neither Manstein nor Hoth can be blamed for the débâcle. The former was appointed too late and did not have final authority over Paulus; the latter did not have strong enough forces with which to make a successful breakthrough to the city. Had Paulus been a man of more ardent and aggressive temperament, like Höpner, Guderian or Model, things might have been different; but the blame must largely rest with Hitler's insistence on giving up no foot of ground, and Göring's grandiloquent boasts that the garrison could be supplied by air.

Just after the fall of Stalingrad, on 6 February, Manstein flew to Rastenburg to try to get Hitler to shorten the whole Russian front. It was a vain attempt. 'All Hitler actually had to say about the operational position was to express the belief that the S.S. Panzer Corps would be able to remove the acute threat to the middle Donets front . . . . His faith in the penetrating power of this newly established S.S. Panzer Corps was apparently unbounded.' Hitler reluctantly agreed to previous requests from Manstein and Kluge to retire to the Mius and abandon the Rzhev salient. In the north Demyansk had also been given up to bring some stability to the Leningrad front. Manstein's Army Group Don was renamed Army Group South.

On 17 February Hitler visited Manstein at his headquarters, intending to dismiss him because Group Lanz, which consisted of the S.S. Panzer Corps and Corps Raus, had given up Kharkov against Hitler's orders. General of Mountain Troops Hubert Lanz had withdrawn only because the S.S. Corps had retreated, he claimed; nevertheless he was dismissed and replaced by General of Panzer Troops Werner Kempf, and the Army and S.S. continued to hold each other responsible for the loss of Kharkov. Manstein now proposed a counter-offensive against the Russians in his rear who had got to within thirty miles of the Dnieper and were only 50 miles from his head-quarters. Hitler agreed. The attacks of both Manstein and Kluge were successful in a limited way, and left the Germans with much the same positions they had held in the winter of 1941. The S.S. Panzer Corps under Hausser distinguished itself in these operations.

The next major operation was the battle of Kursk, for which planning began in March. Several of the leading commanders involved, especially Model, were against it; and Manstein after some doubt thought it had been left too late, as indeed it had. But Hitler and Zeitzler won the day over all objections. Model in the north had twenty-one divisions and over 900 tanks, but relied upon the infantry attacking first, whereas Manstein in the south had twenty-two divisions, of which eleven were infantry (though only seven took part), and about the same number of tanks. Unlike Model, Manstein relied upon his tanks to lead the assault. But it was not to be like his last victory with Hoth in February on the Dnieper–Donets front, which, though limited, had smashed six Russian tank Corps, ten rifle divisions, and six independent brigades. On 21 June Manstein had asked whether the Donets region was to be held or the Russians made to bleed themselves to death on the Dnieper, and O.K.H. had replied, 'The Führer wants both!' Now, when operation 'Citadel' finally got under way several weeks late on 4 July, the Russians were ready for it. Model's forces in the north ran into trouble early, and the Russians penetrated near Orel in his rear, causing von Kluge to suspend his attack. But Manstein in the south, using Hoth's 4th Panzer Army and Army Detachment Kempf, won a hard-earned success with their tanks, particularly those of Hoth, and had the Russians at a disadvantage. Losses were heavy on both sides and the German tank crews in Hoth's

Army became exhausted, but Manstein was convinced that he was on the point of breaking the Russians, when Hitler suddenly called the offensive off, mainly because of the Allied invasion of Sicily. Kluge was quite agreeable, but Manstein protested: 'Victory on the southern front of the Kursk salient is within reach. The enemy has thrown in nearly his entire strategic reserves and is badly mauled. Breaking off action now would be throwing away victory!' He proposed that Model should tie down the enemy in the north and that Hoth and Kempf should continue their battle south of Kursk. Kluge would not agree, and was backed by Hitler, who merely allowed Manstein to continue on his own until 17 July, when the offensive was abandoned finally. By August Manstein's troops were back on their start-lines.

On 3 September 1943 von Manstein and von Kluge flew to East Prussia and presented vital requests to Hitler. The most important was not for reinforcements, essential though those were, but for the abolition of the existing High Command system, the appointment of a single C-in-C for the Eastern front with overriding powers, and the creation of a new integrated command under a single Chief-of-Staff responsible for all theatres of war. These sensible requests would have meant two things unacceptable to Hitler—relinquishment of his own supreme command, and the end of the O.K.W. under his henchmen Keitel and Jodl, as it now existed. Naturally enough he rejected the proposals out of hand. Even in March Göbbels had recorded how Göring had told him that Manstein had once wanted to suggest that Hitler should give up the supreme command. He had not actually done so, but Hitler had got to hear of the plan and ever since had been looking for an excuse to get rid of Manstein, who was kept on only because of his outstanding ability.

Now Hitler would not countenance the large-scale withdrawals which the two field-marshals wanted, from the Donets Basin and behind the Dnieper. He merely allowed Kluge to retire his southern wing behind the Desna and let Manstein give up the Kuban bridgehead, moving 17th Army to the Crimea, and withdrawing 6th Army from the Mius to the 'Tortoise Line'. He would not agree to formations being transferred from other theatres to strengthen the troops in Russia. No doubt this was because on the very evening of the meeting Allied troops landed in southern Italy.

By 7 September Hitler was still refusing to allow Manstein to pull his forces back to the Dnieper, though Manstein pointed out that the Russians were strengthening their front, which already was their focus of effort. His Army Group was facing fifty-two divisions and two tank Corps.

The following day Hitler did fly to Zaporozhye, Manstein's headquarters, to discuss matters, which he realized were serious. He was in a bad mood, for Italy was on the point of surrendering. Again

Manstein proposed that Army Group Centre be pulled back to the Dnieper, thereby shortening the front by a third; again Hitler refused, but he did promise Manstein a total of eight divisions to buttress the Dnieper crossings and consolidate the front beyond them. These Manstein did not get, Kluge refusing to let go the four which should have come from his Army Group Centre. Next day, Manstein telephoned Zeitzler to warn him that any time now the Russians would make a disastrous breakthrough to the Dnieper. He ended by saying: 'If some foresight had been shown and if the reinforcements, now made indispensable by the situation, had been made available in good time, the present crisis, which may well lead to the final decision in the East and hence of the war generally, would have been avoided.' This was clear criticism of the Führer's leadership—but there was no reaction.

On 14 September came the expected Russian breakthrough on the Voronezh front towards Kiev, Kremenchug, and Cherkassy. Without waiting for Hitler's orders Manstein immediately withdrew 8th Army and 1st Panzer Army towards the Dnieper, and ordered the withdrawal next day of 4th Panzer Army similarly on both sides of Kiev 'to prevent the Army being encircled in small groups and smashed in the front of the river'. Kluge had also signalled that withdrawal to the Dnieper of most of his forces was unavoidable. Hitler summoned Manstein to see him. The Field-Marshal's opening words were, 'What is at stake now is no longer the holding of the Dnieper line or of the economically important regions of the Donbas, my Führer, but the fate of the Eastern front.'

At last Hitler agreed Manstein should withdraw to behind the Dnieper and the Desna, with 6th Army in the south still holding the Wotan Line east of the Dnieper from Melitopol to Zaporozhye. Manstein's front extended some 600 miles, and though he had on paper sixty-three divisions with which to hold it, many of them were no more than of regimental strength. He had now to supervise a withdrawal on a 450-mile front of three of his four Armies, some fifty-four divisions pulling back several hundred miles under fierce attack across six bridges over one of the world's largest rivers. It was a tremendous operation, involving scores of thousands of civilians and supply workers, both German and Russian, with hospitals, depots, repair workshops and factories set up.

Hitler would not countenance the simultaneous withdrawal of 17th Army from the Crimea to help Manstein in the Dnieper battles, so it was virtually cut off. In October the Russians took Zaporozhye and on 6/7 November Kiev fell to them, and then Fastov, through which ran all the supply lines to Manstein's northern sector. Then Zhitomir, west of Kiev and the chief supply area for Hoth's 4th Panzer Army, was taken. In desperate counter-attacks Manstein's forces stabilized the front north of Zhitomir at Korosten, and recaptured the area

230

between Zhitomir and Fastov, but they could not recapture Kiev itself.

By December 1943 Army Group South had withdrawn some 250 miles along its whole front, and the Crimea was cut off. The Russians held the northern stretch of the Dnieper bend, and on 29 December Manstein withdrew General Hube's 1st Panzer Army northwards to join General Raus's 4th Panzer Army on the threatened flank. On 4 January 1944 Manstein flew to persuade Hitler to abandon the Dnieper bend entirely, and to pull back the southern wing of his Army Group, even if this meant giving up the Crimea. Hitler refused, and again turned down Manstein's proposal that a single unified command under an independent professional soldier should be entrusted with the war in Russia. Kluge in the centre was still under heavy pressure and complaining about frightening troop deficiencies, and only on the north on Küchler's Leningrad front were things still comparatively inactive—for the time being. Manstein had conducted a successful and masterly retreat, but the omens for Germany were very grave indeed.

In February 1944 came another reverse. Nearly 60,000 men from six-and-a-half German divisions of Lieutenant-General Theobald Lieb's XLII Corps and General of Artillery Wilhelm Stemmermann's XI Corps Group were cut off in the Korsun pocket (sometimes known as the Cherkassy pocket) on 7 February. On 10 February, without consulting Hitler's headquarters, Manstein acted on an uncompromising report from Major-General Wenck, Chief of Staff of 1st Panzer Army, and ordered an immediate break-out to the west. In terrible weather perhaps half the encircled men fought their way back to safety, though without all their heavy equipment, and Major-General Koll's 1st Panzer Division held open the Lysanka bridgehead across the Gniloy Tikich river for nine days. General Stemmermann was killed in action, and the six-and-a-half divisions no longer existed as such.

Army Group South was already badly weakened by months of hard fighting, and now Manstein expected a full-scale Soviet offensive towards Poland on his northern sector, south of the Pripet Marshes. This was forecast by Colonel Gehlen's Foreign Armies East bureau, which also foresaw a Russian wheel southwards towards the Dnestr River to turn the area east of it into a trap for the 1st and 4th Panzer Armies; and on the southernmost front a drive across the Bug into Wohler's 8th Army, with the intention of breaking through towards Rumania. These warnings were ignored at Hitler's headquarters, though they later proved to have been accurate.

Manstein had moved his headquarters to Lvov on the Polish front, expecting the worst attack to come where he feared a breakthrough between his own Army Group and Army Group Centre, and where he was weak. But when the Russian attacks did come on 4 and 5 March they came along the whole of the Ukraine front. Zhukov, with the strongest forces, the 1st Ukrainian Front, attacked Manstein's left or northern wing, and tore a hole in 4th Panzer Army. General A. Hauffe's XIII Corps was forced back west and north-west, while its neighbour, Lieutenant-General Friedrich Wilhelm Schulz's LIX Corps (both were parts of 4th Panzer Army) had to retreat south into 1st Panzer Army's area. Manstein had held two Panzer Corps in readiness for just such an emergency, under two of the most experienced commanders of armour, Generals of Panzer Troops Breith (III Panzer Corps) and Balck (XLVIII Panzer Corps), and by forming 'hedgehogs' and mounting counter-attacks on the Tarnopol area they somewhat stabilized the situation.

Meanwhile in the south Wöhler's weakened 8th Army could not contain a strong attack by Konev's 2nd Ukrainian Front, which took Uman, crossed the Bug, and pushed on towards the Dniester. On the lower Dnieper Hollidt's 6th Army was prevented from helping Wohler by Russian attacks from two more Armies. Konev's forces cut the Lvov–Odessa railway, the principal supply route for the Germans in the south, on 16 March. Next day they crossed the Dnestr River, and turned north-west to encircle 1st Panzer Army. By 26 March they had reached Rumanian soil. In the north their successes were not so marked, but there was still the fearsome gap between 4th and 1st Panzer Armies, and though Breith managed to hold the Bug for a time, Zhukov to his west pushed through to the Dnestr and on 29 March captured Cernauti.

Thousands of Russian troops were now threatening the rear of Manstein's Army Group, in which Colonel-General Hans-Valentin Hube's 1st Panzer Army now seemed trapped in a large pocket between the Bug and the Dnestr. Hube was one of the ablest and toughest commanders in the Army. He disposed of twenty-two divisions, six of which were very good panzer ones. On 23 March Manstein asked Hitler for reinforcements so that he could re-establish contact with Hube, who was being supplied partly by air, but was keeping mobile to avoid encirclement. Next day Hitler replied: 'The 1st Panzer Army will hold its front on the Bug and will re-establish its severed rearward communications by its own efforts.' Manstein was very angry; he replied: 'The order to hold on and simultaneously to seal the big gap between 1st and 4th Panzer Armies is unrealizable. Please inform the Führer that I shall give 1st Panzer Army the order to break out unless I have his binding assurance by 1500 hours that reinforcements will be sent to me.' Determined to avoid another Stalingrad, Manstein was delivering an ultimatum. An hour later Hitler's head-quarters replied that while Hube could break out westwards he must hold his entire front as before. This was eating one's cake and having it with a vengeance, and Manstein complained to Zeitzler, who agreed with him but said that Hitler did not fully understand the seriousness of the situation. Then, on the evening of 24 March, Manstein was summoned to the Berghof next day.

At Berchtesgaden Manstein explained how Hube must force his way west to link up with Raus. Some fifty miles of Russian-held territory would have to be taken and Raus, C-in-C 4th Panzer Army, needed urgently at least one panzer corps to reinforce him. Hitler refused to give any new troops. He said the whole scheme was pointless, and that 1st Panzer Army must clear up its rear by its own efforts; and as for Manstein, all he did was fall back. Manstein retorted that Hitler himself was solely to blame—for eight months he had given the forces on the southern wing one strategically insoluble task after another, and he himself had been granted neither adequate reinforcements nor freedom of movement. He must now give Hube the order to break out immediately or he would be lost. It was almost unheard of for a general to criticize Hitler so badly. Hitler refused to make a decision on the spot, and walked out, whereupon Manstein told Schmundt that if Hitler could not agree with his views the Führer must find another Army Group commander.

Hube now came through on the telephone to Manstein to say that a breakout to the south, across the Dniester, would entail less risk than to the west and would greatly increase the gap between the two Panzer Armies. Manstein saw Hube's point, but a southwards breakout would leave the Russians free to press on unopposed to Galicia; also, Hube might well walk yet into another encirclement with his back to the Carpathians. He was certain the breakout should be westwards, and because his monitoring staff had broken the wireless codes of Zhukov's armies he had a very good idea how to achieve it.

Hitler, in a changed mood, agreed with Manstein's decision to go west, and even promised him the two panzer divisions of II S.S. Panzer Corps in France, and a Jäger division from Hungary. So in spite of Hube's protest that the terrain to his west was impossible, in the early hours of 26 March he was ordered to make ready for the western breakout. He was to link up with Raus's 4th Panzer Army, though Raus still had to try and save the garrison at Tarnopol, now also cut off.

Zhukov, meanwhile, confident that Hube would go south, had switched the bulk of his attacking force towards the Dniester to intercept him and chase 1st Panzer Army back to the Carpathians. Hube formed two big breakout groups, northern and southern; Corps Group von der Chevallerie, which formed a bridgehead over the Zbruch and then forced the Seret and established bridgeheads there; and Corps Group Breith, which forced a crossing of the Zbruch at Okopy. When Zhukov realized what was happening he reversed the direction of his main tank force northwards. By 5 April Hube had thirty miles to make good; meanwhile II S.S. Panzer Corps and the Jägers had arrived to strengthen Raus and were pushing towards Hube's men. On 6 April the S.S. troops took Buchach and linked up with the advance formation of Hube's Army. By 9 April the whole of 1st Panzer Army, after travelling 150 miles west, had joined up with 4th Panzer Army, and the day was saved. Although much heavy equipment and supplies were lost, the dangerous gap had been eliminated. It was a classic denial of disaster by Manstein, Hube, and Raus.

For this brilliant achievement, Manstein's reward was to be summoned to Berchtesgaden to be dismissed. He was decorated with the Swords to the Knight's Cross as a sop, but Hitler told him: 'The time for operating is over. What I need now is men who stand firm.'

Field-Marshal von Manstein had more than his share of reverses as well as of successes. His plan so brilliantly executed in France in 1940, his 150-mile drive to Dvinsk at the opening of the Russian campaign, his capture of Sevastopol—these had been great achievements. But his withdrawal to the Dnieper and his salvation of 1st Panzer Army were also great achievements. He was trusted by his Staff and by his commanders as a general who thought carefully, took risks when he thought them justified but not unless, and usually thought ahead of the enemy. His colleagues' near unanimity in choosing Manstein as their greatest brain and best commander has been echoed by military commentators of the Allied countries.

Blumentritt called Manstein 'the most brilliant strategist of all our generals'. Westphal wrote: 'Of all the officers of the General Staff von Manstein . . . possessed the greatest strategic and general military gifts. Forward-looking, always full of new, good, and often brilliant ideas, an organizer of genius, a difficult subordinate and a generous superior, he was always in the front rank where the interests of the Army were at stake.' Paul Carell described Manstein as 'the finest general on the Eastern front'. Liddell Hart stated: 'The ablest of all the German generals was probably Field-Marshal Erich von Manstein. That was the verdict of most of those with whom I discussed the war, from Rundstedt downwards.'

Manstein's favourite tactic was to allow Russian penetration in a particular area on purpose, and then fall upon the attackers when they had been lulled into complacency. This successful ruse showed that he did not think merely in terms of fixed lines, but was constantly regrouping his forces in his mind's eye. To Hitler, of course, this was unacceptable, for he would not abandon terrain even for a future victory; but Manstein said, when taxed with losing Kharkov, 'I'd rather lose a city than an Army'.

Hitler's own opinion of Manstein, given to Jodl in 1944, was this: 'In my eyes Manstein has a tremendous talent for operations. There's no doubt about that. And if I had an army of, say, twenty divisions at full strength and in peace-time conditions, I couldn't think of a better commander for them than Manstein. He knows how to handle them, and will do it. He would move like lightning—but always under the condition that he has first-class material, petrol, plenty of ammunition. If something breaks down ... he doesn't get things done. If I got hold of another army today I'm not at all sure that I wouldn't employ Manstein because he is certainly one of our most competent officers. .... [He] can operate with divisions as long as they are in good shape. If the divisions are roughly handled I have to take them away from him in a hurry, he can't handle such a situation.'

This is less than just to Manstein, who constantly had to fight with under-strength formations. He thought that after Stalingrad it was still possible to force a stalemate on the Russian front, but his plans involved withdrawals that Hitler would not countenance. He told Hitler before his dismissal that his divisions had been giving of their best under his command, 'and that no one else could get them to give anything more'; and he was proved right.

After the war von Manstein was arraigned as a war criminal, though he was not brought to trial for over four years. There were seventeen charges against him, including responsibility for the execution of Jews in Poland and Russia, the deportation of civilian populations, the distribution and execution of Hitler's Commissar order, and unjustified reprisals against partisans. Only two of the charges were substantiated, though Manstein was found 'accountable' on seven others—which, very questionably, had been modified after his defence had closed. On the Commissar order charge Manstein's defence was that he had ordered it to be ignored. It emerged from the trial that most right-thinking military commentators thought Manstein had conducted himself very well as a commander, and that far from instigating any policies of brutality he had done his best to make life more tolerable for the Russians in his occupied areas. It was, of course, impossible for Manstein personally to supervise the whole of the vast areas under his control, and undoubtedly S.S. Einsatzgruppen were responsible for bestialities in both Poland and Russia. But Manstein was not the sort of man to countenance them.

Nevertheless, the court found him guilty on two charges, and he was given a sentence of eighteen years' imprisonment. This sentence, and indeed the trial as a whole, provoked opposition from some distinguished quarters, which included Liddell Hart. He wrote to *The Times* on 7 January 1950 a letter in Manstein's defence which ended: 'I have studied the records of warfare long enough to realize how few men who have commanded armies in a hard struggle could have come through such a searching examination of their deeds and words as well as von Manstein did. His condemnation appears a glaring example either of gross ignorance or gross hypocrisy.' The original sentence was reduced greatly; and von Manstein died a free man, in 1973.

If it be by his peers that a man's qualities should best be judged, then Field-Marshal von Manstein's reputation is safe for all time.

The other general whom I would class as a great one is Kesselring. The combination of being an outstanding airman and a successful C-in-C Italy, places him in a category all his own. He did what no other general could have done, and it is hardly possible to say he was a lesser man than Manstein.

Albert Kesselring was born in 1885 at Wunsiedel, in the Fictelgebirge, and attended Bayreuth Grammar School. He entered the Army in 1904 as a 'Fahnenjunker' in the 2nd Bavarian Foot Artillery Regiment. In the Great War he served in Lorraine until the end of 1914; as adjutant of the 1st Bavarian Foot Artillery from 1915 to 1916; and of the 3rd Bavarian Artillery Regiment from 1916 to the end of 1917. He was on the Staff of the 1st Bavarian Landwehr Division in Russia in 1918, and then G.S.O. to the II and III Bavarian Army Corps at Lille in 1918.

From 1919 to 1922 he was a battery commander in the Reichswehr, and from 1922 to 1929 a G.S.O.1 to the Chief of Staff, Army Direction. From 1931, when he became a colonel, he was commander of the 4th Artillery Regiment at Dresden and a divisional commander. On 1 October 1933 he transferred from the Army to the Luftwaffe.

Kesselring's Army career had been sound but unspectacular. In the Luftwaffe, where he was a friend of Göring, his rise was fast. He learned to fly in 1933. In 1935 he was made responsible for the administration, feeding, clothing, finance, and airfield construction of the Luftwaffe, and in 1936 he succeeded General Wever as Chief of Staff. He held this position for a year, being succeeded in turn by General Stumpff. In 1938 he was G.O.C. of the Berlin Luftwaffe District, and in 1939 commanded Air Fleet I in Poland. Kesselring had not continued the heavy bomber programme which Wever supported, and in 1937 had been responsible for cancelling the Dornier 19 and Junkers 89 heavy bomber programmes.

On 12 January 1940 Kesselring became head of the 2nd Air Fleet, which he commanded for nearly two-and-a-half years. He promoted the theory of mass air assaults and created the 'rolling attack' whereby individual squadrons co-operated with each other rather than acting on their own. He also did much to better Army-Luftwaffe co-operation, especially in conjunction with von Bock with whom he got on well. The results of this were proved in France in 1940 and Russia in 1941; and he was to be equally successful when 2nd Air Fleet was transferred to the Mediterranean at the end of October 1941.

Of his collaboration with von Bock Kesselring wrote, 'All my commanding officers and I prided ourselves on anticipating the wishes of the army and on carrying out any reasonable requests as quickly and as completely as we could'. The air operations in Poland and France, though admittedly there was little resistance in the former case, were copybook examples of how an attacking air force should work with ground troops, especially panzer forces. Nevertheless he had no false complacency, and was horrified by Göring's claims for what the Luftwaffe would achieve at Dunkirk. Hitler had a fairly high opinion of Kesselring, perhaps because Kesselring had a friend at court in Jodl.

Kesselring was one of the first three Luftwaffe officers, apart from Göring, to be promoted Field-Marshal in July 1940. 'I had no idea at that time', he wrote in his memoirs, 'that many Army officers did not consider the Luftwaffe field-marshals as their equals in rank. I am still today firmly convinced that none of us would have been made field-marshals after the western campaign if Hitler had not believed in the probability of peace . . . . Both Hitler and the German General Staff thought in terms of continental warfare and shied at a war across the sea—a view corroborated by Admiral Raeder. If the Army was reluctant to tackle an operation against Great Britain, the Navy was flatly opposed to it. We Luftwaffe generals, however, including the Reichsmarschall, were more positively minded.'

Kesselring thought that at least until mid-August 1940 a properly prepared offensive might have succeeded, but he was critical of the planning operation for 'Sea-Lion'. 'The most arresting fact about "Sea-Lion" is that the lessons of the German airborne landings in Holland were completely ignored and it was proposed to do without the support of parachutists. With proper planning enough parachutists and glider planes could have been made available to swamp the defence and radar bases on the coastal assault front, and to seize airfields on which the landing of one or two airborne divisions would then have been possible.'

He thought that the air offensive against Britain that preceded the expected date for 'Sea-Lion' was conducted 'on lines quite at variance with those instructions and never harmonized with the requirements of an invasion'. Nevertheless in early September 1940 Kesselring thought that R.A.F. Fighter Command had been so weakened that it was time to switch to bombing London rather than continue the attacks on airfields and radar stations. In this he disagreed with Sperrle, who thought that the R.A.F. was far from finished and still could put up 1,000 planes. But Kesselring's view prevailed.

He had no illusions by then, however, about the prospects of 'Sea-Lion' without enthusiastic naval support and the use of parachutists. 'It was clear to every discerning person, including Hitler, that England could not be brought to her knees by the Luftwaffe alone. . . .' Nicknamed 'Smiling Albert', Kesselring has been accused of undue optimism throughout the war, but this is not always the case. He was also a realist, who could say of the Dunkirk air operation boastfully demanded by Göring: 'The job is completely beyond the strength of my depleted forces.'

In the summer of 1941 2nd Air Fleet, which had operated till then from bases in Holland, Belgium and North-eastern France, with headquarters at Brussels, was transferred to the Eastern front. There it massively backed up von Bock's Army Group Centre, sometimes contributing 1,000 aircraft from its two Air Corps, II under Lörzer and VIII under von Richthofen. After the fall of Smolensk, Kesselring ardently advocated an all-out attack on Moscow in early September. Towards the end of the year, however, his command was transferred to Italy and Sicily, where nominally he came under Mussolini. His brief was to back up Rommel in the dessert, gain air mastery over the Mediterranean, secure communications, and keep Malta 'in subjection'.

On 2 December 1941 Kesselring was appointed Commander-in-Chief, South, and moved to Rome. This was a big promotion for a Luftwaffe officer.

As an air commander in the Mediterranean Kesselring earned a big reputation, but he had to wear at least two hats. He was the superior of Rommel, but never enjoyed with him the kind of close and successful relationship that Alexander had with Montgomery. He also had to deal with the Italian Commando Supremo, represented by Marshal Ugo Cavallero, frequently an arduous and disappointing task. His main difficulties were the demands of the Italian allies, and Rommel's requirements of supplies and equipment. Although Kesselring made fairly frequent visits to Africa, he was basically confined to Rome; and, as the expert and experienced General Enno von Rintelen, German Military Attaché there since 1936, observed: 'It is not possible to interfere in tactical decisions.' Kesselring may be criticized for having taken too optimistic a line with the Italians, right through to the time when in 1943 he accepted Badoglio's false assurance that Italy would fight on.

Rommel certainly found Kesselring too optimistic, and was often irked by his rulings, believing he saw things only from an Air Force point of view. Later, however, Rommel was to be more complimentary and he refers to Kesselring's 'splendid leadership' in the defence of Italy.

An example of Kesselring's optimism is his claim in 1942 that 'the planned air attack on Malta between 1 and 9 April has, in my opinion, eliminated Malta as a naval base'. Von Senger also refers in June 1943 to Kesselring's 'over-optimistic view of the situation, for this restricted the influence of Rommel, who was in a better position to judge. To me also it seemed that Kesselring rated the possibility of defending Sicily too favourably. . . .' It may also be said that at first Kesselring did not appreciate the significance of the Allied landings in North Africa, having been over-impressed by the German repulse of the Dieppe raid.

Yet Kesselring fully appreciated the importance of Malta, which he wanted to take before Tobruk in the spring of 1942. He thought that the end of April would be the right moment for an attack on Malta, and Mussolini agreed. But Hitler continued to believe that a landing was impracticable, and told O.K.W. that any landing on Malta was bound to end in failure. Therefore he would not allow the operation; only theoretical planning was permitted to go ahead. In many ways it was 'Sea-Lion' all over again.

It must have been a bitter blow to Kesselring; after Rommel had captured Tobruk in June the Malta prospect faded out, and he was alone in raising objections to the further advance of the exhausted and ill-supplied troops. It was not surprising that, like Rommel, he believed the German High Command failed to appreciate the importance of the Mediterranean theatre. Hitler sometimes backed Rommel, sometimes Kesselring, in the frequent disputes which arose.

On 26 June 1942, for example, when Rommel undertook to reach the Nile in ten days, Kesselring had disagreed strongly, because he thought the supply problem still unsolved. He had told Rommel, Cavallero and General Bastico: 'The Luftwaffe badly needs rest. My crews are exhausted, and their planes in need of overhaul. As an airman I say it is madness to rush on against an enemy whose air bases [in Egypt] are still intact. In view of the vital role the Luftwaffe would have to play, I must, for this reason alone, disagree with pushing on to Cairo.' On that occasion, Hitler backed up Rommel.

The Italians were proving more of a liability than a help. Its Army had been bled white by losses in Greece, Africa, and Russia, and von Rintelen estimated that by the end of June 1943 only twenty out of eighty-five divisions were effective. Re-equipping and supplying the Italian forces was a major headache for Kesselring. They wanted as much independence as possible, yet continually required more support from Germany. When the pro-German Cavallero was forced out of office, things became even more difficult, and Rintelen observed of the Italians, 'they are only of value as a weak stop-gap of a strong ally'.

Kesselring was proved wrong in his estimate that the Badoglio Government would continue Mussolini's support of Germany, and after Italy's ignominious exit from the war had the problem of disarming or disbanding the Italian troops. On 23 November 1943 Kesselring became C-in-C South-West and Army Group 'C', with Rommel officially commanding an Army Group in Northern Italy. But it was on Kesselring's broad shoulders that the defence of Italy was to devolve when the Allies landed in Sicily in July 1943 and began their drive north. He disposed of two Armies—the 10th, under Colonel-General von Vietinghoff, and the 14th, first under Colonel-General von Mackensen and later under General of Panzer Troops Lemelson.

Field-Marshal Earl Alexander wrote in his memoirs: 'Every time we attacked Kesselring in Italy we took him completely by surprise; but he showed very great skill in extricating himself from the desperate situations into which his faulty intelligence had led him.' But Kessel-

239

ring in his own memoirs gives no hint that he was ever particularly astonished by an American or British attack. He displayed the greatest talent in making use of his resources, and never allowed himself to panic. He was favoured very often by the Italian terrain and by mountain ranges which made defence far easier than attack, but he was inferior in the air, had a potentially and sometimes actively hostile population with which to deal, and did not enjoy the normal defensive preponderance in numbers to his attackers. He was probably most upset by losing ten divisions from Italy after the Allied landings in Normandy. He was also very worried by the partisans, witness his order of 17 June 1944: 'The Partisan situation in the Italian theatre, particularly central Italy, has recently deteriorated to such an extent that it constitutes a serious danger to the fighting troops and their supply lines as well as to the war industry and economic potential. The fight against the Partisans must be carried on with all the means at our disposal and with the utmost severity. I will protect any commander who exceeds our usual restraint in the choice of severity of the methods he adopts against Partisans. In this connection the old principle holds good that a mistake in the choice of methods in executing one's orders is better than failure or neglect to act.' Three days later he repeated and reinforced this order.

Kesselring had been over-optimistic about his chances of holding Sicily in July 1943, but his defence on the island, through command of the very efficient General Hube, caused the Allies a longer delay than they would have wished. In the end, 60,000 German troops were evacuated safely. Fred Majdalany writes, in *The Fall of Fortress Europe*: 'In this campaign Kesselring perfected the science of holding up a stronger advancing army by frequent demolitions on mountain roads, the booby-trapping and mining of abandoned towns and villages, the employment of mobile guns, leap-frogging back from one twist in a mountain road to the next, so that the advance was constantly held up by the necessity to build bridges, create traffic diversions around road gaps, or by the necessity to mount set-piece attacks with artillery and air support.

In Italy, aided by the atrocious winter weather and by the natural defensive topography, Kesselring continued his tactics of slow withdrawal from one obstacle to the next. To the attacking Allies it seemed that there was always a next ridge, just as there had been in the desert, always a next mountain, or river, or marsh, or barren gully with which to deal.

Though he narrowly failed to defeat the Allied landing at Salerno Kesselring withdrew in good order to the Garigliano River north of Naples, and thence to the Gustav Line through Cassino. Cassino was not taken until mid-May 1944, after severe battles there and on the Rapido River, in several of which the Germans were successful. In late January 1944 the Allies made a landing at Anzio, some thirty-five miles from Rome and well in the rear of Cassino. But the caution of the American commander, Lieutenant-General John P. Lucas, the shortage of Allied landing craft for tanks and heavy equipment, and the quick reaction of the German commanders, meant they failed to exploit their first surprise.

Kesselring was now in charge of the whole of Italy, Rommel having been transferred to France. In their long defensive campaign up Italy, he and his troops wrote an honoured page in German military history. He had a narrow escape at Valmontone, thanks to General Mark Clark's diverting his armour away from Kesselring's line of retreat towards Rome, in his eagerness to gain the prestige of capturing Rome himself. The next main defence line was the Pisa-Rimini or Gothic line, which again held up the Allies. Hitler was fully aware of the importance of tying down as many Allied troops as possible in Italy, and even gave Kesselring some reinforcements. The Allies were weakened in July by the diversion of seven divisions to the landings in southern France, where they were not needed nearly as much as in Italy. Hitler laid down that defences should be prepared from the Alpine approaches to the Adriatic coast, and in August 1944 gave Kesselring Colonel-General Gustav-Adolph von Zangen to construct them. Zangen had been the last commander of 15th Army in France, Belgium, and Holland, and had distinguished himself in organizing the successful evacuation of most of it across the Scheldt. He had large numbers of Todt Organization labour force units at his disposal, and also the former Mountain Staff, Italy.

Kesselring had his differences with both his army commanders, and in the end he got rid of von Mackensen in June 1944; von Vietinghoff was sent to command Army Group Courland between January and March 1945, but returned to Italy for the final days.

On 8 March 1945 Field-Marshal Kesselring was summoned to Berlin, where Hitler appointed him C-in-C West in place of von Rundstedt. It was a dubious honour, for nothing now could save Germany. Kesselring wrote later: 'I was appointed C-in-C West in one of the sharpest crises of the western campaign. After I had formed a picture of the general situation I felt like a concert pianist who is asked to play a Beethoven sonata before a large audience on an ancient, rickety and out-of-tune instrument.'

By the time that Kesselring succeeded Rundstedt—he actually took over in the West on 10 March—the German front was crumbling, and too disorganized for him to rally it. His strict orders to Model and other commanders not to give ground were bound to be ineffective, and he himself did not believe in the military defence of the Ruhr.

As the war stumbled to its end at the close of April, Kesselring became C-in-C South, with authority over south-eastern Germany, most of Austria, half of Czechoslovakia, northern Italy, and a piece of Yugoslavia. For some days he did his best to sabotage the peace negotiations that had been progressing under cover for some time under the leadership of, rather surprisingly, S.S. Colonel-General Wolff, who had made contact with Allen Welsh Dulles, of the Office of Strategic Services, and British intermediaries in Switzerland. He even had von Vietinghoff and his Chief of Staff, General Hans Röttinger, who had been involved in the negotiations, relieved of their duties and threatened with court-martial at the end of April. Of course nothing came of this, and in the end Kesselring gave in and agreed to the capitulation on the Italian-Austrian front. It was evidently distasteful to him to surrender as long as Hitler was alive, but after Hitler's death Kesselring informed Dönitz on 3 May 1945 that he was ready to approve the already negotiated surrender of Army Group South-West.

After the war Kesselring was indicted for war crimes in Italy, including responsibility for the deaths of numerous Italian civilians. He protested that the real responsibility lay with Himmler's S.D. gangs which, however, came under his authority. Although distinguished men such as Field-Marshal Alexander were prepared to testify on his behalf, he was found guilty and condemned to death by a British court in May 1947. In October 1947 the sentence was commuted to life imprisonment; and in October 1952 Kesselring was pardoned and set free. Later he became head of the nationalistic veterans' association, the Stahlhelm.

Kesselring considered himself a lucky general, notably at Anzio when —with forces split before Rome—the Allies failed to make the most of their advantage. In Berlin Kesselring was thought to be too pro-Italian; he certainly advocated sparing Italian towns from bombing and useless defensive stands, and this policy stood him in good stead when he had to cope with the disarming of large bodies of Italian troops after Italy's surrender. Lieutenant-Colonel A.P. Scotland, who interrogated many senior German officers after the war, thought him 'the best of a bad bunch'. He died in 1960.

242

The Panzer Leaders

The name of Colonel-General Heinz Guderian will always be remembered for the lightning panzer thrusts that carved up the Polish and French armies, with the dash to Abbeville on the Channel coast in 1940, and with the initial tank successes in Russia.

Guderian was born in 1888 at Chulm, on the Vistula, in Poland, to a family of west Prussian landowners and lawyers in the Warthegau. In 1907 he joined the 10th Hanoverian Jäger Battalion as an ensign, and passed through a year's course at the War Academy just before the Great War. During that conflict he was employed much of the time as a signals officer both at the front and at higher formation, including Army headquarters. He also held various General Staff appointments and briefly commanded the 2nd Battalion, 14th Infantry Regiment. His signals experience was to stand him in good stead in his later handling of armoured formations.

Guderian was not the father of Germany's Panzer troops. This honour belongs to General of Panzer Troops Oswald Lutz, who as a colonel in the late 'twenties was Chief of Staff to the Inspectorate of Motorized Troops. But Guderian was in at their birth. In late 1929 Lutz gave him command of the 3rd (Prussian) Motorized Battalion at Berlin-Lankwitz, and in 1931 he made Guderian, now a lieutenant-colonel, his Chief of Staff. When von Fritsch became Army C-in-C in 1933, things became easier for the devotees of armour; Lieutenant-Colonel Guderian demonstrated the earliest Mark I tanks to Hitler at Kummersdorf, and the new Chancellor told him excitedly: 'That's what I need! That's what I want to have!'

In the spring of 1934 a Motorized Troops Command Staff was set up under Lutz, the Inspector of Motorized Troops; and in the summer this was elevated to a Motorized Troops Command. Then in October 1935 the first three Panzer Divisions were formed, the 1st at Weimar under von Weichs, the 2nd at Würzburg under Colonel Guderian, and the 3rd at Berlin under Major-General Fessmann.

Guderian held this post for over two years, becoming a major-general in 1936. In 1938 Lutz was dismissed for his involvement with the unfortunate von Fritsch, and Guderian, promoted Lieutenant-General, succeeded him as head of the panzer arm. He took charge of all the armoured units which entered Austria—not a campaign of unmitigated success, for he himself admitted that 30 per cent of the vehicles

243

suffered breakdowns. Nevertheless, by 1939 Guderian was a full general of panzer troops and in charge of the '*Schnelltruppen*' or 'Fast troops'. Although other tank experts included von Weichs, von Vietinghoff, Höpner, Hoth, Schmidt, and Reinhardt, his position as Germany's leading tank general was a strong one. It was thus natural that von Manstein should consult Guderian when revising the German plan of attack on France and the Low Countries.

Guderian was an uncompromising, tough, burly figure at his best in handling aggressive operations. This suited his personality, essentially that of a hard-striking armoured leader prepared to take risks. His critics have accused him of being bull-like in his methods, and he was not, certainly, a man of subtlety, but he was too well trained and expert in the handling of armour to be foolhardy. But he was somewhat choleric and dictatorial in his methods, and was not an easy man to command. He was popular with his troops, with whom he maintained a breezy yet demanding relationship, and was admired by most of the panzer commanders.

Guderian's dash, technical skill and whole-hearted belief in the massed use of armour—'Not driblets, but mass'—were given ample opportunity in Poland and France, and at every turn were vindicated. So was his belief in air co-operation, and neither the Poles nor the French could stand up to the combined onslaught of panzers and Stukas. Guderian handled his forces in XIX Panzer Corps, consisting of 1st, 2nd and 10th Panzer Divisions and some smaller motorized formations, with confidence and brilliance, and its breakthrough at Sedan and dash to the Channel at Abbeville and Calais will always be remembered. Very much a frontline commander, Guderian was always well up with his troops, urging them on and frequently risking his own mobile head-quarters. The units of his Corps wore a 'G' painted on their vehicles, a practice which he was the first to introduce. Though primarily an attacking general, Guderian was by no means scornful of defence. In the early days he had much to do with the formation of anti-tank companies in the armoured divisions.

The essence of the German Panzer victories was a concentrated punch in conjunction with low-level bombing and strafing, rapid mobility and follow-up, then a fanning out, with the ability to keep moving. Such an unexpected and determined armoured thrust could cause chaos and a slump in morale among the enemy, especially when the tanks got behind a formation. In view of the huge distances and often uncertain going in Russia, perhaps these tactics were bound to be less effective than in Poland and France. It was a very different matter to bolster a successful panzer thrust with strong follow-up infantry formation at high speed in the vast steppes and unending forests of Russia, than doing the same thing in the built-up and restricted areas of France.

An apostle of German–Russian rapprochement and a great advocate of the Nazi-Soviet Pact of 1939, Guderian was disgusted when he first heard about Hitler's plan to invade the Soviet Union, and of Halder's view that Russia could be defeated in eight to ten weeks. Guderian conveyed his views to O.K.H. with no effect at all. One day his two senior Staff Officers returned starry-eyed from a briefing by Halder on the forthcoming Operation Barbarossa. 'When they spread out a map of Russia before me', says Guderian in his memoirs, 'I could scarcely believe my eyes.' He hoped the whole thing was mere bluff, but was to be disillusioned. He was the more sceptical because most of the vehicles given to the new divisions that Hitler was creating for the Russian campaign were captured French ones, 'in no way capable of meeting the demands of warfare in eastern Europe'. Nevertheless Guderian had proved he could successfully move his panzer divisions hundreds of miles without too many breakdowns or casualties, and as long as the good weather lasted in Russia he was equally successful.

The worst enemy of the German Army in the Eastern campaign was the bad winter weather—mud, frost, and cold. Moreover it suffered from a lack of adequate tank and motor replacements, and of sufficient motorized infantry formations to back up the armoured breakthroughs. Guderian disposed of some 850 tanks in his 2nd Panzer Group, in Russia, but this proved not enough. He had five Panzer divisions, three motorized infantry divisions, and one invaluable horsed cavalry division, split into three Corps; while Hoth, commanding 3rd Panzer Group, had four Panzer and three motorized infantry divisions in two Corps.

During the first five months of the Russian war, Guderian achieved some brilliant successes. They were due partly to his own excellence as an armoured commander, and partly to the high standard of his troops and subordinate commanders. These latter included men like Generals von Geyr, von Vietinghoff, von Löper, and Lemelsen, the first two of whom had commanded Panzer divisions and the third a light division (subsequently Panzer) before the war. There were also such rising stars as Model, Schaal, Hausser of the S.S., von Arnim, Nehring, Kempff, von Thoma, and Colonels Balck and Eberbach. For part of the time Guderian also had under command an outstanding infantryman, General Heinrici. A third factor in Guderian's successes was the splendid air support he got from the fighters of Colonel Mölders and from von Richthofen's 4th Air Fleet.

At the beginning of the Russian invasion Guderian advanced from Brest-Litovsk to the Dnieper in only fifteen days. There he was ordered by von Kluge to await the infantry, but he was convinced that he must cross the Dnieper, and that a swift strike at Moscow could decide the campaign. His confidence persuaded Kluge, though he told Guderian grumpily, 'Your operations always hang by a silken thread'. Smolensk fell on 15 July, and Tula, some 185 miles from Moscow, on 19 July;

but then Hitler shied away from pressing the Moscow drive. On 21 August, after weeks of hesitation, he gave the Ukraine and Crimea priority over the Russian capital.

Bock and Guderian were in despair. The former sent Guderian and Halder to see Hitler on 23 August to try to change the decision. Although forbidden by von Brauchitsch to mention Moscow, Guderian forcefully stated his case. Hitler heard him out, but then adduced economic considerations—Germany needed the grain of the Ukraine and the industrial power of the Donets; it also had to cut off Russian oil supplies from the Caucasus. Guderian was silenced, and the fatal decision was taken to turn north and south.

The Moscow drive was not to be resumed until early October, and while Guderian and Kleist won great victories in the interval—Guderian at Roslavl, Krichev, in the Gomel region, and across the Desna River; Kleist in the Uman encirclement; and the pair in the great Kiev pocket battle in September—the great opportunity had been missed.

Bryansk fell to Guderian; Kaluga, only 100 miles from Moscow, to Höpner; and Vyazma to Hoth; but then the weather broke and by November the Germans were bogged down by mud, frostbite, exhaustion, and casualties all along the front. The number of tanks no longer fit for service was appalling. Guderian encircled Túla with two Panzer divisions on 24 November, but by 5/6 December had to break off his attack and retreat on the southern sector of Bock's Army Group Centre. He wrote to his wife: 'The icy cold, the wretched accommodation, the insufficient clothing, the heavy losses of men and *matériel*, and the meagre supplies of fuel are making military operations a torture, and I am getting increasingly depressed by the enormous weight of responsibility which, in spite of all the words, no-one can take off my shoulders.' He realised that the attack on Moscow had failed, though he was only seventy-five miles south of it.

On 20 December Guderian again had an interview with Hitler, in east Prussia. Now he wanted the German line to withdraw to better positions, a considerable distance if need be. Hitler refused on the grounds that any authorization of retreat would lead to general panic. Guderian stuck to his guns, saying: 'Positional warfare in this unsuitable terrain will lead to battles of *Matériel* as in the First World War. We shall lose the flower of our officer corps and N.C.O. corps; we shall suffer gigantic losses without gaining any advantage. And these losses will be irreplaceable.' Hitler invoked Frederick the Great, and when Guderian went on to say that there seemed no justification to him for sacrificing his soldiers' lives, added: 'I know all about your personal effort, and how you lead your troops from in front. But for this reason you are in danger of seeing things too much at close quarters. You are hamstrung by too much compassion for your men. Things look clearer from a greater distance. In order to hold the front no sacrifice can be too great. For if we do not hold it the Armies of Army Group Centre are lost.'

Guderian was not an easy man to control, and it was particularly unfortunate for him that his immediate superior Bock had been replaced by the more cautious von Kluge, with whom he did not get on, and who frequently complained that Guderian did not carry out his orders properly. On Christmas Eve Kluge accused Guderian of evacuating Chern without authority, creating a dangerous gap of twenty-five miles, and Hitler dismissed him from his command, already alarmed and angered at the talk of tactical withdrawal.

His dismissal sent Guderian into the wilderness for over a year, and was to prevent his ever becoming a field-marshal. It also ended his active command career. It came at a bad time for Germany, for von Brauchitsch and von Rundstedt had just gone, and soon to join them in retirement would be von Leeb and General Küchler at their own request, from Army Group North and 4th Army; Colonel-General Höpner (dismissed with ignominy); General of Infantry Geyer; and General of Pioneers Förster. Colonel-General Rudolf Strauss, G.O.C. 9th Army, also departed the Russian front in January 1942 because of ill-health.

For nearly fourteen months Guderian remained unemployed, with the additional misfortune of a bad heart attack, from which he recovered slowly. Despite the good offices of Schmundt and the S.S. leader Sepp Dietrich, his career seemed over. Guderian's enemies at court prevailed over the sympathetic Schmundt, who reported after an investigation: 'The man has been treated unjustly. His whole army is on his side and believes in him. We must see what we can do to put this business to rights.'

In September 1942, when Rommel went on sick leave before El Alamein, he asked for Guderian to replace him in Africa; but Hitler jibbed, and sent instead General Stumme. Later, Guderian was to think himself fortunate that Hitler had turned down Rommel's suggestion. He thought he would probably have been as unable as Stumme and Rommel to avoid defeat at El Alamein.

Guderian was recalled to service on 1 March 1943 as Inspector-General of Armoured Troops. He had wide powers and exerted considerable influence—but he held no command. Although Hitler assigned to him 'the common powers of an Army commander' and made him senior officer of armoured troops, he did not command any troops directly. More important was the fact that Guderian reported to Hitler himself, and not to O.K.W. or O.K.H. He also exercised direction over the armoured troops of the S.S. and Luftwaffe. Despite the great Panzer victories to which he himself had contributed so much, Guderian was far from satisfied with the production figures and development of German tank production and design, the faults and shortcomings of which he set out to correct. In May 1940 German tank production of all types had been only 125 per month. In late January 1942, Hitler had ordered overall tank production to be raised to a capacity of 600 per month; and now in April 1943 Guderian got the figure raised to 1,955.

But when Hitler held an important conference at Munich on 4 May 1943 to discuss the proposed double envelopment attack against the Russians west of Kursk, 'Operation Citadel', Guderian spoke strongly against it. His objections were based on the fact that neither the Panther tank nor the Ferdinand, an electrically-driven assault gun based on the Tiger tank, were yet properly ready. Both were suffering from teething troubles and Guderian was dissatisfied that the Ferdinand, having no machine-gun armament, was hopelessly unsuitable for close combat. Nothing positive was decided that day, so Guderian took the opportunity in Berlin on 10 May, when Hitler had summoned him to discuss Panther production, earnestly to beg him not to attack in the East that year, Kursk being a matter of supreme indifference to the outside world. Half convinced, Hitler replied, 'You're quite right. Whenever I think of this attack my stomach turns over.' All the same, the attack was made, with disastrous results.

Guderian next turned his attention to the problem of defending the Western Front. In 1944 the problem became urgent, and he made several visits to France to see von Rundstedt, von Geyr the armoured commander, whom he knew well, and other Panzer leaders. There were nine Panzer divisions and one Panzer grenadier division in France, and forty-eight infantry divisions. Guderian also saw Rommel, whom he knew as a former commanding officer of the Goslar Jäger (10th Hanoverian) Battalion, his own old regiment, with which he had always kept in touch. Guderian is more than fair to Rommel's abilities in his memoirs, stating that 'he had great understanding of his men and, in fact, thoroughly deserved the reputation that he had won for himself'. Since Rommel to a large extent had supplanted Guderian as the Panzer leader foremost in the Führer's favour, this was generous of him. But on the question of the employment of the tank forces when the Allies invaded, there was clear disagreement between the two. Guderian sided with von Rundstedt and von Geyr, who wanted to keep the armour well back from the coastal areas and then use it in a massive co-ordinated counter-attack to sweep back the invaders. Rommel, because of his experiences in Africa and then in Italy, was convinced that the superiority of Allied air power negated the possibility of moving large bodies of armour about once the invasion had started.

The argument can go on for ever. But it is doubtful whether, whatever course the Germans had chosen, they could long have resisted the ruthless impetus of the Allied attack in Normandy and north-western France.

The events of 20 July 1944 shocked Guderian, as they did the whole officer corps. According to his memoirs, he knew absolutely nothing about the assassination plot, and for this we must take his word. But Guderian is less than frank about the various approaches made to him previously by the conspirators, mentioning only one by von Tresckow in July 1943. This was the year in which von Hassell, writing on 20 April, noted that, 'At the moment, for a change, some hopes are put on Guderian'. The opposition to Hitler was manifestly barking up the wrong tree here. Guderian would have no part in a conspiracy against Hitler. He was against the assassination attempt because, he claimed, assassination was wrong in itself and because he doubted in any case whether a change of régime would be of any avail to the war effort. But he was acutely aware of the tragic horrors and grievous implications for the Army and the General Staff that resulted from 20 July. He was particularly affected by Rommel's wretched end. The fate of the conspirators—and of many others only loosely connected with the Plot, or even not at all connected—was brought doubly home to Guderian because, against his will, he had to serve as a member of the military Court of Honour which sat chiefly to dismiss the accused from the armed services preparatory to their arraignment before the People's Court.

Nevertheless, the fact that—even in his murderous rage following the 20 July assassination attempt—Hitler should have chosen Guderian to head the General Staff, shows that he had no doubts of the validity of Guderian's Nazi convictions. His appointment to be Chief of the General Staff after the July plot in 1944 came as a surprise, but by now Hitler was using the Chief of Staff as little more than a glorified messenger boy, and it is doubtful whether Guderian should have accepted the post. As it was, if he believed at this late stage that he would be able to influence events decisively, he was mistaken. He had no more influence on Hitler than Zeitzler had—and whereas the latter had gradually become less and less pliable, Guderian to his discredit supported Hitler's Nazi line almost slavishly at first.

Already in May 1943 he had written a letter, intended for Hitler's eyes only, in which he characterized the General Staff as a body of weak-kneed defeatists. On his first day in office, when the Chief of Staff, Army Group North, had told him that Colonel-General Friessner believed that the course Hitler was pursuing would lose him the Baltic States and 16th and 18th Armies, Guderian sneeringly declared that he expected 'General Friessner will be man enough to give the necessary orders [to surrender] in the event of a catastrophe'.

On 29 July 1944 he addressed an order to all the officers of the General Staff which began: 'Every General Staff officer must be a National Socialist officer-leader, that is not only by his knowledge of tactics and strategy but also by his model attitude to political questions and by actively co-operating in the political indoctrination of younger commanders in accordance with the tenets of the Führer . . .' and ended: 'I expect every General Staff officer immediately to declare himself a convert or adherent to my views. . . .'

It was as if he had become mesmerized by Hitler's personality, a reaction common to many men.

But the old dogmatism reasserted itself, and from November 1944 his readiness to stand up to Hitler provoked many bitter and even violent clashes between them.

For example, Guderian requested again and again that the wasted Army Group of 16th and 18th Armies, consisting of twenty infantry and two Panzer divisions, in Courland, be evacuated and used elsewhere; but repeatedly Hitler demurred, claiming that it was tying down large Russian forces, and using Dönitz's tepid enthusiasm for such a marine operation as an excuse to postpone it. Guderian was doubtful about the Ardennes offensive, and when he saw early on that it had failed he pleaded on 24 December 1944 for Hitler to break it off and use the troops for reinforcing the threatened eastern front. He correctly forecast 12 January 1945 as the date of the next big Soviet attack. Hitler would have none of it. Twice more Guderian tried to convince him of the urgent straits of the troops in the east and of the impending Soviet attack, but Hitler ridiculed Major-General Gehlen's intelligence reports as 'completely idiotic'.

There were arguments about Hungary and the relief of Budapest, about Poland, about the performance and appointment of generals. Guderian fought in vain in January 1945 to keep Colonel-General Josef Harpe in his post as C-in-C Army Group 'A'. Hitler insisted on replacing this gallant and intelligent commander with one of his own favourites, the Nazi Schörner. Colonel-General Reinhardt, another first-class and experienced armoured leader, was dismissed from Army Group Centre, as was General of Infantry Friedrich Hossbach, C-in-C 4th Army, who had made an unauthorized disengagement in the face of encirclement. Hitler overruled Guderian's suggestion that Field-Marshal von Weichs be appointed C-in-C Army Group Vistula, and instead made the ludicrous appointment of Himmler. Hitler also removed the very capable Colonel-General Erhard Raus, an Austrian, from command of 3rd Panzer Army.

An eye-witness to events, Captain Gerhard Boldt, has written: 'Their mutual hostility was partly due to basic differences of opinion about military tactics; but a strong additional factor, and one which will always redound to Guderian's credit, was the way in which the General mustered the courage, time and again, openly to contradict and warn Hitler. He was one of the very few men in Hitler's entourage who stood by his own views and who was bold enough to contradict the Führer without restraint at that time.'

The last clash came when Guderian was defending General Theodor

Busse, commander of 9th Army, whom Hitler was holding responsible for the failure to relieve Kistrin. This scene, in the Reich Chancellory on 28 March 1945, almost defies description or belief, Hitler was ranting and raving against the Army, the General Staff, the whole Officer Corps, and the Generals. Guderian more and more hotly criticized Hitler's military leadership and the abandonment to their fate of the people of East Germany. In the end it looked as though he would provoke a physical assault from the Führer, now quite out of control with rage. Horrified onlookers had to separate them by force. Afterwards Hitler said: 'Colonel-General Guderian, your physical health requires that you immediately take six weeks' leave.' It was a dismal and almost farcical end to the career of a one-time favourite.

By his own lights Guderian was faithful to his caste, and it is to his credit that he stuck by Keitel and Jodl as his 'comrades', even after their deaths. But though his memoirs provide a fascinating account of the German Army before and during the war, as seen from a special and outspoken vantage point, what they omit is as interesting and provoking as what they declare. Guderian speaks little about his real attitude to National Socialism and to Hitler, and he withholds moral judgement, though he admits that Hitler lacked the wisdom and moderation of Frederick the Great and of Bismarck. 'Abandoned by his good fairies, he ended in utterly destroying his own handiwork, and with him a fine, upstanding, hard-working, and loyal nation was cast down into the depths.'

At the end of the war Guderian surrendered to the Americans; denazification proceedings were instituted against him, but were dropped in June 1950. In 1954 Colonel-General Heinz Guderian, Panzer leader par excellence, died at the age of sixty-six.

Without question, the name of Field-Marshal Rommel is the one which, even today, will come first to the lips of Britons asked to name one German general of the last war. For many Rommel remains *the* outstanding enemy general. Yet in 1939, even in Germany, he was more or less unknown outside a limited professional circle, a new and junior major-general, promoted that August.

Erwin Rommel was born near Ulm in Württemberg on 15 November 1891, the son of a provincial schoolmaster of typical bourgeois Swabian stock. In 1910 he entered Infantry Regiment 124 of the Royal Württembergian Army, in which he served as a platoon commander and later adjutant, with a brief spell on detachment to an artillery regiment. After distinguishing himself on the Western Front and being wounded, he joined the newly formed Württemberg Alpine or Mountain Battalion in October 1915. In 1917 this *élite* battalion was posted to the Alpine Corps on the Rumanian front, and in the Carpathian Mountains he achieved further successes.

His battalion was then transferred to the Italian front, and at Caporetto Rommel did spectacularly well, capturing a complete Italian position in two days' fighting and taking prisoner 150 officers, 9,000 men, and eighty-one guns. He followed up this success by another at Longarone where 10,000 Italians with twenty guns and a transport column surrendered. For these exploits Rommel was awarded the *Pour le Mérite*. His encounters in battle with the Italians were to leave a lasting feeling of suspicion, even of contempt for them, that served him ill in the African campaigns of the Second World War. For most of the last year of the Great War Rommel held a Staff appointment. After the war, when his own regiment was disbanded, Rommel served as a captain for nearly nine years in Infantry Regiment 13 at Stuttgart. He then went as an instructor for nearly four years to the Infantry School at Dresden, under von Falkenhausen; with him and another instructor, Heinrich von Stülpnagel, he became friendly.

It was not until 1933, at the age of nearly forty-two, that Rommel achieved his first command as a lieutenant-colonel, that of a mountain battalion of Infantry Regiment 17 (Jäger Goslar). It was during his two year's command that he first met Hitler. In 1935 Colonel Rommel was posted to the War Academy at Potsdam, and in 1938 made Commandant of the War Academy at Wiener Neustadt. Given the job of supervising the military training of the 'Hitler *Jugend*', he had tangled in 1937 with the Reich Youth leader, Baldur von Schirach. Rommel's textbook on infantry tactics, *Infantry Greift An*, attracted the interest and approbation of Hitler, and when the Führer invaded the Sudetenland in October 1938 he chose Rommel to command his headquarters bodyguard, the Führergleitbataillon. He continued in this post in the Prague campaign in March 1939. He was rewarded by being given the command of a division. As he had expressly asked for a Panzer Division (though himself an infantryman, he had noted the success of German tanks in Poland) he was given 7th Panzer Division.

Although he had the opportunity, Rommel never became a member of the General Staff; he regarded himself as essentially a regimental officer. He did, however, have some friends in high places, notably the Bavarian General List, a Corps commander in Dresden in 1938 and an Army Group commander in Vienna in 1939. Rommel had been something of a protégé of List since 1928.

Rommel took over 7th Panzer Division in February 1940 from Lieutenant-General Stumme, who had trained it well and fought with it successfully in Poland. Rommel's immediate superior was his Corps commander, General of Infantry Hermann Hoth, an experienced armoured commander. On 24 May Hoth was given an Armoured Group and Rommel came directly under General of Panzer Troops Rudolf Schmidt's XXXIX (Panzer) Corps, responsible to Hoth. Schmidt was also experienced in tanks, having commanded 1st Panzer division for two years before the war. It is worth noting that in 1940 the German Army in the West mustered ten full Panzer divisions, and three motorized ones; with all their numerous tanks the French disposed of barely four armoured divisions, and the B.E.F. just one, which never fought as an integrated formation.

Rommel took to tanks like a duck to water; he had clearly spent his time well in observing their use in the Sudetenland, Austria, and Poland.

In the first phase of the French campaign Rommel did brilliantly in crossing the Meuse and advancing rapidly, sometimes by night, to Le Cateau and Cambrai. In the second phase he was given a nasty shock by the British counter-attack near Arras. However he rallied his division and completed the encirclement of Lille, which led to the trapping of nearly half the French 1st Army. Always up with his leading tanks, he was often exposed to danger. On 3 June Hitler, paying a visit behind the front, told him: 'Rommel, we were very worried about you during the attack.' Rommel was awarded the Knight's Cross to add to his Iron Cross.

In the latter part of the campaign Rommel drove from the Somme to the Seine, splitting the French 10th Army and capturing many French and British prisoners. In the last phase of free-wheeling pursuit, he covered 150 miles in one day starting east of Laigle and ending at La Haye-du-Puits, south of Cherbourg; then on to Cherbourg itself.

Often out of touch with his Staff because of his insistence on travelling at the front, Rommel broke the rules but got away with it. During the whole campaign the division lost only forty-two tanks, and captured over 100,000 prisoners, more than 450 tanks and armoured cars, and 300 pieces of ordnance. In March 1941 he was given a retrospective award of the Oak Leaves to his Knight's Cross.

In January 1941 Rommel was promoted Lieutenant-General, and the following month appointed commander of the German Afrika Korps. This initially comprised only two divisions, the 5th Light and 15th Panzer, to be sent to Libya to help the Italians. At this time the situation in Africa from the Axis point of view was grave. Wavell had taken Benghazi and looked ready to advance into Tripolitania. On 12 February Rommel reported to the Italian commander in Africa, General Gariboldi, under whose orders he now technically came, and then lost no time in taking to the air daily to study the African terrain and troop dispositions.

Although in theory Rommel came under the Italian C-in-C in Africa, he received his orders direct from O.K.W., and made little attempt to work closely with the Italian commanders or adhere to directives from Rome. The Italians were jealous of German interference in what they regarded as an Italian theatre of war. On the other hand they baulked at taking Malta, which Rommel rightly considered necessary for a successful guarantee of getting enough supplies. Rommel continually told his staff in 1941 and 1942 that he could not understand why the High Command did not take Malta. He thought it should have been attacked in preference to Crete in May 1941. The Italian Navy was unable to control the Mediterranean, and Rommel had little opinion of its worth, just as for the most part he underrated and even despised the Italian divisions in Africa. His independent attitude led to friction with the Italian senior commanders.

Rommel would also have preferred the Luftwaffe in Africa to be subordinated to his own command, instead of operating under its own command system responsible to Kesselring. All this made more difficult the already hard task of General Enno von Rintelen in Rome, German military attaché since 1936, and plenipotentiary as 'German general in the headquarters of the Italian armed forces'. It was due to von Rintelen's tact, experience, and understanding of the Italians that many major difficulties were avoided but Rommel saw him in a different light, as an obstructionist sitting on his backside in Rome who did not understand his supply difficulties and did far too little to solve them.

On 19 March 1941 Rommel was told firmly by von Brauchitsch that there was no intention of striking a decisive blow in Africa in the near future. But although 5th Light Division was not yet complete, and 15th Panzer not due to complete its arrival before the end of May, Rommel now proceeded totally to disregard his instructions. He had already told Lieutenant-General Streich to prepare an attack on El Agheila, and on 24 March this was carried out successfully against light and unprepared British forces. On 31 March Rommel's forces took Mersa el Brega, and though Wavell thought the Axis unlikely to make any big effort for another month, it seemed from Rommel's reconnaissance on land and by air that the British were tending to withdraw. He therefore seized his opportunity and decided to strike at the whole of Cyrenaica. On 2 April Agedabia fell to him, and next day Benghazi. The British, over-estimating the size of Rommel's small force, went on falling back. Rommel was berated by Gariboldi for ignoring orders from Rome, but was saved by a signal from the German High Command giving him complete freedom of action.

As he wrote to his wife on 3 April: 'I took the risk against all orders and instructions because the opportunity seemed favourable.' By 5 April Ben Gania had fallen, and by 8 April Rommel's German and Italian troops were in Mechili and Derna. He directed the battle partly from the air and partly up with the leading troops. On 10 April he announced that his objective was the Suez Canal, but that Tobruk, now heavily reinforced by the Australians under Major-General Morshead, must first be taken. This proved easier said than done, though from 10 April Tobruk was encircled and its investment was completed next day, when Bardia, further along the coast, fell.

Rommel's stock stood high; but by 2 May he realized that Tobruk was not going to fall easily into his hands. Meanwhile in Berlin Colonel-General Halder, who neither appreciated Rommel nor understood desert warfare, was having second thoughts. His spies reported that Rommel was 'in no way equal to his task', so Halder sent out his Deputy Chief of Staff, Lieutenant-General Friedrich Paulus, to make an on-the-spot investigation, believing Paulus to be 'perhaps the only man with sufficient personal influence to head off this soldier gone stark mad'. Paulus was an admirable staff officer, a contemporary of Rommel, and like him a product of the south German lower middle class. In nearly all other respects they were the opposite of each other. After witnessing an unsuccessful new attack on Tobruk, Paulus reported back that Rommel was too weak logistically, and put an embargo on further attacks towards Egypt. Later he was to characterize Rommel as 'this thick-headed Swabian', though he admitted that he was 'an enterprising leader of men'.

On 15 May General L.H.C. 'Strafer' Gott surprised Rommel by capturing Sollum and Capuzzo in a quick dash, and the British retired from all points except Halfaya Pass. On 27 May the Germans recaptured Halfaya Pass, and Rommel ordered strongpoints to be constructed between Sollum, Halfaya, and Bardia. During the summer Lieutenant-General Gause, a former pioneer, arrived from O.K.W. with a large staff. Although he had been told not to place himself under Rommel's command, he was immediately co-opted and soon became Rommel's Chief of Staff.

On 15 June, full of misgivings because of the slowness and vulnerability of British tanks, Wavell launched the 'Battleaxe' offensive. Rommel had been waiting for it, although he only had thirteen 88 mm. dual-purpose guns, he had skilfully dug them in at Halfaya with their barrels horizontal so that these basically ack-ack guns were practically invisible. He now had the complete 15th Panzer Division with eighty tanks under Lieutenant-General Ludwig Crüwell. (Its original commander, Major-General von Prittwitz, had been killed by an anti-tank shell near Tobruk soon after arriving.) He also had the 5th Light Division, which contained a Panzer battalion. The Germans probably mustered some 150 tanks, the British over 200.

The British troops directed by Lieutenant-General Beresford-Peirse included the 7th Armoured Division, 4th Indian Division, and 22nd Guards Brigade. Their Crusader tanks proved unreliable, and in the centre eleven of the twelve leading Matildas were destroyed by the dug-in 88s. After heavy fighting all through 15 June the Guards succeeded in taking Capuzzo. Next day 15th Panzer launched a severe attack on the ninety Matildas of 4th Armoured Brigade and the infantry of 22nd Guards Brigade, but lost thirty of their eighty tanks. Further west the 5th Light Division's tanks fought a violent but successful action against the Crusaders of 7th Armoured Brigade. In Rommel's view this was the turning-point of the battle, for very early on 17 June he was able to push in a two-pronged surprise attack on Sidi Suleiman by 5th Light and 15th Panzer, after which the two divisions went on to Halfaya. The British were now in confusion and short of petrol and ammunition. By the time Wavell arrived to inspect the situation Major-General Messervy had ordered 4th Indian Division in the north to retreat, so Wavell told Major-General O'Moore Creagh, G.O.C. 7th Armoured Division, to conform. He sent a signal to General Dill in London which began, 'I regret to report the failure of "Battleaxe".' Rommel had won a decided victory.

Rommel was now promised large reinforcements which, however, did not materialize. Had they done so, 'We would have been strong enough to destroy the British in Egypt in the spring of 1942, and could have advanced into Iraq and cut off the Russians from Basra.' It should be remembered that Rommel commanded only a corps so far. It consisted of 5th Light Division, soon to be renamed 21st Panzer and 15th Panzer Division, each with two tank and three infantry battalions. These comprised the Afrika Korps. In August 1941 when Rommel's command was upgraded to a Panzer Group and he was promoted General of Panzer Troops, the 90th Light Division was formed from independent units. Though it had no tanks it was very strong in fire power, and under Major-General Kleeman was to become a byeword to its British opponents. Lieutenant-General Crüwell, who was promoted General of Panzer Troops in December 1941, became commander of the Afrika Korps in August, with Colonel Fritz Bayerlein as his Chief of Staff. Rommel also had under command the Italian XXI Infantry Corps and the XX Motorized Corps consisting of the Ariete and Trieste Divisions.

Despite Rommel's success, O.K.W.—now preoccupied with Russia and the Balkans—did not reinforce him adequately. Though it was agreed that Tobruk should be taken as a first step towards the conquest of Egypt, Hitler still shied off the capture of Malta, deterred by the heavy parachutist casualties in Crete. Halder still mistrusted Rommel, who he thought was not facing up to the realities of the supply situation. Meanwhile the Western Desert Air Force was daily growing stronger and regularly attacking Rommel's lines of communication.

At the end of October Field-Marshal Kesselring was appointed C-in-C South, with orders to gain control of both air and sea between Italy and Africa. During the summer both sides in the desert made preparations for attack. The British had 477 tanks in Lieutenant-General Willoughby Norrie's XXX Corps, including 173 American Stuarts and 210 Crusaders. In Lieutenant-General Godwin-Austen's XIII Corps they had 135 in 1st Army Tank Brigade, and 126 in 2nd Army Tank Brigade, nearly all Matildas and Valentines. They also had about 200 tanks in reserve, which were used up at the rate of some forty a day. Rommel disposed of some 400 German and Italian tanks, of which 150 were Mark IIs and 55 Mark IVs, and 342 available aircraft out of a total of 536. The Afrika Korps practised co-ordinated tactical moves between tanks and 88 mms. acting in concert, a highly important manoeuvre. Rommel also formed a heavy artillery support group under Lieutenant-General Böttcher. His eyes were still on Tobruk.

As it happened it was General Cunningham's 8th Army which struck first. 'Crusader' was launched on 18 November, achieving tactical surprise, and Rommel abandoned for the time being his plans to take Tobruk.

He did not immediately appreciate the size of the British offensive, and thus forebore to concentrate his armour sufficiently. Cunningham, however, made a worse mistake. Baffled by Rommel's lack of reaction to the appearance at Gabr Saleh of 4th Armoured Brigade, he split his armoured force, sending 22nd Armoured Brigade to attack the Ariete at Bir el Gubi and 7th Armoured Brigade to Sidi Rezegh. On 19 November Rommel gave Crüwell's Afrika Korps a free hand, and with confusion on both sides the Germans had the better of various tank engagements. But a British sortie from Tobruk on 21 November complicated the situation, and early on 21 November Rommel thought the situation critical. The armoured battle joined at Sidi Rezegh on 21 November was to last for three days of unprecedentedly severe tank fighting.

General Scobie's break-out from Tobruk cost him hard in tanks and men. Scobie knew that he might be forced to give up the ground so hardly won, and expected an all-out German assault on Tobruk at any time. To Rommel, however, unaware of the weakness of Scobie's force, the break-out seemed 'a heavy attack'.

The first part of 'Crusader' resulted in a German victory, due primarily to the splitting of the British armour and to the fine leadership of Lieutenant-General Ludwig Crüwell. It was he rather than Rommel who was the mainspring behind the German attack of 21–23 November. On 22 November Crüwell led Major-General Neumann-Silkow's 15th Panzer Division east, evading all British vigilance, and regrouped them in depth against the long northern flank of Cunningham's forces. While Major-General von Ravenstein's 21st Panzer Division attacked the airfield at Sidi Rezegh and threw back the British and South Africans, 15th Panzer attacked Bir Sciaf-Sciuf successfully and pushed on during the night, overrunning 4th Armoured Brigade headquarters. On 23 November Crüwell drove 15th Panzer south to Sidi Muftah, en route to link up with the Italian Ariete and Trieste Armoured Divisions in the Bir el Gobi area. Here a violent tank battle broke out, but by afternoon Crüwell had reached a point south-east of Hagfed el Haiad—as Rommel noted, 'deep in the enemy's rear'.

257

Meanwhile the leading tanks of the Ariete had arrived, and Crüwell soon launched the combined German and Italian force northwards against the British rear, trying to surround him and force him back into 21st Panzer's arms at Sidi Rezegh. By the end of 23 November the 5th South African Brigade was more or less a write-off, and 4th and 22nd Armoured Brigades had lost heavily in tanks—so heavily that, with 7th Armoured Brigade casualties added, the British had lost two-thirds of their armour. German losses were not light either; by the evening of 23 November Rommel had lost about 100 of his original 260 German tanks. But the British, firing 2-pounders helplessly against 88s or 75s, had lost twice as many. 4th and 22nd Armoured Brigades were late in arriving, thus the British armour was never fully concentrated; part of 22nd Armoured Brigade went astray; and 7th Armoured Brigade had therefore to bear the brunt of the German attack for most of the day. By 25 November 7th Armoured Brigade had ceased to exist and its remnants were sent back to base.

Rommel put together a scratch force under the artilleryman, General Böttcher, to prevent any attempts to raise the seige of Tobruk. Then he decided to thrust to the frontier and Sollum with 21st Panzer, while Neumann-Silkow attacked Cunningham's headquarters at Fort Maddelena, and a third force moved on the Bir Habata railhead and its supply dumps. This was on 24 November; the Afrika Korps and the Ariete reached Sidi Omar that evening, and Rommel led 21st Panzer Division straight through 4th Indian Division into the Sidi Suleiman area to seal off the Halfaya front. 15th Panzer attacked at Sidi Omar, but without success; and 21st Panzer, after moving through the Halfaya position, became involved in costly fighting at Capuzzo, which had been taken by the New Zealanders.

Rommel's deep raid had caused chaos: Cunningham had lost control of the battle and prepared to withdraw over the frontier. But now the British C-in-C, General Auchinleck, showed his mettle; he refused to countenance withdrawal and on 26 November replaced Cunningham with Lieutenant-General Ritchie, his own Chief of Staff. Now Lieutenant-Colonel Siegfried Westphal, Rommel's Operations Officer, off his own bat recalled 21st Panzer to El Adem, much to Rommel's initial fury. But it turned out to be a sound decision. On 25 November Scobie at Tobruk was told that the New Zealanders expected to capture El Duda next day on their way to Sidi Rezegh. Thus Scobie launched another attack the following day, which was contained only with difficulty by Böttcher and his mixed German-Italian force. That afternoon the Tobruk garrison greeted with wild cheers the red flares from the advancing New Zealanders, and the garrison with new heart pressed on towards El Duda. On 27 November they linked up with the New Zealand infantry and a squadron of British tanks, and General Godwin-Austen made his signal: 'Corridor to Tobruk clear and secure. Tobruk is as relieved as I am.' But on 30 November Rommel repulsed all attacks, and next day the Afrika Korps launched a heavy offensive which destroyed most of the New Zealand Division. Thus the British garrison was once more confined in Tobruk.

In the first week of December 1941 Rommel made a last desperate attack at El Duda and towards Bir el Gobi. But the Italians had virtually given up by now, and Auchinleck reinforced 8th Army with two infantry brigades. R.A.F. raids on Axis lines of communication and supply columns were ceaseless and successful, and the New Zealanders retook Bel Hamed. The last German attack on 7 December was a failure with heavy casualties. The Axis forces were played out, and reluctantly Rommel decided to abandon Tobruk and disengage. After 242 days the siege of Tobruk was finally raised, and by 12 December Rommel's troops were back on the Gazala line.

The Italians now raised furious objections to giving up Cyrenaica, and on 16 December General Cavallero, backed up by Kesselring who was particularly anxious not to lose the airfield at Derna, demanded that the order to retreat be countermanded. But things had gone too far, and Rommel would not be swayed. On 25 December his retreat to Agedabia, some 300 miles away, was complete. His troops left on the Halfaya–Bardia front were in sore straits. Those at Bardia surrendered on 2 January, followed by Sollum, and on 17 January by Halfaya, with a total loss to the Axis of 4,000 German and 10,000 Italian prisoners.

Rommel has been criticized severely for his raid towards Libya, yet had it come off he would have been hailed as a genius. Victory, it has been said, has many godparents, while defeat is an orphan. Crüwell would have preferred to concentrate against Tobruk after the initial success, which was much of his making. Lieutenant-Colonel (later Major-General) von Mellenthin was convinced that 'if we had kept the Afrika Korps in the Sidi Rezegh area, we would have won the "Crusader" battle'.

Worse in a way than any tactical errors was the manner in which Rommel had antagonized his Italian allies. Kesselring who—unlike Rommel—thought politically, did his best to smooth things down, as did von Rintelen in Rome, with the result that Rommel was often angry with both of them. But the Italians felt deeply the retreat in Cyrenaica, and politically Rommel failed in his job. To Kesselring, whose position was by no means easy, Rommel was, in Ronald Lewin's words, 'a successful nuisance'. To Halder and the General Staff he was not to be trusted. Fortunately for Rommel, Hitler and Göbbels believed in him; Hitler was never one to write down the freebooting qualities of a former Free Corps leader.

But Hitler's attitude to the war in Africa was ambivalent. He rejoiced in Rommel's successes there, but he was unwilling to promote the Mediterranean beyond a secondary theatre of the war. Rommel's forces were better mechanized and motorized than those sent to Russia but they were still far below the minimum of four armoured divisions that a General Staff officer had recommended as necessary for success in October 1940.

Although Rommel's German command amounted to little more than an enlarged Corps for the greater part of the African campaign, his supply problems were serious, and the further he advanced east the greater they became. Had Malta been captured Rommel might have been able to hold out indefinitely, though even with the port facilities of Tripoli and Benghazi operating there were enormous distances to be covered.

In January 1942 the British lost command of the sea in the eastern Mediterranean. At the same time, due to Japan's entry into the war, Auchinleck lost some important fighting formations, and some bomber and fighter squadrons. The British front line was weak, for 7th Armoured Division, the most experienced desert formation, had been withdrawn to rest and refit, and its successor, 1st Armoured, was barely trained for the desert and lacking 22nd Armoured Brigade. Rommel, never afraid of taking risks decided to attack.

He kept both his allies the Italians, and the German High Command, in the dark until his offensive had achieved surprise. When it went in on 21 January 1942 the British were caught napping. They lost Agedabia on 22 January, the day that Rommel's command was elevated to Panzer Army and his own rank to Colonel-General. Ritchie wrongly assessed Rommel's move as no more than a reconnaissance in force, which was what General Cavallero on the Italian side wished it would remain. But Rommel's Afrika Korps struck in strength, and on 24 January Lieutenant-General Godwin-Austen, G.O.C. XIII Corps, advised Ritchie that he could no longer contain the Germans and recommended a general withdrawal to Mechili. General of Panzer Troops Crüwell halted the Afrika Korps at Msus, because of threats to his rear communications. On 28 January Ritchie was taken in by a feint with part of Crüwell's force towards Mechili, while the main thrust was directed against Benghazi. Colonel Erich Marcks of the 90th Light Division made a brilliantly successful outflanking attack on the town, and on 29 January Benghazi, its harbour, and large quantities of supplies fell into Rommel's hands. The British had again to give up a large area of Cyrenaica, and withdraw to a line south of Gazala. Rommel had achieved a small but pronounced success, and the situation now drifted into stalemate until late May.

Rommel's chief problems now were reinforcements and supply, despite the capture of Benghazi, which the Germans soon had working at peak capacity. There were no major ports to the east short of Alexandria, for Tobruk's capacity was limited and it was always a target for bombers of both sides. He was aware of the very heavy demands upon the

Wehrmacht in Russia, but he wrote later that 'in the summer of 1942, given six German mechanized divisions, we could have smashed the British so thoroughly that the threat from the south would have been eliminated for a long time to come. There is no doubt that adequate supplies for these formations could have been organized if the will had been there'. After March 1942 his supply situation improved, due to Kesselring's air forces achieving superiority, but it was still evident that the 8th Army could be reinforced more speedily than the Germans.

Rommel was banking on an Axis assault on Malta by Italo-German parachute and airborne forces before his next offensive. But Hitler doubted Italian fighting spirit and the capabilities of the Italian Navy, and he was troubled with the German parachute casualties suffered at Crete. At the end of April he agreed with Mussolini that the attack on Malta should be launched early in July—after Rommel's offensive; but he decided to drop the Malta operation when Rommel took Tobruk, arguing that Malta could be by-passed by sending supplies via Crete.

By May 1942 the tank situation, previously so favourable to Rommel, had changed. In sum, Rommel had some 320 German tanks and 240 inferior Italian ones; the British mustered nearly 900. In the air things were fairly level: the Desert Air Force had 604 front-line strength; the Luftwaffe and Regia Aeronautica had 542, but 120 of these were Messerschmitt 109Fs which outclassed the Hurricanes and Kittyhawks of the British.

On 26 May the Italians under General Crüwell attacked the Gazala Line frontally. But this was a feint, for Rommel had directed his main striking force—the Afrika Korps, 90th Light Division, and the Italian XX Corps—to go south of Bir Hacheim, then north to outflank the Gazala Line. 90th Light, making excellent progress, actually reached El Adem next morning, but the Afrika Korps collided with the British 4th Armoured Brigade and the Indian 3rd Motor Brigade south-east of Bir el Harmat, with the British 1st Armoured Division joining in the fierce tank battle that afternoon. 90th Light was out of touch with the Afrika Korps, and Rommel admitted later that his underestimation of the British armoured strength was the cause of his failure to overrun the British forces behind the Gazala Line.

During the first day's fighting over one-third of the German tanks were lost. Yet Ritchie had again failed to concentrate his armour sufficiently. On the night of 28 May 90th Light, which had been stuck out on a hazardous limb, disengaged from the British and got back to near Bir el Harmat, and the Ariete filled the gap between it and the Afrika Korps. Meanwhile the Italian attack in the north had come to a halt against well-prepared British defensive positions, and General Crüwell, whose Storch reconnaissance plane had been shot down, was a prisoner—a sad loss to Rommel. Indeed during the space of three or four days he was to lose not only Crüwell but Lieutenant-General von Vaerst of 15th Panzer, his own Chief of Staff, General Gause, and his chief operations officer, Lieutenant-Colonel Westphal, all wounded. The first phase of the battle of Gazala had left 8th Army in an advantageous position.

But the British were slow to exploit it, and now Rommel pulled off a daring stroke. To ensure a supply route he carved a way through the British minefields from the east (the British rear), using X Italian Corps; and then, using the main part of the Afrika Korps as a defensive screen, attacked Got el Ualeb. It fell on 1 June after severe fighting; and Bir Hacheim, held by the Free French under General Koenig, also fell.

Elsewhere there was something of a lull, which Rommel used to recover some of his knocked out tanks and repair others. On 5 and 6 June Ritchie's head-on attack against Rommel's armour was beaten off with heavy losses.

As Auchinleck's despatch was to state, 'The failure of Eighth Army's counter-attack on 5 June was probably the turning point of the battle'.

At Bir Hacheim the French fought gallantly and with resource, leading Kesselring to complain to Rommel about the slow progress of the attack, which had cost the Luftwaffe nearly forty dive-bombers on one day alone. But on 10 June Colonel Baade broke into the main defensive position north of Bir Hacheim with his combat group, and thenceforward its fate was sealed.

Rommel's tail was now up and he moved north the same day 'to seek a final decision without further delay'. By 12 June El Adem was again in his hands. Early on 15 June units of 15 Panzer crossed the Via Balbia in the north and reached the Mediterranean. The 8th Army, disorganized and defeated, was retiring to the Egyptian frontier, with Tobruk left as the main outpost to tie down Rommel's forces. Rommel was determined to exploit the great success of Gazala, perhaps his finest battle, and speedily strike while the iron was hot and the enemy depressed and confused. On 21 June he accepted the surrender of the garrison commander, the South African Major-General Klopper.

Rommel now stood at the summit of his African achievement: on 22 June 1943 Hitler promoted him, at the age of fifty, Field-Marshal. What sort of man was this youngest field-marshal in the German Army? In many ways he was typically Swabian, unsophisticated, self-sufficient, hard-headed, provincial. Tough and impervious to hard living (despite his illnesses), he was abstemious in his tastes, drinking little, and not caring what he ate. He was warm-hearted and a devoted husband. Like Hitler he had *Fingerspitzengefühl*, that knack of sensing in his finger-tips the vital occasion and opportunity. He had complete mastery of his profession, and enormous personal drive and magnetism. His enemies—and not a few in Germany were jealous of him—dismissed him as a swashbuckler with no Staff training, and Halder consistently underestimated him and even found his independence quite irresponsible.

Von Senger considered him 'the prototype of an energetic and confident divisional commander', but noted Rommel's failure to work smoothly with the Italians, and the antipathy of Rommel's staff for Kesselring. The hostility between Rommel and Kesselring has probably been exaggerated, since on reflection both spoke well of the other.

To his troops Rommel was an inspiration, especially because he was so often with them in the front line, sometimes to the despair of his Staff. He made great demands upon his subordinates, but shared every danger and hardship. He was essentially chivalrous and honest. He burned Hitler's order to kill all captured commandos; and later, in 1943, when there was trouble with the behaviour of S.S. troops in Milan, he sent to Berlin a long list of officers who should be punished. On 17 June 1944, at the Margival conference with Hitler, he demanded that the members of the S.S. 'Das Reich' Division responsible for the massacre at Oradour-sur-Glâne should be punished.

To his Staff he posed great problems, being volatile, unpredictable, often likely to tear up the book of rules. Major-General von Mellenthin, who served him in a senior position as a Lieutenant-Colonel, said: 'He was not an easy man to serve; he spared those around him as little as he spared himself. An iron constitution and nerves of steel were needed to work with Rommel.' He also wrote: 'Between Rommel and his troops was that mutual understanding which cannot be explained and analysed, but which is the gift of the gods. The Afrika Korps followed Rommel wherever he led, however hard he drove them ... the men knew that Rommel was the last man to spare Rommel.' Lieutenant-General Fritz Bayerlein, for some time his Chief of Staff in Africa, plainly adored him, and in France later one of his admirers, rather surprisingly, was the intellectual General Speidel, though he doubted whether Rommel ever in his life had read a book not to do with war. The British, in their peculiar way, admired and even hero-worshipped him, so that Churchill in the House of Commons praised his skill, and Auchinleck was provoked to issue an ill-judged Order of the Day which—though designed to show that Rommel was no superman—in effect underlined his magical reputation by its very appearance.

It is not surprising that Hitler for long made Rommel a favourite. He was successful, apparently accommodating though full of initiative, not a Prussian, not on the General Staff, and not highly born—he was thus hand-made to become a National Socialist hero. Dr Göbbels, with all the resources of his propaganda machine behind him, soon made Rommel a household name, a pleasant task for Göbbels because he genuinely believed in Rommel. In his diary for 24 January 1942 he writes, 'Rommel deserves it, and he is such an exemplary character and outstanding soldier that propaganda on his behalf can do no harm.

For once propaganda is being done for the right person'. More than any other German general (unless for a time Dietl) Rommel's uncompromising features adorned the public prints, and the Services magazine *Signal.* He became a national hero.

After the fall of Tobruk, Rommel was determined to press on without giving the 8th Army time to reorganize. He wrote later, 'I knew that the fall of Tobruk and the collapse of the Eighth Army was the one moment in the African war when the road to Alexandria lay open and virtually undefended, and my staff and I would have been fools not to have gone all out to seize this unique opportunity'.

Now he abandoned the premise that Malta should be taken before his onslaught on Egypt, extracting from Mussolini approval to allow him freedom of movement, which meant pursuit of the British. With every mile he progressed towards Cairo Rommel's supply difficulties became greater, but Hitler and Mussolini had acute reservations about an attack on Malta, and it was this fear of grasping the nettle that may have cost them Africa. Rommel may have been counting on an extra two panzer divisions being prepared for desert warfare in Germany, but in the event O.K.W. sent them to Russia. He had said on 22 June: 'Hitler has made me a field-marshal. I would much rather he had given me one more division.'

Rommel decided to attack without a firm supply system, for the longer he waited, the stronger would 8th Army and the Desert Air Force become. He wanted to cause a British collapse before large shipments from Britain or America arrived to bolster 8th Army, even though eighty-five per cent of his own transport still consisted of captured British vehicles. Clearly his decision meant taking an enormous risk. The fact that it failed in the end does not mean that he was wrong, only that he underestimated the supply difficulties and perhaps put too much trust in promises of reinforcements.

Rommel was on the move across the Egyptian frontier on 23 June. His first target was Mersa Matruh, needed as a supply port, where he hoped also to destroy much of the British Infantry: he failed in this, though British casualties were heavy, but won a decisive tactical victory, with the last fortress port in the western Egyptian desert falling on 29 June.

From 1 July, with the bulk of the British infantry digging in on the Alamein Line, Rommel launched a succession of hard-fought attacks. But there was a new sense of resolution in 8th Army. Auchinleck himself had taken over command on 25 June, and though the Alamein front became more or less static in mid-July, he launched vigorous local attacks, particularly against the Italians, who were Rommel's soft spot. Well before the end of the month Rommel had lost the initiative, and was desperately short of tanks and infantry; meanwhile 8th Army was being steadily strengthened.

At the end of August, nevertheless, Rommel decided to attack, conscious that this was his last chance. He now faced a fresh opponent in General Bernard Montgomery, who took over from Auchinleck during August. As Ronald Lewin observed: 'Montgomery's dispositions imposed his will on his opponent before the battle started'; when the Germans attacked on the night of 30/31 August the tanks were forced to negotiate a series of depressions which hampered their mobility and offered good targets for the R.A.F. The advance was slower than Rommel had wanted. Additionally, the first phase of the attack suffered when Lieutenant-General Graf von Bismarck was killed by a mine, depriving the 21st Panzer Division of its commander; and General Nehring, commander of the Afrika Korps, was wounded during an air attack.

Rommel was now in two minds whether to call off the operation. He turned the 15th Panzer Division north on 1 September, only to lose over twenty tanks to the dug-in tanks and guns of 22nd Armoured Brigade. R.A.F. bombing activity and a serious lack of petrol now hampered the Afrika Korps, and Rommel himself was lucky to escape injury. Again Rommel debated breaking off the battle, for on the night of 1 September Panzer Army Afrika had only one petrol issue left, and on 2 September he finally made up his mind to retire. His withdrawal began next day. Montgomery has been criticized for not unleashing the British armour to cut off and destroy the Afrika Korps, but he was already planning the decisive blow at El Alamein, for which he wished to keep 8th Army intact.

Alam Halfa had not been a large battle, but its implications were enormous. For the first time Rommel had failed to win an armoured battle.

It was Allied air superiority at Alam Halfa, and later El Alamein, that dictated Rommel's conviction in France in 1944 that the enemy must be met on the beach-heads. He never forgot how the tide of battle had turned against him because of air power.

Because of his gastric trouble Rommel flew back to Germany on 23 September, handing over command of the Panzer Army to General of Panzer Troops Georg Stumme. Stumme was a newcomer to the desert, but an able and experienced armoured commander who had done well in Russia. Most of the corps and divisional commanders were also replaced because of wounds or illness. General of Panzer Troops von Thoma, a highly regarded armoured expert, took over the Afrika Korps.

The battle of El Alamein opened on 23 October—on the very next day Stumme died of a heart attack while under attack in his command car at the front. He had suffered from high blood pressure, and in Rommel's opinion should not have been sent to the desert. Rommel flew back to resume command on the evening of 25 September.

Hitler had promised him more supplies, a Nebelwerfer rocket brigade, forty Tigers and more self-propelled guns. None of these were to arrive.

Montgomery had the advantage of an almost two-to-one superiority in tanks and men—195,000 troops against 50,000 Germans and 54,000 Italians; and over 1,000 tanks against 510, 300 of which were Italian. The air situation was even less favourable to the Axis, for by now the Desert Air Force had complete superiority.

Nevertheless there was bloody, bitter, and costly fighting at El Alamein, a long set-piece battle, and it was only when Montgomery—persuaded by General McCreery—switched his main punch further south that a breakthrough was achieved. By the night of 4 November the Germans and Italians were in full retreat for Fuka.

Alamein destroyed the power of the Panzer Army in Africa. From now on Rommel knew that he was fighting a losing battle, and began to be completely disillusioned with Hitler, whose unrealistic promises had continually let him down. He began to cease to believe in an ultimate German victory in the war, and his letters home grew shorter and more pessimistic. Still, however, he looked at all times to the safety and salvation of his troops, and by a series of masterly strokes made his retreat across Cyrenaica back to Tunisia a fighting withdrawal rather than a rout.

On 10 December 1942 Panzer Army Tunisia was established, but not under General Nehring, in whom Rommel had confidence. The new commander was Colonel-General Jürgen von Arnim from the Russian front, where he had commanded a Panzer Corps. Rommel had little time for veterans of the East Front, perhaps foolishly, but at this juncture it would certainly have been wiser to leave the trusty and desert-experienced Nehring as the Tunisian commander. There was little rapport between Rommel and von Arnim and it would have been better to have one unified command, for as Rommel noted there was little co-ordination between the new one and his own. Kesselring, despite Rommel's criticisms of him, backed Rommel as the Supremo, but in the event Rommel never got control of Arnim's forces until too late. By the time Rommel was nominated C-in-C of a new 'Army Group Africa' on 22 February 1943 with authority over not only von Arnim but the Italian C-in-C Messe as well, his successes at Kasserine and Tebessa had been wasted by Arnim's failure to exploit them. From late January 1943—according to Bayerlein—Keitel, Jodl, Kesselring, and the Italians were all scheming to oust Rommel. On 26 January 1943 he was told that on account of his bad health he would be released from command once the Mareth Line was reached.

At the end of February von Arnim launched his 5th Panzer Army towards Medjez el Bab and, a complete surprise to Rommel, Beja. Despite an early breakthrough his forces were soon heavily counter-attacked and bad weather bogged down most of his tanks, so that the attack petered out with heavy casualties. Rommel, who was now both unwell and despondent, agreed with Messe that it would be better to attack in the Gabes area further south, but they were overruled by Hitler and the Commando Supremo. This led to Rommel's last attack, which he did not even plan in detail himself, leaving it to Messe and the new commander of the Afrika Korps, Arnim's erstwhile Chief of Staff, Lieutenant-General Ziegler. It was a measure of Rommel's tiredness and despondency that the Medenine battle was left a week too late, by which time Montgomery was ready for it in strength.

It was the end for Rommel in Africa. On 9 March he flew to Rome, having handed over his command to von Arnim. Next day he went on to Hitler's headquarters in Russia, where Hitler refused him permission to continue his command, told him to take sick leave, but talked of his resuming command later for operations against Casablanca, which merely showed how out of touch with reality the Führer was. On 11 March Hitler decorated Rommel with the Oak Leaves with Swords and Diamonds to his Knight's Cross.

For most of the rest of 1943 Rommel played little significant part in military events. At first, after he was well again, he served as a military adviser, without much say, to Hitler: then was appointed to command a skeleton Army Group north of the Alps for reinforcing the Italian front; then was sent in July to Salonika to report on conditions in Greece; and finally in August his Army Group H.Q. was established in northern Italy to prepare the Gothic Line and supply the Germans in the south with reinforcements. In late July he had warned Hitler that the Badoglio Government would not continue to fight on the German side, though Kesselring had optimistically asserted that they would. Although Rommel was proved right, the supreme command in Italy was given to Kesselring.

In November Rommel received a worthwhile assignment directly from Hitler—to inspect the coastal defences of France and the Atlantic Wall. On 12 December, as a result of representations by von Rundstedt, the C-in-C West, Rommel's position was regularized and he was made C-in-C Army Group 'B', under Rundstedt, and charged with coastal defence from Holland to the Bay of Biscay. This command consisted of Colonel-General Hans von Salmuth's 15th Army between Ostend and Le Havre, and Colonel-General Friedrich Dollmann's 7th Army between Le Havre and the Loire, in Normandy and Brittany. Later Colonel-General Johannes Blaskowitz was put in command of Army Group 'G' at Toulouse watching the coast from the Loire to the Bay of Biscay, with General of Infantry Kurt von der Chevallerie's 1st Army at Bordeaux and General of Infantry Georg von Sodenstern's 19th Army at Avignon.

Von Rundstedt cynically referred to the Atlantic Wall as a 'Propaganda Wall', but Rommel tirelessly travelled round the Low Countries and

France, accompanied by his naval adviser, Vice-Admiral Friedrich Ruge, who became a close friend. His batteries re-charged, between mid-December 1943 and the spring of 1944 he greatly reinforced the Atlantic defences from Holland to France, and then the French Mediterranean ones, tripling the mines laid down and getting anti-glider and boat obstacles set up on the coasts and foreshores. But Rommel had no authority over Field-Marshal Sperrle's 3rd Air Fleet, the Luftwaffe ack-ack defences, or Admiral Theodor Krancke, the Naval C-in-C Atlantic in Paris, who did not readily co-operate, and thus in 1944 could not dispose of all the troops in France as he wished.

On 23 April Rommel wrote to Jodl urging him to place the Panzer divisions under his command.

If, in spite of the enemy's air superiority we succeed in getting a large part of our mobile forces into action in the threatened coast defence sectors in the first few hours, I am convinced that the enemy attack on the coast will collapse completely on its first day . . .

My only real anxiety concerns the mobile forces. Contrary to what was decided at the conference on 21 March, they have so far not been placed under my command. Some of them are dispersed over a large area well inland, which means that they will arrive too late to play any part in the battle for the coast. With the heavy enemy air superiority we can expect, any large-scale movements of motorised forces to the coast will be exposed to air attacks of tremendous weight and long duration. But without rapid assistance from the armoured divisions and mobile units, our coast divisions will be hard put to it to counter attacks coming simultaneously from the sea and from airborne troops inland. Their land front is too thinly held for that.

But his pleas went unheeded, and his performance as an Army Group commander in Normandy cannot, therefore, be assessed without understanding the great difficulties under which he was operating. He did not have a free hand. 'My functions in Normandy', he wrote later, 'were so restricted by Hitler that any sergeant-major could have carried them out. He interfered in everything and turned down every proposal we made.'

The Allies landed in Normandy on 6 June. And Rommel, after all his preparation for their coming over the past seven months, was not there. For fourteen vital hours at the very start of the landings, when his power of immediate decision was needed urgently to get the panzer divisions, all still well back from the coast, to the beach areas, he was absent from the battle area.

Rommel had left his headquarters at La Roche Guyon near Paris on 5 June to consult with Hitler at Berchtesgaden, and to go on next day to his home near Ulm to celebrate his wife's birthday. He came hurrying back to a situation which was already out of hand. His nearest panzer division was the 21st at St. Pierre-sur-Dives, some miles south-west of Lisieux; and the 12th S.S. Panzer, which he would have liked in the Cotentin Peninsula, was still east of Falaise, even father away. The Panzer Lehr was at Le Mans, 90 miles from Caen, even more distant from the invasion beaches. As Rommel had correctly feared, these divisions—and others to come after them—were to suffer greatly from Allied air strikes by day, so much so that they could only move with safety by night and often took several days to cover comparatively small distances, incurring losses all the while on their approach marches. And not even von Rundstedt was able to move these divisions without special permission from Hitler and O.K.W. Lieutenant-General Edgar Feuchtinger's 21st Panzer Division, only some fifteen miles from the coast, was directly under Rommel's Army Group B command; but though he received a report in the early hours of 6 June that parachutists had been dropped near Troarn, within his prospective defence area, he received no orders from Army Group 'B', nor indeed from any other quarter. He thus wasted six hours waiting for orders and then decided to attack the British 6th Airborne Division on the Orne off his own bat. Shortly after making this decision he was told that he was now under command of Dollmann's 7th Army, but again got no orders. At 9.00 a.m. nearly nine hours after his first report of enemy action, Feuchtinger came under direct command of General Marcks at LXXXIV Corps at St Lo, but it was not until 10.00 a.m. that he got his first orders—to stop his tanks engaging the airborne troops and to send them west to help defend Caen. By the end of the day he had lost a quarter of his 170 tanks.

As soon as Rommel returned he ordered 21st Panzer to attack immediately with or without reinforcements, but this was a relayed rather than a personal order and Feuchtinger does not appear to have followed it probably because it was superseded by a decision of Rundstedt on 6 June that three Panzer divisions were to attack the next day and throw the invaders back into the sea.

The Germans were caught on the wrong foot all round on D-Day. Colonel-General Dollmann was conducting a map exercise at Rennes, to which, naturally, all his available Corps and Divisional commanders had come. Colonel-General 'Sepp' Dietrich of the S.S., commanding I Panzer Corps, was at his headquarters in Brussels, far from the scene of action. He was summoned by von Rundstedt to Paris and told, at 5.00 p.m. on 6 June, that his Corps, consisting of 12th S.S. Panzer Division 'Hitler Jugend' (Brigadeführer S.S. or Major-General Kurt Meyer), Feuchtinger's 21st Panzer, and Panzer Lehr (Lieutenant-General Fritz Bayerlein) would attack from the Caen area. Feuchtinger, aware that Bayerlein could not possibly get his tanks up in time, advocated postponing the attack until all three divisions were in position and ready, but Dietrich insisted on him going in with only two. Meyer had petrol difficulties, and never reached his proper start-line, so concentrated was the Allied artillery and naval gunfire, and so effective the

British anti-tank guns. Meanwhile Bayerlein, the ablest of the three tank divisional commanders, was not allowed to wait until nightfall to move his division on its long approach march, and as a result lost nearly half his tanks from air action and breakdowns in the two days that it took him to get to Tilly, west of Caen. All in all, the first German attempt to oust the invaders was a dismal failure.

By 9 June there had still been no proper Panzer attack and on 10 June the British moved forward in strength. By 15 June Bayerlein had to pull out of Tilly and the chance of a successful panzer Corps drive to the sea was lost for ever. All of this might have been different if Rommel had been at his H.Q. when the invasion began. But it would also have needed General Geyr von Schweppenburg to be put in charge of an immediate armoured attack instead of Sepp Dietrich; for Hitler to have woken up earlier to the fact that the Normandy invasion was the real one and not just a smokescreen for a more dangerous one in the Pas de Calais area; and for the German chain of command to have been less diffuse and complicated.

General Marcks, the LXXXIV Corps commander in the Normandy invasion area, was authorized to use 21st Panzer Division only on the afternoon of 6 June—some eight hours after the beach landings. General von Geyr was appointed by Rommel ground commander from east of the Dives River to Tilly on 8 June, a sensible move; but on 9 June his headquarters at La Caine, north-east of Thury-Harcourt, was wiped out by a bombing raid, and Staff officers were killed. This raid effectively prevented the organization of a German armoured Corps thrust in the days that followed.

Rommel had wanted a strong Flack force in Normandy, and German troops from Norway, Southern France, and the Channel Islands (where a complete division sat out the war doing nothing), but he had been refused. Thus the four million mines that had been laid off the coast and on it by 20 May failed entirely to stop the invaders.

Rommel again was unfortunate in that the brilliant Allied Pas de Calais deception plan worked so well. The Germans were fooled into believing that a greater invasion Army under General Patton was about to spring on the Calais coast, and the constant and imaginative radio traffic between mostly non-existent formations led O.K.W. into making the decisive mistake not to move troops from Colonel-General Hans von Salmuth's 15th Army on the Channel coast east of the Seine to the Normandy front.

In the south of France there was the complete Army Group 'G' under Colonel-General Blaskowitz. South of the Loire Blaskowitz had two Armies: the 1st, under General of Infantry Kurt von der Chevallerie, with headquarters at Bordeaux, responsible for the Mediterranean coast; and the 19th, under General of Infantry Georg von Sodenstern, with headquarters at Avignon, further inland. The later Allied landings in the south of France probably did not make a significant difference to the eventual outcome; and, in the event, bringing Blaskowitz to reinforce Dollmann up north in the very early days would have been a wise move. But Rommel had not the power to utilize von Salmuth's troops against Hitler's wishes, still less those of Blaskowitz until it was too late.

Rommel would have been better off if Blaskowitz and Dollmann were in each other's places, for though neither had seen action since the early days of the war Blaskowitz was highly regarded by his fellows. As it was, Dollmann could exert little influence on the battle; he had a stroke at the end of June and died before he was replaced, as he surely would have been. Geyr, as we have seen, early had his head-quarters destroyed and was later himself removed by Hitler. He was a commander who had no real chance to show his merit in Normandy. Marcks, the local Corps commander in Normandy, died of wounds on 12 June. Lieutenant-General Karl Wilhelm von Schlieben, who commanded 709 Infantry Division, was holed up in Cherbourg and surrendered it after a good defence. S.S. Colonel-General Paul Hausser, who took over 7th Army from Dollmann, was thoroughly capable, the best of the S.S. Generals, but by July he could not stem events, and in late August he was wounded, for the second time, in the Falaise pocket. In the first dozen days of the invasion four divisional commanders and one Corps commander were killed in action or died of wounds.

By 19 August, as Field-Marshal Viscount Montgomery relates with gusto, forty German divisions had been 'eliminated or badly mauled' and the Normandy battle was over. Twenty German generals had been killed or taken prisoner, two were wounded, and Rundstedt and von Kluge had been dismissed. How right Rommel had proved his assessment, of 23 April to be; and how vital his absence from command when the attack came.

Rommel was terribly shaken by the German casualties. 'It was one terrible blood-letting. Sometimes we had as many casualties in one day as during the whole of the summer fighting in Africa in 1942. My nerves are pretty good, but sometimes I was near collapse. It was casualty reports, casualty reports, casualty reports, wherever you went. I have never fought with such losses. If I hadn't gone to the front nearly every day, I couldn't have stood it, having to write off literally one more regiment every day.' It was this senseless destruction of the youth of Germany more than anything else that finally turned Rommel against Hitler.

Rommel thought the attempt on Hitler's life 'stupid', believing that peace negotiations should have been arranged in the West with the Allies; for then Hitler would have been faced with a *fait accompli*. During his last days at the front Rommel and his Chief of Staff, General

Speidel, worked to this end. His latest military achievement was correctly to estimate Montgomery's 'Goodwood' armoured attack, and to take steps to repulse it; but he was not to see it, for on 17 July a low-flying R.A.F. plane shot up his car as he was being driven near the village of Ste Foy de Montgommery, close to Livarot, and he was severely wounded. It was the end of Rommel's military career.

As far as the resistance to Hitler is concerned, Rommel was certainly a late-comer. He was first and foremost a professional soldier. It was only when he was thoroughly disillusioned with Hitler after Africa that he began to appear to the conspirators a possible candidate to command the Army or the Wehrmacht after a successful *coup de main.* In France and Belgium in 1944 the two military governors, Generals von Stülpnagel and von Falkenhausen, were long-standing and ardent conspirators; and Rommel's new Chief of Staff, General Speidel, was also deep in the conspiracy. These men and others, including Dr Strölin, Lord Mayor of Stuttgart and a fellow officer from the Great War, turned their persuasive powers upon Rommel, and he agreed with them to the extent of telling Strölin, 'I believe it my duty to come to the rescue of Germany'.

Whatever exactly this meant, there can be no doubt that—with his enormous prestige and popular reputation—Rommel would have been a great asset to the conspirators had their plans come off. Wheeler-Bennett dismisses Rommel too easily as a 'Johnny-come-lately' of the Resistance and a 'band-wagon jumper' on the level of the fumbling von Kluge and the devious Fromm. It is true that he kept aloof until 1944, and his motives then were to save the German Army and the State rather than hatred of Hitler or what he stood for. Even von Rundstedt, though not prepared to intervene himself, thought that Rommel, with his enormous popular appeal, should act. What would have happened had Rommel not been wounded that day in July near Livarot is problematical, but certainly as a man of action rather than a ditherer like von Kluge he would have done something.

His enforced suicide, on 14 October 1944, compelled by two revolting lackeys of Hitler unfit to wear an officer's uniform, Generals Burgdorf and Maisel, was a tragedy for Germany, which Rommel might well have served notably after the war.

His reputation lingers on. Has it been exaggerated? Brigadier Desmond Young's near-idolatrous book did nothing to play it down, but in the 'fifties there were some attempts—notably by Professor Hugh Trevor-Roper and Lieutenant-General Sir Brian Horrocks—to cut Rommel down to size.

Rommel was a great leader of men, whose personality stamped his whole command. Liddell Hart pointed out that 'the outstanding feature of Rommel's numerous successes is that they were achieved with inferiority of resources and without any command of the air'. He was not only personally courageous and a front-line leader *par excellence,* like Guderian, he had great organizing ability and an acute tactical brain. He took risks, sometimes unjustifiably, because risks had to be taken with his strained supply situation and poor backing from O.K.W. Had Hitler given Rommel stronger forces and his full backing, things might have been very different; even so, offices in Cairo were reduced to burning their files in a rush of anxiety by Rommel's advance. Montgomery is typically unforthcoming of praise of Rommel in his *Memoirs*, but he certainly did not underestimate him. One must agree with Liddell Hart's description of Rommel: 'Exasperating to staff officers, he was worshipped by the fighting troops, and what he got out of them in performance was far beyond any rational calculation.'

Rommel lacked political sense, did not get on well with the Italians as it was his business to do, put his own Staff to unwarranted pressures, was often out of touch during critical moments of a battle, and perhaps worried unduly, doubtless because of his ill health.

For these reasons, very high as Rommel must be rated, like Guderian whom he so closely resembled in style of command, he does not rank among the greatest commanders. He nevertheless remains the Third Reich's most famous warrior.

One of the most underestimated German generals and Panzer experts is Colonel-General Hermann Hoth, already a General of infantry when war broke out. He was to have the distinction, albeit a dubious one since the Germans were defeated, of commanding the largest force of German armour ever assembled on the Russian front, in the fierce tank battle of Kursk–Orel in 1943.

Hoth was steady rather than dashing, cool, a good strategist and tactician, unflappable, and well liked by his troops and colleagues, to whom he became known as 'Papa' Hoth. He commanded the 18th Division at Liegnitz as a major-general and lieutenant-general from 1935 to 1938. On 1 January 1938 he stood fiftieth in seniority on the Army List. He was then given the XV Army Corps at Jena in 1939, which he took to Poland.

In France in 1940 he commanded the Hoth Panzer Group, having under him Höpner and Rudolf Schmidt, both armoured experts. (Von Kleist in his parallel Group had their equals in Guderian and Reinhardt.) Successful in France, he was rewarded with promotion to Colonel-General and command of the 3rd Panzer Group for the invasion of Russia in 1941.

By 26 June Hoth had reached Minsk; two days later he took it and on 10 July Vitebsk fell to his 20th Panzer Division, commanded by Lieutenant-General Stumpff. By 15 July Hoth had isolated Smolensk, cutting its road and rail links with Moscow. He and Guderian had encircled half a million Russians in four Armies. Like Guderian he was all for pushing on to Moscow in August, but it was not to be.

When the assault on Moscow was begun too late, Hoth's tanks linked up with Höpner's at Vyazma on 7 October 1941, encircling hundreds of thousands of Russian troops. On 14 October Kalinin, ninety-three miles north-west of Moscow, fell to 1st Panzer Division under Lieutenant-General Rudolf Kirchner.

By November 1941 one of Hoth's Corps commanders, General Reinhardt, had taken over 3rd Panzer Group, now promoted to 3rd Panzer Army, and Hoth was given command of 4th Panzer Army. In June 1942 he was sent with this Army to the Voronezh front, under von Weichs, where his tanks acted as the striking force. Hoth won a victory, but for the first time the Russians refused to get engaged in large numbers and retreated swiftly across the Don. In July, when Field-Marshal List's Army Group 'A' was directed on the Caucasus, Hoth's first objective was Voroshilovsk; however, not until the bulk of 4th Panzer Army had been switched north, at the very end of July, to come under von Weichs again in Army Group 'B' and strike at the Russians in the Kalach area before Stalingrad, did the town fall to Lieutenant-General Breith's 3rd Panzer Division.

Hoth had to leave a Panzer Corps behind on the Caucasus front, and another with General Paulus's 6th Army which was making the main attack on Kalach. He got his Corps back from Paulus after Kalach was taken on 8 August, but was still short of a Corps for his advance from the Kalmyk steppe to Tunutovo, thence to Voroponovo and Pitomnik, in late August and on 1 September. During this time Paulus was under fierce pressure in the Don bend opposite Stalingrad. Had he been able to link up quickly with Hoth they might have trapped two Soviet Armies, and Stalingrad would surely have fallen. As it was, Paulus could not disengage enough troops, and the Russians to his south escaped. When the infantry of General of Artillery Walther von Seydlitz-Kurzbach's LI Corps finally linked up with Hoth's advanced armour on 3 September, it was just two days too late. By disengaging his armour from the hilly country and changing his approach, Hoth had done all he could, and been successful. Paulus could not match his progress.

The German attack on Stalingrad was left to 6th Army, reinforced on 17 September by Lieutenant-General Ferdinand Heim's XLVIII Panzer Corps from Hoth's 4th Panzer Army. But it was a set-piece battle with tired troops. Paulus received no other new formations and lacked the strength to take the industrial area by storm. On 19 November, just as Paulus was launching another attack, the Rumanians to their north and south were heavily attacked by the Russians and broke completely. The Russians poured through the gap and headed for Kalach, covering some thirty miles to cut off and encircle 6th Army, and splitting Hoth's Panzer Army.

Hoth had been let down by the Rumanians before. When they

fled south of Stalingrad, he reported: 'German commands which have Rumanian troops serving under them must reconcile themselves to the fact that moderate heavy fire, even without an enemy attack, will be enough to cause these troops to fall back, and that the reports they submit concerning their own situation are worthless since they never know where their own troops are and their estimates of enemy strength are vastly exaggerated.' Later Hoth was to recommend that Rumanian divisions should be entrusted only with very narrow fronts, and that one German division should support every four Rumanian ones.

When the Russians took Kalach on 23 November, 6th Army found itself shut in a trap. By immediately abandoning any attempt to take Stalingrad, Paulus could have salvaged most of 6th Army, but Hitler ordered him to hold on and await air supply. When Hoth launched his relieving attack on 12 December his troops needed to cover sixty miles, which proved in the end too much for them; they only made good half the distance. 6th Army's chance of survival was a break-out to meet him half way, but Paulus was so worried by the lack of petrol, and pressure from Hitler, that he stood fast.

Hoth fought many battles on the Eastern Front, and won many victories. One of his greatest was the third battle of Kharkov. In the last part of February and on 1 March 1943, between Dnieprop-etrovsk and Kharkov, the Soviet 6th Army and Popov's Tank Corps were utterly crushed at Krasnoarmayskoye, Pavlograd and Barvenkovo by General Siegfried Heinrici's XL Panzer Corps and General Otto von Knobelsdorff's XLVIII Panzer Corps. As a result the Russians lost 615 tanks, 400 guns, 600 anti-tank guns, 23,000 dead and 9,000 prisoners; and by mid-March Kharkov was in his hands.

In the great battle of Kursk which started on 4 July 1943, Hoth again served in von Manstein's Army Group. With some 700 tanks in his 4th Panzer Army, he commanded the larger part of the Army Group's more than 1,000 tanks. He had 3rd and 11th Panzer Divisions as well as the S.S. Panzer Divisions 'Grossdeutschland', 'Liebstandarte', 'Das Reich', and 'Totenkopf', under Hausser. Some 300 tanks were mustered by General of Panzer Troops Werner Kempf, in Army Detachment Kempf, on Hoth's right below Belgorod, in 6th, 7th, and 19th Panzer Divisions.

Guessing from air reconnaissance reports that if he obeyed O.K.H. orders to link up directly with Model at Oboyan the Russians would catch him on the flank with their main armoured force, Hoth decided to deal with them at Prokorovka before pushing on to Kursk. Kempf's forces were to push across the Donets, act as flank guard, but then join him to smash the Russian armour. Unfortunately for Hoth's plan, Kempf's forces to his right rear got bogged down against stiff Russian opposition so that the III Panzer Corps commander, the reliable Lieutenant-General H. Breith, could not make the necessary speed to link up on 9 July. On 11 July, his leading formations were still twelve miles from Prokorovka, though some of Hausser's S.S. units had crossed the Psel River between Bogoroditskoye and Vesselyy and were pushing on towards Prokorovka between the Psel and the railway.

In the north, Model's forces advancing from the direction of Orel were on the point of breaking through at Teploye between Orel and Kursk. On 12 July General Rotmistrov's 5th Guards Army, which Kempf had failed to intercept, crashed with 850 tanks (mostly T.34s) against Hausser's 600 in a huge armoured battle. Kempf's much-needed tanks were now only twelve miles away at Rzhavets on the Donets River, but Model's forces in the north were drawing no closer, having been attacked in their rear.

On 13 July 6th Panzer was tied down near Alexsandrovka after capturing Rzharets in a night attack, but the tanks of 7th and 19th Panzer Divisions crossed the river and poured forward to help Hausser's tanks at Prokorovka.

And now, when all was to play for, Hitler suddenly called off 'Citadel' as a result of the Allied landing in Sicily on 10 July. Field-Marshal Manstein was horrified; 'Victory on the southern front of the Kursk salient is within reach. The enemy has thrown in nearly his entire strategic reserves and is badly mauled. Breaking off action now would be throwing away victory.'

But Hitler could not be persuaded to continue the offensive at full pitch. He did allow Manstein to continue the southern attack, but since this had relied partly upon Model's pressures from the north, it could not hope to succeed. On 17 July Hitler ordered the immediate withdrawal of Hausser's S.S. Panzer Corps from the battle, intending them to be sent to Italy. In the event, they remained in Russia for several months, but it meant the end of 'Citadel'. Despite their major gains, Hoth and Kempf in the end had to admit failure.

In August the Russians exploited a dangerous gap of over thirty miles between Hoth's 4th Panzer Army and Army Detachment Kempf, and threatened to retake Kharkov and push on to the Dnieper.

In November 1943, after Hitler in October had vetoed a most promising armoured attack with which Hoth wanted to break up enemy concentrations in the Lyutezh area, the Russians attacked 4th Panzer Army heavily in the Kiev region. On 6 November Kiev fell to the Russians; and while the Germans succeeded in restoring the situation elsewhere, Kiev could not be retaken. In mid-November Hoth was sent on long leave, relinquishing command of 4th Panzer Army to General Haus, and in December 1943 was dismissed. The colonel-general who had proved himself in France in 1940, in the summer drive of 1941 in Russia, at Rostov and Kharkov, on the Don, the Dnieper, and the Donets, was made the scapegoat for Hitler's mistakes and pushed aside without thanks. 'A bird of ill omen', Hitler called him; 'an instigator of defeatism of the worst sort.' He was never again given a command.

For the rest of the war Colonel-General Hermann Hoth lived quietly in retirement. He was sentenced to fifteen years' imprisonment at Nuremberg for war crimes on 27 October 1948.

Broken Swords and Withered Oak Leaves

In 1945 Hitler said bitterly: 'They will have to write on my gravestone, "He was a victim of his generals".' Many German generals since the end of the war have claimed the opposite. Halder, von Manstein, von Rundstedt, Guderian, and others, have stated their conviction that victory after victory was lost because of the Führer's interference in command. The greatest victims, of course, were the German people. For what their country was reduced to, where should they place the blame?

Three events during the 1930s were responsible for tying together the destinies of the Führer and the Army. These were the murder of Lieutenant-General von Schleicher and Major-General von Bredow in 1934; the oath of loyalty to the Führer in 1935; and the dismissal of von Fritsch in 1938. In the beginning the Army generals threw in their lot with Hitler because they seemed to have common objectives. Hitler wanted a strong Army, and the Army desperately wanted to regain its status in Germany, and Germany to regain its status in Europe. For this reason with the honourable exception of a very few, they made a compact with Hitler and turned a blind eye to the political excesses of which they certainly disapproved. By the time of the Blomberg-Fritsch crisis in 1938 they held a tiger by the tail.

Many of them have since justified their passivity at that time by their oath of allegiance to Hitler. But Hitler himself had taken an oath—an oath to respect the Constitution, which guaranteed the rights of men to political freedom, and which he broke shamefully on many occasions even before the oath of loyalty was drafted. 'Consider your honour as a gentleman of more weight than an oath', said Solon. A few—a very few—generals did, and should always be honoured for it.

So by the beginning of the war Hitler already held supremacy of political power, which he could not have had without the support of the generals; and when he appointed himself supreme head of the Army also, in December 1941, he was only acknowledging by title what he had always effectively been in practice. Thereafter the price the generals had to pay for their promotions, decorations, and rewards of money or land was a bitter one.

Although we have seen in these pages how often Hitler's judgement was at fault, it would be absurd to claim that he was invariably wrong. The victories he won were astonishing—the conquests of Poland, France,

278

the Low Countries, Norway, Greece, Yugoslavia, and much of western Russia were brilliantly planned and executed. He was better prepared for war than any of the Allies, his troops were better trained and better led, he enjoyed superiority in tanks and aeroplanes, the army was battle-hardened in Spain, Austria and Czechoslovakia, and they had invented and developed such modern methods of warfare as the *blitzkreig* and the close co-operation of armour and aircraft. Few historians could be found to state that—from a purely military point of view—he was wrong to go to war in 1939.

But he made many big mistakes, and his cardinal one, of course, was the decision to attack Russia in 1941, from which many of the other failures stemmed, for he was committed to fighting a war on two fronts. Everything about the Russian campaign staggers the belief —the vast extent of the fronts, the numbers concerned, the casualties on both sides. It is healthy for a westerner to try to appreciate the scale of the fighting and to accept that the war was won and lost there, not in the Western Desert, Italy, or Normandy, creditable as were the successes of the Allies in those theatres. Until September 1943 German Army strength in Russia never fell below $2\frac{1}{2}$ million men— excluding their allies, and the Luftwaffe, and the S.S. Even in the spring of 1944, a year from the war's end, it was not much below $2\frac{1}{4}$ million. The Red Army at that time was over 6 million. It was nothing unusual, as we have seen, for an Army Group commander to control fifty or even sixty divisions (Von Bock in Army Group Centre commanded a million men). Compare this with the figure of—at the most—fifteen divisions in the B.E.F. of 1940 or the British 2nd Army of 1944.

Another overwhelming failure on Hitler's part was to fail to trust his staff and senior commanders. The team of Brauchitsch and Halder was, despite certain weaknesses, a formidable one, and as long as it existed there remained a sense of coherence in the German Army. But when Hitler took over in 1941 it was the end of professionalism. For all his intuitive powers, Hitler was not suited to exercise the highest military command. He was psychologically incapable of delegating authority, and persistently interfered in the chain of command even down to brigade level. The dismissal of such men as Höpner, List, Hoth, von Manstein, and von Weichs could not be supported, even in an army so rich in talent as the German one.

'The sky over Germany has grown very dark', wrote Rommel in 1944, but to many of his colleagues it must have been clear that the war had been lost since 1943. Stalingrad, Alamein, and Kursk had sealed the fate of Germany.

But to say that Hitler, as supreme commander, should accept the sole blame for these mistakes is to ignore the fact that it was the generals themselves who were responsible for putting him there. In the words of Lord Justice Geoffrey Lawrence at Nuremberg:

They have been responsible in large measure for the miseries and suffering that have fallen on millions of men, women, and children. They have been a disgrace to the honourable profession of arms. Without their military guidance the aggressive ambitions of Hitler and his fellow Nazis would have been academic and sterile ... Many of these men have made a mockery of the soldier's oath of obedience to military orders. When it suits their defence they say they had to obey; when confronted with Hitler's brutal crimes, which are shown to have been within their general knowledge, they say they disobeyed. The truth is they actively participated in all these crimes, or sat silent and acquiescent, ...

According to General Westphal there were 1,242 generals in the Army List in 1944. He reports that some five hundred of these were either dead or missing, and presumably those dismissed are included in the latter category. But the casualty figure was enormous: in Russia some thirty-five generals were killed or taken at Stalingrad alone; twenty were killed or taken prisoner in Normandy; and at least a dozen were killed or taken prisoner in Africa. In the Luftwaffe, which contained at least another 150 generals, the casualty figure was not so great, but it was still substantial.

Many were to spend a few years in captivity, a few received the death penalty, the bulk faded away into the mists of history. Yet these men had commanded the mightiest army the world has ever seen and held most of Europe in their sway. As they are remembered for their military prowess, so must they be remembered for its results.

Von Brauchitsch said that Hitler was the fate of Germany, and that that fate could not be stayed. But the generals could have done it. For their failure, Germany and Europe have had to pay a terrible price.

Maps

German/U.S.S.R. boundary 1939 (Sept)
Limit of German advances into U.S.S.R.

0   100   400
                                  miles
       100   600   km

Volga

alinin

⦿ MOSCOW
● Mozhaysk

sk
●

Vyazma

Kaluga ●   ● Tula

S.   R.

● Orel

● Voronezh

Kursk ●

Belgorod ●   Stalingrad
                                                   Volga
Kharkov ●

E

Kremenchug   Donets   Don   Astrakhan ●

A   I   N   ● Dnepropetrovsk   **CASPIAN**

Zaporozhye ●   Rostov
                    ● Taganrog   **SEA**

ayev   Dnieper

                              Kuban

CRIMEA   ● Maikop

Sevastopol ●   **C A U C A S U S   M O U N T A I N S**

L A C K   S E A

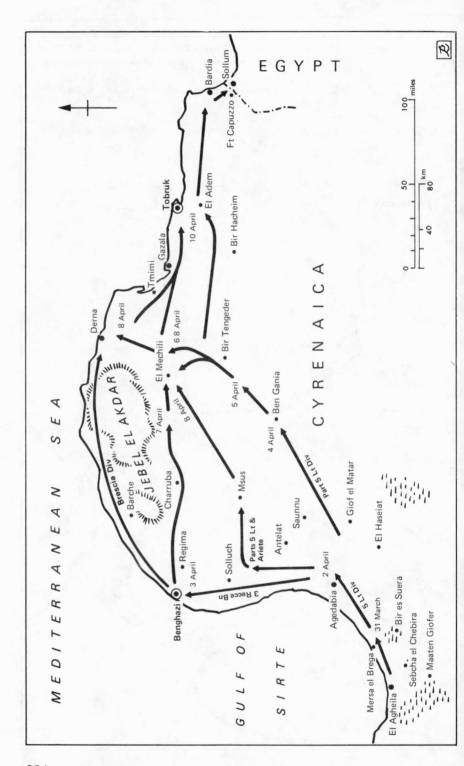

284

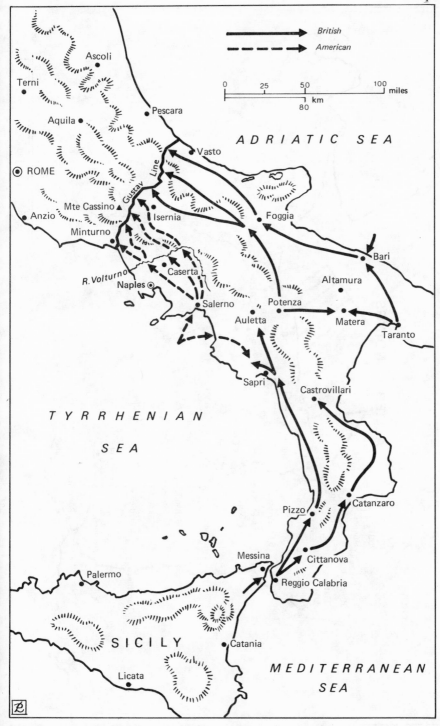

British

American

0   25   50   100 miles

km
80

ROME

Terni

Ascoli

Aquila

Pescara

ADRIATIC SEA

Vasto

Mte Cassino

Anzio

Isernia

Minturno

Foggia

R. Volturno

Caserta

Bari

Naples

Altamura

Salerno

Auletta

Potenza

Matera

Taranto

Sapri

Castrovillari

TYRRHENIAN

SEA

Pizzo

Catanzaro

Messina

Cittanova

Palermo

Reggio Calabria

SICILY

Catania

MEDITERRANEAN

Licata

SEA

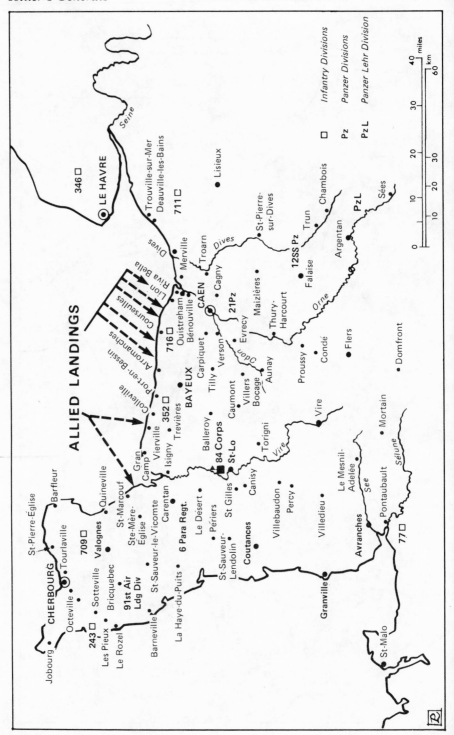

Appendices

Appendix One: Armed Forces Chain of Command

Supreme Commander
Adolf Hitler

O.K.W.
(Armed Forces High Command)

Chief
Field-Marshal Wilhelm Keitel

Chief of Staff
Colonel-General Alfred Jodl

NAVY

C-in-C
until '43
Grand-Admiral Erich Raeder

from '43
Grand-Admiral Karl Dönitz

LUFTWAFFE

C-in-C
Reichsmarschall Hermann Göring

Chief of Staff
until Aug. '43
Colonel-General Hans Jeschonnek

Aug. '43–July '44
Colonel-General Gunther Korten

Aug.–Oct. '44
General of Fliers Werner Kreipe

Nov. '44–May '45
Colonel-General Karl Koller

O.K.H. (ARMY HIGH COMMAND)

C-in-C Army
until Dec. '41
Field-Marshal Walther von Brauchitsch

from Dec. '41
Adolf Hitler

Chief of General Staff, Army
until Sept. '42
Colonel-General Franz Halder

Sept. '42–July '44
Colonel-General Kurt Zeitzler

July '44–Mar. '45
Colonel-General Heinz Guderian

Mar.–May '45
Colonel-General Hans Krebs

WAFFEN S.S.

Reichsführer
Heinrich Himmler

C-in-C Army
Chief of Army General Staff

Army Group
C-in-C a field-marshal or colonel-general

Army
C-in-C a colonel-general or general

Corps
G.O.C. usually a lieutenant-general

Division
G.O.C. usually a major-general or lieutenant-general

Brigade Group / Battle Group
major-general or colonel

Brigade
usually a colonel

Regiment
a colonel

Battalion
a lieutenant-colonel or major

Company
a captain or lieutenant

Note: O.K.W. had responsibility for all theatres of war with the exception of Russia, which was the responsibility of O.K.H.

Appendix Two: Some Armed Forces Commands 1939–1945

POLAND 1939

Army

C-in-C Col.-Gen. von Brauchitsch
Army Group North Col.-Gen. von Bock
  4th Army Gen. of Arty. von Kluge
  3rd Army Gen. of Arty. von Küchler
Army Group South Col.-Gen. von Rundstedt
  8th Army Gen. of Inf. Blaskowitz
  14th Army Col.-Gen. List
  10th Panzer Army Gen. of Arty. von Reichenau

Air Force

C-in-C F.-M. Göring
1st Air Fleet Gen. of Fliers Kesselring
4th Air Fleet Gen. of Fliers Löhr

Navy

C-in-C Gen.-Adm. Albrecht

NORWAY 1940

Army

C-in-C Gen. of Inf. von Falkenhorst
G.F.C. Lieut.-Gen. Dietl

Air Force

5th Air Fleet Col.-Gen. Milch

Navy

C-in-C Vice-Adm. Kummetz

FRANCE AND LOW COUNTRIES 1939–1940

Army

C-in-C Col.-Gen. von Brauchitsch
C-of-S Gen. of Arty. Halder

Army Group 'B' (Holland and Belgium)
  28 divisions inc. 3 panzer
  18th Army Gen. of Arty. von Küchler
  6th Army Col.-Gen. von Reichenau
Army Group 'A' (France and Belgium)
  44 divisions inc. 7 panzer
  2nd Army Gen. of Cav. Baron von Weichs
  4th Army Col.-Gen. von Kluge
  12th Army Col.-Gen. List
  16th Army Gen. of Inf. Busch
Army Group 'C' (Central France to Swiss frontier) 17 divisions
  1st Army Col.-Gen. von Witzleben
  7th Army Gen. of Arty. Dollmann

Air Force

C-in-C F.-M. Göring
  2nd Air Fleet Col.-Gen. Kesselring
  3rd Air Fleet Col.-Gen. Sperrle

AFRICA 1941–1943

Army

C-in-C (23 Feb. '41–9 Mar. '43) F.-M. Rommel
C-of-S Lieut.-Gen. Nehring; Lieut.-Gen. Gause; Col. Westphal; Lieut.-Gen. Bayerlein
C-in-C Tunisia (Sept.–Dec. '42) Gen. of Panz. Nehring; (until 13 May '43) Col.-Gen. von Arnim
C-of-S Lieut.-Gen. Ziegler

Air Force

C-in-C F.-M. Kesselring (as G.O.C. 2nd Air Fleet, Mediterranean)

Desert Air Force Commander
   (until Apr. '42) Gen. of Fliers Frölich;
   (Apr.-Aug. '42) Gen. of Fliers von
   Waldau; *(from Aug. '42)* Gen. of
   Fliers Seidemann

Navy

C-in-C Vice-Adm. Weichhold

ITALY AND SICILY 1943–1945

Army

C-in-C (1 Dec. '41–24 Oct. '44;
   14 Jan.–10 Mar. '45)
   F.-M. Kesselring;
   (24 Oct. '44–14 Jan. '45;
   11 Mar.–2 May '45) Col.-Gen. von
   Vietinghoff
C-in-C Army Group 'B' (Northern Italy)
   F.-M. Rommel
   10th Army (until 15 Feb. '45)
      Col.-Gen. von Vietinghoff;
      (from 15 Feb. '45)
      Gen. of Panz. Herr
   14th Army (Sept. '43–June '44)
      Col.-Gen. von Mackensen;
      (June '44–May '45)
      Gen. of Panz. Lemeisen
   Sicily Lieut.-Gen. Hube

Air Force

C-in-C (12 June '43–27 Oct. '44)
   F.-M. von Richthofen
Air Fleet 2 (28 Oct. '44–May '45)
   Gen. of Flak Arty. von Pohl
Sicily Lieut.-Gen. Mahncke
Sardinia Lieut.-Gen. Lungershausen

Navy

C-in-C Naval Forces Italy Vice-Adm.
   Ruge;
   Vice-Adm. Weichhold (Rome)

REPLACEMENT ARMY, GERMANY

C-in-C (until 21 July '44)
   Col.-Gen. Fromm;
   (21 July '44–27 Apr. '45)
   Reichsführer S.S. Himmler

BALKANS

C-in-C (1 Aug. '42–26 Aug. '43;
   25 Mar.–8 May '45) Col.-Gen. Löhr;
   (June–Oct. '41) F.-M. List;
   (25 Oct. '41–31 July '42)
   Gen. of Pion. Kuntze;
   (26 Aug. '43–25 Mar. '45)
   F.-M. von Weichs
German Troops, Croatia 1941 Gen. von
   Glaise-Horstenau
Southern Greece (June '41–Oct. '42)
   Gen. of Fliers Felmy
South-East (10 June–15 Oct. '41)
   F.-M. List
Serbia (June–Aug. '41) Gen. of Flak
   Arty. von Schröder

C-in-C WEST

(until 25 Oct. '39) Col.-Gen. von Leeb;
   (June '40–15 Mar. '41)
   F.-M. von Rundstedt;
   (15 Mar. '41–28 Feb. '42)
   F.-M. von Witzleben;
   (1 Mar. '42–6 July '44)
   F.-M. von Rundstedt;
   (7 July–17 Aug. '44)
   F.-M. von Kluge;
   (18 Aug.–5 Sept. '44)
   F.-M. Model;
   (5 Sept. '44–10 Mar, '45)
   F.-M. von Rundstedt;
   (10 Mar.–2 May '45)
   F.-M. Kesselring
Occupied France (1 Nov. '40–6 Feb. '42)
   Gen. of Inf. Otto von Stülpnagel;
   (6 Feb. '42–20 July '44) Gen. of Inf.
   Karl-Heinrich von Stülpnagel;
   (Aug. '44) Gen. of Fliers Kitzinger
Commandant of Paris Gen. Streccius;
   (7 Aug.–25 Aug. '44) Gen. of Inf.
   von Choltitz
Occupied Belgium and Northern France
   ('40–'44) Gen. of Inf. von
   Falkenhausen; *(July–Sept. '44)*
   Gen. of Inf. Grase
Occupied Holland Gen. of Fliers
   Christiansen

G.F.C. (Nov. '44–Feb. '45)
  Col.-Gen. Student; *(Feb–May '45)*
  Col.-Gen. Blaskowitz
Occupied Channel Islands ('40–'41)
  Colonel von Schmettow;
  (1941) Maj.-Gen. Müller;
  ('41–'45) Lieut.-Gen. von
  Schmettow;
  (1945) Vice-Adm. Huffmeier

OCCUPIED NORWAY

C-in-C (24 Apr. '40–18 Dec. '44)
  Col.-Gen. von Falkenhorst

OCCUPIED DENMARK

C-in-C (9 Apr. '40–'41) Gen. Kaupisch
  ('41–Oct. '42) Gen. Lüdke;
  (24 Jan–8 May '45)
  Col.-Gen. Lindemann

OCCUPIED POLAND

C-in-C Army of Occupation 1939
  Col.-Gen. Blaskowitz
Commander of Troops in Government
  General Gen. von Gienanth;
  Gen. of Arty. Ulex

OCCUPIED ITALY 1943–1945

C-in-C F.-M. Kesselring;
  Col.-Gen. von Vietinghoff

OCCUPIED CRETE

C-in-C ('41–'44) Maj.-Gen. Kreipe

OCCUPIED SLOVAKIA

Supreme Commander German Forces
  S.S. Col.-Gen. Berger

BOHEMIA AND MORAVIA

Wehrmacht Plenipotentiary Gen. Friderici

Supreme Commander (until June '42)
  S.S. Col.-Gen. Heydrich;
  S.S. Col.-Gen. Daluege

RUMANIA

Chief of Military Mission ('41–'44)
  Gen. of Cav. Hansen
Air Force Gen. of Fliers Gerstenberg

NORTH–WEST GERMANY 1945

C-in-C F.-M. Busch

SOUTH GERMANY 1945

C-in-C F.-M. Schörner
Commandant of Vienna (until Mar. '42)
  Gen. Streccius; Gen. von Bünau

FINLAND

O.K.W. Military Representative ('41–'44)
  Gen. of Inf. Erfurth

FRANCE AND NORTH–WEST EUROPE 1944–1945

C-in-C F.-M. von Rundstedt;
  F.-M. von Kluge; F.-M. Model;
  F.-M. Kesselring
Army Group 'B' (Northern France)
  F.-M. Rommel; F.-M. von Kluge;
  F.-M. Model
  7th Army (until June '44)
    Col.-Gen. Dollmann;
    S.S. Col.-Gen. Hausser
  15th Army (until July '44) Col.-Gen.
    von Salmuth; *(from Aug. '44)*
    Col.-Gen. von Zangen
Army Group 'G' (Southern France)
  1st Army Gen. of Inf. von der
    Chevallerie
  19th Army (until July '44) Gen. of Inf.
    von Sodenstern; *(from July '44)*
    Gen. of Inf. Weise

Army Group 'H' (Holland and North-West
  Germany) (Nov. '44–Feb. '45)
  Col.-Gen. Student; (Feb.–May '45)
  Col.-Gen. Blaskowitz
Luftwaffe Command West F.-M. Sperrle
Adm. Commanding Group West ('43–'44)
  Adm. Krancke

RUSSIA 1941–1945

Army Group North (June '40–Dec. '41)
  F.-M. von Leeb;
  (Jan. '42–Jan. '44)
  F.-M. von Küchler;
  (Jan.–Mar. '44)
  F.-M. Model;
  (Mar.–July '44) Gen. of Cav.
  Lindemann;
  (July '44) Col.-Gen. Friessner;
  (July '44–Jan. '45) Col.-Gen.
  Schörner;
  (Mar. '45) Col.-Gen. Weiss
Army Group Courland (Jan. '45)
  F.-M. Schörner; (Jan.–Mar. '45)
  Col.Gen. von Vietinghoff;
  (Mar. '45) Col.-Gen. Rendulic;
  (Apr. '45) Col.-Gen. Hilpert
Army Group Centre
  (June–Dec. '41) F.-M. von Bock;
  (Dec. '41–Oct. '43) F.-M. von Kluge;
  (Oct. '43–June '44) Col.-Gen. Busch;
  (June–Aug. '44) F.-M. Model;
  (Aug. '44–Jan. '45)
  Col.-Gen. Reinhardt;
  (Jan. '45) F.-M. Schörner;
  (25 Jan.–11 Mar. '45)
  Col.-Gen. Rendulic
Army Group South (June–Dec. '41)
  F.-M. von Rundstedt;
  (Dec. '41–Jan. '42) F.-M. von
  Reichenau;
  (Jan.–July '42) F.-M. von Bock

Army Group 'A' (July–Sept. '42)
  F.-M. List;
  (Sept.–Nov. '42) Adolf Hitler;
  (Nov. '42–Mar. '44) F.-M. von Kleist
Army Group South Ukraine
  (Mar.–July '44) Col.-Gen. Schörner;
  (July–Oct. '44) Col.-Gen. Friessner
Army Group South (Oct. '43–Apr. '44)
  Col.-Gen. Wöhler;
  (Apr. '45) Col.-Gen. Rendulic
Army Group 'B' (July '43–Feb. '43)
  Col.-Gen. von Weichs
Army Group Don (Nov. '43–Feb. '43)
  F.-M. von Manstein
Army Group South (Feb. '43–Mar. '44)
  F.-M. von Manstein
Army Group North Ukraine
  (Mar.–Aug. '44) F.-M. Model
Army Group 'A' (Sept. '44–Jan. '45)
  Col.-Gen. Harpe;
  (Jan. '45) F.-M. Schörner
Army Group Vistula (Jan.–Mar. '45)
  Reichsführer S.S. Himmler;
  (Mar.–May '45) Col.-Gen. Heinrici;
  (May '45) Col.-Gen. Student
C-in-C Northern Finland ('42–'44)
  Col.-Gen. Dietl
C-in-C Northern Norway ('41–'43)
  Gen. of Mtn. Troops Schörner
Luftwaffe C-in-C Reichsmarschall Göring.
  For the invasion of Russia the 1st
  Air Fleet under Col.-Gen. Keller
  supported von Leeb's A.G. North,
  the 2nd Air Fleet under F.-M.
  Kesselring supported von Bock's
  A.G. Centre, and the 4th Air Fleet
  under Col.-Gen. Löhr supported von
  Rundstedt's A.G. South. The 5th
  Air Fleet under Col.-Gen. Stumpff,
  operating from Norwegian and
  Scandinavian bases, also supported
  operations in Russia and Russian
  waters

Glossary

Abwehr	German Military Intelligence
Allgemeine S.S.	General S.S.: section of S.S. which dealt with recruiting, training, administration, etc.
Blitzkreig	'Lightning attack'
Bund Deutscher Mädel	League of German Maidens, counterpart of Hitler Jugend
Gestapo	Geheimestaatspolizei (Secret State Police)
Hitler Jugend	Hitler Youth, boys' organization of German National Socialist (Nazi) Party
Luftwaffe	German Air Force
O.K.H.	Oberkommando des Heeres (Army High Command)
O.K.W.	Oberkommando der Wehrmacht (Armed Forces High Command)
Ostelbien	Provinces east of the Elbe
Panzer	Armoured vehicle
Reichswehr	German Army
S.A.	Sturmabteilung, Storm Troops, the 'brownshirts', a para-military organization banned in 1932
Schwerpunkt	'Heavy punch' or concentrated attack
S.D.	Sicherheitsdienst, Security Service of Party and S.S.
S.S.	Schutzstaffeln, Protection Squads or Shock Troops, originally in parallel with S.A. but increasingly separate and powerful
Volkssturm	People's Force, equivalent to Home Guard
Waffen S.S.	Armed S.S.: military formations of the S.S.
Wehrkreis	German military district centred on an important city
Wehrmacht	The Armed Forces including Army, Navy, Air Force, and Waffen S.S.

Bibliography

Alanbrooke, Visct. *The Alanbrooke War Diaries 1939–43, 1943–46* (ed. Arthur Bryant): London 1957

Alexander of Tunis *The Alexander Memoirs 1940–1945* (ed. John North): London 1962

Bailer, Seweryn *Stalin and his Generals*: London 1969

Bekker, Cajus *The Luftwaffe War Diaries* (tr. and ed. Frank Ziegler): London 1966. *Hitler's Naval War*: London 1974

Blumentritt, Gunther *Von Rundstedt, the Soldier and the Man*: London 1952

Boldt, Gerhard *Hitler's Last Days* (tr. Sandra Bance): London 1973

Bottger, Gerd *Narvik im Bild*: Berlin 1941

Bullock, Alan *Hitler—A Study in Tyranny*: London 1955

Carell, Paul *Hitler's War With Russia*: London 1964
      Invasion, They're Coming! (tr. Ewald Osers): London 1964

Clark, Alan *Barbarossa: The Russo-German Conflict 1941–1945*: London 1965. *The Fall of Crete*: London 1962

Craig, A. Gordon *The Politics of the Prussian Army*: London 1955

Creswell, John *Sea Warfare 1939–1945*: California 1967

Deakin, F.W. *The Brutal Friendship: Mussolini, Hitler and the fall of Italian Fascism*: London 1962

De Guingand, Francis *Operation Victory*: London 1947

Deutsch, Harold C. *Hitler and His Generals: The Hidden Crisis, January–June 1938*: Minnesota 1974

Dicks, Henry V. *Licensed Mass Murder*: London 1972

Dietrich, Otto *Auf den Strassen des Sieges*: Munich 1940

Douglas-Home, Charles *Rommel*: London 1973

Dulles, Allen Welsh *Germany's Underground*: New York 1947

Ellis, L.F. *Victory in the West*: London 1962
      The War in France and Flanders, 1939–1940: London 1953

Fishman, Jack *The Seven Men of Spandau*: New York 1954

FitzGibbon, Constantine *The Shirt of Nessus*: London 1956

Fleming, Peter *Invasion 1940*: London 1957

Friedin, Seymour, and Richardson, William (eds.) *The Fatal Decisions*: London 1956

Galland, Adolf *The First and the Last* (tr. Mervyn Savill): New York 1954

Gallo, Max *The Night of the Long Knives* (tr. Lily Emmet): New York 1972

Gilbert, Felix *Hitler Directs His War*: New York 1950

Gilbert, G.M. *Nuremberg Diary*: London 1948

Giles, O.C. *The Gestapo* (Oxford Pamphlets on World Affairs): Oxford 1940

Gill, Ronald, and Graves, John *Club Route In Europe*: Hanover 1946

Göbbels, *The Göbbels Diaries* (ed. Louis P. Lochner): London 1948

Görlitz, Walter *The German General Staff*: London 1953
        Paulus and Stalingrad (tr. R.H. Stevens): New York 1964
Grunberger, Richard *Hitler's S.S.*: London 1970
Guderian, Heinz *Panzer Leader*: London 1952
Halder, Franz *Hitler als Feldherr*: Munich 1949
Hanfstängl, Ernst ('Putzi') *Hitler—The Missing Years*: London 1948
Hart, W.E., *Hitler's Generals*: London 1944
Hassell, Ulrich von *The von Hassell Diaries, 1938–1944*: London 1948
Heiden, Konrad *Hitler*: London 1945
Heiss, Friedrich *Der Sieg im Osten*: Berlin 1940
Hinsley, F.H. *Hitler's Strategy*: Cambridge 1951
Hoth, Hermann, *Panzer-Operationen*: Heidelberg 1956
Humble, Richard *Hitler's High Seas Fleet*: London 1971
Irving, David *The Rise and Fall of the Luftwaffe*: London 1971
Kesselring, Albert *A Soldier's Record* (tr. L. Hudson): New York 1954
Killen, John *The Luftwaffe: A History*: London 1967
Kramarz, Joachim *Stauffenberg* (tr. R.H. Barry): London 1967
Langer, Walter C. *The Mind of Adolf Hitler*: New York 1973
Leach, Barry A. *German Strategy Against Russia 1939–1941*: Oxford 1973
Lee, Asher *Goering—Air Leader*: London 1972
Lewin, Ronald *Rommel*: London 1968
Liddell Hart, B.H. *The Other Side of the Hill*: London 1948
        (ed.) *The Rommel Papers*: London 1953
Lochner, Louis P. *What About Germany?*: London 1943
Macintyre, Donald *The Naval War Against Hitler*: London 1971
Majdalany, Fred *The Fall of Fortress Europe*: London 1968
Mannerheim, Carl Gustav *Memoirs of Marshal Mannerheim* (tr. Count Eric Lewenhaupt): London 1953
Manstein, Erich von *Lost Victories*: London 1958
Manvell, Roger *The Conspirators: 20th July 1944*: London 1971
Martienssen, Anthony K. *Hitler and his Admirals*: London 1948
Molony, C.J.C. *The Mediterranean and Middle-East* (Official War History, vol. v): London 1973
Montgomery of Alamein, *Memoirs*: London 1968
Moorehead, Alan *African Trilogy*: London 1944
Muck, Richard *Kampfgruppe Scherer*: Berlin 1943
Neave, Airey *The Flames of Calais*: London 1972
O'Neill, Robert J. *The German Army and the Nazi Party, 1933–39*: London 1966
Papen, Franz von *Memoirs*: London 1952
Playfair, L.S.O. *The Mediterranean and Middle-East* (Official War History, vols. i, ii and iii): London 1954
        and Molony, C.J.C. *The Mediterranean and Middle-East* (Official War History, vol. iv): London 1966
Raeder, Erich *The Struggle for the Sea*: London 1959
Rauschning, Hermann *Makers of Destruction*: London 1942
Reitlinger, Gerald *The S.S.—Alibi of a Nation*: London 1956
Riess, Curt *The Self-Betrayed: Glory and Doom of the German Generals*: New York 1952

Robichon, Jacques *The Second D-Day* (tr. Barbara Shuey): London 1969
Ryan, Cornelius *A Bridge Too Far*: London 1974
               The Last Battle: London 1966
               The Longest Day: New York 1959
Schacht, Hjalmar *Confessions of 'The Old Wizard'* (tr. Diana Pyke): Boston 1956
Schirer, William L. *Berlin Diary*: London 1941
               The Rise and Fall of the Third Reich: London 1960
Schröter, Heinz *Stalingrad* (tr. Constantine FitzGibbon): New York 1958
Seaton, Albert *The Battle for Moscow 1941*: London 1971
               The Russo-German War 1941–1945: London 1971
Senger und Etterlin, Frido von *Neither Hope Nor Fear* (tr. George Malcolm): London 1963
Shulman, Milton *Defeat In The West*: London 1947
Soviet Government *Adolf Heusinger's Crimes*: Moscow 1962
Speidel, Hans *Invasion 1944*: London 1951
Spencer, John Hall *Battle for Crete*: London 1962
Stevens, E.H. *The Trial of Nikolaus von Falkenhorst*: London 1949
Taylor, Telford *The Breaking Wave*: London 1967
               The March of Conquest: London 1959
               Sword and Swastika: London 1953
Thursfield, H.G. (ed.) *Führer Conferences on Naval Affairs*: London 1947
Thyssen, Fritz *I Paid Hitler*: London 1941
Toland, John *The Last 100 Days*: London 1966
Trevor-Roper, H.R. (ed.) *Hitler's War Directives 1939–1945*: London 1964
Turney, Alfred *Disaster at Moscow: Von Bock's Campaigns 1941–1942*: London 1971
Van der Porten, Edward P. *The German Navy In World War II*: London 1971
Westphal, Siegfried *The German Army in the West*: London 1952
Wheeler-Bennett, John W. *The Nemesis of Power*: London 1953
Williams, John *France: Summer 1940*: London 1969
Wilmot, Chester *The Struggle for Europe*: London 1952
Wiskemann, Elizabeth *The Rome–Berlin Axis. A Study of relations between Hitler and Mussolini*: London 1966
Young, Desmond *Rommel*: London 1950
Ziemke, Earl F. *The German Northern Theatre of Operations 1940–1945*: Washington 1959

Index

305